ENIAC in Action

History of Computing

William Aspray and Thomas J. Misa, editors

ENIAC in Action

Making and Remaking the Modern Computer

Thomas Haigh, Mark Priestley, and Crispin Rope

The MIT Press
Cambridge, Massachusetts
London, England

Set in Sabon by Toppan Best-set Premedia Limited. Printed and bound in the United States of America.

Cataloging-in-publication information is available from the Library of Congress.

10 9 8 7 6 5 4 3 2 1

dedicated to Douglas R. Hartree,
who could do a great deal with ten million multiplications

Contents

Acknowledgments

This project was generously funded by Mrs. L. D. Rope's Second Charitable Settlement. With this support we were able to bring together the skills and resources to comb through mountains of archival materials and dig deep into the world of early computing practice. Peter Sachs Collopy did most of the work needed to obtain archival documents from the collections at the University of Pennsylvania. Nate Wiewora, Alan Olley, and Stephanie Dick all procured specific documents from other collections. Susan Abbey provided handwriting analysis services to clarify the authorship of numerous documents. Haigh's research assistant, Ann Graf, carefully reviewed the manuscript and verified citations.

Thanks are owed to archivists and curators Susan Dayall at Hampshire College, Lynn Catanese at the Hagley Museum and Library, Susan Hoffman and Arvid Nelsen at the Charles Babbage Institute, Nancy R. Miller at the University of Pennsylvania, Valerie-Ann Lutz and the other members of the archival staff at the American Philosophical Society, Debbie Douglas at the MIT Museum, David E. Pfeifer at the Institute for American Thought at Indiana University–Purdue University Indianapolis, and members of the staff of the Library of Congress Manuscripts Reading Room.

Peggy Kidwell of the National Museum of American History was particularly helpful in pointing us toward the earliest known use of the term "stored program" and in helping us clarify the locations and the ownership of many surviving parts of ENIAC. Kim D. Todd at the Jean Jennings Bartik Computing Museum provided several images, including what may be the earliest surviving record of an ENIAC set-up used in practice. George Dyson and Marina von Neumann Whitman shared with us unpublished material from the latter's personal collection of papers concerning Klara von Neumann. Anne Fitzpatrick, Steve Aftergood, Robert Seidel, J. Arthur Freed, and Alan B. Carr all did what they could to help us navigate the maze of restrictions surrounding access to historical materials from Los Alamos, though alas our Freedom of Information Act requests have yielded no fruit more than two years after they were submitted.

William Aspray, Jeff Yost, Atsushi Akera, Doron Swade, Bill Mauchly, Paul Ceruzzi, and Martin Campbell-Kelly kindly answered our questions on specific topics and shared their perspectives on computing in the 1940s.

Some material from the project was initially published in *IEEE Annals of the History of Computing* in article form. We benefitted from suggestions made by anonymous reviewers and by those who discussed the draft at the informal Workshop on Early Programming Practice organized by Gerard Alberts and Liesbeth De Mol.

Portions of chapters 6 and 11 were previously published in Haigh, Priestley, and Rope, "Reconsidering the Stored Program Concept," *IEEE Annals of the History of Computing* 36, no. 1 (2014): 4–17 and in Haigh, "'Stored Program Concept' Considered Harmful: History and Historiography," in *The Nature of Computation. Logic, Algorithms, Applications*, edited by Paola Bonizzoni, Vasco Brattka, and Benedikt Löwe (Springer, 2013).

Portions of chapters 8 and 9 were previously published in Haigh, Priestley, and Rope, "Engineering 'The Miracle of the ENIAC': Implementing the Modern Code Paradigm," *IEEE Annals of the History of Computing* 36, no. 2 (2014): 41–59.

Portions of chapters 7 and 11 were previously published in Haigh, Priestley, and Rope, "Los Alamos Bets on ENIAC: Nuclear Monte Carlo Simulations, 1947–48," *IEEE Annals of the History of Computing* 36, no. 3 (2014): 42–63.

List of Recurring Characters

A number of people make repeated but short appearances in this book, several of them under multiple names because of marriage. To minimize confusion without making endless re-introductions, we have prepared this list.

Barnes, Gladeon Marcus
Chief of Research and Development for the Ordnance Department, and therefore responsible for Aberdeen Proving Ground, of which the Ballistic Research Laboratory (BRL) was a part. Represented the Ordnance Department at the ENIAC launch event.

Bartik, Jean
Married name of Betty Jean Jennings.

Bilas, Frances
One of the first of the ENIAC operators selected in 1945, having worked as a computer and differential analyzer operator for the BRL since 1942. Married Homer Spence.

Brainerd, John Grist
A senior member of the faculty of the University of Pennsylvania's Moore School of Electrical Engineering who was designated director of the ENIAC project.

Burks, Arthur W.
A mathematician turned philosophy PhD turned ENIAC engineer who made substantial contributions to ENIAC's design, produced the first detailed plans for the trajectory computations, and later wrote extensively on the early history of electronic computing.

Clippinger, Richard

A mathematician who was employed at the BRL from 1944 to 1952. He became involved with ENIAC in 1946 as a user interested in simulating supersonic wind flow, and later took part in planning the conversion of ENIAC's programming system.

Cunningham, Leland

A Harvard University astronomer who worked at the BRL during World War II. He helped to shape ENIAC through its design process and served on the BRL's Computations Committee to plan ENIAC applications.

Dederick, Louis S.

A senior BRL civilian scientist, appointed head of the BRL's Computing Laboratory in 1945. He retired from the laboratory in 1953.

Eckert, John Presper, Jr.

A young electronic engineer who led the detailed design and construction of ENIAC as "laboratory chief." One of the two ENIAC inventors credited in its patent. Left the Moore School in 1945 to co-found the first computer company.

Gillon, Paul

A computational specialist and member of the BRL staff who was responsible for the BRL's joint development of differential analyzers with the Moore School. Herman Goldstine's direct supervisor during the early part of ENIAC development, he was later a supporter of the project from within the Army's Office of the Chief of Ordnance.

Goldstine, Adele Katz

A mathematician who trained and recruited human computers and who in 1947 drafted an early plan for the conversion of ENIAC to its new programming mode. Wife of Herman Goldstine.

Goldstine, Herman Heine

A mathematician assigned as the BRL's liaison to the Moore School, initially to oversee the human computers working there. He was the Army's primary liaison to the ENIAC project and was deeply involved in its daily progress. Later he worked with John von Neumann at the Institute for Advanced Studies in Princeton. Husband of Adele Goldstine.

Holberton, Frances Elizabeth "Betty"

Married name of Elizabeth "Betty" Snyder.

Holberton, John
A BRL staff member who was selected in 1945 to head ENIAC operations, which he did during its time at the Moore School and after its move to Aberdeen. Married Elizabeth "Betty" Snyder.

Jennings, Betty Jean
One of the initial cohort of ENIAC operators hired by the BRL in 1945. Leader in 1947–48 of a contract programming group that worked on the plans to convert ENIAC to its new programming mode. Became Jean Bartik upon marriage in 1946.

Lehmer, Derrick Henry
A mathematician with a particular interest in prime numbers. He spent part of World War II at the BRL and served on the computations committee responsible for planning ENIAC applications.

Lichterman, Ruth
Hired by the BRL as a human computer, she became one of the first ENIAC operators in 1945. She became Ruth Teitelbaum upon marriage.

Mauchly, John W.
A physicist and a member of the Moore School's faculty who instigated the ENIAC project. One of the two ENIAC inventors credited in its patent. Left the Moore School in 1945 to co-found the first computer company.

McNulty, Kathleen Rita "Kay"
Hired by the BRL as a computer in 1943, she operated the differential analyzer before becoming one of the initial cohort of ENIAC operators in 1945. Married John Mauchly in 1948.

Metropolis, Nicholas Constantine
A physicist and Manhattan Project veteran who remained active after World War II in developing computational methods at Los Alamos while on the faculty of the University of Chicago. In 1948 he returned to Los Alamos, where he led development of its first electronic computers. He reconfigured ENIAC's programming mode in 1948 immediately before the first computerized Monte Carlo simulations were run.

Pender, Harold
Dean of the Moore School, where ENIAC was created under contract to the BRL.

Sharpless, Thomas Kite
An ENIAC design engineer, nearly always referred to as T. Kite Sharpless.

Simon, Leslie E.
A scientist who served as director of the BRL and was responsible for overseeing ENIAC's construction and use.

Snyder, Frances Elizabeth "Betty"
One of the initial cohort of ENIAC operators hired by the BRL in 1945. Left the BRL in 1948. Married John Holberton.

Spence, Homer
Began maintenance work on ENIAC in 1945 as an enlisted soldier. Returned as a civilian employee to the BRL, where he then oversaw maintenance work. Married Frances Bilas in 1950.

Teller, Edward
Physicist, Manhattan Project veteran, and co-inventor of the hydrogen bomb.

Travis, Irven
Moore School faculty member since 1931. In 1940 proposed construction of an electronic differential analyzer with close parallels to the later ENIAC proposal. After returning to the Moore School from a wartime assignment, he oversaw contract research, including ENIAC and EDVAC work.

Ulam, Stanislaw M.
Physicist, Manhattan Project veteran, one of the originators of the Monte Carlo method, and co-inventor of the hydrogen bomb.

von Neumann, John
A mathematician who was involved in the ENIAC project from approximately August 1944 on. Helped to shape plans for its successor, EDVAC, as expressed in the hugely influential "First Draft of a Report on the EDVAC." Also credited with the idea for converting ENIAC to EDVAC-like operation, he was responsible for bringing several teams from Los Alamos to Philadelphia, and later to Aberdeen, to work with ENIAC. Husband of Klara von Neumann.

von Neumann, Klara
Coded and helped to run a series of Monte Carlo simulations run on ENIAC for Los Alamos between 1948 and 1950. Wife of John von Neumann.

Archival Collections Used

Thanks in large part to research associated with the ENIAC litigation that was concluded in the 1970s, many ENIAC documents are held in more than one of the institutional and personal collections listed below. Where we can do so, we have cited the collection in which an original copy of a particular document is held.

AWB-IUPUI
Arthur W. Burks Papers, Institute for American Thought, Indiana University–Purdue University Indianapolis. The papers are stored in file drawers. Because the folders are not numbered, no precise locations can be given. Finding aid: http://liberalarts.iupui.edu/iat/uploads/docs/Arthur_Burks-Finding Aid-Jan2012.pdf.

AWB-NCSU
A. Wayne Brooke Collection, 1948–1986, Special Collections, North Carolina State University, Raleigh. Each citation is followed by a box number and a serial number. Finding aid: http://www.lib.ncsu.edu/findingaids/mc00268.

ETE-UP
ENIAC Trial Exhibits, Master Collection, 1864–1973, University of Pennsylvania Archives and Records Center, Philadelphia. Finding aid: http://www.archives.upenn.edu/faids/upd/eniactrial/eniac.html. A searchable database can be used to locate items by title and author. This is a microfilm collection consolidating photocopied trial materials from the University of Pennsylvania, the Charles Babbage Institute, and the Hagley Museum and Library. The microfilms are also accessible at those institutions. When the paper copies are held at University of Pennsylvania, we generally cite ETR-UP instead as ETE-UP.

ETR-UP
ENIAC Patent Trial Collection, 1864–1973, University of Pennsylvania Archives and Records Center, Philadelphia. Finding aid: http://www.archives.upenn.edu/faids/upd/eniactrial/upd8_10.html.

GRS-DC
Papers of George R. Stibitz, 1937–1979, Dartmouth College, Hanover, New Hampshire. Each citation is followed by a box number and a folder name. Finding aid: http://ead.dartmouth.edu/html/ml27_fullguide.html.

HHG-APS
Herman Heine Goldstine Papers, American Philosophical Society, Philadelphia. Each citation is followed by a series number and a box number. No finding aid is available online, but an unpublished draft of a finding aid is available from the archivists of the American Philosophical Society.

HHG-HC
Herman H. Goldstine Collection, 1941–1971, archives, Hampshire College, Amherst, Massachusetts. Each citation is followed by a box number. Finding aid: http://asteria.fivecolleges.edu/findaids/hampshire/mah1.html.

JGC-MIT
Papers of Jule G. Charney, MC.0184, Massachusetts Institute of Technology Archives, Cambridge. Each citation is followed by a box number and a folder number. Finding aid: http://libraries.mit.edu/archives/research/collections/collections-mc/mc184.html.

JvN-LOC
Papers of John von Neumann, Manuscripts Division, US Library of Congress, Washington. Each citation is followed by a box number and a folder number. Finding aid: http://lccn.loc.gov/mm82044180.

JWM-UP
Papers of John W. Mauchly, University of Pennsylvania Kislak Center for Special Collections, Rare Books and Manuscripts, Philadelphia. Processing in progress at the time of writing.

KvN-MvNW
Papers related to Klara von Neumann retained in the personal collection of Marina von Neumann Whitman. We did not see the originals; we worked from extracts transcribed by Whitman and scans sent to us by George Dyson. The originals have subsequently been donated as part of the Marina von Neumann Whitman Papers, 1946–2013, Schlesinger Library, Radcliffe Institute for Advanced Study, Harvard University, Cambridge, Massachusetts.

MSOBM-UP
Moore School of Electrical Engineering, Office of the Business Manager Records, 1931–1948, UPD-8.3, University Archives and Records, University of Pennsylvania, Philadelphia. Each citation is followed by a box number and serial number. Finding aid: http://www.archives.upenn.edu/faids/upd/upd8_3invtry.pdf.

MSOD-UP
Moore School of Electrical Engineering, Office of the Director Records, 1931–1948, UPD 8.4, University Archives and Records, University of Pennsylvania, Philadelphia. Each citation is followed by a box number and a folder name. Finding aid: http://www.archives.upenn.edu/faids/upd/upd8_4invtry.pdf.

NARA-ENIAC
Records Relating to the Development and Use of the Electronic Numerical Integrator and Computer (ENIAC), 1943–1947, National Archives at Philadelphia. Each citation is followed by a box number and a folder number. Finding aid: http://research.archives.gov/description/636248.

SMU-APS
Stanislaw M. Ulam Papers, American Philosophical Society, Philadelphia. Each citation is followed by a series number and a folder name. Finding aid: http://www.amphilsoc.org/mole/view?docId=ead/Mss.Ms.Coll.54-ead.xml.

UV-HML
Sperry Rand Corporation, UNIVAC Division records, Accession 1825.I, Hagley Museum and Library, Wilmington, Delaware. Each citation is followed by a box number and a folder name. Finding aid: http://findingaids.hagley.org/xtf/view?docId=ead/1825_I.xml.

Introduction

In October of 1946, Douglas Hartree took up the post of Plummer Professor of Mathematical Physics at the University of Cambridge. His inaugural lecture was published the next year as an influential little book on recent developments in "calculating machines."[1] A few months earlier Hartree had been visiting the University of Pennsylvania, where he had a rare opportunity to use the newly constructed Electronic Numerical Integrator And Computer (ENIAC), an urgent wartime project rushed from conception in 1943 to completion in 1945 under the direction of J. Presper Eckert Jr. and John W. Mauchly. Hartree's lecture centered on the opportunities for science presented by this electronic marvel. Its "speed of operation" was "of the order of a thousand times faster than anything else at present available." Thus, "a calculation involving ten million multiplications may take only about nine hours." Hartree noted with wry understatement that "one can do quite a lot with ten million multiplications."

The present book is about how and why a small group of mathematicians, scientists, engineers, and Army administrators came together to propose, authorize, and design the unusual machine. It is also about the women and men who built, programmed, and operated ENIAC, and about the uses scientists found for all those millions of multiplications. Access to millions (and eventually billions and trillions) of automatically sequenced arithmetic and logical operations transformed the practice of science during the second half of the twentieth century. ENIAC established the feasibility of high-speed electronic computing, demonstrating that a machine containing many thousands of unreliable vacuum tubes could nevertheless be coaxed into uninterrupted operation for long enough to do something useful.

During an operational life of almost a decade ENIAC did a great deal more than merely inspire the next wave of computer builders. Until 1950 it was the only fully electronic computer working in the United States, and it was irresistible to many governmental and corporate users whose mathematical problems required a formerly infeasible amount of computational work. By October of 1955, when ENIAC was decommissioned, scores of people had learned to program and operate it, many of whom went on to distinguished computing careers. Within limits imposed by its design, ENIAC could be programmed to combine its basic computational operations in whatever order was needed for the problem at hand. It could select a course of action on the basis of results it had so far obtained—for example, to calculate a shell's trajectory only to the point where the shell hits the ground. Previous calculating devices had either required human intervention at such moments or been limited to problems of a particular kind. That new capability gave ENIAC great flexibility. Among other things, it calculated tables of sines and cosines and tested for statistical outliers, simulated explosions of hydrogen bombs, plotted the trajectories of bombs and shells, searched for prime numbers, ran the first numerical weather simulations, modeled the flow of air at supersonic velocities, and analyzed data from experimental firings of captured German V-2 rockets.

This is the first scholarly book devoted to ENIAC and the first comprehensive examination of its use as a scientific instrument. But ENIAC has never been an obscure machine. Widely publicized at the time of its creation, it was later at the center of a series of high-profile legal proceedings, and it figures prominently in standard histories of computing. It is still frequently written about, and it features in a number of major museum displays. Yet previous accounts have neglected many aspects of ENIAC's story in favor of casting it in one of two traditional roles: either as a candidate for the title of the "world's first computer" or as merely one of a series of steps leading to development of the modern computer. In recent years discussion has focused on ENIAC as the site of another "first": the workplace of the first computer programmers. All three narratives focus almost entirely on episodes in ENIAC's initial development and experimental use, as the turning point in computer design or programming practice is assumed to have come during that phase. Much less has been written about ENIAC as a physical machine changing over time, as a busy workplace, or as a scientific instrument.

Books that focus on material objects often signal the importance of their subjects by presenting them as inflection points in world history. The titles of dozens of books have tried to lure a broad audience to an obscure topic by touting an idea, a fish, a dog, a map, a condiment, or a machine as having "changed the world." George Dyson recently argued for John von Neumann's computer, built at the Institute for Advanced Studies in Princeton a few years after ENIAC, as the "point source" of origin for "the digital universe." Similar claims might be made at least as persuasively for ENIAC: Was ENIAC an essential agent in the construction of the modern world, like cod, salt, or the Irish? Were its creators miraculously ahead of its time, as Ada Lovelace, Leonardo da Vinci, and Alan Turing are said to have been? Was it the work of a lone genius defying the lazy wisdom of inbred elites?

One of the luxuries of writing an obscure academic book is that one is not required to embrace such simplistic conceptions of history. As the title *ENIAC in*

Action suggests, this book focuses on the many different ways in which ENIAC was used. It is a nod to Bruno Latour's *Science in Action*, a foundational work of science studies.[2] Like Latour, we are interested in how artifacts, such as ENIAC and its components, act in conjunction with humans. The concept of action, in this broad sense, runs through the entire book. It applies not only to the use of the physical ENIAC to carry out computations but also to the use of initial sketches of ENIAC to mobilize resources at the beginning of the project and to more recent attempts to enlist ENIAC to bolster the participation of women in computing. Reducing this rich history to an argument that some particular feature of ENIAC "changed the world" would sacrifice a great deal. Instead we try to position ENIAC within various historical chains connecting earlier technologies and practices to later ones. We document these connections not only in the area of computer design but also in the areas of programming practice, computing labor, and scientific practice.

We tell ENIAC's story in a broadly chronological way, moving through invention, construction, use, and modification to obsolescence, but from a number of different perspectives. Each perspective offers a different view of what ENIAC was or is, and thus of why it matters. In the rest of this introduction we introduce some of those perspectives, sketching how our approach differs from previous accounts and situating our work on ENIAC within several distinct historical traditions.

ENIAC as a Machine of War

The electronic computer was, like radar and the atomic bomb, a technology developed for and during World War II, a period of exceptionally rapid innovation. For example, nearly every military aircraft that was flying in 1939 was obsolete before the end of the war. The Mitsubishi Zero fighter dominated early engagements, but by the war's end it was fit only for kamikaze duty. Advances in anti-submarine warfare obliterated the formerly invincible German U-boat fleet. Communications and cryptography advanced dramatically. Nations transformed themselves. Industrial production quickly shifted from civilian to military needs, new goods and foodstuffs were introduced to replace those that were unavailable because of wartime disruption, and government bureaucracies were established and staffed in record time. Boats and planes were mass produced on a scale unknown before or since. Technologies moved from lab to battlefield in months. People everywhere were working harder than usual, sleeping less, and looking for ways to get things done without delay. All this created opportunities for the young and ambitious to win approval for unconventional ideas. The war ended after two bombs destroyed two cities, an unprecedented leap in destructive power.

Many of the apparently sudden breakthroughs of the war resulted from the application of money and enthusiasm to implement ideas that had been proposed years earlier, only to languish during the Great Depression. The jet engine, for example, had been patented in 1930 but was not incorporated into a fighter until 1944. Amateur rocket enthusiasts had been promoting their technology ever since the 1920s, but only the war provided German rocket builders with the money and slave labor they needed to push the technology into practical use. The atomic bomb depended on recent advances in theoretical and experimental physics, but could be built only thanks to the labor of many thousands of people within specially constructed industrial cities. Such a commitment of effort would have been unlikely in peacetime.

ENIAC was small by the emerging standards of postwar "big science," or even in comparison to the largest scientific projects launched by the government during the war.[3] The Manhattan Project alone cost about 4,000 times as much. Historians have focused on the wartime Office of Scientific Research and Development (OSRD), headed by Vannevar Bush, as a crucial institution in bringing thousands of scientists, the government, and vast sums of money together in pursuit of military advantage. The Massachusetts Institute of Technology alone received $117 million in research funding during the war. We do not have much to say in this book about the roles of OSRD and other high-profile agencies in supporting, opposing, or shaping ENIAC. Other historians have ably documented these connections, and we have little to add to their accounts.[4] The construction of ENIAC was justified by a specific wartime need—to produce firing tables at a time when human computational labor was scarce—and was made possible by the huge sums of money that the federal government allocated to the Army. Nevertheless, we see it as fundamentally a bottom-up, local initiative in which staff members of the University of Pennsylvania's Moore School of Electrical Engineering allied themselves with the management of the Ballistic Research Laboratory, and with that lab's patrons in the Army's Ordnance Department, to launch a project of mutual interest.[5]

If ENIAC had never existed, history would surely have followed some other path to the development of computer technology. So we are particularly concerned with aspects of ENIAC's design and use that were shaped by its specific context as a machine rushed into existence during wartime. ENIAC is a milestone on only one of many possible paths to the modern computer, and that particular path is one that would never have been taken in peacetime. Every aspect of ENIAC was influenced by the war: the task for which it was crafted, the design compromises made to produce it more quickly, the scale on which it was constructed, even the way it was staffed and operated. Without the war, no one would have built a machine with its particular combination of strengths and weaknesses.

Our story has more to say about changes in scientific practice during the twentieth century's wars than it does about the development of federal science bureaucracies. ENIAC belongs to the tradition, reaching back as far as Charles Babbage, of devices intended to reduce the labor involved in producing mathematical tables. In ENIAC's case, these were artillery firing tables, affected by tactical developments in World War I that greatly increased the computational challenge of producing them. These tables were still needed after World War II: we estimate that ENIAC spent at least a fifth of its productive life calculating trajectories for them.[6]

But ENIAC's more profound contributions to advances in military science and technology came with Cold War work that would have been prohibitively expensive to attempt by hand. ENIAC simulated explosions of atomic and hydrogen bombs, airflow at supersonic speeds, and designs for nuclear reactors. With the considerable assistance of John von Neumann, it established the digital computer as a vital tool within the emerging military-industrial-academic complex carrying out cutting-edge research and development work during the early years of the Cold War. A few years later, IBM launched its first commercial computer, the Model 701, as the "defense calculator" and sold it almost exclusively to defense contractors. The United States Government even managed the delivery queue for IBM, making sure that computers were dispatched first to the firms doing the most important work.[7]

ENIAC was particularly important as a test-bed for algorithmically driven simulation, a fundamentally new approach to modeling. The Monte Carlo simulations carried out from 1948 to 1950 on behalf of Los Alamos were landmarks in the history of scientific practice as well as in the history of computer programming. The historian of physics Peter Galison made ENIAC's role in the development of computer simulation famous, but in chapters 8 and 9 we provide the first clear and in-depth exploration of exactly what the simulations did and, drawing on the dissertation work of Anne Fitzpatrick, illuminate the contributions they made to the progress of the atomic weapons program.[8]

ENIAC as the "First Computer"

New acquaintances learning that someone is a historian of computing often ask "What was the first computer?" The case for caring about ENIAC has usually been expressed a "first" of some kind, and it is ENIAC's status as the "first computer" that continues to dominate public discussion, for example in the "talk" section of its Wikipedia page, reviews posted on Amazon of books related to early computers, or the comments threads of online news articles. Feuds between the supports of rival claimants seem to return to life however assiduously historians try to steer discussion in more productive directions.[9]

Some firsts record historical events understood by participants and spectators as dashes to a defined goal, making the order in which contestants reach the finish line crucial. The celebrated "races" to get humans to the North Pole, the summit of Everest, the surface of the moon, or moving faster than the speed of sound fall into this category. The question of priority can also be of great importance in patent law, and in fact legal proceedings around ENIAC's patent profoundly shaped discussion of its place in history. Yet the computer projects of the 1940s have only in retrospect been perceived as races toward a well-defined goal. Thus, questions of influence and legacy are more historically revealing than those of priority. For example, while we show that in 1948 ENIAC was reconfigured to become the first computer to run a program written in the modern code paradigm we also found that no one who was involved appears to have seen that as particularly momentous at the time and that it did not have a discernible direct influence on other computer projects.

ENIAC was not the first electronic digital computer, even though for some decades it was generally believed to have been. The basic idea of a programmable computer is usually traced back a century earlier—to Charles Babbage, who worked for years on the design of a hand-cranked "Analytical Engine" but did not build it. In Germany, Konrad Zuse built an automatic mechanical calculator in his family's apartment in the 1930s, and during World War II he was given government resources to create a variety of successors based on relay technology. Even the use of electronic devices to hold and manipulate numbers was not unprecedented. From 1937 to 1942, the physicist John Atanasoff worked to build an electronic computer that would be able to solve systems of simultaneous linear equations. It never quite worked, but that failure is attributable to its external storage system (intended to burn intermediate results onto paper) rather than to its electronic components.[10]

Beyond this well-documented series of experimental machines lay a variety of special-purpose digital devices designed for different applications. Adding machines, calculating machines, and cash registers represented numbers digitally using systems of interlocking cogs. Punched-card machines stored data as patterns of holes in small rectangular cards, and by the 1930s letters as well as numbers could be represented. Machines specialized for particular tasks, such as sorting or punching cards, were configured by setting switches or wiring plugboards.

The first fully operational electronic digital computer, however, was a British machine, or rather a series of machines, called Colossus. Like ENIAC, Colossus was intended to address specific challenges and was shaped profoundly by the urgency of war. It was developed at the Post Office Research Establishment in London and deployed, under great secrecy, on a sprawling private estate in southern England that had been converted to house a scientific assault on the cyphers that the Germans were using to protect communications. Secrecy was paramount, since the codes could easily be modified if the Germans began to suspect that their contents were no longer secure. The very existence of Colossus was thus top secret throughout the war (and, thanks to the instinct for secrecy prevalent in the intelligence community, for decades afterward). Its creators were unable to take public credit for their historic achievements, and the machines, their blueprints, and other records of the project were systematically destroyed after the war.

Like Atanasoff's computer, the Colossus machines are usually classed as special-purpose machines confined to a single application, although they have widely been recognized as "programmable" because they could be reconfigured to apply different sequences of steps to decryption work.[11] Because of the secrecy surrounding it, Colossus had no influence on the ENIAC project. Even in Britain it had only an indirect and underappreciated influence on later developments, as its veterans were not able to explain the source of their ideas or to justify their confidence in particular techniques. Tommy Flowers, Colossus' primary designer, received little recognition until the very end of his life. Even after Colossus was embraced as part of Britain's national heritage, many still assumed that it had been Alan Turing's creation.

Scholars addressed the continuing feuds between the creators of these and other early computers by agreeing on the appropriate series of adjectives to insert between the words "first" and "computer" to reflect the unique contribution of each pioneer. Introducing a conference devoted to early computers, the historian Michael Williams asked his colleagues "not [to] use the word 'first'—there is more than enough glory in the creation of the modern computer to satisfy all of the early pioneers, most of whom are no longer in a position to care anyway."[12] In the same address, Williams said: "If you add enough adjectives to a description you can always claim your own favorite. For example ENIAC is often claimed to be the 'first electronic, general purpose, large scale, digital computer' and you certainly have to add all those adjectives before you have a correct statement."[13] We endorse that sentiment, and we have no interest in perpetuating these squabbles by anointing ENIAC (or one of its rivals) as the singular "first computer." We are concerned instead with establishing what was new about ENIAC, and what was not. However, that does not mean that we accept the distinctions drawn by these adjectives as a full description of what was historically important about ENIAC. They are more useful for defining metaphorical rosettes to be pinned to the various machines than for understanding their actual historical legacies and the influence each machine exerted on other early computing projects.

ENIAC as an Obligatory Point of Passage

The consensus on ENIAC as the first electronic, general-purpose, large-scale digital computer defined its importance primarily as a milestone on the road leading to the "first stored-program computer." That journey was recently recounted as a "creation myth" by George Dyson in his book *Turing's Cathedral*, but in less romantic form it is also the basic structure of standard scholarly accounts.[14] For example, the narrative of Martin Campbell-Kelly and William Aspray's *Computer* takes the shape of an hourglass, with ENIAC as a narrow isthmus linking various areas of pre-World War II technological practice to the postwar world of electronic computing. This mirrors the diagram reproduced here as figure I.1, an influential diagram prepared by Arthur and Alice Burks in their classic paper on ENIAC. While arguing that the basic technology of the electronic digital computer was appropriated from Atanasoff, they nevertheless reinforced the centrality of ENIAC to the story of modern computing.

Earlier technologies were represented as contributions to the development of ENIAC, in which they were embedded. ENIAC, in turn, led to later generations of computer hardware. This made ENIAC what sociologists of scientific knowledge have called an "obligatory passage point" in historical narrative, a role it took quite literally in the long-running Information Age exhibit at the Smithsonian.[15] The first exhibit hall displayed a range of technologies for calculation, communication, and clerical work. As visitors progressed, the walls closed around them, forcing them through a narrow opening into a chamber holding as much of ENIAC as would fit in a small room while leaving space for a few mannequins and museum goers. Nearby monitors looped video clips in which the machine's creators discussed its role. History opened up again as the visitor emerged from ENIAC into the modern world of digital computing. The display dramatized ENIAC, almost literally, as the machine that gave birth to modern computing.

In such narratives, ENIAC fills much the same role as John the Baptist in the New Testament: that of an essential supporting player remembered primarily for heralding the coming of the central character. In the New Testament that is, of course, Jesus; in the history of computing it has traditionally been the "stored-program computer," the "modern computer," or, more precisely, the approach to computer design first documented in John von Neumann's "First Draft of a Report on the EDVAC" (1945) and almost universally adopted by the electronic computer projects of the late 1940s. EDVAC was planned as a successor to ENIAC, and so the ideas described in the First Draft were developed in collaboration with ENIAC's creators.

As we will show in chapter 6, the new approach to computer design was deeply influenced by ENIAC both as a tangible demonstration of what could be achieved with electronics and as a challenge to find much simpler and more efficient ways to control computations automatically. John the Baptist's head made a messy exit on a plate. ENIAC vanishes from most narratives shortly after being switched on for experimental use at the Moore School.

ENIAC as a Material Artifact

Much discussion of ENIAC has continued to be framed in terms of the extent to which it anticipated or influenced later computers. Insofar as the objective of any

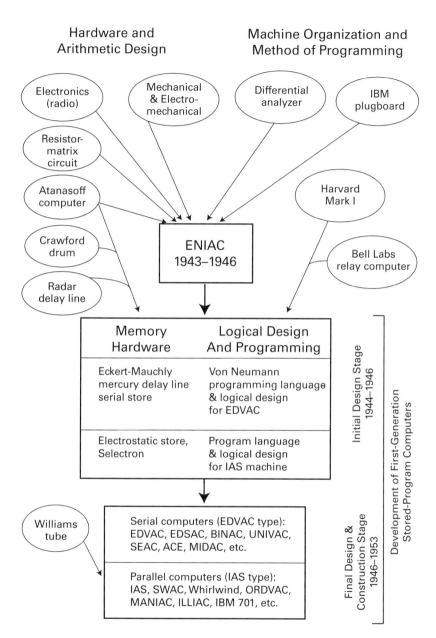

Figure I.1
Arthur and Alice Burks saw ENIAC as an obligatory passage point in the development of the modern computer. This diagram is from their article "The ENIAC: First General-Purpose Electronic Computer" (*Annals of the History of Computing* 3, no. 4, 1981: 310–389; ©1981 IEEE; reprinted, with permission, from *Annals of the History of Computing*).

overview history of computing is to explain the emergence of modern computer technology, that is entirely natural. ENIAC really was an indispensable link in a causal chain of innovation leading from hand-cranked calculating machines to modern supercomputers. Yet to remember ENIAC only as a stepping stone on the way to the digital world reduces it to a single moment, even if it boosts its significance. The actual machine and its career as a productive piece of scientific equipment disappear under the symbolic weight of world-changing importance.

One of our objectives is to use the rich archival evidence to re-engage with ENIAC as a physical artifact, following the recent revival of interest in "materiality" as a topic within science studies.[16] Historians have written about ENIAC's pioneering use of vacuum tubes, but not about the difficult challenges its creators faced in procuring and assembling its many other components (high-precision resistors, custom power supplies, even steel frames) in wartime. In chapter 3 we show that difficulties with these components, rather than vacuum tubes, caused the greatest concern as the computer's completion date slipped again and again during 1944 and 1945.

In focusing on ENIAC more as an idea than as a physical object, historians have naturally been more concerned with the engineers who designed the machine than with the dozens of "wiremen" who built it. We show that nearly all of the "wiremen" were women who, unlike the female ENIAC operators today lauded as the first computer programmers, have not been remembered by posterity. Blue-collar work has been less useful as a source of female role models, but without the toil of these forgotten women there would have been no ENIAC.

We reconstruct the rather shabby environment in which ENIAC was produced at the Moore School, documenting both a flood caused by the crumbling building that housed it and a fire sparked by flaws in the machine's cooling and safety systems. We also chart the difficulties caused by its move to its permanent home at the Ballistic Research Laboratory in Aberdeen, Maryland. The new space constructed for it at the BRL, which had air conditioning and a suspended ceiling, protected ENIAC and showcased its striking modernity.

ENIAC was a site of scientific spectacle.[17] Many delegations from companies and research groups were ushered inside the machine while it was still being built. Once it had been completed and installed at Aberdeen Proving Ground, work was often interrupted by parties of military visitors eager to witness it in action.

ENIAC was also a site of frequent frustration, to an extent that previous histories have not fully conveyed. In chapter 5 we show that ENIAC was only occasionally functional for more than a year after its arrival at Aberdeen. During four weeks in early 1948 a succession of failures, intermittent errors, and human errors meant that only the equivalent of one day of uninterrupted work was accomplished. This highlights the importance of maintenance work, another kind of labor previously neglected by historians of computing. Thanks to the efforts of the machine's operations and support teams in the next few years, ENIAC was eventually able to spend most of its time performing useful work, a transition we explore in chapter 10 along with the various modifications made to the machine over its operational life.

There is another sense in which ENIAC remained "in action" long after its first use in 1945. ENIAC was an exceptionally flexible piece of technology. Its hardware and its programming capabilities were repeatedly upgraded by its users. In 1948, after a long period of planning, ENIAC was reconfigured to use a programming method very similar to the method planned for the newer computers then under construction. We describe this process in chapter 7. It became the first computer to run a recognizably modern program. ENIAC had originally been a kind of modular kit from which a computer designed to solve a specific problem could be constructed by interconnecting wires and turning dials spread over several dozen bulky units. After its conversion, the wires and dials remained largely fixed in place until its retirement, implementing a number of generalized instructions. Programs were coded using these instructions and were stored on a set of read-only switchboards. This was a quite literal remaking of ENIAC around the new models of automatic computing to which it had given rise.

ENIAC as the Origin Point of Computer Programming

ENIAC's first six operators were hired in mid 1945. In a book titled *The Innovators* and subtitled *How a Group of Hackers, Geniuses, and Geeks Created the Digital Revolution*, Walter Isaacson demonstrates the extent to which their place in popular memory has come to overshadow that of the people who designed and built the machine. Isaacson writes dismissively of "the boys with their toys" who "thought that assembling the hardware was the most important job." In fact, he writes, "all the programmers who created the first general-purpose computer were women."[18] That baffling statement highlights both the extent to which the work of those women has come to overshadow the rest of ENIAC's story and a general lack of understanding of how "ENIAC programming" fits within the machine's overall story.

The women did play important roles in the success of ENIAC during the year it spent running problems at the Moore School, as did their less well-known successors who tended to ENIAC during its years in Aberdeen. We explore the full scope of their work, which included physically reconfiguring ENIAC, running cards through it and its auxiliary punched-card machines, and participating in the planning work we now think of as programming. Indeed, the fact that they are now celebrated exclusively as programmers rather than as operators is another sign of the technology world's disinclination to celebrate work seen as blue-collar. As Wendy Hui

Kyong Chun has noted, "reclaiming these women as the first programmers … glosses over the hierarchies … among operators, coders, and analysts."[19]

Discussing this early work poses some linguistic and conceptual challenges. Though it has become common to speak of the work of configuring ENIAC to carry out the mathematical operations needed to tackle a particular problem as "programming" the computer, at the time such work was usually called "setting up" ENIAC for the problem. We likewise respect contemporary usage by calling the necessary configuration, which was documented on "set-up forms," a "set-up" rather than a program.

We also illuminate several less familiar aspects of ENIAC's contribution to the development of programming practice—for example, the establishment in 1947 of a team of programming contractors led by Jean Bartik (formerly Betty Jean Jennings), one of the initial operators. This is the first known example of programming being fully separated from other forms of work. Along with Adele Goldstine, this team contributed significantly to the conversion of ENIAC to the new programming mode that made it practicable to write complex programs for Monte Carlo simulation. This was the first modern computer code to be executed, and remarkably complete archival materials allow us to document (in chapter 8) its development from an initial mathematical plan through several generations of flow diagrams to a complete program listing. That process required the application of fundamental programming techniques such as loops, conditional branching, and arrays; it also required a well-developed methodology for the transformation of mathematical statements into programs.

ENIAC as a Site of Technical Analysis

One thing that sets this book apart from most histories of computing written by professionally trained historians in the past 20 years is its systematic engagement with aspects of the technical history of computing: the development of computer architecture, the evolution of programming practice, and the mutual shaping of mathematical practice against computational capabilities. We guide the reader through some fairly detailed examinations of computer designs, flow diagrams, and code. Those passages include an examination of the development of conditional control in chapter 2, a close reading of von Neumann's "First Draft of a Report on the EDVAC" and its relationship to ENIAC in chapter 6, a discussion of the design process and programming techniques used to implement the first computer Monte Carlo simulation in chapter 8, and a comparison of ENIAC's capabilities with those of other early computers in chapter 11. Further technical material, including various primary sources and an annotated version of the Monte Carlo code, is presented on the book's companion website (www.EniacInAction.com).

We see this as part of a broader re-engagement of historians with the specifics of computer technology and the concerns of computer science. The history of science as a whole made a turn toward social and cultural analysis a generation ago, influenced by the emergence of science studies. Since then the wisdom of attempting to pry open the black boxes of technical knowledge and peer inside has been much debated.[20] Some scholars within science studies, such as Donald MacKenzie, have argued for the importance of understanding esoteric technical concepts well enough to demonstrate that even the most impersonal details of high technology are inseparable from social concerns. Others, such as Langdon Winner, have viewed the pursuit of technical detail as a distraction from social and political engagement.[21]

Within the history of computing, a relatively new and rather insecure subfield of the history of science and technology, the process of scholarly professionalization has been marked by a fairly uniform disengagement with technical detail in favor of stories about institutions, ideology, and occupations. Early historical work on computing, like early historical work on many other topics, was done by pioneers and other participants. They tended to produce detailed technical stories about particular computers, pioneering institutions, and the proper allocation of "firsts." Most of those entering the field as graduate students in history programs and science studies programs have lacked the technical background to appreciate or produce such stories, and have in any event sought instead to increase the scholarly respectability of the history of computing and their own potential employability by patterning their work on established models in better-developed historical fields. The development of the history of computing in a more scholarly direction has also been defined largely as a move away from technical history and technical details. Martin Campbell-Kelly, one of the field's most distinguished scholars, wrote a detailed exploration of the programming of early machines as his doctoral dissertation but later confessed to being embarrassed by that youthful indiscretion and turned to business history.[22] For a long while now, detailed examination of computer code or programming practice has been almost unknown in scholarly history of computing, seen at best as a guilty pleasure.

The change in methods was accompanied by a change in historical time frames. Scholars specializing in the history of computing paid relatively little attention to the machines of the 1940s, ENIAC included, from about 1990 to about 2010. Their stories had been well documented, and there were neglected topics of great importance in later eras. The publication in 2000 of the edited volume *The First Computers: History and Architecture* seemed for a while to represent the end of work on the topic rather than a new beginning.

In the past few years historians have begun to re-engage with the electronic computers of the 1940s and to bring some new questions and perspectives to their research. We have, in particular, grown more interested in questions of use and practice. This has reflected, in part, the incorporation of perspectives from this history and philosophy of mathematics in which technical exploration of the internal content of mathematical work has remained more prominent than in other areas of the history of science. Liesbeth de Mol and Maarten Bullynck have been particularly active in this area, examining ENIAC's use by Lehmer and its planned use by Haskell Curry.[23] ENIAC has begun to pop up as a supporting character in work on particular kinds of applied science. Most notably, its use for the first numerical weather simulations in 1950 and 1951 has been treated in some detail by Paul Edwards and Kristine C. Harper in two recent books.[24] As with Peter Galison's earlier discussion of ENIAC's role in early nuclear simulation, these narratives shift our understanding of ENIAC away from its traditional portrayal as one link in a chain running from primitive to modern computers and toward its work as an instrument for the creation of new kinds of scientific practice.[25] This parallels developments in the humanities outside existing work on history of computing, particularly attempts to establish fields such as "platform studies," "critical code studies," and "software studies."[26] The challenge is to re-surface from the sea of technical details clutching treasures that justify the dive.

This book is, in part, an experiment in the re-integration of technical detail into history influenced by the perspectives of science studies, labor history, institutional history, memory studies, and gender history. We see no essential boundary between these "social" perspectives and our more "technical" analysis. ENIAC's designers, builders, administrators, operators, programmers, and users were all, at the moment of their engagement with the machine, operating in both arenas, and we try to respect that when telling their stories.

ENIAC as an Object of Contested Historical Memory

ENIAC's history does not stop with its decommissioning in 1955. ENIAC has spent more time generating relics and parables than it ever did crunching numbers and punching cards. In chapter 12 we use some perspectives from the field of memory studies to explore its changing place in popular awareness during the intervening decades, from its role as a convenient yardstick to gauge the superiority of newer computers to its recent renown as a computer programmed by women.

It is not possible to fully separate this topic from the earlier narrative chapters. In attempting to reconstruct many aspects of ENIAC's history, such as the training of its operators, its public announcement, and the collaboration between its designers and John von Neumann to shape the next generation of computers, we found ourselves constantly grappling with contradictory statements made decades later by important participants. To some extent this may be blamed on the vagaries of human memory and on the mental processes by which people later make sense of their own actions by stitching them into coherent narratives. Many of the disagreements, however, are directly tied to the lengthy and unpleasant series of legal proceedings stemming from Eckert and Mauchly's June 1947 application to patent ENIAC, and with it the digital computer. They spent much more time arguing about ENIAC than they had spent building it. Less than three years after the first ENIAC contract was signed they had already left the University of Pennsylvania to try their luck as entrepreneurs. In contrast, 30 years went by between the start of work on ENIAC and the eventual invalidation of the patent in October of 1973.

From the 1950s on, many participants in the ENIAC project were repeatedly questioned, deposed, hired as consultants, or called to testify by lawyers representing various companies. They learned to speak cautiously and selectively about issues such as the influence, or lack thereof, of particular earlier projects on their own work. By the 1970s, sworn statements by ENIAC veterans enrolled on opposing sides were describing quite different versions of major events. The same people (among them Arthur Burks, Herman Goldstine, and Jean Bartik) went on to write extensively about ENIAC and its place in history.[27] Their accounts provide details and insights that are not available elsewhere, but they are also profoundly shaped by the positions of their authors in later battles. For example, Arthur Burks, who had designed much of ENIAC, later attempted to have himself added to the patent as a co-inventor so as to obtain license payments.[28] He and his wife Alice wrote the definitive technical history of ENIAC and wrote extensively about the capabilities and fate of Atanasoff's earlier computer.[29] They were careful researchers, and in places we rely on technical details from their work. We also include a number of quotations from Arthur's unfinished book on early computing. Yet their work—particularly Alice's book *Who Invented the Computer?*—is profoundly shaped by their experience in the lawsuit.[30] Her book is full of judgments against Mauchly's character and vituperative attacks on perceived enemies and is fixated on questions that no longer have consequence for anyone but the participants and their immediate family members.

At several points in the book we pause to engage with contradictory claims, exploring how narratives changed over time and, when possible, using archival evidence to evaluate the plausibility of particular stories. The incidents become case studies in the construction of historical memory. Many previous accounts uncritically accepted stories told in memoirs or oral history interviews, so we believe it is important to engage with these pervasive stories rather than simply ignoring them to substitute, without comment, our own narratives.

The reliance of historians and journalists on oral histories and memoirs, and in particular on a number of quotable anecdotes, has profoundly skewed dominant understanding of many aspects of ENIAC. For example, a great deal has been written about the process by which ENIAC was set up to demonstrate the calculation of shell trajectories for its public unveiling in February of 1946. Credit for that task has been vehemently disputed; however, participants and historians have tended to agree that work for the task began only a few weeks, or at most a few months, earlier, and that little attention had been given to ENIAC programming methods before the hiring of the first operators. This has given the job in question an almost mythic status as the first programming done for the first programmable computer.[31] All this has perpetuated a misconception that ENIAC was designed and engineered with no more than a vague appreciation of how it would be configured to carry out useful work.

Returning to the original archival materials enables us to present a more complex picture and to place the evolution of ENIAC programming within the broader context of the problem as a whole. In fact, planning for the calculation of shell trajectories was carried out very early in the project, starting in the autumn of 1943 with the production of configuration and timing diagrams. This took place in parallel with, and helped to shape, the detailed design of ENIAC's basic building block, the accumulator, and had been largely completed before significant design work took place on many of the machine's other units and long before the operators were hired. In this area, and in several others, our goal is not so much to provide the answers to controversial questions as to find different and better questions that steer us toward a deeper understanding of ENIAC's remarkable history.

1

Imagining ENIAC

Dozens of people worked for years to make ENIAC a reality, but John Presper Eckert Jr. and John William Mauchly are its acknowledged inventors. Theirs were the two names on the patent application filed in 1947, and when a federal judge eventually invalidated that patent he gave them the meager satisfaction of dismissing claims that several others had contributed enough to its overall design to be considered co-inventors.[1]

ENIAC's Inventors

The idea of building an electronic computer originated with Mauchly, the older of the pair. Then in his mid thirties, he was, according to the historian Atsushi Akera, a financially precarious middle-class man whose dreams of emulating his father's research career had been largely thwarted by the generational mistiming inherent in graduating with a PhD in molecular physics near the start of the Great Depression. Mauchly was employed as the only physics teacher at Ursinus, a small teaching-oriented college near Philadelphia, while looking for opportunities to build a research record and gain skills in areas of science with rosier career prospects. He was drawn to electronics, and particularly to the use of circuits to automate control and to count quantities digitally. By 1940 he had begun to investigate the prospects for an electronic machine to automate statistical work for meteorological research and had come into contact with others who were thinking along similar lines. In June of 1941, on John Atanasoff's invitation, he traveled to Iowa to see the electronic computer that Atanasoff was building with Clifford Berry at Iowa State College in Ames. According to Akera, Mauchly's career was "transformed" when he decided to forgo paid summer employment to enroll in a special program at the University of Pennsylvania in which scientists were being re-trained to meet anticipated wartime needs.[2]

It was in these classes that Mauchly met Eckert, a bright young master's-program student with a remarkable talent for electronics who was running the course's teaching laboratory. Eckert, from a wealthy local family, had attended an elite private school, to which he reportedly had been chauffeured.[3] His love of engineering had drawn him away from the family's real-estate business and toward the laboratory.

Electronics and the War

The summer program that Mauchly attended was organized by the Moore School of Electrical Engineering, established in 1923 and as of 1941 still led by Harold Pender, its energetic founding dean. Electrical engineering was by then firmly established as a profession and a field of study, having joined the older disciplines of military, civil, and mechanical engineering. During the 1940s the University of Pennsylvania as a whole was, despite its venerable roots, not seen as belonging in the front rank of American universities. Engineering, which tended to draw practical students from ordinary families, was outside the mainstream at Ivy League schools, where students were known as much for their privileged backgrounds as for their academic drive. The Moore School had a solid reputation, but was smaller and less focused on large-scale research and the integration of the latest scientific discoveries into engineering practice than, say, MIT's electrical engineering department.

Why the urgent need for scientists with knowledge of electronics? By the 1940s engineers had begun to think of some novel uses of electricity as the domain of the new discipline of "electronic engineering." That term needs some explanation, since electricity is by definition the flow of electrons through a conductor. Electrical power had been successfully commercialized since the 1880s and was typically used to heat something or to turn something by means of a motor.

Electronics originated as an extension of the techniques of radio engineering. In radios, electricity was used not to turn or to heat mechanical components but to amplify signals. Diodes and triodes, the fundamental building blocks of electronic systems, were first implemented during the 1920s in the form of vacuum tubes. Vacuum tubes had evolved from incandescent light bulbs—glass bubbles in which delicate metal filaments shielded from the atmosphere could conduct electricity without burning out. But whereas light bulbs were intended simply to turn current into visible light, vacuum tubes manipulated current in a variety of ways. Diodes conducted in one direction only. Triodes had three terminals and were the basic building block of amplifiers. Together with other, more specialized kinds of tubes, they became essential components of radios, of telephone and telegraph networks, and of televisions. The availability to the Moore School of a critical mass of engineers with skills in electronics owed a great deal to the maturity of radio technology and to the emergence of Philadelphia as a center for the production of vacuum tubes and radios.

The prospect of war created an urgent demand for new forms of electronic transmission. One of the most important new technologies was radar, first put into useful operation by the British in the late-1930s. Radar enabled ground stations, and eventually portable airborne stations, to detect aircraft when they were too far away to be seen or when they were obscured by clouds or darkness. The crucial step separating useful radar systems from unsuccessful earlier experiments was the shift from transmission of a continuous signal to illuminate the target (as in conventional radio applications) to transmission of a series of pulses. Targets were sensed by measuring how long it took a pulse to return after being reflected, rather than by looking for changes in its frequency. In the terminology of the time, this was a change from analysis of information contained in the "frequency domain" of the signal to analysis of information contained in the "time domain." The technologies needed to reliably generate rapid pulses and process them through electronic circuits were essential to the later development of electronic digital computers.

Eckert later wrote that "the influence of radar switching and timing circuitry was more important and significant" than his "experience with analog computers," which "was no great help in building the digital ENIAC."[4] His first experience with counting circuits had come when, while working on a radar project the Moore School was conducting jointly with MIT, he attempted to measure digitally the time a radar pulse took to return.[5] When Mauchly stated at the end of his life that there was not a "shred of truth" to the idea that radar inspired ENIAC, insisting that his digital approach to computation was to "a large extent, based on the 'scaling circuits' of nuclear and cosmic ray laboratories,"[6] he was discussing the sources of his determination to apply digital electronics to scientific computation. (The patent dispute provided a strong incentive to downplay any influence from Atanasoff's project.) However, the surge of interest in radar associated with the war played an important part in realizing such ambitions by spreading the skills and equipment needed to work with digital pulses to places such as the Moore School and to men such as J. Presper Eckert and Homer Spence, an unsung hero of the ENIAC story who stayed with the machine for almost its entire operating life and who did more than anyone else to keep it functioning reliably.[7]

Conceiving ENIAC

In September of 1941 Mauchly began work at the Moore School, having been hired by Dean Harold Pender to help fill the gaps left in the Moore School faculty as it reorganized to support war-related projects.[8] His long-standing desire to work on electronic computing technology was satisfied in April of 1943 when the ENIAC proposal he and Eckert had drafted was approved. This proposal was profoundly influenced by the environment of the Moore School, and in particular by its wartime collaboration with the Ballistic Research Laboratory at the Aberdeen Proving Ground in nearby Maryland.

The Aberdeen Proving Ground was a showpiece for the modern American military, having been created during World War I in what the historian David Alan Grier called "the Manhattan Project of its age." Built on the shores of Chesapeake Bay for proximity to Washington, military installations, and munitions producers, its construction involved the eviction of 11,000 people who were living on its 35,000-acre site.[9] Aside from frequent explosions of shells, dropping of bombs, and test firing of small missiles, conditions there were quite bucolic. Scientific work having to do with all kinds of ordnance was carried out there, but the work most important to ENIAC's development was the mathematical labor involved in the production of firing tables.

Firing Tables

Pistols and rifles are aimed by pointing them at a target. Even over the maximum effective range of expert snipers during the 1940s (perhaps 1,000 yards), the adjustments needed to compensate for the pull of gravity or the influence of wind could be made by eye or by simple heuristics. But the procedures used by artillery gunners, whose targets might be several miles away, were quite different. They used controls to set the direction and elevation of a gun's barrel, but the distance a shell traveled was also influenced by the type of ordnance being used, by the altitude (and hence the density of the air), and by the velocity of the wind. The firing tables supplied with each gun specified the elevation required to fire a shell of a certain type at a target a certain distance away, and supplementary correction tables allowed a gunner to compensate for the temperature of the gunpowder, the cant of the carriage's axle, and other variables.[10]

Different information was required for different types of fire. Anti-aircraft batteries, for example, fired shells that were exploded by timed fuses, and so gunners needed to know the height of a shell at regular intervals during its flight so that shells would explode in the vicinity of the target aircraft.

Producing firing tables involved a complex mix of empirical and mathematical work for each combination of gun and ammunition. The process began on the BRL's test range, where about ten rounds were fired at various elevations. The distances traveled by the shells were measured and used to fit "reduction trajectories" to the observed data. The process yielded numerical coefficients that then could be plugged into standard ballistics equations. In the most time-consuming part of the process, ballistics equations were solved repeatedly in order to plot the trajectories of shells fired at many different elevations. Each calculated trajectory provided the information for a single row in a complete firing table.

1	2	3	4	5	6	7	8	9	10	11	12	13	14	15	16	17	18	19	20
			Change in elevation for 100-yd change in range	Change in range for 1-mil change in elevation	Time of flight	Probable Error Range	Probable Error Deflection	Height of burst	Slope of fall	Line no. of metro message	Deflection effect Drift	Deflection effect Lateral wind of 1 m.p.h. (+)	Complementary angle of site for each +1 mil of site	Complementary angle of site for each −1 mil of site	Range effect of increase of — One per cent in weight of projectile standard weight 15.96 lb.	Range effect — One foot per second in MV	Range effect — Air temperature 1° Standard is 59°	Range effect — Rear wind 1 m.p.h.	Range effect — One per cent in air density
Range	Elevation	Fork	c	1 mil	Time	ePr	ePd		Slope	Line	Dft.	W-D			Wt.	VE	Temp.	W-R	Den.
R	El	F	m.	yd.	sec.	yd.	yd.	m.	1/-	No.	m.	m.	m.	m.	yd.	yd.	yd.	yd.	yd.
yd.	m.	m.																	
4000	122.0	2	4.6	22	10.2	11	1	1	5.5	1	R4	.4	+.01	−.01	−1	+2.3	+1.1	+3.7	−14
4100	126.6	2	4.6	21	10.5	12	2	1	5.3	1	R4	.4	+.01	−.01	−1	+2.4	+1.2	+3.8	−14
4200	131.4	2	4.8	21	10.9	12	2	1	5.1	1	R4	.4	+.01	−.01	−1	+2.4	+1.2	+4.0	−15
4300	136.2	2	4.8	21	11.2	12	2	1	4.9	1	R4	.5	+.02	−.02	0	+2.4	+1.3	+4.2	−15
4400	141.0	2	4.8	20	11.6	12	2	1	4.7	1	R4	.5	+.02	−.02	0	+2.5	+1.4	+4.4	−15
4500	146.0	2	5.0	20	11.9	12	2	1	4.5	2	R4	.5	+.02	−.02	0	+2.5	+1.4	+4.6	−16
4600	151.6	3	5.0	20	12.3	12	2	1	4.3	2	R4	.5	+.02	−.02	0	+2.5	+1.5	+4.8	−16
4700	156.0	3	5.0	19	12.6	12	2	1	4.2	2	R4	.5	+.02	−.02	+1	+2.5	+1.6	+5.0	−16
4800	161.2	3	5.2	19	13.0	12	2	1	4.0	2	R5	.5	+.02	−.02	+1	+2.6	+1.7	+5.2	−17
4900	166.6	3	5.2	19	13.3	12	3	1	3.9	2	R5	.5	+.02	−.02	+1	+2.6	+1.7	+5.4	−17
5000	172.0	3	5.4	19	13.7	13	3	1	3.7	2	R5	.5	+.02	−.02	+2	+2.6	+1.8	+5.6	−18
5100	177.6	3	5.4	18	14.0	13	3	1	3.6	2	R5	.5	+.02	−.02	+2	+2.6	+1.9	+5.8	−18

Figure 1.1
An extract from a firing table for a 75-millimeter gun, with trajectory information given for equally spaced range intervals. (Paul P. Hanson, *Military Applications of Mathematics*, McGraw-Hill, 1944, 84)

TRAJECTORY DATA FOR 3-INCH ANTIAIRCRAFT GUN M1917, M1917MI, M1917MII, AND M1925MI

AA Shrapnel, Mk. I   FT 3 AA-J-2a
Part 2a   Fuze, Scovil, Mk. III
(MV=2,600 f/s)

Quadrant elevation (φ)=500 mils					*Quadrant elevation (φ)=600 mils*				
Time of flight	Fuze setting	Horizontal range	Altitude	Angular height	Time of flight	Fuze setting	Horizontal range	Altitude	Angular height
t	F	R	H	ϵ	t	F	R	H	ϵ
(Sec.)	(Sec.)	(Yds.)	(Yds.)	(Mils.)	(Sec.)	(Sec.)	(Yds.)	(Yds.)	(Mils.)
1	1.2	706	372	494	1	1.2	666	440	594
2	2.4	1,316	683	488	2	2.4	1,239	809	588
3	3.5	1,850	946	481	3	3.5	1,745	1,123	582
4	4.6	2,325	1,169	474	4	4.6	2,196	1,393	576
5	5.7	2,755	1,360	467	5	5.6	2,603	1,627	569
6	6.8	3,149	1,526	460	6	6.7	2,977	1,832	562
7	7.8	3,515	1,670	452	7	7.7	3,326	2,013	555
8	8.8	3,860	1,795	443	8	8.7	3,656	2,173	547
9	9.8	4,191	1,904	434	9	9.7	3,972	2,316	538
10	10.9	4,511	1,998	425	10	10.7	4,278	2,444	529

Figure 1.2
Detailed trajectory information from an anti-aircraft gunnery manual, given for equally spaced intervals of time.
(War Department, Coast Artillery Field Manual. Antiaircraft Artillery: Gunnery, Fire Control, and Position Finding, Antiaircraft Guns (FM 4–110), Government Printing Office, 1940, 314)

Calculating Trajectories

The calculation of individual trajectories is central to the production of firing tables of all kinds. The path of a shell once it has left the barrel of a gun is the subject of *exterior ballistics*.[11] This path is defined by a pair of second-order differential equations defining the shell's horizontal and vertical distances from the muzzle as a function of time. Although the equations are quite simple, solving them is complicated by the need to model air resistance, which varies in a nonlinear manner according to the shell's velocity. No amount of rearranging symbols, checking substitution rules, or looking up integrals yields an exact analytical solution. Unlike a calculus teacher, who selects only equations that respond to elegant methods, the mathematicians at the BRL couldn't ignore wind resistance or assign a different problem. Like most differential equations formulated by scientists and engineers, ballistics equations require messier techniques of numerical approximation.

Before World War I, most artillery was fired on rather flat trajectories that could be approximated to a high degree of accuracy using methods developed by the Italian mathematician Francesco Siacci. However, trench warfare demanded higher gun elevations to fire shells safely over friendly troops and down onto the enemy beyond. The new problem of anti-aircraft fire also demanded much higher gun elevations than had been necessary before. Siacci's methods did not work well for these trajectories, and after that war the U.S. military gradually adopted the more versatile method of numerical integration, breaking each trajectory into many small time intervals.[12] Equations described how the horizontal and vertical velocities of the projectile changed. The velocities might be calculated first after 0.01 second, then again after 0.02 second, and so on. Using these velocities to repeatedly update an estimate of the projectile's position provided a trace of its entire aerial trajectory. Though mathematically simple, these calculations were very time-consuming. It was not feasible to compute most firing tables directly; instead, generalized ballistics tables were used to derive firing tables for particular weapons. Nevertheless, the series of firing tables begun after World War I was not completed until 1936. Fortunately, developments in automatic computation were about to come into play.

The Differential Analyzer

At the beginning of the 1930s, Vannevar Bush and his colleagues at MIT developed the differential analyzer, a machine that for the first time enabled differential equations to be solved mechanically.[13] At the heart of the imposing device were shafts to which operators attached mechanical integrators and other components in problem-specific configurations. A pen-like drawing arm was used to trace input curves, which the machine transformed into solutions drawn on a separate sheet of paper. Inside the analyzer, numbers were represented in analog form by the rotation of the shafts. The integrators added up the values of these constantly changing quantities, for example to provide a running total of the distance traveled by a projectile as a function of its velocity.

The differential analyzer brought the Moore School into close contact with the Aberdeen Proving Ground. Irven Travis joined the Moore School's faculty in 1931, quickly becoming its "machinery expert."[14] Struggling with the solution of nonlinear differential equations, he had the idea of obtaining federal Depression relief funds to build an analyzer at the Moore School.[15] Travis visited MIT to learn more, but because a government sponsor was needed in order to obtain funding he also turned to the nearby Aberdeen Proving Ground.[16] Vannevar Bush had previously suggested that the analyzer might be of use in producing firing tables.[17] A deal was now struck: the Moore School would come up with a suitable design, and relief funds would then be used to construct one machine for the Moore School and one for the proving ground. In the event of war, the proving ground would be able to take over the Moore School's analyzer.[18] The Moore School's analyzer was completed in late 1934. The proving ground's analyzer, which became operational in 1935, was housed in the Computing Section of the new Research Division, renamed the Ballistic Research Laboratory in 1938.[19]

At the Moore School, Travis continued to take an active research interest in the analyzer. In 1940 he produced a report for General Electric describing a digital version of the analyzer that would use off-the-shelf adding machines rather than specialized analog integrators.[20] Another person with an interest in the machine was John Grist Brainerd, the director of research at the Moore School and the faculty member overseeing liaison with the Aberdeen Proving Ground, who in the early 1940s published a number of papers on computational approaches to various topics in applied mathematics.[21]

The analyzer could compute a single trajectory in about 15 minutes, whereas a person with a mechanical desk calculator needed two full work days (though the human did deliver more accurate results). But because each firing table required the calculation of hundreds of individual trajectories, the backlog of work continued to grow.[22] In 1940, with war looming, the Ballistic Research Laboratory invoked its contractual right to take over the Moore School's analyzer.[23] Staff members at the Moore School were trained to maintain and operate the analyzer, and in addition a manual computation group was set up at the school. The manual computation group was staffed by a team of mostly female "computers" who worked largely by hand.

Electronics to the Rescue

By 1942 America was at war, and the demand for firing tables continued to grow. Existing tables covered only a limited range of factors and were reported to have an unacceptable error rate.[24] The case for replacing them was easy to make. Most

Figure 1.3
The differential analyzer, operated by Kay McNulty, Alyse Snyder, and Sis Stump in the basement of the Moore School.
(U.S. Army Photograph, courtesy of the Jean Jennings Bartik Computing Museum, Northwest Missouri State University)

battlefield casualties on both sides were caused by mortars and other artillery.[25] Because the first few volleys—before the soldiers being targeted could take cover— were the most deadly, even a small boost to the accuracy of the early volleys would appreciably benefit the war effort.[26]

The Moore School's firing-table group was pushing the limits of what the available workforce could do with existing technology. Toward the end of 1942, more than 100 women had been assigned to the group, working six days a week in two shifts in a small building on the University of Pennsylvania's campus.[27] As their output fell further behind schedule, it was becoming apparent that the job would not be completed until long after the war was over.

Mauchly was well aware of these developments. During 1941 and 1942 he took time to familiarize himself with the workings and the use of the analyzer. He discussed the possibilities of electronic calculation with Travis before the latter left for service in the Navy in June of 1941.[28] He was also involved with manual computation, supervising a group carrying out calculations evaluating a new type of radar antenna, and his wife, Mary, was a member of the computing group working on firing tables.

The looming backlog of calculations provided Mauchly with a new opportunity to argue for the development of electronic calculating technology. In an August 1942 memo titled "The Use of High Speed Vacuum Tubes for Calculating" he outlined a machine that would, he suggested, speed up trajectory calculations greatly.[29] Brainerd returned the report to Mauchly in January of 1943, commenting "it is easily conceivable that labor shortage may justify development work on this in the not too far distant future." But the immediate spur to progress was provided by Lieutenant Herman Goldstine, the BRL's liaison officer at the Moore School overseeing the work of the computing group. Goldstine held a PhD in mathematics from the University of Chicago. In spring 1943 he read Mauchly's memo and became convinced that a machine such as Mauchly had described would deal effectively with the severe delays his teams were experiencing.

Goldstine discussed Mauchly's ideas with Colonel Paul Gillon, who had been Goldstine's first supervisor when at the BRL but who had soon been transferred to the Research and Materials Division of the Office of the Chief of Ordnance. They "agreed on the desirability of the Ordnance Department underwriting a development program at the Moore School looking toward the ultimate production of an electronic digital computer for the Ballistic Research Laboratory."[30] The BRL requested a more formal proposal from the Moore School. Brainerd, Mauchly, and Eckert quickly prepared a "Report on an Electronic Difference Analyzer."[31] That novel term was chosen to exploit the familiarity of their audience with the Moore School's differential analyzer.[32] The proposal emphasized the structural similarities between the two machines; in fact, the "difference analyzer" bore a strong overall resemblance to the digital version of the differential analyzer that Irven Travis had described in 1940.[33]

The Moore School's representatives visited Aberdeen on April 9 to discuss the proposal, and "shortly thereafter Colonel Simon, in charge of the Ballistic Research Laboratory, indicated that he was inclined to include $150,000 in his budget for the project." After a further meeting on April 20, Gillon "stated that the possibilities were so important that the Army should invest the money in the development."[34] The April report formed the basis for the formal contract finalized in June, even though descriptions of circuits were conspicuously absent and the computer's control method remained fuzzy.

Brainerd promised the BRL that "the analyzer" would "perform most of the work" that was then handled for the Aberdeen Proving Ground "by the computing branch of approximately 200 persons, by the mechanical differential analyzers at Aberdeen and at the University of Pennsylvania ... and by many of the IBM machines at Aberdeen," and that "in addition, certain large-scale projects such as extensive ballistics tables, not now undertaken, might be turned out." This work, he promised, would be done more rapidly and more accurately than was currently possible. It would include "virtually all processes which a human computer can do with a computing machine," allowing "the preparation of a complete firing table" and "thus eliminating the large amount of manual and machine work which now follows mechanical analyzer runs."[35]

ENIAC's initial design departed dramatically from previous computers in only one respect: vacuum tubes were used to build its control units and arithmetic circuits and to store the numbers on which it was working. Earlier machines had represented digits by the positions of cogs on shafts, by holes punched in cards, or by the positions of electrically operated relay switches. Even if numbers could be added quickly, they still had to be read from such a medium, and the result then had to be written back before the next step in the calculation. The mechanical components worked thousands of times more slowly than the purely electronic circuits planned for ENIAC.

Relying on vacuum tubes as the only storage mechanism for numbers modified during the execution of a program was indeed radical. The tradeoff was one of speed (very high) versus cost (also very high), capacity (rather limited), and complexity (spectacular). Electronic counting circuits were not entirely unknown, but remained a difficult and esoteric area of electronics. Nancy Beth Stern has pointed out that industrial development labs such as those of NCR and RCA had struggled to get them to work, and that the leaders of the National Defense Research Committee, a group established to coordinate wartime technical projects, had deep reservations about whether the technologies needed for a digital computer were mature enough to produce useful results in time to contribute to the war effort. They also had reservations about the ability of the Moore School, a respectable research center but not an elite one, to pull off this feat.[36]

ENIAC in the Original Proposals

From the very beginning, ENIAC's design was bound up with conceptions of the problems it was intended to solve. In 1942 Mauchly characterized these as being represented by "formulas which can readily be put in the form of iterative equations." He expected that its major application would be to the numerical solution of differential equations, such as those used in the calculation of trajectories, by means of difference equations. This approach led to "step-by-step" solutions of problems, each step, or cycle, repeating a sequence of operations until the required solution was obtained.[37]

Design work on what eventually became ENIAC appears to have taken as a starting point Irven Travis' 1940 proposal for a digital differential analyzer.[38] Travis had shown how to solve difference equations by interconnecting units that performed the elementary operations of arithmetic. His examples used three types of units: accumulators (which could store a number and add other numbers to it), multipliers (which formed the product of two numbers), and adders (which added numbers together and transmitted the result instead of storing it).

The transition from analog to digital meant that the units had to be explicitly coordinated. On the analog differential analyzer, numbers were represented by the rotation of the shafts connecting the units, and gears and integrators transformed the rates of rotation as was required. Computation was, in a sense, continuous. But if the integrators were replaced by adding machines, computation and the communication of numbers between units would become sequences of discrete events. How could the actions of the different units be coordinated so that data would be automatically transferred from one unit to another when that was required and individual operations would be initiated in the correct order? The differential analyzer did not suggest answers to these questions, and Travis had done no more than point out that some kind of timer would be required.

Mauchly faced the same problem, and in 1942 he was almost as vague about how to solve it. He envisaged the set of arithmetic units as if it were a team of human computers, each working on a specific subcomputation and exchanging intermediate results only when that was necessary. To solve equations numerically, the new machine would "perform a number of multiplications, additions, subtractions or divisions in sequence" and carry out "a cycle of operations which will yield a step by step solution of any difference equations within its scope." Mauchly proposed that the machine include a "program device" that would coordinate the transfer of numerical results between units and would be capable of "arranging a cycle of different transfers and operations … with perhaps fifteen or twenty operations in each cycle," but he gave no details of how the device would do that.[39]

In their 1943 proposal, Eckert and Mauchly built on Travis' modular approach. They adopted the accumulator to store numbers and to provide for addition and subtraction. That made the adder unnecessary, but they proposed dedicated units to perform multiplication and division and a "function generator" to provide values of functions. Looking up values from tables was a pervasive feature of manual computation, and Travis had also included a function generator in his plans. A "constant transmitter" and a "recorder" for input and output completed their proposed roster of units.

Eckert and Mauchly's proposal included a "block diagram," similar to those drawn by Travis, for a simple problem. It showed "in" and "out" terminals on each unit connected so as to pass numbers directly between units. The connecting wires therefore played the same communicative role in the machine that the rotating shafts played in the analyzer.

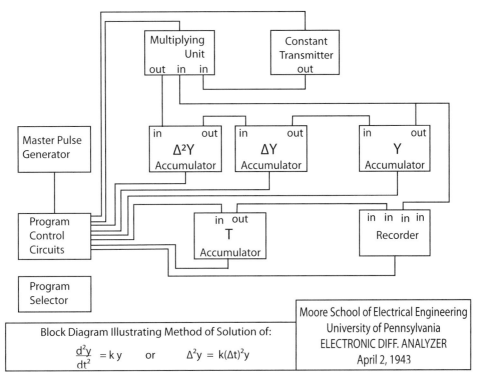

Figure 1.4
The 1943 proposal that launched the ENIAC project included this sketch of how the machine could be set up to solve the harmonic equation.
(University of Pennsylvania archives)

The proposal also described in more detail how the coordination problem would be solved. A "program control unit" containing "the necessary control circuits for initiating the various steps of the calculation in their proper order" would be connected to all the other units. It would determine when units read and transmitted numbers through their data terminals and when accumulators were cleared. The block diagram shows a highly centralized control system with a dense web of wires spreading out from the program-control circuits to the computational units. Control signals would take the form of pulses produced by a "master pulse generator" and passed along these wires. Exactly how the desired sequence of operations would be encoded wasn't clear, although there was a brief mention of a "program selector" capable of reading data and sequencing information from punched cards.[40]

A more detailed example (presented here in redrawn form as figure 1.5) showed "one of many possible ways of setting up a program for the step-by-step solution

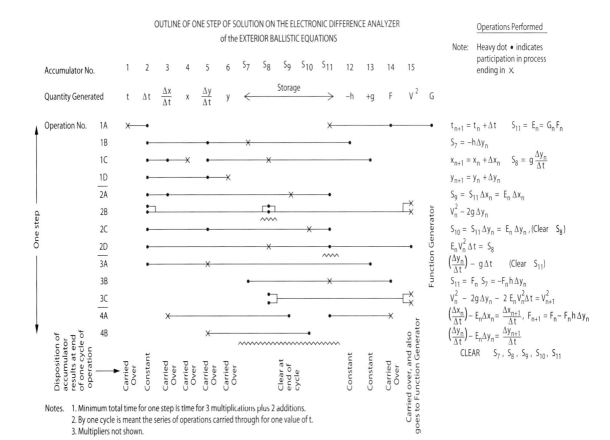

Figure 1.5
The 1943 ENIAC proposal included this detailed sketch of how the machine's components could work together to carry out the series of operations needed to calculate a trajectory.
(University of Pennsylvania archives)

of a pair of equations commonly used in exterior ballistics" and gave a clearer idea of how computations would be structured on the difference analyzer.[41]

The computation was represented in tabular form, recalling the sheets used in manual computations. Those sheets were typically divided into columns, each corresponding to a mathematical variable, into which the (human) computer wrote successive values of the variable as the calculation proceeded. In Eckert and Mauchly's diagram, the columns represented accumulators, each annotated with an expression describing its contents. Rather than actual numerical values, however, the table showed when and how the operations corresponding to equations written to the right of the table were carried out. Each row specified the accumulators from which the arguments of an operation were taken and those in which the result would be stored. To save computing time, operations that could be performed simultaneously were grouped together—for example, all the operations in group 1 were started at the same time, and not until all of them had been completed could the operations in group 2 commence. This capability of performing logically distinct operations at the same time was to remain a basic feature of ENIAC's design.

Getting Started

Preparatory work began well before July of 1943, when what was code-named Project PX would formally commence. Harold Pender noted that "numerous purchases" and some project work were done in April and May of 1943, "at a time when our PX # 1 contract had definitely been decided upon but before an account was set up."[42] In May, a detailed list of necessary electrical components and instruments was drawn up, the War Department was provided with a list of project staff so that background checks could be carried out, and security measures to be put in place to protect the project's workspace were discussed.[43]

In early June, the Ordnance Department sent a formal letter of intent to the Moore School and the administrative details of the project were finalized. Pender described "a $150,000 project spread over fifteen months," meaning that ENIAC would be finished by September of 1944.[44] The initial contract was for only six months, with supplemental contracts to be awarded if progress was satisfactory. By the end of June, Brainerd had sent a detailed budget to the Moore School's accountants.[45]

Staffing the Project

Mauchly, Goldstine, and Eckert remained at the center of ENIAC planning and development through mid 1945. Mauchly was recognized as the initial leader of the project, though his official role was merely that of a consultant. Because of Eckert's superior knowledge of electronics, his role grew ever more prominent as the design of the machine came into focus and as its construction neared. Eckert and Mauchly remained employees of the Moore School, and Goldstine was the Army's primary representative, but all three men came to identify more strongly with the ENIAC project itself than with their employers, and worked as a team to ensure that it received the resources it needed.

Of the three, only Eckert was initially assigned to work full time on the project. Goldstine was expected to continue his supervision of the Moore School's computing group and to contribute to various other projects the Ballistic Research Laboratory was involved with (among them projects having to do with high-altitude bombing and with meteorology).[46] The Moore School expected its faculty members, including Mauchly, to carry out their teaching and administrative duties even when working on wartime contracts. In February of 1943, shortly before the ENIAC proposal was prepared, the Moore School had only nine full-time faculty members, "about two thirds" of whom were already working on government contracts. Even with the addition of dozens of research and laboratory engineers, assistants, and machine-shop workers, their burden was heavy.[47] Soon Project PX was larger, in terms of revenue and personnel, than the school's dozen or so other projects combined. As it progressed, Mauchly shifted into, and then back out of, full-time commitment.

The initial budget, covering the period June 1943–May 1944, called for the partial support of eighteen named individuals from project funds. Salaries were the largest budgeted category, followed by supplies. Brainerd was listed as the project's director, Eckert and Mauchly as "laboratory supervisors." Three "research engineers" were specified, including Arthur W. Burks (part time) and T. Kite Sharpless. Burks, like Mauchly, was a PhD who had been re-trained for electronics work in the Moore School's special summer course, though his doctorate was in philosophy rather than science or engineering. The number of research engineers eventually grew to nine. Burks remained the most important addition to the design team. The initial roster was filled out with five laboratory engineers, three junior engineers to be hired from the graduating class, four technicians, one assistant technician, and a secretary. All the junior members of the staff were full time.[48]

Getting the lab ready entailed obtaining equipment such as lamps, hand tools, drawing tables, drawers, and the light machine tools needed to set up a small shop.[49] Ordnance Department staffers inspected the Moore School's facilities and recommended "plant protection measures" such as the addition of window grills, lockable doors, and fire extinguishers to safeguard the room in which project work would take place. A night watchman was also suggested.[50]

Even in peacetime, computer design projects tend to take a toll on the personal and emotional well-being of their participants. ENIAC was built during wartime, when normal personnel policies were suspended. Vacation days were limited, Saturdays were official work days, and for much of the duration of the project there were two shifts. After it was all over, John Brainerd wrote: "To build a staff, obtain materials, and carry on at double quick speed during the middle of the war was … a task of 60 to 80 hours per week for the leaders, with much of the work futile, promises unkept, goods diverted, and mental breakdowns lurking around each weekend."[51] He was not exaggerating.

Numbers and Accumulators

In notes on a meeting held on July 10, 1943, T. Kite Sharpless mentioned "J. W. Mauchly holding forth" and explaining that the team's first task was to build an "electronic version of [an] ordinary computing machine."[52] Communication within the machine was to be carried out by the transmission of electrical pulses; the number 7, for example, would be transmitted by passing seven pulses down a wire.[53] The first requirement was, therefore, for a circuit capable of counting pulses. The team initially hoped to obtain counters from an external source. Details of several electronic counting circuits, most of them designed by scientists for specific purposes such as measuring cosmic radiation, had been published. A number of circuits were tested, including a new "positive action ring counter" designed by Eckert and a thyratron counter developed by NCR.[54] None of those circuits was suitable, however. Eventually the team settled on a new design for a counter that they called a "decade," which operated reliably over the full range of operating frequencies planned for ENIAC.[55]

A decade was the electronic equivalent of a wheel storing a single decimal digit on a mechanical calculator. It had ten distinct states, or stages, moving from one to the next whenever a pulse was received. Numbers larger than 10 would be transmitted and stored digit by digit. As Mauchly had explained in 1942, the number 1,216 could be stored on four decades and transmitted using ten pulses: six on a units line, one on a tens line, two on a hundreds line, and one on a thousands line.[56] A special two-stage counter, dubbed the PM counter, was used to record the sign of a number. (P stood for "positive" and M for "minus.") Negative numbers were stored using a "tens complement" scheme: if four-digit numbers were stored, for example, 15 would be represented by P0015 and –15 by M9985.

By September of 1943, the team had come up with a concrete proposal for "accumulators" and "transmitters."[57] An accumulator was to contain eight decades and a PM counter, thus accommodating a single integer of up to eight digits. In addition to counting incoming pulses, it would be able to reset itself to zero or to round off the number held to a specified number of significant figures. Transmitters were responsible for signaling the number held in an accumulator by emitting the appropriate numbers of pulses. Adding two numbers together was little more than a special case of counting. If two pulses and then three more pulses were received by a decade, the decade would register all five pulses. After receiving ten pulses, a decade would wrap around from 9 to 0 and send a "carry" pulse to the next decade, implementing electronically a well-established mechanical technique.

The use of complements made it easy to implement subtraction. An accumulator had two output terminals and so could transmit a stored number (from terminal A) or its complement (from terminal S). Adding the number transmitted from terminal S had the effect of subtracting the number actually stored in the accumulator. This technique wasn't familiar in 1943. Burks devoted several pages of his notebook to checking that it worked for all combinations of positive and negative numbers.[58]

Determining the Size of the Accumulator

Mauchly's proposal described a machine that would solve differential equations by iterative numerical methods, and the team quickly enlisted Hans Rademacher, a mathematician on the University of Pennsylvania's faculty, to investigate its likely accuracy on such calculations. They were lucky to find him, as expertise in numerical methods was then more widespread among scientists and engineers (who had to deal with numerical methods) than among mathematicians (to most of whom numerical analysis generally appeared esoteric and dull—for example, the computer scientist Grace Hopper later recalled that she had learned error analysis, important in numerical approximation, in a chemistry course, having heard nothing of it during her long education in mathematics).[59] Rademacher set to work, and by November of 1943 he had produced a report on the relevant mathematical topics, including an annotated bibliography on the topic of rounding-off errors.[60]

The most important question was how many digits an accumulator had to store to ensure adequate precision of the final results. Early plans called for eight digits, which matched the procedures used by the Moore School's human computers.[61] ENIAC's speed would allow some changes to mathematical procedures, for example by calculating intermediate results over shorter time intervals, and it was important to be certain that any such changes would not affect the accuracy of its results.

Rademacher explored the effects of the two main kinds of error introduced by numerical integration techniques. Truncation (or intrinsic) errors were caused by using discrete time intervals to model continuous physical processes, whereas rounding errors were a consequence of working with a limited number of digits. These errors were complementary: truncation errors could be reduced by working with smaller time increments, but this increased rounding errors as more mathematical operations were performed.[62] Rademacher investigated a number of approaches, including a method of numerical integration, devised by the German mathematician Karl Heun, that seemed to offer an appropriate balance between the two sorts of errors.[63] Trial calculations indicated that Heun's approach would introduce four or five digits of rounding error into each result. To ensure the desired five-digit accuracy of the results, the size of the accumulators was therefore increased to ten digits.[64]

2

Structuring ENIAC

In the first months of the project, good progress had been made toward clarifying various details of ENIAC's design, including the number of digits needed in each accumulator and the basic structure of the circuits in which numbers would be stored. The hardest and most important issue to resolve was that of control. How would ENIAC's arithmetic circuits be directed to perform the right operations at the right times?

ENIAC's unique control system is usually described in terms of the capabilities of its many specialized units. In this chapter we instead explore its origins as a response to careful analysis of the process of calculating trajectories, its co-evolution with programming and diagramming practices, and its use to structure the process of computation. We dispel two pervasive myths: that programming was an afterthought to which no attention was paid until ENIAC was completed and that the capability for "conditional branching" (automatically choosing between different courses of action depending on how things were going) was not added to ENIAC until its main design had been completed.

Decentralizing Control

In order to establish the feasibility of their plans for electronic computation, Eckert and Mauchly decided in the fall of 1943 to build and test a minimal ENIAC prototype in parallel with continuing design work on the complete machine.[1] The accumulator was ENIAC's fundamental unit, but one accumulator on its own could not carry out any meaningful computation. The test system would therefore consist of two accumulators and the circuits needed to connect them and to coordinate their behavior. Completing such a system before the original target date of August 1944 would show that the Moore School could build a reliable computer around vacuum tubes, demonstrating tangible progress to justify contract extensions and budget increases. The project's leaders later defended their design choices by pointing to the urgent need to move on to construction while there were still enemy forces to bombard.[2]

As Atsushi Akera has pointed out, that decision had implications for the design of ENIAC's automatic control system. Early design work had assumed that a central control mechanism would "switch various accumulators into and out of connection with each other" and would tell them when to receive and transmit numbers by sending electronic signals, known as "pulses" and "gates."[3] Those signals might stimulate an accumulator to clear the stored number, transmit it, or add to it a number received from another accumulator.

Pushing ahead to build the two-accumulator system meant that the design and the construction of ENIAC would overlap, and that plans for the accumulators would have to be finalized before the overall programming system had been fully thought through. That constrained the role of the proposed program-control unit. As work progressed, that unit's central role was replaced by a distributed system in which programming information was spread around ENIAC's various units. As ENIAC was eventually built, it consisted in large part of a platoon of accumulators marching side by side to the beat of the cycling unit and occasionally receiving new orders from a "master programmer" unit.

The new approach began to emerge as the design of the accumulator unit was completed in October and November of 1943. A high-level view is provided by a sketch of an accumulator's "program unit" in T. Kite Sharpless' lab notebook that shows a number of dials and switches built into the accumulators.[4] These dials and switches were grouped into "program controls," each defining a single operation to be performed by the accumulator—for example, to clear the accumulator when that was necessary, or to transmit or receive a number. Some controls would repeat an operation as many as nine times. Operations were triggered by special "program pulses" carried into special input and output terminals attached directly to the program controls on a network of wires known as "program lines." When the operation finished, the control emitted an output pulse, which was routed directly to the program controls, on the same unit or on different units, controlling the next operation to be performed.

In this distributed programming model, a program pulse was a signal to initiate an operation, but what action would be triggered depended entirely on which control the wire carrying the pulse led to and on what that control had been configured to do. For example, sending a number from one accumulator to another involved two program controls: one on the first accumulator that was set to transmit the stored number and one on the other accumulator that was set to receive it. When a program pulse stimulated both controls simultaneously, the effect was to add the number from the first accumulator to the contents of the second. Accumulators were synchronized by a "cycling unit," whose standard sequence of pulses and gates became ENIAC's heartbeat. Among other things, that sequence defined when numbers and program pulses were transmitted, so that information sent by one accumulator could be safely received by others.

A block diagram of the circuits that were needed inside the accumulator to implement the operations defined by its program controls was discussed at a meeting on November 20, and the high-level design of the accumulator was then essentially complete.[5] Although details of the circuitry and the number of controls changed as work progressed, the principles of distributed control and the provision of both arithmetic and programming circuits within each unit remained unaltered and were applied in the rest of ENIAC's design. That allowed many decisions, such as details of the mechanism used to output data from ENIAC, to be deferred.

The question "Who designed what?" was of primary importance in the ENIAC patent trial. The judge found that the designing of the individual units had been decentralized within the engineering team, ruling that T. Kite Sharpless had been largely responsible for the cycling unit and the multiplier, Robert Shaw for the function table, the master programmer, and the constant transmitter, and Arthur Burks for the multiplier, the divider, and the master programmer.[6] Decentralization meant that the details of a unit's internal circuitry and its local control capabilities weren't relevant provided that the unit was compatible with the physical connectors and adhered to the standard system of pulse signaling.

Planning the Trajectory Calculations

Much of the responsibility for early work on the problem of calculating trajectories fell to Arthur Burks, and in response he developed an overview of ENIAC's structure and the use of its control system. In October of 1943, Burks considered how the problem might be solved using decentralized control and pasted a preliminary sketch of an ENIAC "set-up" to calculate a trajectory into his notebook.[7] That sketch was then worked up into a complete solution expressed as a pair of diagrams, which were included in the progress report produced at the end of the year. Among other things, this work enabled the team to get a sense of how many accumulators would be needed to calculate trajectories, and for numerical matters such as the precision of the numbers stored. In an unpublished manuscript, Burks later claimed, not unreasonably, that this was "the first program drawn up for an electronic computer," though it would not have been referred to as a program in 1943.[8]

Modern computers are sometimes called "universal machines," but a machine that can do almost anything requires a great deal of configuration to make it do something in particular. We now call this work programming, and the control information a program. As David Alan Grier has observed, this terminology descends from the ENIAC project.[9] Grier ties the use of the word "program" to contemporary

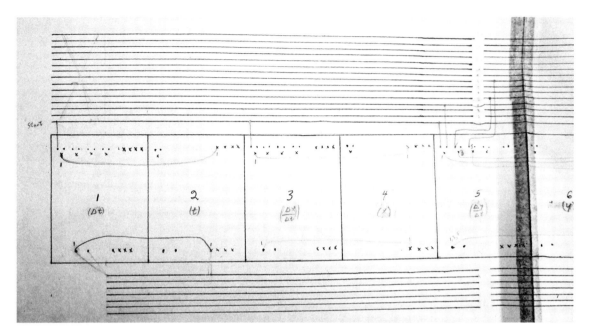

Figure 2.1
A detail from a sketch of the trajectory problem set-up that Arthur Burks pasted into his notebook in October of 1943. Each rectangle represents one of ENIAC's panels, holding a specific variable during the calculation. Program lines are shown above the panels and data transmission lines below. The diagram shows the connections between terminals on each panel and the program and data lines that formed part of a complete ENIAC set-up.
(from notebook Z16, MSOBM-UP, box 1, serial no. 16, University of Pennsylvania archives)

usage in control engineering and military logistics. However, we feel that a clearer antecedent may be found in the work of programming schedules—for example, programming a concert series or a weekly schedule of radio broadcasts. Such programming comes down to answering two basic questions. First, what combination of the various possible choices should be scheduled to take place? Second, in what order should the selected items be scheduled? A program of lectures or concerts encodes the answers to both questions by specifying a sequence of events.[10]

The meaning of "program" when used by ENIAC project members was more complex than has previously been acknowledged. In Mauchly's original 1942 memorandum for the Moore School, the word "program" appears only in the phrase "program device."[11] In the 1943 proposal, the "program device" became the "program control unit," which was responsible for ensuring that accumulators and other units carried out operations in the correct order. The word "program" was also used in passing to refer to the sequence of operations carried out in each iteration of the computation.[12] When control was decentralized, however, "program" lost the sense of a sequence of arithmetic operations. As was discussed above, a "program control" was a collection of switches on one of ENIAC's units that specified a single operation to be carried out in response to an input "program pulse," and the circuits that directed the unit according to the switch settings were placed in its "program unit."[13] In other words, "programming" no longer denoted the activity of a central unit in coordinating the overall flow of a calculation; it now referred to the internal activity of an accumulator or some other unit in generating a sequence of micro-operations to perform a single operation—for example, to transmit the complement of the stored number.[14] The overall configuration of ENIAC to solve a particular problem, which we would now think of as the "program," was called a "set-up."[15] The word "program" came to mean the settings for a single operation on a program control, though toward the end of 1945 it regained a wider meaning.[16]

The end-of-year progress report described a three-stage process, similar to that used for the differential analyzer, for setting up a problem on ENIAC.[17] First, the mathematical equations describing the problem had to be reduced to a form that allowed them to fit onto ENIAC and to be solved by ENIAC using only its basic arithmetic operations. Second, the problem was to be laid out in two diagrams, a "setup form" and a "panel diagram," showing the scheduling of the operations and their distribution across ENIAC's many units. Third, switches were to be set and cables plugged in to prepare ENIAC physically for solving the problem. In illustrating this approach, Burks worked out in detail how to use ENIAC to compute solutions to the trajectory equations using Heun's method. We believe that he was considering the specific case of anti-aircraft fire. Unlike ground-to-ground fire, in which shells explode on impact, anti-aircraft shells have a timed fuse, which is set to explode the shell in the vicinity of the target. The calculation of the trajectory could therefore stop after a fixed number of iterations once the shell had passed the altitude of any intended target. Furthermore, to set a fuse correctly a gunner needs to know the intermediate positions of the shell in flight, not only the final distance traveled as in ground-to-ground fire. Burks' computation was therefore designed to print out the position of the shell at one-second intervals up to a maximum of 40 seconds of flight.[18] He used 0.02 second as the basic time interval for an integration step, which meant that ENIAC would carry out 50 integration steps for each printed result, a total of 2,000 steps.

Burks documented his set-up for the trajectory calculation using the two types of diagram mentioned in the progress report. The first, the setup form, had the same basic tabular format as the diagrams given in the 1943 proposal for solving ballistics equations.[19] Each column in the table represented one of ENIAC's units. As one read down the diagram, the rows described the sequence of simple operations into which the calculation was broken down. Detailed notations showed which units participated in each operation, what their roles were, how various switches on their

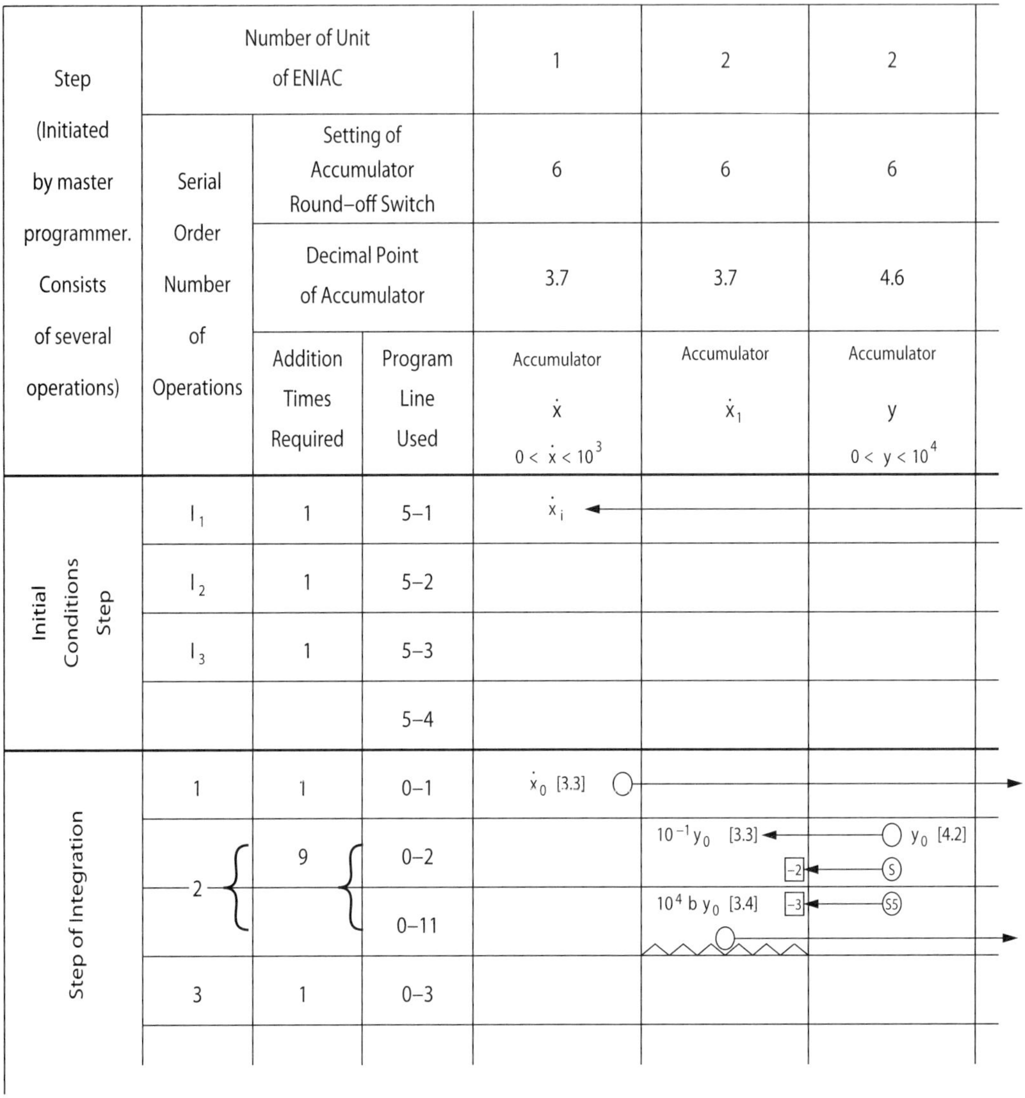

Step (Initiated by master programmer. Consists of several operations)	Serial Order Number of Operations	Number of Unit of ENIAC		1	2	2
		Setting of Accumulator Round–off Switch		6	6	6
		Decimal Point of Accumulator		3.7	3.7	4.6
		Addition Times Required	Program Line Used	Accumulator $\dot{x}$ $0<\dot{x}<10^3$	Accumulator $\dot{x}_1$	Accumulator y $0<y<10^4$
Initial Conditions Step	I_1	1	5–1	$\dot{x}_i$ ←		
	I_2	1	5–2			
	I_3	1	5–3			
			5–4			
Step of Integration	1	1	0–1	$\dot{x}_0$ [3.3] ○		
	2 {	9 {	0–2		$10^{-1}y_0$ [3.3]	○ y_0 [4.2]
					[-2]	Ⓢ
			0–11		$10^4\,b\,y_0$ [3.4] [-3]	㊿
	3	1	0–3			

Figure 2.2
A detail from Burks' late-1943 "setup form" showing the sequence of operations performed to compute a trajectory.
(University of Pennsylvania Archives)

program controls should be configured for each operation, and information about the timing of the operations.

The time taken by the computation was measured by counting "addition times"—how much time ENIAC took to perform the fundamental operation of transferring a number from one accumulator to another. More complex operations, such as multiplication, took several addition times to complete. The setup form listed the number of addition times taken by each operation and showed which operations could take place simultaneously. If two transfers involved different accumulators and data lines, for example, they could take place within the same addition time, and shorter operations such as addition could be scheduled to take place while a multiplication was going on.[20] Burks' analysis showed that a single integration step required 224 addition times, and thus the time taken by a complete trajectory computation of 2,000 steps was estimated as 70 seconds.[21]

Burks' second diagram, the panel diagram, was a refined version of the sketch he had pasted into his notebook in October.[22] It showed a long sequence of rectangular boxes representing ENIAC's panels (the cabinets in which the circuitry of each unit was housed). There were a considerable number of these boxes, and this diagram unfolded horizontally, rather like a scroll. Donald Hunt, a student at the University of Pennsylvania who helped Burks produce panel diagrams in early 1944, recalled that Burks had "prepared a chart many feet long" and that "we even had to design a special drawing board to hold the large sheet."[23] Each box contained a graphical representation of the program controls of a panel, with spaces left for writing in the settings of the various switches. The buses used to transmit data between units were shown as lines drawn above the boxes, and those used to transmit program pulses as lines below.[24] Configuring ENIAC to run a particular task also involved wiring electrical connections between terminals on the panels and the buses. The necessary cables were represented by lines on the diagram linking terminals and buses.

The setup form and the panel diagram contain essentially the same information, but presented in ways that made it useful for different tasks.[25] We conjecture that the setup form was used initially to plan the sequence of operations, something that would be more difficult in the distributed format of the panel diagram. The panel diagram would then be used to map this plan onto ENIAC's physical equipment—a process that would, no doubt, lead to revisions to the setup form. Switching between the diagrams in this way would eventually lead to a consistent pair of diagrams describing the complete computation and the corresponding ENIAC configuration.

The final step was transferring the information on the diagrams to about 200 "program cards," each of which would contain the details of the switch settings and the plugging required for a small portion of ENIAC. The cards would be stored in

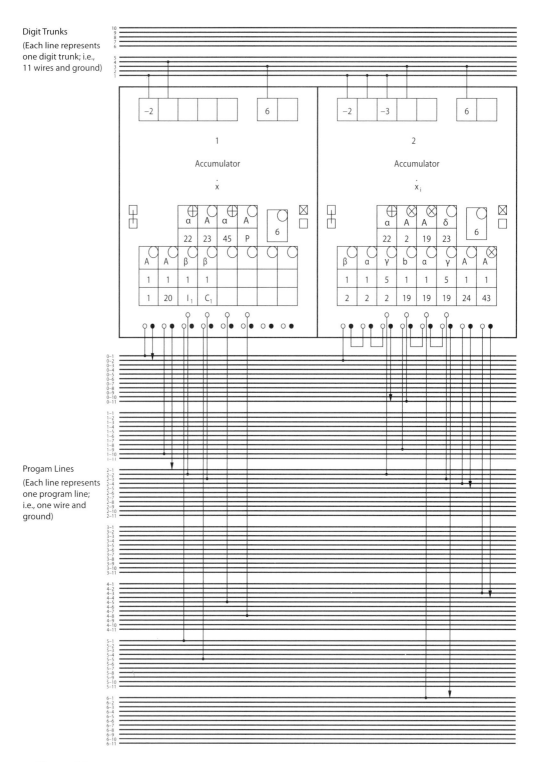

Figure 2.3
A detail from Burks' late-1943 "panel diagram" showing settings of the program controls on ENIAC's first two accumulators and their interconnection via program and data trunk wires.
(University of Pennsylvania archives)

special holders on the machine's panels and would be referred to by the operators who were responsible for physically configuring the machine. The report estimated that this would require about 700 "units of work," such as setting a program control or plugging in a cable, which could be performed by "several people" working simultaneously.[26]

Comparing the polished panel diagram with the October 1943 draft gives a vivid impression of the rate at which ENIAC's design was evolving. The draft diagram shows 22 accumulators and three additional panels for a multiplier. By the end of the year the number of panels had increased to 32, including a range of other units in addition to the accumulators and the multiplier: a divider, a master programmer, a function table, a constant transmitter, and four printer accumulators storing data to be punched onto cards for permanent output.

A few numbers' worth of data storage was needed to hold the initial conditions for a trajectory calculation; several constants also had to be stored. The new constant transmitter was proposed to set these numbers using switches or, for greater speed, push-buttons. A more significant question was how to incorporate into the calculations empirical data about the influence on trajectories of things like the shape of the bullet. In the equations, these empirical data were represented by the values of a function, G, that could not be derived mathematically. Rather than being calculated, the value of this function corresponding to a particular argument was looked up on the function table (a unit that had been designed to hold a significant amount of tabular data).

Once the decision to decentralize control had been made, the team moved quickly to complete the outline of ENIAC's design. The machine described in the progress report written at the end of 1943 and depicted in Burks' panel diagram is recognizably the machine that was completed in 1945. This approach to control incurred significant overhead costs: at the end of 1943, Eckert and Mauchly estimated that 30 percent of the equipment in an accumulator was used for control purposes, commenting that "programming is thus very appreciably decentralized."[27] This approach yielded a flexible framework, however, into which a menagerie of functionally specialized units could be fitted. Some, such as the accumulators and the multiplier, had essentially reached their final forms; others had yet to be considered in detail. This design philosophy contributed to the longevity of ENIAC, as new units were added throughout its life.

Early Conceptions of the Master Programmer

In their proposal, Eckert and Mauchly had explained that ENIAC was designed for iterative computations. Each "step" in such a computation consisted of a sequence of individual mathematical operations, and they included examples showing the details of one step of the solution of both trajectory ("exterior ballistics") calculations and explosive ("interior ballistics") calculations. The decentralized control system could sequence the operations within a step, but it was not obvious how this mechanism could control, for example, how many times a step would be repeated. Also, a complete application would contain more than just the sequence of operations for the numerical integration step. Burks' set-up contained four distinct sequences: in addition to the integration step, there were sequences to set up the initial conditions and print out the results, and also one to test ENIAC by performing the integration step with known data after each set of results was printed.[28] The job of combining these sequences into a coherent computation was given to a new unit called the "master programmer." As shown in Burks' panel diagram, it made the high-level structure of the computation explicit as a sequence of four stages labeled "Initial conditions," "Integration," "Printing," and "Check run." The master programmer would sequence these tasks and control the number of times a particular step would be repeated. The printing and integration steps were nested: results would be printed after every 50 integrations, and the calculation would halt after 40 printings.

The progress report specified in more general and detailed terms the functional requirements for the master programmer. It was to "consist of a number of switching units through which program connections may be established and broken," and it would control the high-level operations of starting a problem, interrupting the normal sequence of operations to print results, and stopping the calculation. More generally, it would control "any other necessary switching from one calculating cycle to another type of calculating cycle," for example "when a somewhat complex sequence of computations can be broken down into two or more different component sequences which occur several times within the complete sequence."[29]

Although it was not yet clear how the master programmer would carry out these tasks, its introduction established a two-level approach to the organization of calculations—an approach that would be retained in ENIAC practice until March of 1948. Simple sequences of operations were set up using the local program controls, and the master programmer coordinated the execution of the sequences, repeating and combining them in different ways according to the demands of the problem. As Burks' diagrams make clear, the master program would initiate a sequence by sending a program pulse to the first control in the sequence, and at the end of the sequence a pulse would be sent back to the master programmer to prompt it to determine what would happen next. The master programmer therefore preserved an element of central program control in ENIAC's organization.

Finalizing ENIAC's Configuration

As has already been noted, ENIAC's exact complement of units and panels changed significantly as Burks was working on the set-up. Discussions on the machine's final form continued. At a meeting held in April of 1944, a configuration with only ten accumulators and with a new unit called a "register" was discussed.[30] This configuration would have had only one function table, rather than the three eventually used. The register would have provided the storage capacity of eight accumulators with much less hardware. Each accumulator could add, so the same arithmetic circuits were replicated twenty times within ENIAC as finally constructed. This was inefficient, as in any application some accumulators would be used purely for storage. The register would need only one set of circuits to send and transmit numbers, versus eight for the accumulators it replaced, and their arithmetic circuits could be eliminated entirely.[31] The register was never constructed, but the idea of separating storage from arithmetic probably reflected the new approaches to computer design being developed within the team at this point (discussed in chapter 6).

User input played an important part in finalizing ENIAC's structure. Leland Cunningham, the head of the BRL's machine computation group, was, according to Burks, the project's closest contact at Aberdeen and the most knowledgeable member of its staff with respect to digital computing.[32] ENIAC's final configuration was decided at a meeting with Cunningham in April. Burks' notebook reports that during that meeting "plan of # of units, etc., of ENIAC [were] finally arrived at." ENIAC was to consist of 29 units spread across 36 panels: 20 accumulators, three function tables, and one each of the specialized multiplier, a divider–square rooter, a constant transmitter, a cycling unit, a printer, and a master programmer. That configuration was later described as "ample for solving [the ballistics equations] with a setup as extensive as that required by the Heun method."[33]

The Evolution of Conditional Control

The emergence of the "conditional branch" within ENIAC's design has been of considerable interest to historically minded computer specialists. As we shall see in a later chapter, this capability was subsequently identified as the crucial advance setting true computers aside from mere automatic calculators. In an examination of the development of ENIAC's conditional branch capability, Marcus and Akera suggested that it was a "very clever afterthought" developed as late as 1945, asserting that ENIAC "lacks any hardware obviously intended to implement conditional branches" and that it had "no particular mechanism by which the course of computation can be affected by the particular values that the machine is manipulating. A program can loop some number of times before terminating but the total number of iterations must be explicitly programmed … . There is simply no obvious hardware mechanism by which the machine can be programmed to, say, terminate a computation when some computed value reaches 100,000."[34] Their conclusion has been accepted by others, but project records make clear that the need for this

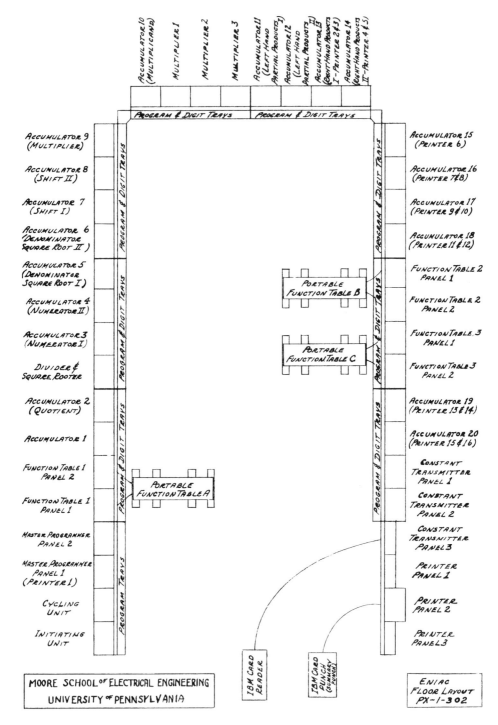

Figure 2.4
ENIAC's 1945 configuration, as installed in the Moore School, was very similar to that agreed upon with Leland Cunningham in April of 1944.
(U.S. Army diagram)

capability had, in fact, been identified by the end of 1943. The task was assigned to the master programmer unit, which was expected to include special circuitry for the purpose. The discussion of conditional control was a small part of the larger question of how to structure complex computations, and the solution the team arrived at does not map exactly onto later conceptualizations. Because this conditional control capability was crucial to the design of ENIAC, and because it illustrates the interplay of logic, hardware, and application planning, we will examine it in some detail.

Automation at Electronic Speeds

There was nothing new in the idea of a calculating machine that could automatically perform sequences of operations. The Harvard Mark I, which became operational about two years before ENIAC, was controlled by instructions read one at a time from rolls of paper tape not unlike those used to drive a player piano. Like a player piano, Mark I would perform exactly the same operations each time a tape was run. A computation consisted of a number of sequences of operations, coded as holes, punched on separate instruction tapes. There was only one tape reader, so detailed instructions were prepared to tell the machine's operators when to unload one tape and load another. To repeat a sequence of instructions, the ends of the tape were glued together, creating a physical loop known as an "endless tape." (This may have been the origin of the use of the term "loop" in this context.) Mark I's capability to automatically stop a calculation and alert the operator when "a given quantity ... is less in absolute magnitude than a selected positive tolerance"[35] relied on detecting when the result of a certain test was negative rather than positive, and it allowed iterative processes to be halted when sufficiently accurate results had been obtained.

Mark I was constrained by the speed with which relay switches could flip. It took six seconds to perform one multiplication, and a full minute to compute a logarithm or a trigonometric function using its specialized hardware. Any computation complex enough to justify the use and programming of such an exotic machine would involve a lot of multiplications. Thus, even if it took an operator a minute or two to recognize that Mark I had finished processing a step in the calculation and was now ready to move on with the next instruction tape, that would hardly slow its overall progress. During its design, no urgent practical need to provide multiple instruction tapes or any other mechanism for branching had been identified.

ENIAC's designers shared with the Mark I's designers the notion that a computation was built up from straightforward sequences of operations, though the operations were set up on program controls rather than being read from paper tape. ENIAC's electronic logic units worked so fast that it would be slowed unacceptably if it had to wait for the next instruction to be read from tape. Waiting for human input before moving from one stage of the calculation to the next would be even less practical, as the machine would spend most of its time waiting for its operator to notice that it needed attention. Burks' set-up for the trajectory calculation therefore relied on the master programmer to automate the sequence switching performed by Mark I's human operators, as well as performing the more complex task of controlling the number of times sequences were repeated. ENIAC had no control tape, but Burks' set-up would still repeat exactly the same series of operations regardless of the input data fed into it or the results obtained in the course of the computation.

An Early Proposal for Branching Units

The shortcomings of the player-piano approach to automatic control soon became apparent. Richard Bloch, one of Mark I's first programmers, referred to the lack of conditional branching as a "major flaw" that became particularly apparent in mid 1944 when John von Neumann brought a complex differential equation from Los Alamos for Mark I to solve.[36]

The ENIAC team was also aware at an early stage of the need to enable their machine to change its course of action according to the results of the calculation so far, as evidenced by the numbers stored in its memory. Computer scientists view this as one of the crucial characteristics making a computer "universal," meaning that with sufficient time and storage space it could simulate the behavior of any other computer and thus run any program that any other computer could run. Such discussions often treat the conditional branch as a unitary capability that a computer either had or did not have. Rather than setting out to provide ENIAC with this single capability, however, the team conducted a broader investigation into how to automate computations consisting of multiple instruction sequences that had to be combined in complex and unpredictable ways.

The need for some flexibility in control was discussed in the 1943 end-of-year progress report. Burks' set-up would compute and print the position of a shell at regularly spaced intervals of time (the "independent variable"), but for regular time intervals (1 sec, 2 sec, and so on) the distance traveled by the shell (the "dependent variable") would vary by irregular amounts. It would also be useful to tabulate the shell's flight time for regular intervals of distance (10 yards, 20 yards, and so on). As the report put it: "It is frequently desired to print the results at evenly spaced intervals of some dependent variable."[37] That could be done by repeating the integration step until the calculated distance equaled the next value at which printing was required. To ensure that the value would be determined with adequate precision, the report proposed using a longer time interval (0.01 second) "until the value of the dependent variable was within close range of the value to be printed," and then taking smaller steps (0.001 second) "until the desired value had been exceeded."[38]

This meant setting up two versions of the integration step and picking the appropriate one on the basis of the current value of the calculated distance.

As in Mark I, the condition that was used to decide when to make the switch was a certain calculated quantity's changing from positive to negative. The difference between the value at which the switch was to be made and the calculated distance would become negative once that value had been reached. The sign of a number was held in an accumulator's PM counter, from which pulses were transmitted only if the number the accumulator held was negative. The key idea was to use these pulses to control what happened next. As the report put it, the "fact that a given quantity was in a specified range could be indicated by the reversal of a PM counter, which could be used to govern the programming."[39]

The actual branching capability was to be provided by the master programmer, in the form of "about 30 units which are capable of receiving program pulses on one line and transmitting them on either of two lines in accordance with pulses received on another line."[40] "Such a unit," the progress report continued, "could be used, for instance, to enable sets of values along evenly spaced intervals of a dependent variable to be printed. The completion of a given interval would be indicated by a change of sign (the reversal of a PM counter) in an accumulator. This information could be automatically transmitted to one of these units so that the integration could be stopped and the results printed." These units would support the equivalent of thirty "IF... THEN ... ELSE" control structures. A program pulse arriving at the master programmer at the end of an integration step would be routed through one of the branching units to trigger the first operation in one of two alternative sequences. Which path it followed would depend on whether or not a particular PM counter had changed sign, but no details were given as to how the sign pulses would be used to configure the switch. These simple units, each providing a binary decision point, would be coupled with other devices to provide more complex control structures. The report noted that "several counters will be available" and that "these may be used in conjunction with the units just described." The master programmer would incorporate switches on which the operator could set values such as "the number of steps of integration performed before each printing and the number of times the values are printed before the ENIAC stops."[41]

Sequence Programming

By the end of 1943, then, the ENIAC team had recognized a need for conditional branching and had proposed what might, to present-day eyes, seem an elegant and general mechanism for accomplishing it: simple hardware units implementing binary decision points to shift control along one path or another. But development of the master programmer did not follow a smooth path toward implementation of these ideas. Instead, deeper consideration was given to the more general issue of "sequence programming," and the simple branching units were never constructed. As the master programmer's design emerged in the next six months, the team decided that the requirement for conditional branching could be met more efficiently by merging the capabilities of these switches with the counting and control capabilities already needed for other purposes.

By the time of the 1944 mid-year progress report, the basic design of the master programmer was complete. The project's official engineering notebooks shed little light on intermediate design steps. Burks later claimed to have come up with "the basic design" of the master programmer after a discussion with Eckert and Mauchly in the spring of 1944.[42] The clearest insight into the design process, however, can be gained by looking at some previously unexamined drawings, in Mauchly's hand, that outline several design alternatives.[43]

In ENIAC's two-level model of control, basic sequences of operations were set up on the local program controls of each unit. Most problems would require many such sequences. The controls responsible for ensuring that these sequences would be carried out in the correct order and repeated the appropriate number of times were said to be performing "sequence programming."[44] The local program controls in a sequence were physically connected by wires into what Mauchly described as a "program circuit." It would be easy to repeat a sequence by making a connection from the last control back to the first; however, like Mark I's endless tapes, this would provide no way to move on when the desired results had been obtained. The solution adopted by ENIAC's designers was to include in the circuit a device able to break the loop by diverting the flow of program pulses onto a different branch.

To implement a two-way branch, Mauchly described a "bifurcator" with control lines to set a flip-flop circuit determining which of two output lines would receive an input pulse. Mauchly also discussed a "sequence unit" or "stepper" using a ring counter in place of a flip-flop to provide multi-way branching. This had one output line for each stage of the counter. An input pulse on the control line would move the counter from one stage to the next.

Mauchly's sketches represented these control units as abstract devices with a number of program input and output lines. (See the diagram reproduced here as figure 2.5.) A pulse arriving on an input line (P_i) would be transmitted on certain of the output lines (P_o), depending on the state of the device. The state was controlled by input on separate control lines (P_s). The choice of notation shows that Mauchly was already abstracting the idea of logical decision points, at which one of several courses of action would be chosen on the basis of previous results, from the details of particular circuit designs.

Mauchly noted that the PM counters on ENIAC's accumulators could drive either the control line or the input line of a stepper, changing the course of a calculation when particular quantities went from positive to negative. The decision point was

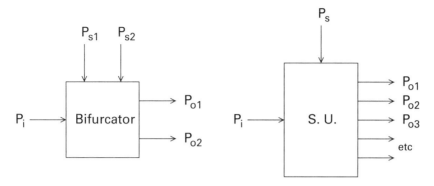

Figure 2.5
A simplification of Mauchly's schematic for a bifurcator (left) and recreation of his schematic for a stepper (sequence unit) (right).
(based on original drawings in the collection of the Hagley Museum and Library)

preceded by the calculations that were needed to manipulate the sign of the number in question. For example, someone wishing to branch if one variable was greater than another would subtract the first variable from the second. ENIAC's implementation technique was particular to its unique system of distributed control, but the concept of changing the course of the computation depending on whether the result of an arithmetic operation was positive or negative has been enshrined in computer instruction sets ever since.

Mauchly showed how a stepper could be combined with counters to sequence and repeat sequences of operations set up on ENIAC's other units. This met the requirement for the master programmer to trigger each step in the trajectory calculation repeatedly before moving on to the next step. The diagram shown here as figure 2.6 shows an example he described as executing "20 programs of Calc. I," 50 of calculation II, 20 of calculation I, six of calculation III, and one "print cycle" before repeating the whole sequence. When a stepper dispatched a pulse on one of its output lines, this triggered a sequence of operations, but could also increment a counter. When the counter reached its maximum value, it emitted a pulse on the control line P_s to advance the stepper to its next stage.[45] As the mid-year progress report put it: "It is a stepper operating in conjunction with a counter which receives the pulse given out at the end of the sequence and feeds it back into the beginning of the sequence the desired number of times. This procedure is called sequence programming."[46]

Mauchly's notes also showed how steppers and counters could be used to control the Heun method, in a sketch diagram in which two interlinked steppers repeated Burks' basic sequences so that the integration step would be repeated 50 times between prints, and 40 print cycles performed in all. The output from stage B of

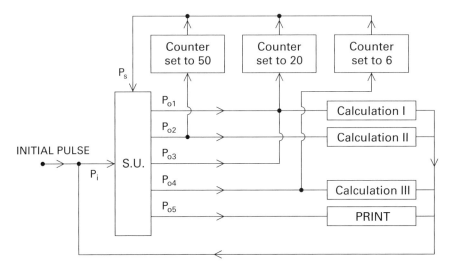

Figure 2.6
A re-creation of Mauchly's diagram illustrating the control of sequence repetition using a stepper (sequence unit) and counters.
(based on an original drawing in the collection of the Hagley Museum and Library)

the left-hand stepper in the diagram shown here as figure 2.7 triggers an integration step, which then passes its output pulse to the right-hand stepper. The counter associated with stage B1 ensures that the integration step is performed 50 times before the stepper moves to stage B2, sending an output pulse to trigger the print sequence. In that diagram, Mauchly illustrated in detail how a combination of steppers and counters could control the computation that ENIAC was being built to carry out, improving on the method illustrated in figure 2.6 in two ways. Firstly, as well as triggering the initialization sequence, the output from stage A of the left-hand stepper is sent back to the stepper itself to move it on to the next stage. Second, the output from stage B2 of the right-hand stepper is directed to a "clear" input on the stepper to reset it to the first stage. Both of these features would reappear in the final design of the master programmer.

Mauchly's notes described other devices for sequence programming which, like the bifurcator, did not make it into ENIAC. One was a "multiple program unit" containing a number of flip-flops, each controlled by a separate input line. An incoming program pulse to the unit would generate output pulses on all those lines whose flip-flops had been set, triggering the simultaneous execution of any desired combination of the controlled sequences. This unit was never built, but the computational pattern it supports resurfaced in plans to use the function table as a program-control device, which will be discussed in chapter 7.[47]

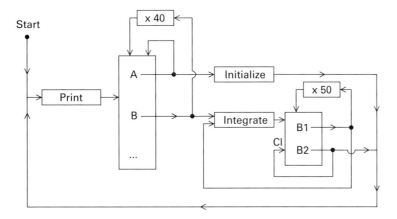

Figure 2.7
A re-created excerpt from Mauchly's diagram showing the use of two steppers to control the nested loops in Burks' trajectory set-up.
(based on an original drawing in the collection of the Hagley Museum and Library)

The Master Programmer

As finally constructed, the master programmer combined ten steppers with twenty single-digit counters. Counters were switched to particular steppers as needed for each problem, reducing the total number of tubes needed for counters.[48] Each stepper had six stages. Switches set the number of times the sequence controlled by the stage should be triggered. The diagram shown here as figure 2.8 shows how the nested loops of Burks' program would be represented in the notation later used to describe the control structure of ENIAC computations. Rather than representing steppers and counters separately, this notation showed the six stages of a stepper and the number of times the sequence programmed by each stage was to be repeated. Each stepper had three input terminals. In the diagram, the middle one receives normal program pulses and the bottom one resets the stepper to its first stage.

In their final form, steppers could also be used to terminate loops when a particular condition was satisfied, rather than after a specified number of repetitions. The mid-1944 progress report revisited in detail the problem of printing trajectory data at regular increments of the dependent variable: "The specified increment of the dependent variable can be stored in an accumulator and the actual value of the dependent variable subtracted from it step by step. At the end of each step of integration the PM signal of the accumulator is transmitted to the stepper. Thus the change in sign of the quantity held in the accumulator may be used to change the programming of the ENIAC."[49]

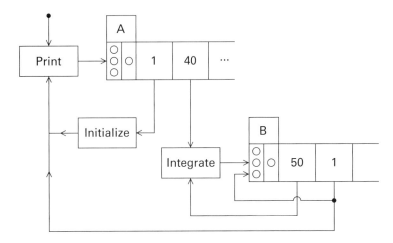

Figure 2.8
A re-creation of Mauchly's diagram showing nested loops expressed in the final master programmer
notation.

Program pulses and data pulses usually circulated on two separate networks
of trunk lines and cables. To "change the programming of ENIAC" on the basis
of the contents of an accumulator, some method had to be found for transferring
pulses from the data network to the program-control network. The team fleshed
out the idea, discussed in the 1943 progress report and Mauchly's notes, of transmitting the pulses emitted by the PM (sign) counter of an accumulator to the
programming circuits so that they would act as program pulses. Because all of
ENIAC's pulses were of the same shape, this presented no fundamental challenges.
However, there were some timing problems to consider, and special cables were
built with adaptors that picked out PM pulses for transmission to a program line
or control.

The third input terminal on a stepper, the direct input terminal, provided the
means whereby pulses from the PM counter could affect the subsequent course of
a computation. This was the "particular mechanism" for conditional branching that
Marcus and Akera believed ENIAC lacked. A pulse (or multiple pulses) received at
this terminal would cause the stepper to advance immediately to the next stage. A
possible set-up for controlling the tabulation by values of a dependent variable is
shown in the diagram reproduced here as figure 2.9. The two alternative sequences
are set up on the first two stages of a stepper. When the difference is computed, the

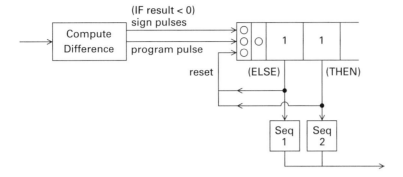

Figure 2.9
The equivalent of an "IF ... THEN ... ELSE" statement set up on one of the master programmer's steppers.

sign pulses from the result are transmitted to the stepper's direct input terminal. If the result is positive, there are no pulses, and the stepper remains in the first stage. If the result is negative, the sign pulses will move the stepper to the second stage. The normal program pulse is then transmitted to the stepper, and the appropriate sequence is initiated.[50]

When designing the master programmer, then, the ENIAC team created an elaborate unit to combine sequences into complete set-ups in highly complex ways, including the repetition of a sequence a fixed number of times and functionality equivalent to the originally imagined two-way branching units. It could even be used to provide a basic subroutine facility: "[W]ithin a given step of integration a certain interpolation process may be used several times. This sequence need be set up only once, by means of a stepper the same sequence can be used whenever needed."[51] The role of the stepper here was to provide the equivalent of the return address in later programming practice: control would pass from the interpolation sequence to the stepper, then back to the appropriate place in the integration step as determined by the current state of the stepper.

Exploring Conditional Control

With the design of the master programmer completed, the team devoted some attention to thinking in more abstract terms about conditional control. The 1944 end-of-year progress report described some new ways of achieving this capability without using the master programmer.

The use of the pulses emitted by a PM counter to control the course of a calculation, depending on whether a stored number was positive or negative, was now termed "sign discrimination." The team discovered that by combining features already built into the accumulator this could be achieved without using the master programmer. Transmission of a positive number would yield no sign pulses on the A ("add") output terminal of an accumulator and nine sign pulses on its S ("subtract") terminal, and conversely for a negative number. Transmitting a number through both terminals simultaneously and sending the sign pulses to the initial controls of two different program sequences meant that one of them would be initiated if the stored number was positive and the other if the number was negative.[52] Using this variant method for a control branch freed a stepper on the master programmer but wasted an entire accumulator. The 1946 ENIAC manual noted that "no numerical programs other than one magnitude discrimination program can be carried out in an accumulator so set up, since both digit output terminals of the accumulator are completely associated with the magnitude discrimination program."[53]

To ensure that the operation triggered had time to complete normally, its initiation was delayed until the start of ENIAC's next addition time (analogous in this context to an instruction cycle in later terminology) by routing the pulses through a "dummy program control." This was not a new device; it was a clever repurposing of the circuits and controls already provided on each accumulator. The sign pulses were transmitted through the special "program adapter" cable to an unused program-control input on an accumulator. This "dummy control" was set to do nothing but emit a program pulse at the start of the next addition time. This delayed the pulse without requiring the construction of any new circuitry.

Once the principle of using the sign pulses of numbers to control the course of a computation was established, it was natural to extend this to number pulses generally, termed "digit control." One example of this was used in the mid-1944 progress report to illustrate the flexibility of the master programmer. A single function could be set up across ENIAC's three function tables. If the first digit of the function argument (0, 1, or 2) was sent to the direct input of a stepper, it could "step a stepper to one of three positions, and would thus determine which of the three function tables would be used" to look up a particular value.[54]

By the time ENIAC went into operation, many of those working on it were familiar with the simple and flexible conditional transfer mechanism that had been devised for its proposed successor, EDVAC. Nevertheless, ENIAC programming was still conceptualized primarily as use of the master programmer to structure a range of specialized actions, such as conditional loop termination and digit control.[55]

Later misunderstanding of ENIAC's implementation of branching as a late and clunky addition to the basic structure of the computer betrays the enduring influence of the aesthetic standards of the modern approach to computer architecture that the ENIAC team was, even then, in the process of devising with John von Neumann.

We shall discuss the new aesthetic later, but here we will note that within the overall design paradigm of ENIAC the master programmer design was quite an elegant solution. Implementing branching as an application of conditional loop termination made efficient use of the master programmer's capabilities, effectively re-using circuits and tubes already required for other purposes. "Branching in the ENIAC was clumsy," Arthur Burks himself wrote many years later, "and more program equipment could have been added to make it simpler. But the equipment used already existed, and so there was no point in adding more electronics to the machine to simplify the operation."[56]

3

Bringing ENIAC to Life

We now turn from the ENIAC team's efforts to structure the automatic control of computation at electronic speeds to the parallel engineering development of ENIAC. The biggest challenge, and the one most familiar from previous historical accounts, was to develop techniques to keep thousands of vacuum tubes working reliably. However designing and building ENIAC quickly during wartime involved a host of other challenges, from the procurement of components to the grueling hands-on work of the women who wired ENIAC's panels and assembled its components.

The advantage that the ENIAC project gained from being run by an engineering school full of people trained in reliable design, shop management, and project management is easy to overlook if the challenges of innovation are assumed to lie primarily in logic or theory. Procurement is seen as a dull topic even by business historians, and almost nothing has ever been written about the history of manufacturing techniques in the computer industry. Yet consider the track record of earlier computer projects. Many computer projects, including Charles Babbage's Difference Engine, John Atanasoff's computer, and Konrad Zuse's Z1, were either abandoned during construction or useless once finished because of engineering challenges their creators lacked the resources and skills to overcome. ENIAC succeeded, and so did the Harvard Mark I (built by IBM's experienced engineering staff), the Bell Labs machines (built by the staff of a telecommunications laboratory with exceptional skills in the production of reliable switching mechanisms), and the Colossus machines (likewise). Our research uncovered serious challenges to the project posed by difficulties with technologies that might be dismissed as mundane: resistors, power supplies, solder joints, and even wire. These technologies might seem somehow less essential to ENIAC than vacuum tubes, but even the most exceptional or innovative machine cannot function without attention to all of its material needs.

The Two-Accumulator Test

Design of the accumulator was complete by the beginning of 1944. Intensive work began on the construction of the equipment needed for the planned two-accumulator test. Much of the responsibility for this fell to John H. Davis, whose lab notebook records the systematic and prolonged testing of the various circuits making up the accumulator.[1] In order to operate the two accumulators, a cycling unit was needed to supply control pulses, along with ancillary devices such as power supplies and connectors and adaptors of various sorts. As the team recognized, this amounted to the construction of "a small ENIAC," and the successful test demonstrated "the workability not only of the accumulator but of the design principles of the entire ENIAC."[2]

Work proceeded slowly. By May 17 the accumulators were largely finished. John Brainerd blamed the delay on "a large volume of wiring" within each accumulator "on which only one person could work." This slowed completion of the accumulators, despite rapid progress on the externally assembled "plug-in" units holding standardized vacuum-tube assemblies.[3] Testing began a week later. After a period of debugging, during which "minor design and construction errors" were corrected, the accumulators were fully functional by late June.[4] On July 3, Harold Pender wrote to Herman Goldstine, who was in a hospital recovering from jaundice, with details, noting that, in addition to having their basic arithmetic operations tested, the accumulators had been linked up to "solve the second order differential equation for a sine wave and that for a simple exponential."[5] These calculations had been based on the harmonic equation, a second-order differential equation whose simple form made it a useful test for automated numerical integration. Eckert and Mauchly's 1943 proposal had included a sample four-accumulator treatment of this equation, but for the test a less general version (which, like the example given by Travis in his 1941 report, required only two accumulators) had been used.

"It was intriguing," Arthur Burks recalled, "to watch the contents of the accumulators going up for the exponential function, and up and down for the trigonometric functions as one accumulator displayed the sine and the other the cosine."[6] The experience gained using this simple computer shaped detailed design work on the circuitry and the interface of the cycling unit.[7] This included plans for controls to allow operators to run ENIAC continuously or to step through a calculation, carrying out one addition or even only one pulse, each time a button was pressed.[8] The accumulator design proved largely stable, though tinkering continued after the first two accumulators were built. New blueprints incorporating minor changes were still being produced in the summer of 1945.[9]

Building ENIAC

Building the accumulators was not easy. A large room on the ground floor of the Moore School was designated for construction work. According to Scott McCartney's book, it "took on the irreverent nickname of the Whistle Factory. Each engineer had a worktable up against a wall of the room. Assemblers and 'wire men' occupied the central floor space, where the machine was taking shape."[10] Wires were threaded through ENIAC's panels, and connections were soldered. The cables springing from the front of ENIAC look impressive in photographs, but they were as nothing compared to the miles of wire inside its various cabinets and the half million or so soldered joints holding its circuits together.[11]

On December 17, 1943, when more design work than construction work was underway, the ENIAC project employed eleven engineers, four technicians, and a support staff of five, including a draftswoman, a secretary, and a part-time stenographer. This workforce ballooned as production and prototyping work advanced. The Moore School became a site of industrial production, and the project's management structure was reorganized into four groups to support it. Eckert remained in overall charge, sharing with Mauchly leadership of an Engineering and Test group consisting of seven engineers. Schematics were passed to a three-person Mechanical Design and Drafting team headed by Frank Mural. The blueprints produced by this group went to a three-person Model Making team. Not until the model implementation had been tested and approved by the Engineering and Test group were the blueprints released to instruction. This separation of design, prototyping, and production reflected the introduction of a certain amount of formality to the design and production process, and was accompanied by a directive to avoid giving verbal instructions.[12] These measures might have helped to deal with the problem, later noted by Burks, that production workers suffered from low morale "because we kept changing circuits after they were wired and before they were finished and could be tested."[13]

In contrast to ENIAC's design engineers, whose names are readily available in the historical literature, the production workers have been ignored by historians and journalists. The production team was headed by Joseph Chedaker (an engineer who had moved over from the design team) and a male inspector, but almost all of the "wiremen" and assemblers were women. In May of 1944 the production team was already the largest ENIAC group, with ten members. By the end of that year, the effort needed to complete ENIAC was being estimated on the basis of 34 full-time production workers.[14]

We found the names of the women in the project's accounting records, which reveal that they began as "trainees" but in most cases were promoted after a few months to "assistant assembler," "assembler," or "technician." Turnover was quite high—some trainees were terminated, but more women resigned, sometimes because of pregnancy or because their husbands were relocated.[15] Some Web sources and some newspaper sources suggest that telephone company employees were recruited. That seems a plausible source of labor, as does the local radio industry, but we could not locate any reliable evidence on the recruitment of these women. In mid 1944, during the wartime labor shortage, a technician earned about $2,000 a year after completing training. That was a good wage for an inexperienced female worker. Male technicians earned as much as $2,500 a year, which positioned them somewhere between the group's secretary, Isabelle Jay, whose pay had recently increased to $1,800, and "Pres" Eckert, who at that point was receiving $4,000 as the laboratory's chief. Design engineers' annual salaries began at $3,000.

Like the engineers, the wiremen and the assemblers worked nights and weekends for the duration of the war, deferring their vacations. Brainerd had worried that their planned dismissal at the end of construction meant they would never be able to use their vacation time, but in fact they were still working in two shifts when the war ended, so at least someone benefitted from ENIAC's many delays.

Procuring Components

ENIAC was largely built with standard off-the-shelf components and instruments, including oscilloscopes, resistors, condensers, transformers, chokes, vacuum tubes and their associated sockets and plugs, racks, panels and chassis, and of course wire.[16] Finding all these components required not only money, which the BRL contract was supplying in adequate volume, but also someone with the connections and ingenuity to navigate the wartime bureaucracy. During the war, the economy of the United States was dominated by government agencies. Supplies to civilians of butter, shoes, and even typewriters were rationed to ensure that military needs were met. Factories were turned over to military production. The military itself consisted of many different organizations, each with its own needs, stockpiles, and supply systems. As in the planned economy of the Soviet Union, it was hard to successfully run a project or a factory exclusively by means of formal bureaucratic mechanisms. Barter and exchange of favors via personal networks were often more effective in getting needs met quickly. Much of that work fell to Herman Goldstine, who, as the liaison officer between the Moore School and the Ballistic Research Laboratory, gave the ENIAC project access to formal and informal military supply networks. Many of ENIAC's components were secured by Goldstine from the stockpiles of the Philadelphia Signal Depot. The Army's Signal Corps was a major user of electronic devices, and the Philadelphia depot was its primary procurement hub.[17] Pulling strings on behalf of subcontractors sometimes helped. The Carl E. Reichert Steel Company, a Philadelphia business, received the contract to build ENIAC's main chassis but wasn't able to obtain the necessary steel until Goldstine wrote to a contact in the Philadelphia Ordnance District and asked him to facilitate its supply.[18]

Even something as apparently generic as wire posed procurement challenges. Building ENIAC entailed linking together an unprecedented number of electronic components spread over a large area. Brainerd came across a sample of suitable wire on a visit to the MIT Radiation Laboratory in August of 1943, but wasn't able to find anyone who could identify the supplier. He resorted to mailing small pieces to suppliers and asking if they recognized the wire and if they could supply 26,000 feet of it.[19] Later, Brainerd had to lobby the office of the Chief of Ordnance in the Pentagon for intervention to secure approval of an order of wire from the Lenz Company. Slow delivery of switches and sockets by other suppliers also threatened ENIAC's progress and prompted pleas for intervention.[20]

ENIAC contained more resistors than tubes.[21] Most were small, reliable, and easy to procure, but the design also required a number of exotic high-precision resistors. In August of 1944, Goldstine attributed a production delay to "a terrible tie up" involving the exotic resistors: the project's liaison with the War Production Board would not acknowledge "our needs, either as to quantities or quality." The resistors in question were produced only by the International Resistance Company. It was "exceedingly difficult to impress" the official, who offered only unsuitable substitutes. On this occasion, ENIAC was saved by Dean Harold Pender of the Moore School, a co-founder and a director of International Resistance.[22]

Procurement work continued throughout the course of the ENIAC project. In mid 1945, when the machine was largely complete, Goldstine was still working with the Philadelphia Ordnance District to fulfill a supplemental $45,000 contract from the BRL to provide a range of spare parts, a customized oscilloscope, a special table, and equipment for testing "plug-in" units outside the computer.[23] Even after ENIAC had been moved to Aberdeen, the Moore School was still ordering and dispatching spare parts to complete the contractual checklist.[24]

Designing for Reliability

ENIAC's circuit designs placed unprecedented demands on mass-produced components that had been intended for less demanding uses. Historians writing about ENIAC have uniformly praised Eckert for ingeniously building a tolerably reliable machine out of inherently unreliable parts.

Vacuum tubes were the basic building blocks of ENIAC's logic and memory units. The number of tubes is often quoted as 17,468, a spuriously precise number insofar as the count fluctuated over the years as units were added and modified. Eckert himself tended to round the number to 18,000.[25] Like the light bulbs from which they had evolved, vacuum tubes would burn out after an unpredictable amount of time, usually as they were turned on. If ENIAC's many tubes failed as frequently as the same tubes did under normal conditions (for example, when used in a radio), it would stand virtually no chance of ever powering up and completing a calculation.

Engineers already knew how to improve the odds. Tubes weren't all created equal, and the weak ones usually failed early in their lives. Eckert's team built special

Figure 3.1
Changing one of ENIAC's tubes. Its panels formed a room divider, with switches on the front and the "plug in" units stuffed with tubes exposed at the back for easy removal.
(U.S. Army photo)

equipment to test incoming tubes, verifying the quality of each batch and accumulating data on their failure patterns. The results were fed back into the design process. The chance of a tube's failure had a lot to do with the amount of current stressing it, so Eckert eventually decided that no tube should ever conduct more than 25 percent of the current recommended by its manufacturer. Each tube was "burned in" under stressful conditions, and the weaklings were culled before being installed in ENIAC.[26] Because most tube failures occurred when power was applied and the tubes warmed up, ENIAC was to be turned off as little as was possible; the power was to be left on overnight and on weekends. Together, these measures improved the machine's expected reliability to a point where it seemed plausible that it might one day complete a calculation, or perhaps even an entire uninterrupted shift.

Fortunately, vacuum tubes were mass produced nearby to supply the local radio industry. Eckert standardized as much as was possible on a handful of readily available models produced a few miles away by RCA. Beginning in January of 1944,

Figure 3.2
This plug-in "decade" unit stored a single decimal digit. Its 28 tubes were mounted externally for easier replacement. The work of the "wiremen" is clearly visible in the wires, resistors, and soldered joints inside the unit.

tubes were being delivered in large numbers to support construction of the initial pair of accumulators, and by August the Moore School was purchasing tubes in sufficient bulk to have its account "set up on a manufacturing basis" so that it would receive rebates on its past and future purchases.[27]

Finding one faulty tube out of 18,000 would itself be a significant challenge. ENIAC's design used standard building blocks, known as plug-in units, across its various panels. These held standard sets of vacuum tubes and ancillary components, and could be easily removed and replaced. It was easier to find the plug-in unit responsible for a fault than to find the individual tube responsible. The unit would be swapped out, and ENIAC would quickly be put back to work while the defective component was isolated and repaired.

By 1945, when construction was in full swing, quality assurance became an increasingly prominent part of the team's work. A special "testing table" was built, and a rigorous program of testing and logging the details of each individual tube used was put in place.[28]

Connecting to Other Projects

The project's web of connections provided intellectual as well as material support. ENIAC was classified as "confidential" rather than as "secret" or "top secret" (two designations used for truly sensitive projects). Within the network of wartime scientific projects and military contractors, ENIAC was something of an open secret. Requests to visit the machine were arriving well before it was complete. Indeed, Goldstine appears to have been systematically spreading awareness of ENIAC. He was arranging clearance for visitors as early as August 1944.[29] In addition to computing experts, the visitors he sponsored included potential corporate users—for example, in June of 1945 a delegation from Chance Vought Aircraft.[30] Eventually the Office of the Chief of Ordnance informed Goldstine that, to avoid further delay and distraction, it would "grant no clearance to visit the ENIAC to any person until the ENIAC is completed."[31] Clearance was therefore initially denied to a delegation from the British Post Office, though an exception was eventually made for W. W. Chandler and Tommy Flowers, who had built the far more secret Colossus computers.[32]

One important connection was with Bell Telephone Laboratories in New York. George Stibitz, Bell's expert on automatic relay computers, was a member of the National Defense Research Committee panel overseeing wartime computing projects and the designer of a series of computers built by Bell Labs during the war. His advice regarding ENIAC in November of 1943 had been that "electronic equipment" could carry out the same operations as relay technology at higher speed, but that the "development time ... will be four to six times as long."[33] That would make ENIAC useless for the war effort. Stibitz proposed that he quickly construct a "relay differential analyzer" for the Ballistic Research Lab, an idea that was initially rejected as redundant in view of the lab's investment in ENIAC.[34] Stibitz's commitment to relay technology has sometimes been dismissed as mere conservatism, but his doubts about ENIAC's schedule were well founded; nevertheless, he advised that "the development of the ENIAC is desirable and should be continued."[35]

In January of 1944, Goldstine wrote to Stibitz thanking him for a recent visit to the BRL and hoping to "enlist his aid" in procuring for it a Bell Labs relay calculator.[36] Other exchanges followed, the most important of which was a meeting in Aberdeen on February 1 attended by senior staff members of the Moore School, the BRL, and Bell Labs. Bell Labs was asked to "consider the problem of developing high speed devices for introducing data into and withdrawing data from [ENIAC] on either magnetic or teletype tapes." The participants also decided to consider commissioning Bell Labs to build a relay computer for the BRL and a printer for its differential analyzer.[37] This ensured the further involvement of Stibitz and other members of the Bell Labs staff (e.g., K. T. Kane and Samuel B. Williams) with

ENIAC. The plan to build high-speed tape drives for ENIAC was soon abandoned. Paul Gillon, who retained a close connection with the project from his new position in the Office of the Chief of Ordnance, wrote to Harold Pender that after further discussions he had concluded that Williams and Stibitz were "not at all enthusiastic about undertaking the job" and that "any delay we are compelled to accept … will be of considerable advantage to them in merchandizing the Stibitz equipment."[38] Despite this, Goldstine continued to work with Stibitz, who provided detailed advice on numerical methods for the ballistics equations.[39] And Goldstine and Cunningham continued to lobby, with eventual success, for the BRL to order the relay calculator, of which we shall say more in a later chapter.[40]

ENIAC benefitted directly from the alliance. Its 1,500 relays—miniature switches whose positions could be flipped electrically—came with their own reliability worries. Goldstine arranged for Western Electric, the manufacturing arm of the Bell System, to supply relays, and in September of 1944 he was still working to "expedite their delivery."[41]

Both the Moore School and the Ballistic Research Lab operated differential analyzers. There were only a few such machines running in the United States, and their owners formed a kind of informal club, sometimes exchanging ideas. This provided another pre-existing line of communication between the ENIAC team and institutions such as MIT, which had also been collaborating with the Moore School on a radar project. Correspondence shows that meetings "to discuss the electronic computer" included people from MIT as early as February of 1944.[42]

Evidence of direct connections between the ENIAC project and other computing projects is less clear. The best-documented link is John von Neumann, who was well informed about the Harvard machine by early 1944 and was deeply involved with the ENIAC group from August of 1944 onward.[43] It is not clear whether any aspect of ENIAC settled upon before this date should properly be considered to have borrowed from or to have deliberately departed from the design of the Harvard Mark I.

Subcontracting

The number in each accumulator could be read from that accumulator's neon-light display, but waiting for an operator to write down each result would hardly make good use of ENIAC's unprecedented speed. ENIAC's other input and output equipment was defined quite late in its development. Most of the computing groups of the 1940s encoded input on flimsy strips of five-channel paper tape of the kind used in telex machines. Even though ENIAC would not have to read large volumes of data in order to perform firing-table calculations, the BRL decided that it should read data from punched cards—a decision that would greatly increase ENIAC's usefulness over the next decade. In April of 1944, Goldstine arranged to obtain specially modified IBM card readers and punches suitable for connection to ENIAC. These were faster, more flexible, and far more robust than conventional paper tape, although they still wouldn't keep up with the machine's full speed on calculations producing large volumes of output with relatively little calculation.

As Goldstine put it in a letter to Brainerd, "This construction will not be delayed by the formalities of including a contract."[44] This ability to work outside official procedures sped the completion of ENIAC. By May of 1944 the machines were largely complete, but Goldstine was still working his contacts within the Ordnance Department to finalize terms of the contract.[45] Design of the "constant transmitter," a unit that served as an interface between the punched-card equipment and the rest of ENIAC, was complete by June. With the help of Bell Labs, its construction was finished a year later.[46]

Repeated Delays

In February of 1944, General Gladeon M. Barnes, who oversaw the Ballistic Research Lab as chief of research and development, reminded Harold Pender of the "utmost urgency in the battlefield implications" of ENIAC, which, he said, made it "imperative to this department that no surmountable difficulty be allowed to interfere with the earliest possible accomplishment of this project."[47] Herman Goldstine offered his superiors a succession of estimates of the date by which ENIAC would be completed, beginning with a promise made on May 26, 1944 that ENIAC would "be completed by October 1." Goldstine added that the "only delays that have been encountered this far have been caused by the difficulty of hiring people to do the necessary wiring."[48] The estimated date was never more than four months away. This relentless, even disingenuous optimism may have stemmed from Goldstine's awareness that delays made the ENIAC project vulnerable to cancellation as the war's end approached.

On June 8, 1944, two days after the invasion of Normandy, John Brainerd received a message from the Chief of Ordnance, Major General Levin H. Campbell, expressing "full confidence in the results of your renewed and continued efforts on behalf of the troops who are fighting for you on the battlefields of the world."[49] Other encouragement was less subtle. In July, Goldstine warned Pender that Samuel Feltman, "head of the Ballistics Branch of the Office of the Chief of Ordnance," was "a little concerned about the rate at which the ENIAC is being manufactured." Goldstine had assured Feltman that "the accumulator design had just been satisfactorily completed and that the manufacture of duplicate units could go forward at a goodly rate." He cautioned Pender that "the necessity for the speedy building of the ENIAC" was therefore "extremely great," as it was "imperative that we complete this machine before the Ordnance Office decides to cut back on long term research projects."[50]

Early in September of 1944, Goldstine reported to Paul Gillon: "Work on the ENIAC is progressing beautifully … . Decades for all accumulators are completed as well as a great deal of the auxiliary gating and switching assemblies. The multipliers, dividers and function table circuits are completed; the ventilating system is on order; and IBM has completed the card input and output machines."[51] The team was "on the fairways." In August, Goldstine promised Colonel Leslie Simon of the BRL that "ENIAC will be virtually completed except for final tests and delivery" at the end of 1944, when the contract would expire.[52] Come December, Goldstine remained upbeat. "We are," he promised Gillon, "in the throes of completing the production of the ENIAC … . within the next two months the machine should be completed."[53]

In February of 1945, Major General Campbell wrote a pointed note to Pender reminding him of the "urgent requirement for the earliest possible completion" of ENIAC, chiding Pender that the backlog of firing tables was then "approximately four (4) times as great as existed when your projects began."[54] ENIAC remained very close to completion throughout most of 1945. In May of that year, Goldstine wrote that ENIAC was "on the home stretch," with all units except the divider "substantially done." Work on ventilation was proceeding, and "we hope to start testing as soon as the ventilating system for the power supply is done—about 2 weeks from now."[55]

Goldstine's reference to ENIAC's power supplies provides another example of a technology that we might assume to have been easy to procure or produce but which in fact had unusual and challenging requirements. A power system able to drive about 18,000 tubes spread over a fairly large room with a cycle speed of up to 100,000 pulses a second was not available off the shelf in 1944. The machine consumed around 150 kilowatts of power during normal operation. ENIAC's designers increased the challenge by making little effort to standardize the voltages used within its many units, and as a result the machine "needed 78 different voltage levels and used 28 separate power supplies to obtain them."[56] A procurement debacle threatened to delay ENIAC's completion long enough to try the patience of the Ordnance Department.

General Electric was the preferred supplier of custom transformers, but owing to its many other military commitments it could not promise to deliver until October of 1945. Maguire Industries (formerly the Auto-Ordnance Corporation) won the contract by promising delivery within a month at a price three times higher than GE's.[57] Maguire Industries had recently diversified into electronic equipment, its fortunes having been lifted by wartime orders for its main product: the Thompson submachine gun.[58] However, it could not begin to deliver on its promises. By the end of February—several weeks after 28 complete and fully tested units were to have been delivered—Maguire had shipped parts of four units.[59] Crisis talks mediated by the Ordnance Department elicited promises from Maguire to expedite delivery, but the transformers delivered in March were shoddily constructed and unable to meet contractual specifications. The specifications had been ignored by the manager responsible, who had assumed that insulation acceptable in normal applications would work for ENIAC. (Eventually, after involving the University of Pennsylvania's law firm and soliciting evaluations from experts, the Moore School won a refund from Maguire Industries.[60])

The failure of Maguire Industries to deliver the transformers left ENIAC without power supplies and the Moore School unable to test its panels properly as the wiremen finished assembling them. Fortunately, the BRL had ordered a full set of spare parts, including a full set of power supplies, having recognized that failure of any one of the unique units would otherwise "tie up the machine for two weeks or more" while a replacement was built.[61] As there was no need to pay Maguire's inflated rush prices for the second set, it had instead been ordered from J. J. Nothelfer Winding Laboratories. Arrival of the backups saved the day, and testing began in earnest shortly thereafter.

By August 22, 1945, ENIAC was approaching completion, after which "final dynamic & static tests" were expected to be conducted at Aberdeen. Burks drew up a list of outstanding tasks, distinguishing between those to be "done right away" and those to be left until after the imminent move to Aberdeen. More than seventy jobs remained to be done, including some work on each of the computer's panels. Burks checked them off in red ink as they were performed.[62] Two weeks later, Brainerd asked members of the core engineering team to work on a two-shift schedule on weekdays, so that work on ENIAC would continue from 8:00 a.m. to 12:30 a.m. five days a week. There was a single shift on Saturdays.[63] Japan surrendered before much headway could be made on the checklist. The war officially ended on September 2, 1945, before ENIAC produced a single firing table. Many other wartime contracts were canceled under special termination clauses, leaving buildings unfinished and weapons unbuilt.[64]

After multiple extensions, the latest ENIAC contract required completion by September 30. But it was clear that the machine wasn't going to be completed by that date, and after six contract supplements the project's cost had increased to $487,125 (with a further $96,200 already budgeted for the transition to Aberdeen).[65] Adjusted for inflation, that amounted to more than $7.6 million in today's dollars.[66] But despite the cost overruns and Major General Campbell's grumbling, ENIAC was not canceled. Instead, an extension to December 31 was granted. ENIAC's flexibility and its potential usefulness for other problems was by now well appreciated—not least by John von Neumann, whose opinions held enormous sway in political, military, and academic circles. Campbell himself commented that ENIAC might "render possible the successful solution of many ballistic problems which cannot now be undertaken because of the prohibitive amount of computational work involved."[67] Besides, war or no war, the Ballistic Research Lab still wanted to calculate its firing tables.

Using ENIAC

Even a fully functional ENIAC would be useless to the BRL without a team of operators to work it. In the summer of 1945 it was time to do something about that. John V. Holberton, an employee of the Ballistic Research Lab and a senior supervisor of the groups that were already carrying out firing-table calculations at the Moore School, was appointed as head of ENIAC operations.[68] Holberton and his operations team were expected to move to Aberdeen along with the machine to provide continuity.

The "Women of ENIAC"

John Holberton and Adele Goldstine selected six women from the existing pool of human computers to form the first cohort of ENIAC operators. In addition to performing the initial physical set-up of a problem, they would be needed to tend to ENIAC's card punch and card reader, to configure and operate the conventional punched-card equipment, and to detect and try to resolve errors and faults when the computer was running. Like most technicians and support personnel before and since, they worked in obscurity, becoming somewhat famous decades later as the "Women of ENIAC" and "the first computer programmers."

In today's senses of the words, neither "operator" nor "programmer" accurately conveys the range of work the women performed. The word originally used, "operator," evokes the intimate, hands-on nature of their relationship with the computer, but from an early stage they were also expected to plan set-ups, working out how the required sequences of mathematical operations could be squeezed onto ENIAC.[69] When ENIAC did not behave as expected, it was hard to separate mistakes made in physically setting up its switches and wires from mistakes in the set-up design. This required operators to gain a deep understanding of the functioning of both ENIAC and the problems running on it. "Computer operator" later came to carry a stigma as lower-status, almost blue-collar work. Retroactively designating the women as programmers has served to highlight the creative and mathematical aspects of their work.

Like hundreds of other firing-table computers at the Moore School, the trainee operators had been performing demanding but mind-numbingly repetitive mathematical labor under cramped conditions for mediocre wages. They were young, unmarried women, generally working a first job, and their accounts convey the excitement of living away from home and enjoying life with new friends in a big city. All six held college degrees (four of them in mathematics), which set them apart from most of the computers. Kathleen "Kay" McNulty (later Mauchly) and her classmate Frances Bilas (later Spence) had majored in mathematics at the Chestnut Hill College for Women in Philadelphia and had been recruited upon graduation in 1942. Frances Elizabeth "Betty" Snyder (later Holberton) had earned a journalism degree from the University of Pennsylvania in 1939. Marlyn Wescoff (later Meltzer) had a degree in social studies from Temple University. Ruth Lichterman (later Teitelbaum) had earned her mathematics degree from Hunter College in New York.[70]

Today, Betty Jean Jennings (later Jean Bartik) is the best known of the "women of ENIAC," having worked hard to tell her story through oral-history interviews and a published memoir. Raised as one of seven children in a religious, teetotaling family on a farm in Missouri, she graduated from Northwest Missouri State Teachers College in June of 1945 with a degree in mathematics. Almost immediately after her arrival at the Moore School, she had transferred to the ENIAC group. Her memoir gives a sense of the zest with which she approached life in the East, where she made exotic new friends and seized opportunities for new experiences.[71]

The ENIAC operators were chosen on the recommendation of their immediate supervisors. The supervisors could not, to the disappointment of at least one, nominate themselves.[72] The six were not, however, the most senior or most highly qualified women working for the Ballistic Research Lab at the Moore School. They already knew Mary Mauchly and Adele Goldstine, who had been responsible for training new recruits to the computation group and who had explained to them the mathematical techniques and the mechanical desk calculators that were in use. Mauchly and Goldstine had recruited many of the women they trained.[73] Goldstine made recruiting trips to many colleges (including Hunter, her undergraduate alma mater, where she snagged Ruth Lichterman for the project).[74]

Adele Goldstine had the best mathematical credentials of any of the women involved with ENIAC, holding a master's degree from the University of Michigan. In 1942 she followed her husband Herman, then serving in the Army, to the mid-Atlantic area. She worked as a public school teacher in Philadelphia, following the default career path of an educated woman.[75] Mary Mauchly was a mother of two young children with a bachelor's degree in mathematics from Western Maryland College. As Akera relates, she had been struggling to maintain a middle-class lifestyle on her husband's meager prewar salary.[76]

Women's Work and Applied Mathematics

Like many other young women of their generation, ENIAC's operators were seizing opportunities that had not existed in peacetime. As men were sent overseas in uniform, women were manufacturing munitions and riveting ships to help the United States increase industrial production to the levels needed to win the war. Hiring women to calculate mathematical tables was a much less radical departure from normal gender roles. Computation was part of applied mathematics, the lowest-status part of the discipline and, not coincidentally, the part most hospitable to women.[77] We tend to think of science and engineering as careers from which women were comprehensively barred before World War II. It is true that women faced terrible discrimination, but some recognized applied mathematics as a haven in which, with sufficient ingenuity and determination, they might build tolerable careers. Women had already been involved in prewar efforts to mechanize computation—for example, Lillian Feinstein became the manager of Wallace Eckert's Colombia University computing laboratory in 1936 and was later called "the senior full-time scientific punched card expert in the whole world" by one pioneer of computing.[78]

Significant numbers of women made it to the highest levels of mathematical education, earning about 15 percent of all PhDs granted in mathematics during the 1930s. Grace Hopper, the best known of that cohort, earned a doctorate from Yale University in 1934.[79] (The persistent myth that Hopper was the first woman, rather than the eleventh, to earn such a degree from Yale tells much about our desire to simplify the uneven history of women's progress within science.) In 1943, Hopper volunteered for the Naval Reserve, and subsequently she was assigned to the staff of the Harvard Mark I computer. She remained prominent as computing grew in the next few decades, gaining broad fame when she returned to the Navy later in life as the public face of its computing work. Another female PhD, Gertrude Blanch, directed the mathematical operations of the federal Works Projects Administration's Mathematical Tables Project. Created in 1938 as an economic stimulus measure to put the unemployed to work producing mathematical tables, this became one of the biggest computation efforts ever undertaken. By June of 1940, more than 400 computers were under Blanch's authority. During the war, her group was mechanized with punched-card machinery and other equipment, shrinking its number of personnel but boosting its output.[80]

In mathematics, as in most fields, women were better represented in lower-status kinds of work. For example, they made up a higher proportion of bachelor's-degree holders than of doctoral-degree holders. However, most of the women calculating wartime tables for the BRL lacked even a bachelor's degree in mathematics—it quickly proved impossible to find enough degree holders to meet the project's expanding needs. The demanding but repetitive labor they carried out as computers did not, in the eyes of the better-educated women, make them mathematicians. As in most fields, roles with poor career opportunities, limited visibility, and low pay were seen as more suitable for women than roles with better opportunities and higher pay. In short, the employment of women as computers was a peacetime practice intensified by the wartime shortage of male labor, rather than a dramatic departure from accepted gender roles.

The decision to select the initial group of ENIAC operators from the existing pool of human computers may seem to have been a more significant departure. However, we see it as a conservative decision, informed by a desire for continuity and a belief in the transferability of their skills and their knowledge of trajectory calculations. Though explained to some extent by the wartime labor shortage, it nevertheless signals confidence in the aptitude of women for computer operations work. As Janet Abbate has noted, labor shortages had not convinced authorities at the Moore School to begin training women to design ENIAC's electronics.[81] For similar reasons, two enlisted men with experience in servicing electronic equipment were selected to maintain ENIAC's hardware. Thus, the hiring decisions of Herman Goldstine and John Holberton suggest that they believed that operating ENIAC had more in common with performing scientific calculations on paper or operating the differential analyzer (roles in which women were well established) than with designing or fixing electronic machinery.

Training the Operators

ENIAC relied on customized IBM punched-card machines to read input data and to output results. Standard machines of other kinds were used to punch input data, to turn output cards into printed tables, and, for many applications, to sort and process cards between runs. Punched-card techniques were not the only techniques the operators would have to understand, but that was a well-established area of practice that they could study while ENIAC was being finished. Without glimpsing ENIAC, the trainee operators were sent from Philadelphia to Aberdeen for six weeks of training in the BRL's punched-card facility. The women shared dormitory rooms and quickly grew to be friends, flirting with soldiers during their free time.[82]

Punched-card machines had been introduced in the 1880s, initially as rather specialized aids to the tabulation of census results. As their use of such machines had expanded into many other areas, later models had been able to print results, to process text as well as numbers, and to calculate results. By the start of World War II, they were widely used to print payroll checks and to update account balances.[83]

Punched-card machines were also increasingly common in scientific computing. Beginning in 1928, Leslie J. Comrie had put punched-card machines to work at the Royal Greenwich Observatory in London to calculate astronomical tables for *His Majesty's Nautical Almanac*. Sailors relied on those tables for navigation, so the British government took their production seriously. Comrie published a series of papers describing his techniques, which were then taken up by others (including Wallace Eckert, an astronomer at Columbia University).[84] In 1940, Eckert published a comprehensive book on the topic, *Punched Card Methods in Scientific Calculation*. He maintained a close relationship with IBM, filling his lab with donated equipment and working with the firm to design and test experimental punched-card equipment.[85]

Betty Jean Jennings later recalled: "We spent much of our time at APG [Aberdeen Proving Ground] learning how to wire the control boards for the various punch card machines: tabulator, sorter, reader, reproducer, and punch. As part of our training, we took apart and attempted to fully understand a fourth-order difference board that the APG people had developed for the tabulator."[86] Coming up with a suitable plugboard configuration for a particular task was far from trivial, requiring an appreciation of the various sensors and counters built into the machine being configured and a creative sense of how its capabilities could be used in conjunction with those of the other machines to automate steps in a particular process. A fully wired plugboard could include hundreds of short wires that were hard to modify without inadvertently disrupting existing connections.

For the women of ENIAC, a more challenging question was "How should one learn to operate a machine that is not yet functional, has not yet been documented, and is still secret?" The training of the first cohort of ENIAC operators is one of the disputed areas in ENIAC's history. Adele and Herman Goldstine later claimed to have played important parts in training the operators, she in a 1956 affidavit produced for submission to the patent office on behalf of IBM and he in a variety of legal materials. In his 1972 book, Herman Goldstine claimed that "they were trained largely by my wife, with some help from me," the Goldstines being "the only persons who really had a completely detailed knowledge of how to program the ENIAC."[87] And indeed Adele Goldstine was the only credited author of the two volumes of ENIAC documentation providing a detailed tutorial on the steps needed to configure the machine, complete with a number of worked examples and a wealth of diagrams.[88]

Passages in affidavits from Betty Jean Jennings and Kay McNulty explicitly disputed Herman Goldstine's suggestion that he and his wife had "taught our programming group, including Mr. Holberton, to program the ENIAC." In fact, both Jennings and McNulty claimed to have "taught themselves to program ENIAC after studying the ENIAC diagrams" and that "any help in this effort received from Dr. (then Captain) H. H. Goldstine, or Mrs. Goldstine, was minimal." The affidavits asserted that Herman Goldstine's authority over John Holberton, and hence over the operators, was purely nominal, and that Holberton's actual orders came from others at the BRL. Similar sentiments were expressed in slightly different words in the affidavits of Marlyn Wescoff, Betty Snyder, and John Holberton.[89] Lawyers had drilled those witnesses into framing their experiences in a particular way. Very similar phrases later appeared in trial testimony and in later oral histories, particularly the insistence on "block diagrams" as the primary source of knowledge. The "block diagrams" provided a functional overview of ENIAC's units, abstracting away from the actual circuitry.[90]

Herman Goldstine was enraged by the aforementioned claims, as Adele Goldstine had died in 1964 and thus wasn't able to press her point. Notes he had received in 1971 from one of IBM's patent teams, as he completed his history book while the legal battle raged, show that he had edited the manuscript to protect IBM's interests. For example, he had added that his complaints about the Moore School "should be tempered by the fact that IBM now has a Scientific Center in Philadelphia whose existence depends in large measure on maintaining good relations with the U of P." Goldstine had been asked by IBM to remove reference to his wife's 1956 affidavit, which wasn't admissible as evidence because it hadn't been given under cross-examination or preserved under a court order. He also had been asked "not [to] mention the fact that there has been any 'controversy' or 'dispute' in regard to the capability of the Holberton group," and he had removed assertions that John Holberton and his group had relied heavily on a draft version of Adele's manual, that they had asked many questions of the Goldstines, and that the very "block diagrams" from which they claimed to learn had been prepared under Adele's direction.[91]

The truth undoubtedly lies somewhere between the two entrenched positions described in the preceding paragraphs. It is clear from later interviews with the operators that they learned a great deal from one another and from other members of the ENIAC project team. They later admitted that they had not simply been locked up with the diagrams and left to figure out how the machine worked. Betty Jean Jennings relates in her memoir that after returning from Aberdeen the women spent several days in a vacant Moore School classroom staring helplessly at block diagrams before John Mauchly happened to stroll in and began to "tell [them] how the blasted accumulator worked." "John," she wrote, "was a born teacher." He encouraged the trainees to ask questions, and they went to his office "every afternoon to ask them."[92] John Holberton shared an office with Mauchly during that phase of the project, so his team would surely have made contact with Mauchly in any event.[93] The operators had fond memories of Mauchly, recalling him as kind, helpful, and approachable. He welcomed their attention, having become much less central to the project as it progressed from conception to detailed design and construction. Later, Jennings wrote that "John Mauchly was the most brilliant, wonderful man in the world."[94] Recollections gathered by W. Barkley Fritz and Bartik's colleagues identified other tutors. Kay McNulty recalled that it had been Burks who was most helpful in explaining the block diagrams, which seems

Figure 3.3
Arthur Burks, seated, holds the control box used to start and stop ENIAC while Betty Jean Jennings
stands to examine the multiplier panels.
(courtesy of Jean Jennings Bartik Computing Museum, Northwest Missouri State University)

reasonable insofar as Burks had devised the first ENIAC set-up for the firing tables
problem back in 1943, had helped to conceptualize the master programmer, and
had played an important role in designing the machine's overall control system.
Betty Snyder told Fritz that Harry Huskey, another engineer, had been her "chief
instructor."[95]

These accounts of frequent exchanges with Mauchly and Burks present rather a
different picture from the complete reliance on block diagrams the operators claimed
in their affidavits. They had help from at least some of the existing members of the
ENIAC team. Training the human computers was the main task that Adele Goldstine
had originally been hired to do, and by late 1945 she was deeply immersed in the

inner workings of ENIAC. Thus, it would have been odd if the members of the
ENIAC team had never talked to her during this period, even if they relied primarily
on Mauchly. In view of the monumental scope of her manual, and insofar as some
of the material had been adapted from progress reports, it is also very plausible that
drafts of some of the manual's text and illustrations would have been available
months before its official publication.

Tensions between Adele Goldstine and the operators may have also been rooted
in the very different positions that the wives and the operators held within the
ENIAC project. Adele Goldstine, like Mary Mauchly and later Klara von Neumann,
performed well in unexpected and demanding roles. Still, all three women owed
their initial involvement with ENIAC to their choice of husbands. They held more
senior positions than the operators, who had been forced to prove themselves while
doing the "grunt work" of manual computation, and they wielded additional influence through their marital alliances with the project's leaders.

The First Los Alamos Calculations

By December of 1945, ENIAC was ready to be exercised on a complete program.
Priorities were changing. Rather than setting up a test routine, or a well-understood
trajectory calculation, its first task was an elaborate calculation to help Los Alamos'
T (for Theory) Division discover whether Edward Teller's design for a hydrogen
bomb was workable. Teller, a brilliant and forceful Hungarian-born physicist, was
deeply attached to the idea of a weapon that could be scaled up to produce a detonation with as much power as was desired. Fission weapons of the kind that had
been used against Japan faced fundamental physical limitations that capped their
explosive power somewhere below the equivalent of a million tons of TNT.[96] That
could destroy a large city with ease, but because of the low accuracy of bomb
delivery at the time it might not suffice for hardened military targets.

Using Los Alamos records not available to other researchers, Anne Fitzpatrick
showed that the main difficulty in determining the feasibility of Teller's "Super"
bomb was determining the kind of hydrogen that was needed to fuel it. Tritium, a
spectacularly rare isotope, could be "ignited" in a self-sustaining fusion reaction by
the small atomic bomb that was to be as a trigger. Deuterium, a relatively common
isotope, was believed to ignite only at an unattainable 400 million degrees.[97]
What was the minimum amount of tritium needed to produce an ignitable mix?
Experimentation wasn't possible. With no tritium stockpile, the United States would
need years to produce "a few hundred grams" even if the sprawling reactor complex
in Hanford, Washington was turned over exclusively to tritium production, sacrific-
ing the plutonium production that was needed for other weapons.[98]

Teller had a tendency to become obsessed with his weapon designs, promoting them over the objections of others even when evidence was lacking. He put a great deal of work into trying to model the bomb's ignition processes only to conclude that it couldn't usefully be modeled with hand calculators or conventional punched-card machines.[99] Two of Teller's colleagues, Nicholas Metropolis and Stanley Frankel, were searching for a faster computer. In February of 1945, Frankel approached Paul Gillon about "the renting of the ENIAC."[100] An unsuccessful attempt to perform the calculations that summer in Wallace Eckert's laboratory left no other option.[101] Herman Goldstine continued to supply Metropolis and Frankel with information about ENIAC over the next few months to help them get ready to use it.[102]

Details of the problem are still classified, but Fitzpatrick states that the calculation "constituted a set of three partial differential equations, meant to predict the behavior of deuterium-tritium systems corresponding to various initial temperature distributions and tritium concentrations." Fitzpatrick also notes that Metropolis and Frankel had to leave out several crucial aspects of the physics in order to accommodate the calculations within ENIAC.

No one working with ENIAC had security clearance for nuclear secrets. Fortunately the computational steps used to implement the model were not themselves classified, so it was possible for the team to help Metropolis and Frankel devise a suitable machine set-up.

Metropolis and Frankel first visited ENIAC in June or July of 1945, talking to its designers and finding out how it worked.[103] Metropolis recalled a second trip some months later to consult with Adele Goldstine as he and Frankel developed the set-up. As directors of the Los Alamos punched-card installation, they were experienced in breaking down complex calculations into numerical procedures fitted to the limits of available machinery. As preparation continued, two of the operators, Kay McNulty and Frances Bilas, were assigned to help. Betty Jean Jennings and Betty Snyder later expressed admiration for the creativity with which the Los Alamos physicists "tinkered" with the machine to get their problem running, inserting cards into readers upside-down and "cutting accumulators" to squeeze several variables into each.[104]

In December, when the problem was actually put on the machine, the operators followed directions as Herman Goldstine stood in the middle of the machine "like an orchestra conductor," reading set-up information aloud to direct the arrangement of switches and wires. This was, according to Jennings, the first time the women had seen ENIAC or met most of its engineering staff.[105]

The computation used nearly all of ENIAC's capabilities and thus served as a demanding stress test for the almost-finished computer. The ENIAC service log book

Figure 3.4
ENIAC's panels enclosed a room within a room that held its operators, portable function tables, and punched-card equipment. Here J. Presper Eckert (left) sets a value on a portable function table while John Mauchly (center) surveys the machine. In the background, Homer Spence (left) examines some accumulators while Herman Goldstine (right) adjusts one of the function-table panels, Betty Jean Jennings (center) sets a switch on another portable function table, and Ruth Lichterman (right) stands next to the card reader.
(from collections of University of Pennsylvania Archives)

notes the beginning of work with the bold heading "Problem A—12/10/45." This is followed by the happy "Machine tested—OK" and page after page of grimmer reports of tube replacements, faulty decades in various units, multiplication errors, subtraction transfer problems, short circuits, carry errors, divider faults, and other varieties of "trouble." The engineers responsible for designing the various panels were there to tend to their creations. Homer Spence and the other hardware specialists replaced tubes and re-soldered joints to eliminate problems as they surfaced.

A million punched cards reportedly were shipped from Los Alamos.[106] People tend to think of ENIAC as a machine that calculated with relatively little input and output, taking a few input parameters and turning out punched cards holding final results for tabulation. In actuality most of its jobs required its operators to feed huge decks of cards into the machine, many of them holding intermediate

Figure 3.5
Many ENIAC jobs involved running thousands of IBM punched cards through the machine. Here Frances Bilas operates the card punch while Betty Jean Jennings tends to the card reader.
(84.240.8 in UV-HM; scanned by Hagley Museum and Library)

data in need of further processing, and to process equally large decks of output cards.

An entry for 6 p.m. on December 17 reads "Everything OK in ENIAC." The machine had managed to punch some cards. Reference to errors in the output followed immediately. Many further errors surfaced over the next few days, but at 4 p.m. on December 20 an "attempt at test run using A-deck" was made. The "problem stops about half way through cards," revealing an error in the set-up. The operators weren't yet accustomed to handling cards, and the test deck was "completely mixed up" during the attempt. Nonetheless, several test decks were running successfully by the end of that day. ENIAC was, fitfully, operational.

Entries made in the next few weeks record many changes to values stored on the function tables and to the machine's set-up. Some of the changes were made to free connections for diagnostic use so that problems could be identified without disrupting the connections needed for the calculations. Errors were becoming less frequent but tended to be intermittent and therefore harder to identify. The team used "break points" (each literally the removal of a wire to break the flow of program pulses) to halt the calculations at particular points so that values stored in memory could be checked. The term "break point" remains in the vocabulary of programmers to this day.[107] On one occasion a number of tubes were damaged when part of ENIAC shut down automatically after internal temperatures hit 120 degrees F because a set screw on an air intake hadn't been properly tightened.[108]

Not all the technological challenges were electronic. On December 23, the "steam pipe going through window ventilator" broke, filling the room with steam. The steam fitters took hours to arrive; however, by turning a valve, opening doors, and adjusting ventilation the team could "reduce [the] amount of steamy air pulled through the machine" enough to keep ENIAC going. They toiled through the holidays. At 9:30 p.m. on December 25, water released by the melting of heavy snow began to leak into the second floor of the Moore School. Mauchly's log entry for 3 a.m., when he went home, mentions "about five men still working, mopping up water and emptying buckets which catch drips."[109] That wasn't the first instance of flooding. In October a storm had destroyed a custom tube tester and several thousand dollars' worth of project supplies.[110] In November, Brainerd had complained that one night "a very large amount of water entered my office through the ceiling."[111]

The first phase of work was completed by the end of January, but Metropolis returned to ENIAC on February 7, 1946, squeezing in further work on the problem around the public demonstrations staged that month.[112] Norris E. Bradbury, head of Los Alamos, thanked Gillon on March 18 for this "extremely valuable cooperation," writing that "the calculations which have already been performed on the ENIAC as well as those now being performed are of very great value to us" and that "it would have been almost impossible to arrive at any solution without the aid of the ENIAC."[113]

Metropolis and Frankel later swore statements that the expedition was intended primarily to experiment with electronic computers and that, in the words of a 1962 affidavit, "we were not interested in answers to practical problems and did not obtain such."[114] Although Metropolis and Frankel had some real reservations about the results, Teller used them at a secret April 1946 conference to proclaim himself vindicated, insisting that the "Super" needed only a modest amount of tritium.[115] The issue was not definitively resolved until another set of ENIAC calculations were carried out in 1950.

From the ENIAC team's viewpoint, the results of the visit were less ambiguous: ENIAC had been subjected to a demanding test and had been shown to work, more or less. Herman Goldstine later wrote that he was "certainly of the opinion that the ENIAC was running satisfactorily prior to the formal dedication." He suggested that by January things had settled down well enough that vacuum-tube failure at the rate of "less than one a day" was the main remaining problem. No tube failures occurred in the course of one entire four-day period.[116] ENIAC's security classification as "confidential" had been removed on December 17, and thus the Ballistic Research Lab and the Moore School were free to announce its existence to the world.[117]

4

Putting ENIAC to Work

Throughout the hectic process of debugging ENIAC, Herman Goldstine was working to ensure that the machine would have a high-profile launch with prominent press coverage. On December 26, 1945, he mentioned to Leslie Simon that planning for the publicity was proceeding and that Paul Gillon hoped "to get General Eisenhower to be the principal speaker at the dedication."[1]

Unveiling ENIAC

In February of 1946 ENIAC made its debut—twice. Invitations to a lunchtime event to be held on February 1 were sent in the name of the Office of the Chief of Ordnance to the "National Association of Science Writers, plus all of the Science and popular magazines carried on our regular mailing list."[2] According to a planning document, the operator "girls" would be deployed as guides to lead groups of visitors around, answer questions, and introduce the engineers.[3] The event included a demonstration of the machine performing four simple mathematical tasks and running a portion of the more complex program used for the ongoing Los Alamos calculations. That enabled the journalists to write, under embargo, stories that could be printed on the day of the official inauguration.

A more elaborate set of demonstrations took place before a distinguished audience on February 15. That evening, a dedication party was thrown for scientific and military dignitaries in Houston Hall, an elegant stone structure claimed by the University of Pennsylvania to be the oldest student union in the United States. The seating chart lists 110 guests. They were treated to lobster bisque, filet mignon, ice cream, and "fancy cakes."[4] Apparently, all the guests were men. The machine's design engineers were present; the women who wired and programmed it were not.[5] At the end of the proceedings, ENIAC was ceremonially dedicated when a button was pushed by Major General Gladeon M. Barnes, Chief of the Research and Development Service of the Ordnance Department. This supposedly turned the machine on, though the team knew better than to ever turn it off.[6] The guests then

Figure 4.1
Leaders of the ENIAC project pose with visiting officials from the Ordnance Department during the dedication event. From left to right: J. Presper Eckert Jr., John Brainerd, Sam Feltman (an Ordnance Department engineer), Herman Goldstine, John Mauchly, Harold Pender, Gladeon Barnes, Paul Gillon. (U.S. Army photo)

made the five-minute walk to the Moore School to be greeted by Arthur Burks, whose demonstration included a newly coded sample trajectory calculation intended to show ENIAC's mastery of the problem for which it had been built.[7]

As Burks narrated, the operators ducked in and out of the room carrying cards between ENIAC and its auxiliary equipment. "We took the cards from the punch to have them printed out as a trajectory on the tabulator, which was out in the hallway," Betty Jean Jennings recalled. "We would also take the cards that had been run through and read from the output tray of the reader and put them back in to be read again for the demonstration to be repeated. The punched cards were read again and again through the tabulator to get enough copies of the trajectory to hand out to everyone as souvenirs."[8]

Figure 4.2
This photograph of ENIAC, used in the 1946 *New York Times* story, remains its most recognizable image. Irwin Goldstein, one of the maintenance engineers, is seen in the foreground using a portable function table. Homer Spence, Frances Bilas, and Betty Jean Jennings work in the background.
(from University of Pennsylvania archives)

The *New York Times* considers itself the "newspaper of record," providing through its coverage an initial judgment on what does and does not deserve to be preserved for future generations. From that viewpoint it handled ENIAC quite well. Newspaper pages were wider then, and the print was smaller, allowing the *Times* to squeeze the beginnings of eleven stories onto the front page. The new machine was front-page news on the day of the dedication, but it wasn't the biggest story of the day. That was a steel strike, a story heralded with a giant headline and flanked by smaller front-page stories addressing related shortages and changes to government wage and price policy. The inaugural session of the United Nations General Assembly also overshadowed news of ENIAC, which was tucked into a small part of the grid, below the fold and under the headline "Electronic Computer Flashes Answers, May Speed Engineering." That headline failed to capture the drama of the story's first sentence, which began with a mention of "one of the war's top secrets, an amazing machine" and then noted that unnamed "leaders" had "heralded it as a tool with which to begin to rebuild scientific affairs on new foundations."[9] The continuation of the story, on an inside page, featured portraits of Eckert and Mauchly beneath a large photograph of the machine showing an enlisted man (Corporal Irwin Goldstein) inspecting a function table in the foreground and several other people working in the background. This is still the classic image of ENIAC.

Was ENIAC Working?

The demonstration trajectory programs run after ENIAC's dedication ceremony featured prominently in later memories of the machine's launch. Lights flashed, the machine calculated frantically, and the simulated shell sped along its virtual trajectory more rapidly than its real-world counterpart. At least that was the claim, although the accuracy of the results obtained was later contested, as was the program's authorship. One of the most crucial points in the patent battle waged into the 1970s was whether the demonstration programs, or any of the programs set up on ENIAC in its first six months of operations, had actually worked. ENIAC, like the computers that followed over the next few years, had some difficulty crossing the gap between "basically built" and "actually working." The question of how long ENIAC spent in that transition became one of the main issues in determining the validity of the patent.

Eckert and Mauchly had begun talking to the Moore School and other interested parties about patents in 1944, but not until June 26, 1947 was a patent application actually filed. Burks later blamed the slow preparation of the application on Mauchly, who was supposed to be focusing on it in 1945 but who missed multiple deadlines, though it is also true that the project's engineers were rather distracted and obtaining sustained assistance from Ordnance Department lawyers was difficult.[10] Whatever its cause, the delay was potentially disastrous because the law gave inventors a year after the date on which an invention was first "on sale" to file a patent application. If no application was filed within that period, the invention was forever in the public domain, owned by no one. In this context, "on sale" did not mean that the machine had actually been perfected and advertised and was available for purchase, but merely that it had been announced to the public and that it worked sufficiently well to be of potential commercial value. Thus, the patent on ENIAC was valid if, and only if, all use before June 26, 1946 was strictly experimental.

The trial run for Los Alamos occurred long before the crucial date, as did the public demonstration and the publication of the front-page story in the *New York Times*. At the time, the Moore School had accepted the Los Alamos computation as the first successful operation of ENIAC. In 1946, for example, Irven Travis had responded to a query from Ordnance Department lawyers as follows: "Regarding date of reduction to practice … . The complete ENIAC was first successfully operated 12-10-45."[11] The Moore School's final construction contract with the Ordnance Department expired on June 30, allowing time for the completion of the necessary paperwork, progress reports, and documentation. Those defending the patent argued that all previous use was exclusively a debugging effort that finished on July 25 with the acceptance of ENIAC by the government.[12]

That position was challenged repeatedly. "Practical problems," Adele Goldstine stated in her 1956 affidavit, "were run on the ENIAC immediately upon its completion, starting in December 1945 and continuing throughout the entire period of my employment."[13] Eckert, Mauchly, and the members of the original six-woman operations team countered by insisting that ENIAC remained so unreliable that its output was of no use whatsoever except as a diagnostic aid. The set-ups in question were, they swore, created and run just to test the hardware and establish the workability of its programming method. A typical assertion, from an affidavit signed by Betty Jean Jennings (by then Jean Bartik), was that "no problems were put on the ENIAC prior to July 1946, the answers of which were intended for or put to practical use, and all operations of the ENIAC at earlier dates were simply to explore and/or show the capabilities of the machine, to aid in learning how to operate it, or to aid in finding defects therein."[14] That point was still in dispute during the decisive 1972 patent trial, in which an impressive lineup of witnesses—including Nicholas Metropolis, Stanley Frankel, Edward Teller, and the mathematician Stanislaw Ulam—were called to testify about the initial Los Alamos calculations. Attorneys representing the Sperry Rand Corporation used their stories to argue that the calculation had been conducted merely to stress the machine and determine whether its programming method was workable, and that no attempt had ever been made to interpret the results or evaluate their reliability.

The apparent success of the demonstration in showing that ENIAC was operational posed a similar threat to the ENIAC patent. Various flaws discovered after the demonstration were also used to cast doubt on the idea that ENIAC had been working properly. The hardware engineer Homer Spence swore an affidavit that problems with ENIAC's cycling unit had rendered the machine useless for a full month after the February demonstrations. These problems "cast grave doubt" on the accuracy of the machine at the time of the demonstration.[15] Spence further swore that the trajectory program that had been run at the demonstration was useless for practical purposes.

The idea of a gap of eight months from completion of ENIAC in December of 1945 to its first useful operation, in July of 1946 is, though hard to square with the historical record, not inherently absurd. Later computers sometimes spent much more time in the liminal state of almost working, and some never fully emerged. No one had ever tried to troubleshoot an electronic device of such complexity before, and ENIAC's high clock speed of 100,000 pulses a second meant that signals had to be transmitted more cleanly, detected more precisely, and processed more rapidly than was usually the case.

Still, it must have hurt the pride of the team to repeatedly swear affidavits and give testimony that the machine had been useless when announced to the world and for months afterward. After the patent was finally invalidated (in 1973), Mauchly quickly began to emphasize the machine's early reliability, claiming that even "before the ENIAC had completed its tests ... it would often work for hours or days at a time without error" and that after the conclusion of the Los Alamos run in January of 1946 "there was no doubt—the ENIAC had been thoroughly tested, and passed to everyone's satisfaction."[16] These assertions are not easy to square with sworn statements Mauchly had made over many previous years.

Programming the Demonstration

Authorship of the trajectory set-up used in the February 1946 demonstration has also been disputed. To Betty Jean Jennings, the set-up eventually came to represent the point at which ENIAC's operators stepped up and began to take a creative role in the programming of the machine in a moment of "history-making impact."[17] That ENIAC had performed the task for which it had originally been designed was a matter of great symbolic importance. The authorship dispute developed during patent and legal proceedings of the 1950s, the 1960s, and the 1970s, although why the issue mattered legally (other than, perhaps, to establish the authority of other statements made by the people involved) isn't clear to us.

Adele Goldstine swore that she had been the direct supervisor of all problems set up on ENIAC before March of 1946, when she had left the ENIAC project. She had had "responsibility to prepare each of the demonstration problems for its solution by the ENIAC and to supervise the setting up of each problem on the machine" for the sessions held on February 1 and February 15.[18] Herman Goldstine later amplified this statement: "The actual preparation of the problems put on at the demonstration was done by Adele Goldstine and me with some help on the simpler problems from John Holberton and his girls." He insisted that, as of February 1946, "the only persons who really had a completely detailed knowledge of how to program the ENIAC were my wife and me" and that the "main calculations and the interrelationship between the various problems" were "prepared solely" by them. He supported his claims with extracts from the ENIAC log book, though the most compelling entries relate specifically to the simpler February 1 demonstration.[19] In regard to the February 15 demonstration, he merely noted a last-minute entry in his handwriting stating "Demonstration problems O.K.!!" and added a recollection that Dean Pender of the Moore School had appeared late at night to present him and Adele with a bottle of bourbon to sustain them as they toiled.

In her 1962 affidavit, Betty Jean Jennings stated that the trajectory problem for the February 1946 demonstration had been set up by her and Frances E. Snyder (later Holberton) and that the "work for this demonstration was not checked by either Capt. or Mrs. Goldstine."[20] In her autobiography she detailed this account, describing how she and Snyder had begun work on a trajectory set-up in October of 1945, with Ruth Lichterman and Marlyn Wescoff assigned to carry out a hand calculation that would exactly mirror ENIAC's operation—a calculation that later proved useful in debugging the set-up. On Jennings' account, after the February 1 demonstration Herman Goldstine had asked her and Frances Snyder if they thought they would be able to get the trajectory calculation installed by February 15.[21] She offered a mirror image of Herman Goldstine's anecdote about the bourbon, in which it had been she and Snyder who had stayed behind the night before the demonstration after the departure of the last commuter train, receiving from a grateful Pender the gift of a "fifth of liquor."[22]

This dispute seems to have become one of the main sources of friction between participants. Betty Jean Jennings never forgave Herman Goldstine for taking credit, growing more bitter (or at least less guarded) in her final interviews. She even alleged that "he forged entries into the logbook."[23]

It is no longer possible to establish which woman was presented with a congratulatory bottle by Harold Pender. We cannot snatch the disputed bottle from either of the ghosts wrestling forlornly for its possession, and will instead hope that Pender purchased liquor by the case to distribute among his many deserving subordinates. The more important historical issue is that these disputes have systematically and fundamentally destabilized historical memory around several aspects early history of the machine, rendering oral histories and memoirs more than usually problematic. They have also served to direct historical attention toward a handful of well-worn anecdotes, and away from the broader archival record showing that the February 1946 set-up, regardless of who produced it, was neither the first nor the most innovative treatment of trajectory computations for ENIAC.

Applications for ENIAC

Although ENIAC was profoundly shaped by Arthur Burks' 1943 work to define a set-up for calculating trajectories, we have found no evidence that comparably detailed work was done for any other problem before the Los Alamos calculation. This does not reflect any unique lack of foresight. Throughout the next decade it was normal for an organization installing its first computer to greatly underestimate the work required to get its problems up and running.[24] As the first team ever to struggle with a computer of such power, ENIAC's creators had a better excuse for this neglect than most of those who followed.

Representing ENIAC Programs

The development practices and notations used for problems designed for ENIAC in its original control mode are only sporadically documented. Potential users faced a two-part challenge: to plan the sequences of operations that ENIAC would carry out and to document the physical configuration required to implement those operations. Eckert and Mauchly addressed both these issues in their original 1943 proposal, and their original diagramming techniques were gradually refined over the years.

The proposal for ENIAC had included a rather crude illustration of black boxes linked by wires, but Burks' late-1943 "panel diagram" showed how all ENIAC's switches should be set and how all its cables should be plugged in order to set it up to perform a calculation.[25] These diagrams, essentially stylized pictures of ENIAC, were still in use in 1946, by which time they had come to be called "set-up diagrams." Burks' original diagram was several yards long and would have been unwieldy and inconvenient to work with. To mitigate this, diagrams were later drawn on pre-printed templates showing four panels to a page. "Program cards" were prepared showing the settings required for individual panels.[26] When attached to the relevant units, these made it easy for operators to check that program settings had been correctly reinstated after a test.[27]

Sequences of operations were described in "set-up tables." These had evolved from Burks' "set up form" showing the sequence of operations in the trajectory calculation, which in turn had built on Eckert and Mauchly's outline.[28] Burks had shown ENIAC's panels along the top, defining columns. Each line in the table could describe a number of simultaneous operations. Individual cells documented the contributions of a particular unit to a particular operation. The set-up table format was used in the December 1944 progress report to illustrate the small example of computing a sequence of squares and cubes.[29] Columns still represented ENIAC units, but now each line showed what happened in a single addition time.[30] Among other things, this enabled a programmer to check that parallel operations were correctly scheduled. Cells in the table showed the switch settings of individual program controls and details of the program lines transmitting input and output program pulses to those controls. Jennings later recalled these diagrams as the origin of "pedaling," a rather idiosyncratic term used by ENIAC's operators. Jennings speculated that the operators called these "pedaling sheets (perhaps because … they showed us what was happening each 'pedal stroke' along the way, or add time by add time)."[31] This suggests a pun on the name of ENIAC's cycling unit, which provided the ability to step through a program for debugging purposes.

Set-up tables showed details of individual sequences, but not their combination in the complete structure of the computation. Because this "sequence programming" was controlled by the master programmer, the team captured it in "master

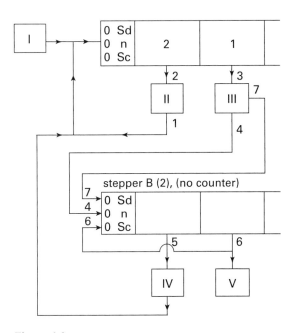

Figure 4.3
This "master programmer connexion" diagram documented the master programmer configuration to convey to readers the structure of one of Douglas Hartree's computations.
(source: W. F. Cope and Douglas R. Hartree, "The Laminar Boundary Layer in Compressible Flow," *Philosophical Transactions of the Royal Society of London. Series A; Mathematical and Physical Sciences* 241, no. 827 (1948): 1–69; reproduced with permission of Royal Society)

programmer link diagrams" showing the numbers set for each stage of the master programmer's steppers, and the connections to be made between steppers and program sequences. The basic sequences were shown as black boxes, their details being documented on the set-up tables. These diagrams convey similar information to the flow diagrams developed a little later by Herman Goldstine and John von Neumann, but in a more concrete way.

An extended discussion of "Programming the ENIAC" was included in an appendix to a report issued in November of 1945.[32] The 1946 ENIAC manual assembled by Adele Goldstine under the direction of Arthur Burks included a number of detailed examples of ENIAC set-ups.[33] These emphasized ballistics problems, including the calculation of trajectories for anti-aircraft tables and for ground gunfire and the use of a drag function in trajectory calculations. Other examples were designed to illustrate particular programming techniques, such as "magnitude discrimination" (a form of conditional branching) and use of the function table to generate program-control pulses. The relationship of these examples to actual practice or to hands-on experimentation with the completed machine is not clear. Some of these diagrams appeared in earlier progress reports and were not drawn by Adele Goldstine, so it isn't clear to what extent she shaped the techniques described in the manual as opposed to serving primarily as an editor to assemble and integrate material produced by the project's engineers.[34] Some set-ups are given in BRL reports, but the only example we have found of detailed documentation for a program that was actually run is a set-up table for part of a calculation carried out by Douglas Hartree in 1946.[35]

In addition to the three forms of diagram already discussed, Goldstine's 1946 manual described "set-up analysis tables" in which the actions performed by sequences and the relationships between them were described in informal English. This was not unlike later practice of documentation via pseudo-code, though some items, such as the conditions for loop termination, were shown in stylized form. We have not located any archival evidence for the use of this technique in actual ENIAC practice. Perhaps it was displaced by the adoption of flow diagrams.[36]

These four notations suggest the outline of a complete process for the development of an ENIAC set-up. The basic program sequences required and their general relationships would be identified, and perhaps documented in an analysis table. A master programmer diagram would then formalize the high-level structures, while set-up tables supported the detailed design of the individual sequences. Finally, the information on these diagrams would be consolidated in set-up diagrams or on cards summarizing the physical configuration of ENIAC for the problem.

In practice the various diagrams were used in flexible and ad hoc ways. For example, the November 1945 report states the basic principle that "in planning a set-up for the ENIAC it is desirable to link the elementary programming sequences into a complex whole by means of the master programmer," but rather than using set-up tables, the details of individual sequences are shown on rather sketchy annotated panel diagrams.[37] Similar informal diagrams and pictures appear in other expository articles.[38] The set-up table for Hartree's 1946 calculation reverts to Burks' earlier practice in which each row of the table corresponds to a mathematical operation (often a multiplication) rather than a single addition time. This computation was dominated by multiplications and so made little use of parallel operations as ENIAC had only one multiplier. Documenting every addition time would bloat the diagram but add little useful information. This casual approach to documentary standards and conventions has been followed by programmers ever since.

Comparing the diagramming methods documented in 1946 with earlier project documents reveals that considerable attention had been paid to programming issues throughout the ENIAC project, and that the basic forms of notation used for planning and describing set-ups had been developed by the beginning of 1945. Although ENIAC's early operators later swore that they had taught themselves to program and had invented their own techniques, it is clear that the methods of diagramming and analysis they used were based on work done long before they were hired.

Problems Run on ENIAC

Buried in the bundles of exhibits that Herman Goldstine assembled in support of the various ENIAC-related lawsuits is a three-page list of problems run on ENIAC through late 1948.[39] Of the eighteen mathematical challenges listed, twelve are topics to which the machine was applied before its conversion to a new programming method. The first eleven seem to have been run, at least in part, at the Moore School. The list includes at least some of the classified problems to which ENIAC was applied, but excludes several applications documented in other sources—among them Derrick Lehmer's sieve for primes. Some other set-ups were designed but never used. Our consolidated list in table 4.1 integrates material from several surviving archival and secondary sources.

Primary set-up work on many of these problems was performed by outside users, as was the case with the three problems run for Los Alamos and the mathematical experiments carried out by Hans Rademacher and Derrick Lehmer. As we saw previously, in mid 1945 Herman Goldstine and John Holberton had seen themselves as selecting machine operators rather than programmers for ENIAC. As important as the creative contributions of the original six ENIAC operators were, they spent less time working the machine and contributed to fewer set-ups than might be assumed from their recent prominence. Our table 4.1 represents a fairly small proportion of the hundred or more distinct scientific problems tackled by ENIAC during its operational lifetime, suggesting that the popular focus on this particular cohort of women rather than their successors at the Ballistic Research Lab is part of a more general fascination with "firsts" and origin stories that has shaped our understanding of other areas of ENIAC's history.

Hartree's Problem

In the summer of 1946 the distinguished British scientist Douglas R. Hartree arrived in Philadelphia to use ENIAC. A physicist by training, Hartree had made important contributions to the development of quantum mechanics in the 1920s, establishing himself as a member of the international community of physicists who were probing the mysteries of the atom and its constituent particles. Within physics Hartree is best remembered for his "self-consistent field method" (more commonly referred to today as the Hartree-Fock method) for calculating atomic structure on the basis of the newly published Schrödinger equation.

During World War I, Hartree's studies as an undergraduate at Cambridge had been interrupted by military service, during which he had assisted one of the university's professors in experimental investigations of anti-aircraft gunnery.

Table 4.1
Problems run on or planned in detail for ENIAC during its time at the Moore School. Except where otherwise noted, all quoted problem names and descriptions are from "A List of Problems the ENIAC Has Been Used to Solve," in HHG-APS, series 10, box 3.

Los Alamos Problem (December 1945–March, 1946).	Calculations to model the workability of Edward Teller's "Super" design for the hydrogen bomb. First problem run on ENIAC, set-up developed primarily by Metropolis and Frankel.
Generation of sines and cosines (April 15–16, 1946).	One of the Feb 1 demonstration problems, and later used to test predictions of error accumulation during numerical integration made in Rademacher's "Theory of Rounding and Truncation Errors." These results were presented at the Moore School lectures as a "particularly simple" experimental investigation.[a]
Table of sines and cosines to ten decimals.	One of the Feb 1 demonstration problems. The table was reproduced locally for use in ballistic work.[b]
Computation of artillery trajectories. (demonstration version, run February 1946)	The task used to justify ENIAC's construction. One of the February 15 demonstration problems.
Laminar boundary layer flow in a compressible fluid for the case of a flat plate at zero incidence. (June–July 1946).	Run by Douglas Hartree to model airflow around a supersonic projectile. Hartree produced his own set-up, but acknowledged Kathleen McNulty for her help making it work and for operating the machine.[c]
Investigations into calculating trajectories.	Two separate cases are mentioned: calculations using x as the independent variable and calculations with t as an independent variable.
Lehmer's Primes Problem (circa July 1946).	An experimental application of the machine to number theory by D. H. Lehmer. Reportedly run over the July 4 weekend.
Calculations in the liquid-drop model of Fission. (July 15–31, 1946).[d]	Another project for Los Alamos. Programmed by Metropolis and Frankel, who thank John von Neumann and the Goldstines "for instructions in its operation" and report their "indebtedness to the capable operating staff of the ENIAC, who proved quite indispensable in the execution of this and a preceding problem."[e]
Trajectory calculations including calculation of director data for 90-mm gun (August 1946).	"Application" of the trajectory calculation.[f] Included provision for meteorological conditions and changes in the time interval without use of the multiplier.[g] At least one set of real firing tables was produced in August of 1946 to meet urgent requirement of the BRL.[h]
Reflection and refraction of shock waves. (September 3–24, 1946)[i]	A Los Alamos problem "programmed and supervised" for Abraham Taub by Adele Goldstine, who had by that point left the Moore School.[j] Jennings also recalled working on the problem.[k] "Numerical solutions for the refraction of plane shocks were obtained … ."[l]

Table 4.1 (continued)

Calculation of zero-pressure properties of diatomic gases (October 7–18, 1946).[m]	According to a later history, "J. A. Goff, dean of the Towne Scientific School, evaluated a mathematical model to obtain zero-pressure properties of certain diatomic gases using the best available spectroscopic … ."[n]
Calculations of the integral [complex integral follows].	Frank Grubbs' problem regarding tests for statistical outliers. Preparatory work was done on this while ENIAC was at the Moore School, but the problem was not run fully until March of 1948 when ENIAC was already in Aberdeen. It is discussed in a subsequent chapter.
Calculation of bombing trajectories, using an analytical drag function.	A cousin of the firing tables problem, concerning bombs dropped from aircraft. Run at the Moore School on behalf of the BRL after it officially took ownership of ENIAC.
Solution of Mathieu's equation.	Mathieu functions are special functions useful in the solution of periodic differential equations. Two hundred trajectories were calculated in twelve hours of computer time, and published by Moore School researchers as contributions to the modeling of electrical circuits. A report notes that this was operated by Moore School staff. However the BRL later returned to the same problem, calculating 1,500 more trajectories, suggesting the equation was also of direct interest to the BRL.[o]
Studies of interpolation methods for ENIAC.	The BRL mathematicians Haskell B. Curry and Max Lotkin carried out detailed preparatory work with Willa Wyatt, one of the senior human computers. Detailed set-ups are preserved, but it does not appear that any of these applications were run.[p]
A shock wave problem for a high-speed projectile.	This problem was fully programmed but abandoned in favor of Clippinger's method."[q]

a. Hans Rademacher, "On The Accumulation of Errors in Numerical Integration on the ENIAC," in *The Moore School Lectures: Theory and Techniques for Design of Electronic Digital Computers*, ed. Martin Campbell-Kelly and Michael R. Williams (MIT Press, 1985); Hans Rademacher, "On the Accumulation of Errors in Processes on Integration on High-Speed Calculating Machines," in *Proceedings of a Symposium on Large-Scale Digital Calculating Machinery, 7–10 January 1947*, ed. William Aspray (MIT Press, 1985); W. Barkley Fritz, "ENIAC—A Problem Solver," *IEEE Annals of the History of Computing* 16, no. 1 (1994): 25–45. The date comes from Travis to Kessenich, 18 November 1946, MSOD-UP box 49 (Letters regarding reduction to practice).

b. "List of ENIAC Problems," n.d., Plaintiff Trial Exhibit 22753, ETE-UP.

c. Cope and Hartree, "The Laminar Boundary Layer in Compressible Flow."

d. Goldstine, *The Computer*, 232.

e. S. Frankel and N. Metropolis, "Calculations in the Liquid-Drop Model of Fission," *Physical Review* 72, no. 10 (1947): 914–925.

f. "List of ENIAC Problems," n.d., Plaintiff Trial Exhibit 22753, ETE-UP.

g. Ibid.

Table 4.1 (continued)

h. "Civil Action No. 105-145 *Sperry Rand vs. Bell Labs*. Deposition of Mrs. Genevieve Brown Hatch," October 18, 1960, GWS-DCA, box 35.

i. Goldstine, *The Computer*, 233.

j. From the paper describing the results of this calculation: A. H. Taub, "Reflection of Plane Shock Waves," *Physical Review* 72 (1947): 51–60.

k. Bartik, *Pioneer Programmer*, 105.

l. Fritz, "ENIAC—A Problem Solver," 44, 48.43.43.

m. Goldstine, *The Computer*, 233.

n. Fritz, "ENIAC—A Problem Solver," 44, 48.43.42.

o. Harry J. Gray, Richard Merwin, and J. G. Brainerd, "Solutions of the Mathieu Equation," *AIEE Transactions* 67 (1948): 429–441. S. J. Zaroodny reports in *Memorandum Report 878: An Elementary Review of the Mathieu-Hill Equations of Real Variable Based on Numerical Solutions* (Ballistic Research Laboratories, 1955) that the findings reported were based on trajectories "made on the ENIAC in 1948." On p. 23 he distinguishes between "Brainerd's Data" and "BRL's Data."

p. De Mol, Carle, and Bullynck, "Haskell before Haskell." This identifies Wyatt as an ENIAC programmer, though she was not one of the six women who operated ENIAC during its time at the Moore School. The planned ENIAC setups are documented in Haskell B. Curry and Willa A. Wyatt, *Report No. 615: A Study of Inverse Interpolation of the ENIAC* (Ballistic Research Laboratory, 1946) and in Max Lotkin, *Report No. 632: Inversion on the ENIAC Using Osculatory Interpolation* (Ballistic Research Laboratory, 1947).

q. "List of ENIAC Problems," n.d., Plaintiff Trial Exhibit 22753, ETE-UP.

Ground-based guns had only occasionally been successful in downing the zeppelins that had raided Britain early in the war. As Hartree was prone to remark in later years, the poor performance of artillery against targets of such bulk and sloth demonstrated that the only flying object anyone knew how to target in 1916 was a grouse.[40] Hartree's first published paper, a short one that appeared in *Nature* in 1920, described a numerical method for the calculation of a shell's entire trajectory.[41] His approach closely paralleled that taken by the American mathematicians at the Aberdeen Proving Ground, whose interest in numerical computation had been shaped by their experience with ballistics computations during the war. As we noted in chapter 1, new tactical demands led to innovations in ballistics theory, and calculating trajectories using the new methods was exactly the kind of problem for which ENIAC was designed.[42]

Hartree became well known as an expert in what would later be called numerical analysis: the solution of mathematical problems using numerical rather than symbolic methods. Unusually for a distinguished scientist of the period, Hartree found profound satisfaction in the act of calculation, spending many thousands of hours computing by hand and with mechanical desk calculators. His particular talent, which he applied to a wide range of physics problems, was reworking equations as systems of differential equations that could be solved with the tools available to

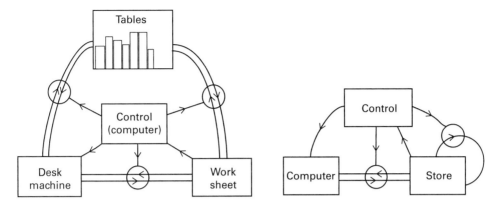

Figure 4.4
Hartree's depiction of the changes and continuities in the organization of computation in going from "hand computation" (left) to "an automatic calculating machine" such as ENIAC (right). (source: Douglas R. Hartree, *Calculating Instruments and Machines*, University of Illinois Press, 1949)

him. That meant understanding the physics of a problem intimately, but it also required the kind of craft knowledge of the interactions of particular kinds of differential equations and numerical methods that came from a lifetime of estimating initial values, cranking handles of calculating machines, recording intermediate results, and gauging the speed with which a solution could be obtained.

Hartree was curious about the latest developments in computing technology. During the 1930s he had overseen the construction of two differential analyzers at Manchester University: an ingenious model built from Meccano parts (Meccano kits were roughly equivalent to the Erector sets played with by American children during the same era) and subsequently a full-scale version.

At the outbreak of World War II, Hartree put the analyzer at the disposal of the Ministry of Supply, and both he and the machine were applied to a wide range of wartime problems. Many of these mirrored the work of the BRL, including calculations related to the trajectories of shells and rockets. He also made calculations relating to uranium enrichment and to the propagation of shock waves from explosions. He spent much time modeling electron flow within cavity magnetrons (the crucial components of portable radar sets), and that work brought him into contact with the latest applications of electronics.

The Ministry of Supply was responsible for the United Kingdom's National Physical Laboratory, which at the end of World War II was setting up a Mathematics Division. Its responsibilities included the construction of computing machinery. Shortly before the end of the war, Hartree, by then a member of the National Physical Laboratory's Executive Committee, visited the United States to familiarize himself with the latest developments. He saw the Mark I operating at Harvard;

however, he was more impressed by ENIAC, which was then nearing completion. He had a detailed description of the new machine ready for publication in *Nature* shortly after it was declassified the following spring. He engaged Herman Goldstine in a detailed correspondence about plans for ENIAC's successor (which we discuss in chapter 6), making "an excellent impression" on Goldstine.[43]

At the beginning of 1946, Goldstine invited Hartree to attend ENIAC's dedication ceremony and to spend some time at the Moore School.[44] That didn't fit into Hartree's schedule; however, after some help from the Americans in arranging passage across the Atlantic, Hartree and his wife arrived in April for a three-month stay. The environment at the Moore School and that at the Ballistic Research Lab was changing rapidly as the urgency of the war receded and the scientists who had been drafted began "streaming back to their Universities."[45] In April, Goldstine wrote to Paul Gillon suggesting a number of ways in which Hartree's expertise and prestige could be put to use to bolster the flagging morale of the staff and to suggest new directions for the use of ENIAC. In particular, Goldstine felt that "every effort should be made to encourage Hartree actually to plan and run" some work related to his aerodynamic investigations.[46] That work concerned the "laminar boundary layer in a compressible fluid," investigating regions where air flows smoothly around an object such as a shell or an airplane wing. Hartree had used the differential analyzer before the war to investigate laminar flow, and as he returned to his personal research he was eager to explore ENIAC's suitability for the task.[47]

His interest in the problem began with attempts to "estimate, if only qualitatively, the effect of the boundary layer on the aerodynamic force coefficients of a projectile" and "calculate the position of separation of the boundary layer," where smooth flow gave way to turbulence. The work was highly relevant to the BRL, which was investigating similar phenomena experimentally in the supersonic wind tunnel. Hartree's paper describing the work, written in collaboration with W. F. Cope, included photographs of bullets in flight, showing various points of separation.[48] Previous work had been confined to the highly simplified case of a flat plate, but the BRL staff knew from photographs taken of bullets in flight that the boundary layers formed around their shapes were significantly more complex.

After a lot of detailed mathematical work, Cope and Hartree succeeded in characterizing the problem to be put on ENIAC in terms of three differential equations defining a set of functions modeling laminar flow. Instead of determining the optimum value to satisfy a single equation, as with the firing-table problem, the calculations had to find values to fit three equations simultaneously. As Hartree explained, such equations are very sensitive to the initial conditions chosen, and solving them with differential analyzers would require a large number of trial solutions with slightly different inputs before a solution was found. Hartree applied his ingenuity to the development of new methods better suited to ENIAC's distinctive strengths and weaknesses. The equations defined functions of different "orders." In the basic case of the so-called zero-order functions, the equations could be substantially simplified. Hartree proposed to solve these equations first, and then to move on to the more complicated and general cases. He considered two approaches to solving the zero-order equations, one a straightforward iterative method and the other a method based on evaluating solutions calculated with "trial values" of certain functions. Although mathematically more elegant, the first approach was rejected because, given ENIAC's limited memory, it would require large amounts of manual card handling. The trial-value approach could, it turned out, be run completely automatically.

A special feature of the equations was that their boundary conditions were given at two points. Boundary conditions express constraints on the allowable solutions for differential equations. If they are all given at one point, as in the ballistics equations, a numerical solution can be obtained by simply calculating from that point on. In Hartree's problem, however, there was no guarantee that once the calculation was run through to the second boundary point the values obtained would satisfy the conditions imposed there. Hartree therefore began with estimated "trial" values for two of the required functions at the first boundary point and ran the calculation. By comparing the results obtained at the second boundary point with the boundary conditions there, he could calculate a better trial value. Repeating this "generate and test" approach produced a solution that satisfied all the boundary conditions reasonably quickly.

ENIAC was therefore set up to integrate the equations from the initial values, to evaluate the results, and to generate a better estimate if one was needed. The master programmer controlled the switching between these tasks and ended the calculation when the solution obtained was sufficiently accurate. ENIAC punched the results of each trial solution on a card so that progress could be tracked. When an accurate solution was obtained, ENIAC ran another integration step, this time printing a card for each value of the independent variable so that the progress of the calculation was fully documented. To prevent numerical errors from building up, small increments of the independent variable were used so that it took 250 separate integrations to cover the full range of values. ENIAC could run eight of these calculations in a second, so one trial solution took about 30 seconds. A typical case required finding about five solutions, requiring a total of about two and a half minutes of computing.[49]

Solutions of the zero-order equations were generated and published for a range of different values of the velocity of the flow.[50] Performing the calculations was very much a team effort. John Holberton, head of the ENIAC operations team, was closely involved, writing detailed notes on Hartree's method and later giving a brief presentation on the calculations at a conference of the Association for Computing

Compressible Laminar Boundary Layer. Zero–order Equations. Set up for integration procedure.

	...	Acc 9	Acc 10	H. S. M.	Acc 11	Acc 12	Acc 13	Acc 14	...
		ier	icand		L.H.P.P.		R.H.P.P.		
Digit Line Shifter Deleter		α β γ δ A 2 1 3 4 1	α β γ δ 1 2 4 2 −1 2			α β γ A 2 3 4 1	α β γ A S 2 1 3 2 1	α β γ A S 2 3 2 4 2 −1	
Pulse from M.P. initiating → A−1		0	0	0	0	0	0	0	
integration sequence		F_0	H_0	A−1 1 α C α O S C 1 A−2			$F_0 H_0$		
		H_0	H_0	A−2 2 β C O C A C 1 A−3			H_0^2		
		F_0	R_0	A−3 3 α C α C A C 1 A−4			$F_0 R_0$	A−3 1 A O 1 H_0^2	

Figure 4.5
A redrawn detail from the "pedaling sheet" prepared by Hartree showing the first three multiplications involved in the integration procedure. (courtesy of Jean Jennings Bartik Computing Museum)

Machinery in November 1947. Douglas Hartree specifically thanked Kathleen McNulty for "instruction, advice and help in organizing the work for the machine, planning the machine set-up for it, and in running the machine," adding that "the active and friendly help received made the work, in addition to being of absorbing interest, a real pleasure."[51]

Figure 4.5 shows a portion of a pedaling sheet for the above-mentioned problem, the only such sheet known to have survived from a problem actually run on ENIAC. Columns represent ENIAC's accumulators and other units, identified in the headings. The first row below the headings specifies digit terminal adaptors and plugging; the next row provides initial values. Each subsequent row represents a successive stage of the computation. Hartree's sense of the computation was centered on multiplications, so he used multiplication operations rather than ENIAC's "add times" to diagram 62 steps spread over four pages. Individual cells contain symbolic representations (using the notations defined in Adele Goldstine's report) of the switch settings and program line plugging active on each unit during each stage and formulas defining the quantities stored in each accumulator.

Hartree then turned his attention to the more complicated requirements of the first-order equations. The particular difficulty with these was not the solution of the equations themselves, but the generation of a large amount of numerical information needed for each solution, itself defined by complex functions. This meant that there was now no alternative but to split the computation. The numerical data would be computed first and would be recorded on decks of punched cards which would then be read while the equations were being solved.

Detailed plans were made for these calculations. Multiple card formats were defined, each holding the values required for a particular step in the calculation.[52] Values were to be calculated on ENIAC and punched onto cards, sometimes in multiple runs. Hartree explained how a full range of values for the variables included in one of these functions was punched manually onto a set of cards, to be duplicated as needed for repeated runs using a specialized machine known as a reproducing punch to create a deck of cards each holding a unique permutation of eight input variables. These were then processed by ENIAC to produce output cards with the values produced by evaluating the function with these arguments, which served in turn as one of several inputs for the program evaluating the overall system of equations.[53] Another specialized punched-card machine, a sorter, could be used to separate the cards according to values punched for particular parameters. Hartree specifically thanked McNulty for suggesting this use of auxiliary punched-card equipment—evidence that the initial training the women received from Aberdeen on the punched-card techniques was boosting the effectiveness of ENIAC. Input decks were prepared, and some preliminary solutions of first-order equations were obtained, but in mid July ENIAC was reassigned to what Hartree described as "higher-priority work." We now know this to have been further Los Alamos calculations run by Metropolis and Frankel, this time on atomic fission.

Hartree later commented that the "small capacity" of ENIAC's high-speed storage was "its main limitation as a general purpose calculator." As his 1946 calculations had demonstrated, one way of getting around this was to punch cards with intermediate results and then read back their contents for further processing. This entailed a great deal of card shuffling, but, as Hartree observed, the operator "is not required to do any calculations … but is only concerned in transferring numbers in large blocks, represented by decks of punched cards, between the different machines. In this way, very powerful use can be made of the ENIAC in cooperation with the punched-card equipment, particularly the reproducing punch and sorter; and though the process is not purely automatic, it may still be fast, and is certainly labour-saving, compared with other methods of carrying out the calculations."[54] When ENIAC was used in this way, its role in the overall calculation process was not unlike that of the specialized electronic punched-card processors later produced by IBM, such as its model 604 Electronic Calculating Punch, in that it served as one of several machines used in succession to process or update a deck of cards.

Shortly after his return to England, Hartree was named the Plummer Professor of Mathematical Physics at Cambridge University. His inaugural lecture describing ENIAC was issued as a small book and provided one of the clearest and most detailed descriptions then available of the machine, and of the new field of electronic computation.[55]

Lehmer's Holiday Computations

Another well-documented calculation from 1946 was carried out by the Berkeley number theorist Derrick Lehmer. Lehmer spent the year 1945–46 at the Ballistic Research Lab as a member of a group helping to plan for ENIAC's use. He experimented with the machine by running "little problems" when it was otherwise not in use.[56] His initials in the service log suggest that by April he was sufficiently familiar with the machine to carry out routine maintenance tasks, such as replacing faulty tubes.[57] This shows that ENIAC remained a quite personal machine, one that could effectively be borrowed and operated by an individual user.

As Derrick Lehmer later recounted, he and his family descended on ENIAC over the July 4 weekend, a weekend during which very little work is done in the United States. (Lehmer's wife, Emma, was a noted mathematician who did much of the computational work required to get ENIAC's output from this visit into publishable form.) With help from John Mauchly, they were allowed to "pull everything off the machine" and set up their own problem.[58]

As a number theorist, Lehmer was interested in different kinds of problems than the differential equations that had constituted most of the machine's work so far. His program tested a method for identifying prime numbers, using a "sieve." An example of this meaning of "sieve" is the familiar "sieve of Eratosthenes," in which numbers with prime factors are progressively sifted out, leaving only prime numbers behind. Lehmer had a particular interest in building automated sieves. During the 1920s and the 1930s he had built electromechanical and photoelectric devices to speed the process, and later he would build a series of special-purpose electronic sieves that as late as the 1970s performed the task much faster than general-purpose computers.

Lehmer credited Mauchly with the idea of implementing a sieve on ENIAC. Lehmer's program, as partially reconstructed by the historians Maarten Bullynck and Liesbeth de Mol, made use of ENIAC's ability to perform several parts of a computation at once.[59] In the reconstruction, fourteen accumulators were used to simultaneously test a single number against different prime numbers.[60] Lehmer's paper does not provide enough information to make it certain that his original implementation exploited that technique, but in discussing the computation he later complained that ENIAC "was a highly parallel machine, before von Neumann spoiled it."[61] He went on to prepare further programs for ENIAC, including a program for Hans Rademacher and a complete set-up to calculate the roots of the Riemann zeta function. However, "before the program could be run, the ENIAC was drastically modified thus rendering it useless for the problem."[62] By that time, Lehmer was back in California. He would soon transfer his affections to other machines.

Departures

ENIAC was officially accepted by the federal government on June 30, 1946, indicating the government's satisfaction that the Moore School had delivered everything it had promised in the contract, including a hefty stack of documentation. Now it was time to move the machine to its permanent home at the Ballistic Research Laboratory at Aberdeen, a little more than 70 miles from Philadelphia. However the building in which ENIAC would be housed was not yet finished, making an immediate move unattractive. Goldstine later offered another motivation for the delay: that ENIAC was already carrying out work that was too valuable to interrupt for a prolonged period. The delay was quite brief. ENIAC was powered down on November 9, 1946.

Planning the Move
In December of 1944, Herman Goldstine had expected that ENIAC would be complete within two months. At that point the plan was to test ENIAC and run trial problems only after the move to Aberdeen, which made the preparation of its new home a matter of some urgency. Goldstine noted that the room assigned to ENIAC, which was within the supersonic wind complex, had been built "to house the induction tunnel." This posed challenges for ventilation and air conditioning "due to the large number of beams and columns stuck into that room," the high levels of humidity, and the "fact that the ENIAC installation will be right next to the water tower for the wind tunnel."[63]

Preparations for the relocation of ENIAC to the BRL began in earnest in January of 1945. In line with the Moore School's system of two-letter codes for its wartime projects, the relocation effort was code-named Project AB. On January 26, 1945, the BRL awarded an initial contract of $15,000 for planning for the move and for the configuration of ENIAC's new quarters.[64] Arrangements were negotiated between

John Brainerd, representing the Moore School, and Herman Goldstine, the designated liaison with the BRL. Agreement was reached quickly on some important matters. The floors around ENIAC would be bare, the walls around it would be soundproofed, and a lobby area with plate-glass windows would give visitors a view of the machine at work. Specifications for wiring, lighting, power, fire prevention, paint, and emergency drainage were agreed upon. A local company, Eggly Engineers, was selected as the contractor to design detailed wiring plans and install the necessary equipment, including a newly designed "ENIAC master control panel" with wall-mounted controls to stop and start the machine.

The plans proved too grand for the humble space originally assigned ENIAC. By January 26 the team faced the prospect of shrinking the showpiece lobby after discovering that the overhead wind-tunnel equipment and maintenance access would allow a ceiling of no more than six and a half feet for the larger area originally planned.[65] By April the situation had been resolved in ENIAC's favor: a new home was found on the third floor of the Ballistic Research Laboratory.[66] The new space—part of an extension to the building known as the Computing Annex—placed ENIAC close to the BRL's other computers. The space was designed around ENIAC, showing it off to best advantage and providing secondary spaces for its punched-card equipment, its testing equipment, and its main panels. The main panels functioned as room dividers, enclosing a smaller inner area in which operators worked.

A contract signed in June of 1945 awarded the Moore School $96,200 to cover the full cost of moving and installing ENIAC, making it the general contractor for the entire relocation process.[67] In view of the cost overruns and the delays that had plagued ENIAC's development, Harold Pender was loath to take on anything that would expose the university to the risk of losing money. He therefore directed that the work "be done primarily by subcontracting" so as to "obtain firm prices from contractors on the basis of an approved plan so that … we will know very closely the costs and will run no appreciable risks."[68] Any unforeseen complications would fall on the heads of Eggly Engineers and the other contractors who had been selected for jobs such as ceiling installation and air conditioning work.

ENIAC on Fire

On the morning of October 26, 1946 ENIAC's guardians discovered that it had been damaged by fire. Insulation around wires carrying power to vacuum-tube heater inputs in one of the function-table panels had ignited after a short circuit, and a small blaze had damaged the panel. The panel's cover had been left off overnight, which may have reduced the effectiveness of its ventilation system. ENIAC's Bakelite sockets, like its plastic and rubber insulation, made it somewhat flammable when hot spots developed. Fortunately the fire did not spread far before automatic safeguards cut off power to the ventilating units fanning it.[69] The rest of the machine could still be operated while the damaged panel was rebuilt by the Reeves Instrument Corporation. Restoration cost $5,794.90—a small fraction of the expense that would have been incurred if the flames had spread between panels.[70]

ENIAC's owners were concerned by the susceptibility of their long-awaited and expensive computer to spontaneous combustion when it was left unattended overnight. A lengthy explanation of the blaze sent to Leslie Simon noted that "as has been customary, recently, both AC and DC supplies were left on the machine overnight." Keeping AC power on continuously was "almost essential from past experience to avoid continual difficulties due to possible failure of one or more of the 18,000 tubes each time the supply is switched. As concerns the DC, recent experience shows that, although less effective than in the case of the AC, continuity in use helps to maintain continuity in operation."[71] This incident, previously overlooked by historians, helps to explain the initial reluctance of BRL staff to leave the tubes' heaters turned on overnight. Mauchly later mocked the Army for what he saw as a shortsighted and bureaucratic error that greatly diminished the machine's reliability.[72]

Rather than merely patch up the damage, the Moore School team proposed what became a $16,000 contract to "eliminate as possible any future fire hazards." Changes included the installation of a switch to cut off DC power, some changes to the function table, and modifications to the fuse systems used with the power transformer. The modifications were incorporated into the relevant parts of ENIAC before it was started up again at Aberdeen Proving Ground.[73]

Leaving Philadelphia

Packing for the move was expected to take about three weeks, and was scheduled to begin on November 11, 1947, with a week or two of full-time effort by one or two people planned for each main unit. Panels were carefully tested and then disconnected from the rest of ENIAC, their vacuum tubes and "plug in" modular units and trays removed for separate packing.[74] All cables and spare parts were also inventoried and crated.

As was true of everything else concerned with ENIAC, the start of packing was delayed a little, in this case to early December.[75] The Moore School paid $2,000 for an insurance policy covering $100,000 in loss or damage incurred in transit and for 30 days thereafter.[76] That policy became active on December 23, presumably marking the first movement of crates and panels.

The Philadelphia company Scott Brothers had won the haulage contract with a proposal for $8,350 of "boxing, rigging, and hauling work," a relatively small part of the overall relocation budget. "Rigging" meant the removal of heavy items, including ENIAC's main panels and the associated power supplies and ventilation gear, by means of power winches through a hole in the Moore School's exterior wall.[77] Partly demolishing and rebuilding the wall was an additional cost and the most dramatic part of ENIAC's exit from Philadelphia.

Breaking Up the Team

Eckert and Mauchly left the Moore School before ENIAC did, and with little more elegance. As far back as the fall of 1944, they had begun what were to prove to be rather unpleasant negotiations with university authorities and other project participants to win the right to submit a patent application granting themselves the rights to the inventions embodied in ENIAC. This was controversial at the time, eroding their relationship with others at the Moore School. Decades later, the judge in the patent trial concluded that the university had yielded its rights to the invention only because Eckert and Mauchly would not otherwise have continued to help the Moore School fulfill its remaining responsibilities under the Army contract.[78] This tension soon began to have a negative effect on work being done at the Moore School to build a new computer, EDVAC, under a follow-up contract awarded in September of 1944. Resentment grew on both sides, and in March of 1946 Mauchly and Eckert both resigned after receiving an ultimatum from the Moore School that their continued employment would require them to release future patent rights to the university and put its financial interests ahead of their own.

Eckert and Mauchly went on to found what eventually became the Eckert-Mauchly Computer Corporation, the world's first computer start-up. Understaffed and undercapitalized, it priced its computers far below the eventual cost of production, which led inevitably to a series of financial crises. In 1950 it was acquired by Remington Rand, the leading office-technology company of the time, and in 1951 the first Univac computer was accepted by the U.S. Bureau of the Census. Though neither Eckert nor Mauchly ever became hugely wealthy, they could plausibly claim to have jointly invented the computer industry as well as the computer. Herman Goldstine and Arthur Burks moved on in 1946, joining a team assembled by John von Neumann at the Institute for Advanced Studies to design an electronic computer.

The ENIAC operating team had originally been recruited with the idea that they would form the nucleus of the group running it at the Ballistic Research Laboratory. However, thanks to the combined effect of marriages, the delayed move, and a long period of restoring the machine to reliable service, only one of the six was still employed by the BRL when ENIAC returned to a reasonably productive work schedule there in the summer of 1948. Betty Jean Jennings and Marlyn Wescoff quit by the end of 1946 rather than follow the computer to Aberdeen, though Jennings continued to work as a contract programmer. Frances Snyder went to Aberdeen, but she left the following year to join Eckert and Mauchly's new computer company. (In another match made by ENIAC, Frances Snyder later married her former boss, John Holberton.)

Three other members of the ENIAC operating team were employed at the Ballistic Research Lab long enough to pass their skills on to the team's new members. Kathleen McNulty's last day at the BRL was February 6, 1948. She married John Mauchly after his first wife's death by drowning in 1946. This is a further indication of the fondness the women of the operations team had for Mauchly, and of its reciprocation. Mauchly had enjoyed the company of the young women, often joining them for lunch and dinner during their time at the Moore School.[79] When Betty Jean Jennings married William Bartik, it was Mauchly, rather than her own father, who walked her down the aisle.[80]

Frances Bilas had married Homer Spence, with whom she must have worked closely while operating ENIAC. Her married name appears in the log book in late March of 1948, but not long afterward she left the BRL after becoming pregnant. Ruth Lichterman stayed longest at the BRL, terminating her employment on September 10, 1948. The reason, reportedly, was marriage. Of the dozens of people who had worked on and with the machine in Philadelphia, there remained only John Holberton and Homer Spence, for whom marriage was no impediment to continued employment.

As will become clear in the following chapters, changes implemented in March of 1948 meant that the work of future programmers and operators would be quite different from that of the original programmers and operators. Programs were now written as a series of instructions, as with other early computers, and were translated to numbers and set up on the computer by turning the knobs on function tables. Thus, programming work was now abstracted from the detailed physical design of the machine, and was less intricately connected with the expertise gained by operating and configuring it. Conversely, the work of operating ENIAC was now more like operating other early computers. All that changed from one task to another was the information coded on the function tables.

5

ENIAC Arrives at the Ballistic Research Lab

In the summer of 1946, the Moore School's contract was successfully completed and responsibility for ENIAC passed to the project's sponsor, the Ballistic Research Laboratory. The BRL had a great need for computer power, even though the urgent need for firing tables that had been used to justify ENIAC's construction had faded somewhat with the end of the war.

A great deal has been written about the building of ENIAC and the team gathered at the Moore School to construct it. ENIAC's time as a working computer at the Ballistic Research Laboratory is much less well understood, even though the BRL commissioned the machine, ran it for eight years, and provided most of the problems to which it was applied. We will therefore begin by putting into focus the BRL and the larger facility of which it was a part: the Aberdeen Proving Ground. These institutions are remembered today, at least by historians of computing, primarily as offstage actors whose greatest contribution to history came from paying the bills for ENIAC. In fact they made important contributions to the development of several areas of science and technology during a transitional era in which the federal government was an increasingly important sponsor of science.

The Ballistic Research Laboratory was created in 1938 in a restructuring of the Aberdeen Proving Ground's Research Division, itself only a few years old. In the second half of the twentieth century, Americans came to take for granted the idea that the federal government would support a wide range of basic scientific research to further the public good, both within its own institutes and through extensive grant programs to universities. The BRL's mission reflected an earlier, more instrumental approach in which the government hired scientists to do applied work in areas of immediate national interest, such as surveying for minerals, boosting agricultural production, and developing new weapons.

The new laboratory bolstered the facility's scientific brain power, hiring more PhDs and more men with degrees from MIT and other prestigious institutions. As the threat of war increased the urgency of its work, the lab was able to attract celebrated scientists such as John von Neumann to its advisory board. This was due in large part to Oswald Veblen, a mathematician who played an important role in coordinating scientific efforts for World War II. Veblen had run Aberdeen's computing group during the earlier war and was now a professor at the Institute for Advanced Study in Princeton. According to Herman Goldstine, it was Veblen who decided to fund ENIAC's construction in the first place. (Veblen's authoritative delivery of the words "Simon, give Goldstine the money," delivered as he walked out of the presentation part way through, featured in one of Goldstine's more memorable anecdotes.[1])

During the 1940s, the BRL was a young institution staffed by highly qualified scientists. When war broke out it grew rapidly, from a small organization of about 40 people to a much larger contingent of about 500.[2] Its leaders were well connected politically and had supporters in the highest circles of American science. In 1944, for example, it had completed the first supersonic wind tunnel in the United States. That project had been headed by Edwin Hubble, the astronomer whose name is today attached both to the law showing that the universe is expanding and to NASA's orbiting observatory.

Goldstine had been the Ordnance Department's point man during ENIAC's development, but he had no desire to remain in military service after the end of the war. ENIAC needed a new master. A Computations Committee had been established in 1945 to provide a group of experts to plan for the arrival of ENIAC at the BRL and to see that it would be applied productively. The members of the Computations Committee included the mathematicians Haskell Curry, Franz Alt, and Derrick Lehmer and the astronomer Leland Cunningham. All of them had come to Aberdeen during the war to assist with the BRL's computational work, and they retained a connection with the lab for several years afterward—some as employees, others as frequent visitors. It is not clear how much the Computations Committee accomplished. Alt later wrote that because everyone at the BRL was still preoccupied with wartime work and ENIAC was still little more than "a jumble of components" the committee was "reduced to working on a few isolated problems, some real, some only for testing."[3]

Something more permanent and more substantial than a committee was needed. In August of 1945 a new Computing Laboratory, headed by Louis S. Dederick, was created as part of a general reorganization within the BRL.[4] Dederick, a civilian scientist, was already an associate director of the BRL, reporting directly to its director, Leslie Simon. Jean Bartik later wrote that "Dederick was a very gentle, considerate man, but quite old, and was being eased out."[5] She also recalled that during her time there he had an office at the Moore School from which he oversaw ENIAC work. Dederick retired in 1953, so although he may have seemed doddering to the young women he still had several years of work left in him.[6]

Installing ENIAC at the BRL

Serious preparations for ENIAC's move to Aberdeen and its installation at the BRL had been underway since January of 1945. The Moore School's contractual responsibilities did not end with ENIAC's arrival, though most of the work involved had been passed on to subcontractors to minimize the school's exposure to risk. The subcontractors mounted ENIAC's various panels to form interior walls, installed the necessary specialized electrical wiring, and mounted suitable air conditioning and ventilation systems. One elegant addition was a master control unit built into the wall, housing the buttons that started and stopped the computer. At the Moore School the same tasks had been performed by a hand-held unit.

ENIAC's owners dithered on the question of a suspended ceiling in the computer room. Such a ceiling had been discussed early in the planning for the machine's new quarters; however, the expenditure wasn't given final authorization until June of 1947, and the ceiling wasn't finished until well into 1948.[7] Leslie Simon had decided not to authorize the ceiling until ENIAC was installed and he would be able to judge for himself if it was needed.[8]

The Register and the Converter
Shortly after ENIAC was delivered to the BRL, the Moore School learned that the BRL had decided to add two new panels built by Eckert and Mauchly's tiny start-up, the Electronic Control Company, "in order to obtain additional programming facilities." On February 18, 1947, Leslie Simon wrote to Harold Pender requesting an estimate of the cost of modifying the installation contract to provide wall space, fans, power, and cabling for the new panels.[9]

The new panels became known as the "register" and the "converter." The register was a delay-line memory, intended to augment ENIAC's tiny writable memory. This was the technology that the Electronic Control Company would have to master to fulfill its ambition to build reliable and affordable commercial computers. Because it was in a more or less permanent cash-flow crisis, the company was desperate for immediate revenues. We suspect that Eckert and Mauchly approached Louis Dederick with the idea of retrofitting the new technology to ENIAC, thereby spreading the development cost of delay-line memory over one more customer. It is less clear what the purpose of the converter was, or how the two new units (now described as an "automatic program selector") would work together.[10]

The notion of "program selection" was not new. Handwritten notes dated August 11, 1945 describe the idea of reading numbers from punched cards to "select from a large number of preset programs."[11] That idea was impractical—ENIAC had only one card reader, and using it for control information would mean either forgoing input data altogether or somehow getting the appropriate control information punched onto the same cards as the data in need of processing. By early 1946 the ENIAC team had come up with the idea of using the function tables, rather than punched cards, to select programs. Adele Goldstine's manual introduced the technique by imagining a situation involving "14 different programs … one or more of which are to be stimulated at various times in a computation."[12] Providing such stimulation in the normal way from the master programmer would soon overwhelm ENIAC's capacity for conditional control. The manual explained how a function table's numerical storage capacity could be used to hold information about what programs were to be stimulated. The table's numeric outputs were connected to program-control lines, and its switches were set to specify particular permutations of program lines.[13] When a particular row was accessed, those connections would trigger the simultaneous execution of up to fourteen sequences (or, as we would call them today, subroutines) set up using the normal ENIAC techniques.

The converter also provided a mechanism for "program selection." In response to receiving a two-digit number, it would emit a control pulse on one of 100 output lines. We conjecture that the converter was intended to trigger subroutines in response to numbers read in sequence from the function table or from the register itself, which would have been an easy way to drive long sequences of subroutines.

Senior staff members at the BRL and at the Moore School shared a desire to avoid relying on the new company. Louis Dederick and Samuel Lubkin, then working at the BRL to design the programming system for EDVAC, met with Irven Travis for a conversation that, unusually, was transcribed. Dederick confided: "Mauchly and Eckert have already quoted us a definite price and the natural thing to do, except for personal considerations or my feeling, would obviously be to let the contract to Mauchly and Eckert. Why go around the bush? But there are these personal considerations. We have been dealing with the Moore School and would like to continue so." Dederick and Lubkin briefed Travis on what was and was not likely to pass muster with Aberdeen's senior management and with federal procurement authorities. "Colonel Simon," Lubkin explained, "would not hesitate" to approve a rival proposal "at a little bit more than Eckert and Mauchly bid."[14]

The contract to build both new panels was issued to the Moore School. As Travis had suggested, it applied a considerable surplus remaining from the existing moving contract toward the cost of the new panels, effectively subsidizing its proposal. The plug-in units for the new panels were manufactured by the Reeves Instrument Corporation of New York City.[15]

Whatever concerns Dederick had regarding the ability of the Electronic Control Company to deliver a reliable memory at the promised low price were borne out over the next few years as the company struggled with optimistic pricing of its Univac computer, unreliable devices, missed delivery deadlines, and chronic undercapitalization. Only a forced sale to Remington Rand in 1950 put the business on a sustainable financial footing. Conversely, the Moore School was crippled by an exodus of talented computer engineers and had no future as a computer builder. Faced with two bad choices, Dederick had chosen the worse one. As it turned out, the Moore School took more than two years to deliver the register, which never worked. Such are the challengers of procuring technologies that have not quite been invented yet. Fortunately the converter would prove useful even without the register.

Staffing ENIAC at the BRL

Two men in crucial positions helped to provide continuity from the construction phase of ENIAC's life through its prime years at Aberdeen despite the generally high rate of staff turnover. John Holberton became Chief of the ENIAC Branch of the BRL's Computing Laboratory. With one title or another, he oversaw the team of ENIAC operators and programmers from its establishment in 1945 at the Moore School until June of 1951, when he left the BRL for the National Bureau of Standards. In 1950 he married Betty Snyder, one of the original operators, who had already left Aberdeen to make a significant contribution to the development of early UNIVAC programming.[16]

Homer Spence features prominently in the remembrances of ENIAC personnel and on the pages of the ENIAC operations log used to record its first few years at Aberdeen. Spence had been a mere Private First Class when he had been sent to Philadelphia during World War II to help get ENIAC finished and working. He had quickly developed an intimate knowledge of its circuits and the little tricks needed to keep them working. Spence moved to Aberdeen with the machine, remaining as a civilian employee after being released from military service. According to W. Barkley Fritz, who worked with ENIAC at the BRL and later did much to document the history of its time there, by mid 1948 "Spence had a small team of maintenance personnel who had the tasks of testing incoming vacuum tubes, preparing and testing plugin circuits, locating the cause of malfunctions, and in general keeping ENIAC in successful operation." He continued to oversee its hardware "during essentially the entire period of its operation."[17]

For most of its career, ENIAC was operated around the clock, and thus three shifts had to be staffed. Demobilization from military service in 1945 ended the special labor conditions that had led John Holberton to pick the first operators from an exclusively female population of computers. Most of the women had left the employment of the BRL by the time ENIAC was properly operational again. Their successors came from a variety of sources. Some (including Winifred Smith, Homé McAllister, Marie Bierstein, and Austin Robert Brown Jr.) had already been working for the BRL as computers. Lila Todd and Helen Greenbaum, who had been assigned to the Moore School as wartime supervisors of work on firing tables, eventually joined the ENIAC team after returning to Aberdeen. Others were new to the BRL. W. Barkley Fritz, for example, had recently earned an MA in mathematics when he talked his way into a summer job with the ENIAC group. In 1952, George Reitwiesner, who had joined the ENIAC team in 1948, married Homé McAllister, continuing ENIAC's matchmaking tradition.[18]

ENIAC as One of Several Tools

The new Computing Laboratory had responsibility for several kinds of computing equipment, inspiring its further subdivision into several "branches." It received custody of ENIAC, the BRL's extensive collection of punched-card machines, and four of the latest relay computers. Even without ENIAC, these holdings would have established the BRL as an important center of scientific computation. Los Alamos possessed nothing more advanced than punched-card machines during this period.

The BRL's first two relay computers were delivered by IBM at the end of 1944 but were returned for significant upgrades the following year.[19] They were constructed around highly modified IBM punched-card machines and, in the punched-card tradition, they were programmed by wiring plugboards. IBM built five altogether, with another pair put to work as the centerpiece of the Columbia University laboratory of Wallace Eckert who had provided many of the ideas behind them. Within the BRL they were usually known as the "IBM relay calculators," though some outsiders called them the "Aberdeen Relay Calculators" and IBM eventually gave them the official designation of "Pluggable Sequence Relay Calculators." The two computers could be linked to work as a single machine. Electromechanical relays could not switch as rapidly as vacuum tubes, but the linked machines still had time to perform 40 calculations in the time it took to mechanically process each input card. They were less complex than the flagship relay calculator of the era, the Harvard Mark I (also built by IBM), but according to Eckert they were optimized for speed, running up to 20 times as fast.[20] To boost throughput they could read an input card while simultaneously punching out the results of the previous set of calculations. They were the fastest calculators of any kind operating in the U.S. for about a year, until ENIAC came to life. Though these machines are interesting as footnotes in the history of automatic computation, and as the electromechanical ancestors of the electronic punched-card calculators IBM introduced in the late 1940s, they were viewed by members of the laboratory staff as unreliable and hard to program. In an internal 1961 history of computing at the BRL, they were dismissed as "unsuccessful" machines that had been used "for a short time."[21]

The BRL's other relay calculator won far more affection from its users. In 1944, the BRL had decided to order the advanced general-purpose relay calculator being designed by George Stibitz and S. B. Williams at Bell Labs. Bell Labs eventually built two Model V relay calculator systems, delivering the second to Aberdeen in August of 1947. Like its IBM rival, it integrated separate calculators with a shared control system. The master unit could direct as many as six calculators, though only two were ever fitted.[22] Model V was much slower than ENIAC, and because it executed its program sequentially from paper tapes it had only limited flexibility to change course according to the results so far obtained.[23] However, it was the most reliable of the BRL's automatic calculators. The Bell Labs engineers had borrowed some of the techniques that had been used to build automatic telephone switching units. Special circuits verified each step of the calculation. Because numbers were stored with redundant bits, errors were detected immediately. When the machine stopped, indicator lights signaled the problem so that it could quickly be restarted without a lengthy expert diagnosis. The Model V found many applications at the BRL until 1955, when it was transferred to Fort Bliss in Texas.[24]

The BRL also continued to operate its differential analyzer. Completed in 1935, it had been used during the war almost exclusively for firing-table calculations, which it performed several times as fast as a conventional desk calculator. The arrival of other calculating machines freed it for other purposes. It was not exactly programmable; however, like other analog differential analyzers of its time, it could be reconfigured to tackle new equations by means of lengthy adjustments with screwdrivers and wrenches. A 1949 report summarized working practices that had been established before the war, noting that a "simple equation" could be set up within hours and that a more complex one "may take several days work to be set up in a reasonably good way," particularly if it wasn't closely related to one tackled previously. Setting up the analyzer involved a good deal of preparatory manual calculation to establish ranges and scales for the variables. Finding a solution for a particular set of input parameters then took from "a few minutes to more than an hour." However, it was "very desirable" to have calculated manually at least one solution against which the first result obtained by the machine could be checked.[25]

The V-2 Calculations

It took the staff of the Computing Laboratory some time to get a feel for the different capabilities of this range of equipment. The first important job for ENIAC at the BRL, and perhaps its only significant work in 1947, was to analyze Doppler data from test firings of German V-2 missiles. The V-2s that the U.S. had retrieved from Germany at the end of the war, the most powerful rockets to have been deployed, provided a template for subsequent American missiles and space-launch systems.

The task of analyzing the Doppler data from the V-2s resembled the tracking and analysis of test firings that the BRL had long carried out for shells as the first step in the production of firing tables. Accurately measuring a V-2's flight path posed a new challenge for the scientists at the BRL, skilled as they were in modeling trajectories. A V-2 flew faster than any airplane and farther than any shell, reaching an altitude of more than 100 miles when launched straight up.

Calculations were performed on ENIAC, on both kinds of relay computer, and by manual methods in what became a comparative trial of the new spectrum of computing options. Three different radar posts logged the frequencies of signals reflected from the rocket. Building on techniques pioneered during the war (for example for proximity fuses), Doppler-effect analysis then revealed the speed at which the rocket was moving relative to the base station. The equipment was something like the radar guns later used by police to catch speeding drivers, but was complicated by a transceiver within the rocket that picked up the incoming signal, doubled its frequency, and beamed it back. The receiving stations sent both the original signal and the modified reflection to a central station, where they were recorded onto 35-millimeter film. About 50,000 sets of values were logged during the flight of a single missile. Determining the position and the velocity of a rocket at a single instant, using successive approximations to home in on the solution, took "around 40 additions, multiplications, divisions and square roots." A human computer with a mechanical desk calculator would take "between 15 and 45 minutes per trajectory point, the actual time required depending on the skill of the individual, his familiarity with the detailed formulae, and the number of approximations necessary."[26] Even after discarding most of the data and calculating only 800 positions on the trajectory, it took weeks to analyze a single flight.

The calculations were overseen by Dorrit Hoffleit, an astronomer then reaching the end of a career detour that had begun with wartime computational work for the Navy. Hoffleit had earned a PhD from Radcliffe College while working at the Harvard College Observatory. She was a talented astronomical observer, best known for her work on variable stars. After volunteering, she was first sent to perform mundane mathematical labor at MIT, where a Harvard astronomer was already calculating naval firing tables. She quit after six months, and was soon invited to the BRL by another Harvard astronomer doing wartime work there. Because astronomers were good at calculating trajectories and analyzing wave forms, many of them came to Aberdeen.

At the BRL Hoffleit became the supervisor of a group of about twenty women computing firing tables for anti-aircraft missiles. As was done at the Moore School, she relied on women with advanced degrees as supervisors. Later she recalled that her trips to the firing range to collect data to estimate drag functions had been the most exciting part of the job. In contrast, she recalled, "the tables as such were horrible."[27]

In her memoir, Dorrit Hoffleit characterizes her stint at the BRL, like most of the rest of her career, as a constant battle against cultures of ingrained sexism.

Leslie Simon refused to allow any women to hold a professional rating because of a belief that they would quickly leave to have children. This, Hoffleit claims, drew the attention of the Army's Inspector General for the district, who objected to the employment of a PhD in a "sub-professional" grade position. Simon's initial response was to make sure that Hoffleit did only menial work suitable for her grade, but eventually he relented.[28] Accounts written decades later cannot be relied upon too closely, but this parallels the difficulty that early ENIAC operators had in obtaining professional job classifications from the BRL, and the eventual upgrading of their positions.

Looking for work more in line with her qualifications, Hoffleit volunteered when she heard of the opportunity to work on analysis of the Doppler data under Thomas H. Johnson.[29] An expert on cosmic rays with a doctorate from Yale, Johnson was then the BRL's chief physicist. Like many others, he had been recruited for wartime work at the lab, where he applied his knowledge of scientific instrumentation to documenting the movement of projectiles and the power of explosives.

Hoffleit's first experimental analysis was done with standard IBM punched-card machines. They had been expected to work more than ten times as fast as humans with desk calculators, but in fact they provided little benefit. The operations involved were too complicated for the machines to automate, and the numbers of digits needed exceeded the capacity of IBM's Model 601 multiplier unit (which tended to break down under the demanding workload).

Next up were the newly arrived IBM relay calculators, wired together to operate as a single unit. Test runs implied that the calculator should handle each trajectory point in five to eight minutes, but reliability problems were already compromising the new machines in their first application. Hoffleit wrote: "Computations for sizable runs of points have not as yet been completed. ... We cannot examine, by use of actual statistics, its long-range dependability."[30]

It took two days to set ENIAC up to calculate the missile's position from the input data. Hoffleit estimated that with one more day the set-up could have been extended to calculate its velocity. ENIAC then spent 15 minutes on calculations that would have taken a human using a desk calculator 10 weeks. Some of the frequent failures were attributable to "warped cards or cards affected by humidity or static charges," others to vacuum tubes and electrical connections.[31]

After ENIAC, the group turned to the relay calculators from Bell Labs. These took five minutes to calculate a single trajectory point, and would thus have had to run around the clock for three days to tackle an 800-point trajectory that ENIAC could perform in 15 minutes. However, they had two advantages for the work at hand. First, they were reliable. Accounts from the BRL insist that they could be left running overnight, with confidence that the day shift would find them still working away or automatically shut down after reaching the end of the calculation. Their results were equally trustworthy: a test run over 1,200 data points produced only one error. Second, it took, according to Bell Labs, no more than five minutes to switch the machine over from one program to another by swapping instruction tapes.[32] Even if ENIAC was available and functional when data from a new test firing were rushed to the BRL for analysis, Hoffleit expected it would take two or three days to set ENIAC up to process the data. Results would come as quickly from the Bell Labs calculators. ENIAC was faster only if the analysis of data from several firings could be batched in "many complete runs of the same type of problem."[33]

By 1948, when Dorrit Hoffleit returned to Harvard to take a tenured position at the university's observatory, another astronomer had taken over responsibility for analysis of the Doppler data. Boris Garfinkel had arrived at the BRL in 1946, having earned a PhD at Yale in 1943. Hoffleit remembers that Garfinkel made considerable improvements in the mathematical procedures that she had "worked … out in a very clumsy way," though her modesty was excessive in view of the success of her work and her subsequent decade as a frequently visiting consultant to the BRL. Still, she felt that her true calling was not as a computational specialist but as a hands-on producer and interpreter of photographic plates documenting her beloved variable stars, as an enthusiastic teacher, and as an institution builder. Over the next 50 years, her career as an astronomer brought her to a research position at Yale, the directorship of the Maria Mitchell Observatory (then a unique institution for training women in astronomical research), and editorship of the *Bright Star Catalogue*.

Boris Garfinkel continued to apply ENIAC to the analysis of data from rocket test firings until 1952, when the White Sands Proving Ground acquired its own computer.[34] Subsequent calculations grew even more complex, with various tweaks to the techniques and equipment used (including an extension to five base stations).[35] Making ENIAC an effective workhorse for that job depended on sustained efforts to improve its reliability and, with the new method of programming, its speed in shifting from one problem to another.

ENIAC's Difficult Period

History books record that ENIAC became operational at Aberdeen on July 29, 1947. That assertion can be traced to a log entry stating "ENIAC starts up again."[36] This does not mean, however, that in mid 1947 ENIAC was able to handle anything like a full workload. As far as we know, the Doppler calculations were the only major new job run on ENIAC between December of 1946 and February of 1948. That had something to do with the unfinished state of its accommodation, with the need to train an almost entirely new staff, and with difficulty in getting new programs ready for the machine. Mostly, however, it had to do with the machine's almost comical reluctance to work properly long enough to finish a job.

Early computers were treated by their owners in much the same way that expensive pieces of industrial equipment were treated by factory owners: as a means by which capital could be substituted for labor. They demanded a major capital outlay and ongoing investment to provide suitable space, to keep power flowing, and to employ a sizable staff of programmers, supervisors, and operators. The useful life of a computer was quite short. The challenge was to get the computer to do as much useful work as was possible, spreading its high fixed costs over a large number of jobs.

The justification for maintaining a state-of-the-art computer operation was to get work done more effectively than would otherwise be possible. The staff of the BRL's Computing Laboratory therefore carefully logged ENIAC's operating performance, compiling statistics showing the number of jobs tackled, the hours of useful production work accomplished each week, time spent on upgrades, repairs, set-up time between jobs, debugging, and idle time. The initial tabulations were far from encouraging. The *New York Times* used the headline "Mechanical 'Brain' Has Its Troubles" to summarize material presented by BRL staff during a December 1947 meeting of the newly formed Association for Computing Machinery. The BRL hosted the event, and John von Neumann was the keynote speaker. The *Times* explained that 5 percent of ENIAC's 40-hour week was spent on set-up, 12 percent on "testing the set up," 31 percent on "locating troubles" of various kinds, 10 percent on "cleaning up" trouble once located, 8 percent on routine hardware checks. Six percent of the time was idle. That only 5 percent of the work time was spent on production work led to the suggestion that ENIAC "works only a two hour week." Its attendants were reportedly optimistic that this could be improved to 6 hours "under changes being made." Another 5 percent was devoted to "checking time," referring to the practice of running each job twice to verify results.[37]

The *Times* took a surprisingly positive tone in breaking the news that a high-profile government project was producing only a fraction of what had been promised. It noted that during its two productive hours the machine did "10,000 man-hours of actual work" and that "if funds and personnel ceiling permitted ENIAC to be operated by three shifts of operators and maintenance workers, the actual output could be increased threefold." Still, unless reliability could be improved, that would require funding ENIAC for 24-hour operation to obtain one hour a day of useful work.

Members of the BRL staff strove to boost ENIAC's productive time by minimizing the time spent on repairs and set-up. A computer that tackled many jobs every month, some of them for scientists and engineers in high-profile organizations across the country, would be a much better advertisement for the BRL's scientific leadership and for the growth of its computer operations. These concerns were behind many changes in work practices around ENIAC, and eventually inspired fundamental changes in the machine itself.

Matters did not improve much in the months immediately after the December 1947 ACM meeting. Many of the staff members were distracted by preparations for the adoption of a new programming method, discussed in chapter 7. The machine's physical environment was still taking shape. Yet the biggest problem was ENIAC itself. In later years, Eckert and Mauchly blamed ENIAC's problems at the BRL on the disruption caused by the move and the inflexibility of Army procedures. Mauchly recalled uptime being "usually over 90%" when the machine was in Philadelphia, claiming that he did not hear any complaints about its unreliability at the BRL until decades later.[38] However some problems were built into the machine itself. For example, tubes were crammed so close together that heat built up to dangerous levels and shortened their life. Despite efforts at Aberdeen to install air conditioning and to position loud and powerful fans to circulate air, the overheating problem was never fully solved.

Entries in the operations log from November 1947 to March 1948 are full of discussions of broken wires, machine errors, visits from Richard Merwin of the Moore School to overhaul problematic units, and other endemic frustrations. Occasional attempts were made to run problems, including the firing-table calculations for which ENIAC was built, but troubles afflicted the function table, the constant transmitter, the power supply, the printer, the accumulators, and the cables. On January 8, 1948 after several days on which no production work was accomplished, the log book noted "At this point we are considering closing down for an overhaul before Moore School takes over for the installation of various items." It was almost a month until the log noted another attempt to use the machine: Harry Huskey turned up on Friday, February 6 to set up a problem he hoped to run by himself over the weekend.

Grubbs' Problem

By March of 1948 two-shift operation was being tried, but ENIAC was still only marginally productive. Its frustrations and its potential are both captured in the progress of what the operations log called "Grubbs' Problem." Captain Frank E. Grubbs was a rising star within the Ordnance Department. When he had been summoned to active duty from the Army Reserve in 1941, his degrees in electrical engineering and statistics had made him an obvious pick for the BRL. Leslie Simon, the BRL's director, was an expert on the application of statistical methods to operations and used the war to boost the lab's capabilities in that area. Grubbs, who became chief of the lab's Surveillance Laboratory in 1942, was a member of an informal community of mathematically minded people who were inventing the field of operations research by applying statistical methods to wartime problems. He had developed methods to assess the hundreds of kinds of artillery ammunition stockpiled around England in preparation for the Normandy invasion. By analyzing the results of thousands of test firings, he showed that the ballistic characteristics of these diverse munitions could be adequately represented by only four sets of possible corrections applied to the standard equations.[39]

When the Army called him to active duty, Grubbs was already several years into PhD work under Cecil C. Craig of the University of Michigan, focusing his research on tests for statistical outliers. Though initially disruptive to his studies, his wartime work ultimately provided his thesis topic and laid the foundation for a long career at the BRL. Statistical practice was then based on producing and using tables. A small community of statistical researchers evaluated new statistical tests and measures. Successful tests were employed by a much broader community, but it was not practical for the users to calculate threshold values for statistical significance. Instead, statisticians supplied tables giving the appropriate values for a range of sample sizes and other parameters, and users looked up the value closest to their own data set. The labor required to calculate these tables was a significant limitation on the diffusion of new statistical tests.

Developing a test for outliers was of more than academic interest to the BRL, as data coming from ballistics tests were "loaded with outliers."[40] Grubbs quickly recognized that ENIAC could generate the statistical tables that had previously required a prohibitive amount of work. Derrick Lehmer and Ruth Lichterman had worked out some of the programming during ENIAC's time at the Moore School, but Grubbs later recalled that "once they got the ENIAC wired for my outlier problem, the Atomic Energy Commission called on Gen Simon and Johnny von Neumann to use the ENIAC to obtain an optimum solution to the problem of imploding the core of a nuclear warhead, with the result … that even though our Computing Laboratory had begged for work, my … extensive calculations to keep them busy immediately got a vanishing priority."[41]

Owing to other demands on ENIAC's time and to its various problems, it was not until March of 1948 that a serious attempt was made to run the calculations. They should not have posed a particularly challenging problem. Ruth Lichterman was still working with ENIAC at Aberdeen Proving Ground, and was charged with running the full calculations along with Helen Mark and Marie Bierstein.[42] The table Grubbs eventually produced held only 96 values, giving expected figures for four different points in the probability distribution for each of 24 sample sizes. To calculate each value, ENIAC had to output intermediate results, which were later read back in for further processing. The card operations slowed the machine, and calculating each value took minutes rather than seconds, but the entire job could still have been completed in only two trouble-free shifts. With two shifts, the team was, under ideal circumstances, looking at a single day of work. But the circumstances weren't ideal, and the job took a month. Little had improved from the situation reported in the *Times*. ENIAC's machine room was barely fit to house a computer, and its operators had to work around scheduled demonstrations. Progress was slowed by programming errors, by mistakes in the numerical methods used, and by breaks for machine upgrades. Most disruptive of all were the hardware errors: power and cooling systems failed, function tables were repaired repeatedly, and the multiplier struggled alarmingly. Historians have tended to think of burned-out tubes as the main problem afflicting ENIAC, perhaps because that peril loomed large in the mind of J. Presper Eckert and the other engineers. In practice, however, the machine lost far more time to "intermittents"—mysterious errors that struck at random to stop the progress of a calculation or to render its results useless.

The ENIAC operations team began setting up Grubbs' problem on the afternoon of Wednesday, February 25. Thursday was lost to repairs to the division and square-root unit. Upgrade efforts trumped operational use when the next day was spent testing the newly installed converter. Eventually, Richard Merwin was called down from the Moore School to spend Friday night tending to it.[43]

On Monday work for Grubbs began in earnest with the "pedaling" of his problem, a term referring to the practice of stepping ENIAC through it addition time by addition time, verifying its behavior against the information contained in the set-up table, or "pedaling sheet." Despite what the log called "some mistakes in the programming indicating that more careful checking and coding is necessary in the future," the team "actually got the problem running and ran the first run."[44]

Previous discussions of ENIAC have given the impression that its effectiveness in its original programming mode was limited primarily by the time and effort needed to set up each new problem. In this case, however, the time spent setting up ENIAC was negligible in comparison with the time spent trying to run the program. Tuesday morning was lost to power supply repairs. In the afternoon the initial results were run again to verify correctness, but the log reads: "The ENIAC failed to duplicate last night's runs. Probably an intermittent." Running input decks through ENIAC twice and comparing the output cards produced was standard practice by that point—the method drew on an existing practice in which important data were keyed twice and a special "verifying punch" was used to check that the same data were provided on both occasions.

On Wednesday, a week after the start of work on the problem, the team "found why it went off base at card 632 for n = 2 and changed shifters etc. so it works." Calculations resumed, and despite a power supply "dumping out a couple of times" a good run was declared for this initial value.[45] Alas, on Friday the team "found out there was an error in the assumptions about the function being integrated in Grubbs Problem." The results were thrown out. Further hardware problems

Figure 5.1
The maintenance engineer Homer Spence (left) played a crucial role in improving ENIAC's reliability to the point where it spent more time working than broken. Here he is removing a digit tray, mounted across several ENIAC panels to transmit numbers between them.
(UV-HML, image 84.240.10)

prevented ENIAC from doing any useful work for another week, though it was readied on Friday to run a demonstration for the Secretary of the Army. He canceled at the last minute, and "all the worry and delay over the demonstration was wasted."[46]

Richard Merwin was back at work on the converter on Monday, March 15, so no attempt was made to run ENIAC. Tuesday and Wednesday were busy days for Homer Spence as he toiled to fix the multiplier and the function tables. Tuesday's night shift was canceled, and Wednesday's was lost to more "intermittents."[47] Grubbs' problem had received every available minute of ENIAC time for three weeks, but had yet to yield a single scrap of useful output. When intermittents struck again on Thursday, the dispirited team resolved nevertheless "to exert every effort to finish Grubbs problem before Nick from [the Atomic Energy Commission] puts the new problem on." Efforts by night-shift workers to "isolate [the] intermittent" proved fruitless, as their "two apparently good runs" again generated different output decks. The log entry concluded with a statement of the obvious: "The machine is in no condition to run the problem."[48]

Early Friday afternoon it was discovered that a single shorted cable was the source of the intermittents. Suddenly finding themselves to be standing inside a reliable computer, the team pushed ahead, being halted only at 4 a.m. on Saturday by "a failure of the constant transmitter or reader." During that 13½-hour period, they ran Grubbs' problem from the initial n = 2 up to n = 22.

A power and cooling failure over the weekend knocked ENIAC out again.[49] Its brief return to operational status on Tuesday afternoon allowed for some numerical experiments. The limited number of digits available to represent a number was an inherent source of computational error. There was a risk that errors would compound every time such numbers were added, multiplied or divided. A program set up on ENIAC for the Signal Corps had recently been abandoned when the operations team had recognized that errors had compounded to the extent that the results were useless. ENIAC was particularly vulnerable to numerical errors, as it was fast enough to carry out many more arithmetical operations in the course of a calculation than other machines. Propagation and accumulation of errors was a matter of immediate and practical concern to Douglas Hartree, John von Neumann, and other early users of digital computers.[50] The ENIAC team carried out a crude mathematical experiment to see if a deliberately introduced error would be eliminated or compounded as the Grubbs calculation was repeated. Additional runs were made "for n = 7, 8, and higher to see if a blank card in the tail end of the series made any material difference." The discovery that "the change that it caused disappeared after 2 or 3 subsequent runs" was reassuring.[51]

The team also had time to verify results by repeating the previous run. On Wednesday afternoon ENIAC overcame more intermittents to duplicate the final set of results. After being demonstrated to five groups of visitors from the Ordnance School, "at 4:30 pm the machine was turned over to Spence for checking & repairing and Grubbs's problem was considered complete, so far as the present set up could handle it."[52]

Frank Grubbs had won for his thesis project a full month of time on the world's only operational general-purpose electronic digital computer. And that was only one of the several computing methods he made use of. ENIAC's results for one of the functions were compared with those produced by one Helen J. Coon using a less accurate process on a conventional mechanical calculating machine. Further calculations on a related statistical distribution were later carried out by two anonymous men and a woman using the relay computers built for the BRL by Bell Labs. Grubbs

published his thesis as a paper in 1950. The paper had a considerable impact—
Google Scholar currently tracks more than 500 citations, despite its bias against
older work.[53] A 1969 tutorial paper incorporating the same table of ENIAC results
garners a report of a further 1,500 citations.[54] Grubbs continued to work on the
statistical detection of outliers, making the topic his own. His name came to be
given to a test widely used by scientists and engineers.

Grubbs' problem was, as far as we can determine, the last problem tackled using
ENIAC's original control method. Three working days later, Nick Metropolis arrived
to begin the process of converting ENIAC. It was about to become a very different
computer. The conversion, rather than the physical move from Philadelphia to
Aberdeen, was the true dividing line between ENIAC's promising but erratic child-
hood and its mature years as a reliable and productive problem-solving machine.
ENIAC's eventual redemption was a team accomplishment, but the two most crucial
factors were the new programming method and the sustained efforts of Homer
Spence and his maintenance team. The successes of the new programming method
and of the efforts of Spence and his team were interconnected. Programming ENIAC
originally involved wiring its panels and setting its switches, in effect creating a new
and untested computer. Troubleshooters had to understand and debug the new
hardware configuration. After the conversion, cables were no longer added or
removed whenever a program was changed. That gradually reduced the rate of bad
connections, one important source of intermittent problems. Freezing the position
of most of the switches on the panels similarly helped to simplify troubleshooting
by fixing their circuits in a single mode of operation.

EDVAC and the First Draft

ENIAC dramatically and publicly proved the feasibility of large-scale electronic computation by tackling a wide range of problems during its time at the Moore School. It was not, however, the template for the next generation of computers. In this chapter we focus on the rapid development of thinking about computer design within the ENIAC team during 1944 and 1945.

In historical discussions, the machines of the next generation have generally been called stored-program computers, and historians have come to describe the crucial ingredient separating them from ENIAC as the "stored program concept."[1] As will become apparent in a chapter 11, we think that term is misleading because it creates an impression that the modern computer is defined by a single abstract idea. We see instead an incremental process grounded in specific technical challenges and motivated in large part by the flaws and inefficiencies the Moore School team became aware of as it worked to build ENIAC and to plan for its application to particular problems.

Rethinking ENIAC

Many aspects of ENIAC's design had been constrained by the need to show rapid and tangible progress. The increasingly large sums of money consumed in ENIAC's construction were justified only by the promise that it would clear up the backlog of firing-table calculations before the war ended. By early 1944, most of the main design decisions had been made. As the project's focus shifted toward detailed engineering work, Eckert, Mauchly, and Goldstine began to turn their attention to future machines.

Memory Technologies

One of ENIAC's biggest shortcomings as a general-purpose computer was its tiny writable electronic memory. Its high speed was possible only because its electronic computing circuits did not have to spend most of their time waiting to read control information and numerical data from a paper tape or a relay memory such as were used by the other computers of the mid 1940s.[2] Instead, instructions and numbers were set up manually on ENIAC's program controls and function tables so that the information was available at what contemporary documents called "electronic speed."[3]

Building a voluminous read-only memory able to keep up with ENIAC was not particularly difficult. Each of the three function tables held 1,248 digits and 208 signs, set by turning mechanical switches. That technique provided cheap and reliable bulk storage of numbers, as vacuum tubes were needed only in control circuitry, but it was not suitable for the storage of variables.

Creating a large, fast, and writable memory was much more difficult. ENIAC's memory contained only 200 digits and 20 signs, spread over its 20 accumulators, which limited its usefulness for many potential applications. Eckert and Mauchly couldn't simply specify that the new machine hold more accumulators, because each modular "plug-in decade" storing a single decimal digit required 28 tubes.[4] That did more to bloat the machine than all the other design decisions put together. The 200 plug-in decades spread over the 20 accumulators held 5,600 tubes, and more were needed for sign storage and for arithmetic, communication, and control circuits. The team had considered building a memory unit containing only the circuits needed to store and transmit numbers, but that would have helped only marginally. Any successor machines would be delivered in peacetime, and the need for rapid delivery would no longer trump the expense and reliability issues raised by extravagant use of vacuum tubes.

Eckert rose to the challenge by inventing the first high-capacity electronic memory: mercury delay-line storage. The delay line originated in the radar project Eckert worked on before ENIAC, giving a strikingly obvious example of the connection between radar technology and early digital computing. Radar dishes rotate constantly, producing blips on the display screen when the scanning beam is reflected back by an object. Stationary objects such as trees and buildings confuse the operator, making incoming planes and other moving objects harder to spot. The goal was to display only moving objects. This meant finding a way to store a set of pulses for exactly as long as it took for the dish to complete one rotation, then comparing them with the new signal to eliminate unchanging blips. Eckert's solution was to turn the electrical radar pulses into sound waves traveling through a tube of mercury.[5] At the far end they would be picked up and turned back into electrical pulses. Changing the length of the tube would change the duration of the delay.

In early 1944 Eckert recognized that the technology could be adapted to store large amounts of computer data and retrieve it at relatively high speeds.[6] A series of numbers to be stored was converted to a train of pulses moving through a delay line. Pulses leaving the line at one end were fed back in at the other so that they cycled continually through the fluid. If the computer needed to read the contents of a particular part of memory, the corresponding numbers would be copied into its vacuum tubes the next time they reached the end of the tank. When it was time to change the number stored in a particular part of the pulse train, the computer provided the delay-line memory controller with an updated value that could be substituted the next time it wrote the corresponding pulses into the tank. Today's memory chips are based on the same insight: any medium able to store data reliably for just a moment can hold it indefinitely if the bits are repeatedly read and "regenerated" before they are lost.[7]

Mercury was not the easiest substance to work with, being both heavy and poisonous. Nevertheless, mercury delay lines were used on many of the earliest electronic computers, including the first commercial Univac and IBM models. Delay-line memory was not perfect, but it was much faster than relay memory and much cheaper than vacuum-tube memory. Because the capacity of a delay-line memory was proportional to its length, a higher capacity line needed no more electronics than a short one. A single delay line storing 200 digits would need only a tiny fraction of the number of tubes required by ENIAC's accumulators. A computer might have to wait for thousands of pulses to go by before reaching the desired datum, but they moved fast enough that this was not a fatal flaw, particularly as programmers learned to arrange the contents of the delay line so that numbers appeared just as they were needed. Delay-line memory and its rival, cathode-ray-tube storage, were the crucial technologies behind computers that were cheaper, smaller, and more powerful than ENIAC. They helped to turn the computer into a practical piece of commercial machinery.

Collaborative Work toward EDVAC

As successful consulting firms and research groups are well aware, one must always be selling the next phase or project before the current one is completed. Indeed, the next contract is usually justified by the limitations of whatever is about to be delivered. Members of the ENIAC team learned quickly and were exploring the potential for a new contract long before ENIAC was completed. They had recognized the limitations of ENIAC's programming system from the beginning. As we have seen, the project began with a vision of centralized program-control circuits directing the operations of the other units. A progress report written at the end of 1943 noted that programming had been "very appreciably decentralized" and that "no attempt [had] been made to make provision for setting up a problem automatically."[8] This was justified by the observation that "the primary objective of the development is to increase the *speed* of ballistic computations" that would be set up once and run many times. As the need for a flexible and general-purpose computer became clearer and the team began to plan for a successor to ENIAC, it returned to the ideas of centralized control and automatic program set-up. These plans were shaped by the involvement of a new participant: the mathematician John von Neumann.

Enter von Neumann

What follows is one of the most frequently repeated anecdotes in the history of computing.

It is the summer of 1944. Herman Goldstine, standing on the platform of the railroad station at Aberdeen, recognizes John von Neumann. Goldstine approaches the great man and soon mentions the computer project that is underway in Philadelphia. Von Neumann, who is at this point deeply immersed in the Manhattan Project and is only too well aware of the urgent need of many wartime projects for rapid computation, makes a quick transition from polite chat to intense interest. Goldstine soon brings his new friend to see the project. The resulting collaboration transforms both computer design and Goldstine's career.[9] For a short period, von Neumann becomes a close collaborator of the team working at the Moore School. He arrives too late to have any known influence on the original design of ENIAC, but he studies it closely and is responsible for many of the problems run on the machine.

Despite a slow posthumous drift from public awareness, von Neumann (1903–1957) was, during his lifetime and for some years afterward, a scientific celebrity, less recognizable than Albert Einstein but more famous than almost any other American scientist. By his mid twenties, having earned both a PhD in mathematics and a diploma in chemical engineering, he had published an astonishing number of important mathematical papers and had begun to show the breadth of engagement across academic fields that would make him famous. He went on to pioneer mathematical approaches to quantum mechanics and to establish the field of game theory by applying mathematical methods to game strategy and related issues in economics. Within pure mathematics his contributions were similarly diverse, advancing areas such as geometry, set theory, and operator theory.

Von Neumann enjoyed material comforts and social stimulation of upper class life, into which he had been born in Budapest. Replicating that social and economic position as an immigrant scientist was a challenge he took up with gusto. By the time he met Goldstine, von Neumann was walking with pride and confidence though the corridors of power in Washington while maintaining an impressive number of consulting commitments with corporations, military centers, and government agencies.[10]

By 1944 he was concentrating on work with direct relevance to military matters. His consulting relationship with the Ballistic Research Lab predated the war and he had been a charter member of the Scientific Advisory Committee that had been formed in 1940 to oversee the Lab's efforts.[11] His most pressing engagement was with Los Alamos, where he was one of the few scientists allowed to come and go from the secret scientific town in the desert. The particular expertise that brought him to the center of wartime science in the United States was in the mathematical modeling of shock waves, which were crucial to the implosion-triggered atomic bombs tested in New Mexico and dropped on Nagasaki. He spent the last years of his life helping to direct American policy on ballistic missiles and nuclear reactors. Despite these various triumphs, it is his work on electronic computing for which von Neumann is most widely remembered today.

A Successor to ENIAC

William Aspray has documented the growth of von Neumann's interest in automatic computation during 1943. After watching automatic accounting machines in use at the Nautical Almanac Office in England, he worked to wire the Los Alamos' punched-card machines and run cards through them. He systematically hunted for new calculating equipment that might help the bomb project, discovering the Navy's computer center at Harvard and the work underway at Bell Labs on relay computers.[12] What was unlikely was not that he stumbled upon ENIAC, but that it took him so long to discover the project.[13] He immediately recognized the potential of electronic computing for Los Alamos. On August 21, 1944, Goldstine wrote to Paul Gillon that "von Neumann is displaying great interest in the ENIAC and is conferring with me weekly on the use of the machine."[14] They estimated that one of von Neumann's blast-wave problems could be solved in ten seconds on ENIAC, as opposed to four hours on a punched-card machine.

Von Neumann catalyzed the refinement of the ENIAC team's inchoate thoughts about their machine's shortcomings into a specific proposal for what was initially framed as an improved version of ENIAC. In July of 1944 Herman Goldstine had informed Harold Pender that he was "extremely desirous" to issue a "new contract with you for improvements in the design of the present machine before the War Department starts retrenching."[15] On August 11, he wrote to Leslie Simon:

Due ... to the necessity for producing the ENIAC in a year and a half it has been necessary to accept certain make-shift solutions of design problems, notably in the means of establishing connections between units to carry out given processes and in the paucity of high speed storage devices. These defects will result in considerable inconvenience and loss of time to the laboratory in setting up of new computing problems ... . It is believed highly desirable that a new RAD contract be entered into with the Moore School to permit that institution to continue research and development with the object of building ultimately a new ENIAC of improved design.[16]

This plea came, according to Goldstine's later recollection, only a few days after he and the Moore School team began to collaborate with von Neumann.[17] Historians have speculated that von Neumann's arrival helped to push the team toward submission of a proposal. This is plausible, as von Neumann was far better connected and more experienced in framing and evaluating large-scale technical projects than the members of the ENIAC team.[18] Things then moved very quickly. By the end of August, a definite proposal to start work on a new machine had been put forward. The crucial decision was made when the Firing Table Reviewing Board met on August 29. Von Neumann was present, as were Goldstine and the higher-level members of the BRL's staff.[19] The board concluded that

a relatively small amount of further development would make possible the construction of a new electronic computing device that will

Contain a much smaller number of tubes than the present … machine, and hence be cheaper and more practical to maintain.
Be capable … of handling many types of problems not easily adaptable to the present ENIAC.
Be capable of storing cheaply and at high speeds large quantities of numerical data.
Be of such a character that the setting up of a new problem on it will require much less time and be much simpler than in the case of the present ENIAC.[20]

It recommended that the laboratory obtain such a machine to further expedite the production of firing tables, expand its computational capability to deal with the complete system of ballistics equations and "many basic research problems," and make use of the data emerging from new research instruments such as the supersonic wind tunnel.

Within the Moore School the new effort was code-named Project PY, indicating its status as a continuation of the ENIAC project, whose code name was PX. John Brainerd produced an estimate of $105,600 for a twelve-month project conducting the "research and development work which might reasonably be expected, but cannot be guaranteed, to lead to the creation" of such a machine.[21] As well as delay lines, Brainerd mentioned "iconoscope tubes," a new development at RCA in which von Neumann was interested, as a candidate technology to hold the "many thousands of values of quantities" required. Work was funded by the fourth in a series of supplements to the initial ENIAC contract.

Initial Conceptions of the "New ENIAC"
Within a year Project PY had produced the outline of a design for a radical new computer, EDVAC. The question of who contributed what to the 1945 EDVAC design is one of the most contentious in the sprawling mess of contested stories concerning the invention of the computer. Correspondence from the first few weeks of the project does not directly resolve this dispute, but it does give a picture of the

technologies with which the team planned to meet these ambitious goals and the applications they had in mind for the new machine.

Along with connections and experience, von Neumann brought a new mathematical challenge: the numerical solution of partial differential equations. He emphasized the importance of this capability, but not, of course, its connection to the urgent and highly secret work of the Manhattan Project.[22] Solving partial differential equations involved large volumes of working data and so needed something like Eckert's delay line to be handled at electronic speed. Just as ENIAC was shaped by the firing-table problem, EDVAC was shaped by the fluid dynamics of the atom bomb. On September 2, 1944, Goldstine wrote to Gillon that he, Eckert, and von Neumann had "formulated quite definite ideas" for the new machine including the use of delay-line storage and a "centralized programming device."[23] The BRL recognized the value of such a machine for its own work, while the Moore School was keen to keep the research funds flowing. In mid September, Brainerd wrote to Gillon highlighting von Neumann's involvement and describing the need for a machine with a larger storage capacity than ENIAC's and able to solve the partial differential equations that arose in "hydrodynamical and aerodynamical problems associated with projectile motion."[24]

The idea of delay-line memory predated von Neumann's arrival but underpinned his collaboration with the ENIAC team. The first three advances promised to the Firing Table Review Board (fewer tubes, broader applications, more memory) would all stem from replacing ENIAC's accumulators with delay-line memory. "Each tank," Goldstine wrote, "will hold 30 numbers and will cost about $100. In this way a new ENIAC can be built for about $30,000 and will contain about 1/10 the tubes in the present one."[25]

The fourth objective, the simpler and faster setting up of problems, was eventually met by storing program information and data in the same high-speed memory. It is not clear if the team had this method in mind when setting the goal, or whether the idea predated von Neumann's involvement.

What other methods might have been considered? As we will discuss in chapter 11, in February of 1944 Eckert had described the possibility of building an electronic calculator that would respond to a key press by reading control codes from rotating disks to sequence the steps needed to carry out a specified operation, such as multiplication. By that time, the team had been exposed, via Bell Labs, to the idea of reading instructions one at a time from paper tape, although its members did not immediately jump to the conclusion that stored instruction codes should control the machine directly. On August 21, shortly before the new contract was approved, Goldstine had written to Gillon regarding "directions in which we should pursue our researches." Goldstine, who had already embraced the potential of delay-line memory for the "future course of the ENIAC," wrote: "Inasmuch as the accumulator is so powerful an instrument, it seems foolish to tie up such tools merely to hold numbers temporarily. Eckert has some excellent ideas on a very cheap device for this purpose."[26] Regarding the control system, however, he assumed the ENIAC approach of setting a mass of special-purpose control switches before the start of a computation rather than imagining a much smaller number of switches that were reset as each new instruction was read. "After talking to S. B. Williams of Bell Telephone," he wrote, "I feel that the switches and controls of the ENIAC now arranged to be operated manually, can easily be positioned by mechanical relays and electro-magnetic telephone switches which are instructed by a teletype tape … . In this manner tapes could be cut for many given problems and reused whenever needed. Thus we would not have to spend valuable minutes resetting switches when shifting from one phase of a problem to the next."[27]

By August of 1944, when the EDVAC project was approved, the team clearly had given some thought to accomplishing the goal of faster and easier problem set-up, but we have found no evidence that it had settled on a single method by which to accomplish it. The board's recommendation, perhaps deliberately, did not constrain the options available.

By early September, the idea of reading instructions one at a time from storage and immediately executing them had been made explicit. Goldstine's letter of September 2 mentioned a "centralized programming device in which the program routine is stored in a coded form in the same type storage [sic] devices suggested above." This had the "crucial advantage" that "any routine, however complex, can be carried out whereas in the present ENIAC we are limited by the number of switches available on the accumulators."[28] The last point makes it clear that Goldstine now expected these stored codes to be executed one at a time to replace, rather than merely set, a distributed system of special-purpose controls.

Progress on EDVAC

From around August of 1944 to early 1946 von Neumann remained closely engaged with work on ENIAC and EDVAC. In view of his many other commitments, this was a surprisingly intense engagement with a relatively small and obscure project. Eckert and Mauchly worked quickly and creatively with von Neumann, Goldstine, and Burks to think through the design implications of a large, high-speed, writable computer memory and to settle on an inspired design. Von Neumann immersed himself in electronic technologies. His correspondence was full of discussions of the merits of particular models of vacuum tubes for EDVAC's circuits and sketches of their performance curves. He dealt most often and worked most closely with Goldstine, who noted in December of 1944 that von Neumann was "devoting enormous amounts of his prodigious energy to working out the logical controls for the machine" and "has also been very much interested in helping to design circuits for the machine."[29]

EDVAC's development proceeded much more slowly than had been planned. In September of 1944, Brainerd had budgeted for the most talented and experienced ENIAC engineers to have finished their work by January of 1945 and to then shift to working on EDVAC.[30] However, many of these engineers worked long shifts on ENIAC all through 1945. In the first Project PY progress report, issued at the end of March 1945, Eckert and Mauchly admitted that it would not be possible to properly set up the planned laboratory until "the need for engineers of PX [ENIAC] decreases." They added that "because of the pressure of work on PX it has not been possible to carry out the terms of the PY budget."[31] What engineering work did take place focused on the procurement of the pulse transformers and crystals needed for an experimental delay-line memory. Goldstine arranged for some of the engineers to visit relevant projects underway at MIT and at Bell Labs and sought help from the Philadelphia Ordnance District in obtaining some of the necessary supplies.[32]

Surviving notes from four Project PY meetings in which von Neumann participated during March and April of 1945[33] give the impression of an energetic and enthusiastic collaboration that had yet to yield a coherent set of design choices. For example, the team had settled on binary number storage but was still pondering whether the arithmetic units should be fully binary or should work with decimal numbers coded as binary. It also discussed possible designs for logic circuits, mechanisms to switch signals coming from delay lines, and the possible use of magnetic tape for storage. Although the decision to store both data and instructions as pulses in mercury delay lines had been made, the team was still undecided about the merits of segregating instructions and data in different parts of the memory with different access pathways.[34] That would have prevented the arithmetic unit from manipulating the content of instructions, suggesting that the idea of allowing EDVAC to modify the address values stored within program instructions, a central feature of its eventual design, was not yet accepted.

The "First Draft of a Report on the EDVAC"
Arthur Burks later characterized the next step as follows: "Johnny [von Neumann] offered to write a summary of our discussions. What we received later was both far more and far less than that. It was far more, because it contained the logical design of a proposed EDVAC (except for the Control) as well as an instruction code for the machine. And it was far less, because it did not even mention our meetings with him or his relation to us and the ENIAC and EDVAC projects."[35] This work eventually became the "First Draft of a Report on the EDVAC," the most influential document in the history of computer design.[36] Discussion of the balance of contributions made to the modern computer by von Neumann versus the members of the ENIAC

team has therefore focused on their relative contributions to this report, narrowing our sense of the gradual evolution of thinking within the group. Von Neumann continued to develop his ideas about the machine's instruction set and design. After receiving comments on the draft from Haskell Curry, a member of the BRL's Computation Committee, he replied that he "must in the first place apologize for the imperfect shape in which I permitted it to get into your hands—it is hardly more than two-thirds finished and besides I feel like changing several things in it already."[37]

Historians have previously dated von Neumann's promise to document a proposed control system for EDVAC to the March 1945 meetings. However, by that time he had already been busy on a proposal for a control system for some time, as is indicated by a letter dated February 12, 1945 in which he informed Goldstine that he was "continuing work on the control scheme for the EDVAC and will definitely have a complete writeup when I return."[38] Reid Warren, the PY project's supervisor, later recalled being told by Goldstine at the beginning of March that von Neumann wished to write a summary of the conclusions of his meetings with the team up to that point.[39] A progress report issued at the end of March noted that von Neumann planned to "submit within the next few weeks" a summary of the discussions "together with examples showing how certain problems can be set up."[40] According to Warren, Goldstine asked if this summary could be mimeographed and circulated within the project team, stating that the material did not have to be classified, as it was an informal report, for internal use only.

The First Draft as we know it was the product of a complex editing and production process. It does not acknowledge the development or the provenance of the ideas it contains, and as a summary of von Neumann's thinking it was significantly out of date even before it was put into circulation. Goldstine received a draft manuscript from von Neumann in April of 1945 as part of their frequent correspondence. On May 8, von Neumann sent Goldstine another letter containing "minor changes and comments concerning the code for EDVAC" and seventeen pages of new material that he said he would incorporate into the manuscript once it had been returned, with comments, from the team. The new material was largely concerned with the format in which programs should be prepared on magnetic input tapes for the new machine, partially remedying the neglect of input and output operations in the draft report.[41]

Meanwhile, under Goldstine's supervision, the manuscript was being typed up for internal distribution. On May 15 Goldstine sent one of the copies along with the manuscript to von Neumann with a disclaimer: "Inasmuch as several dumb typists combined their talents in typing the script there are a lot of errors, which I got discouraged over."[42] The new material in von Neumann's letter was not included in the typescript.[43] In a summary of the team members' initial reactions to the report, Goldstine was, as was usual in his interactions with von Neumann, complimentary.

"All of us," he assured the great man, "have been carefully reading your report with greatest interest and I feel that it is of the greatest possible value since it gives a complete logical framework for the machine."

Von Neumann never produced even a complete second draft of the report. Goldstine sent him the typescript only two months before the test of the first atomic bomb, so his distraction is understandable. Instead, Goldstine circulated a mimeographed version of the report in June, taking advantage of its unclassified status to distribute it quite widely. Initially, 31 copies were sent out.[44] This version of the report was not the same as the typescript prepared in May. Section headings were added, although internal cross-references were left blank to be filled in later. Two sections and six associated figures giving technical details of the delay-line memory were omitted. The additional material sent by von Neumann in his letter of May 8 was still not included in the text, which stopped rather abruptly, after summarizing the original instruction set of the new machine, without explaining the programming techniques required.

The circulated version had von Neumann's name and a date of June 30 on the cover and gave no credit to other members of the EDVAC team. That it lacked the notes and acknowledgments one would expect in a published paper was a source of great and enduring resentment on the part of Eckert and Mauchly.

Immediate responses to the report from EDVAC's sponsors and potential users were very positive and show evidence of close reading and deep engagement with the specifics of the logical design proposed. Haskell Curry wrote that the committee was "very much interested" in the report, noted a few specific errors, and made suggestions for improvements in aspects of the notation.[45] Douglas Hartree, in a letter that was carried to Goldstine by Tommy Flowers, the designer of Colossus, offered specific and detailed responses to the proposed circuit structures, recognizing at once the equivalence of the neuron notation used by von Neumann in the report to a system of logical statements.[46]

Claims for Credit

Mauchly spent much of 1944 and 1945 working on the preparation of patent claims. Ordnance Department lawyers took the lead in this, but the Moore School also had a stake in the process. Eckert and Mauchly found themselves in an increasingly bitter dispute with the Moore School over their plans to patent and personally own the ENIAC inventions. The issue of patent rights was unquestionably beginning to tear the team apart by this time.

Burks later suggested that tensions with von Neumann had developed even before the First Draft. The first EDVAC progress report, dated March 31, 1945, had claimed that "considerable attention is being devoted to the problems of the logical control of the apparatus" during discussions among von Neumann, Goldstine, Eckert,

Burks, and Mauchly, and that a summary could be found in Burks' meeting minutes.[47] Insofar as the minutes included no such discussions, Burks speculated that reading this report "gave Herman and Johnny good reason to believe that Eckert and Mauchly were planning to claim some or all of Johnny's patentable EDVAC ideas."[48] It seems to us more likely that this was a routine exaggeration of progress to a project sponsor, reporting that something planned for the near future was already underway.

Eckert and Mauchly reacted almost immediately to Goldstine's distribution of the First Draft under von Neumann's name. In a July 1945 progress report they distinguished between the logical aspects of the project and its experimental (and therefore patentable) achievements, describing the First Draft as a "report on the general aspects of the design and logical control of a computing machine, with particular emphasis on the logical controls for the EDVAC" which had been "distributed to the engineers on Project PY in order that they may be familiar with the background for the experimental work which they will do on this project."[49]

In September, Eckert and Mauchly issued a much longer and more ambitious report, titled Automatic High-Speed Computing, setting out their own general ideas on computer design and offering two possible designs for EDVAC in reasonable detail.[50] They began with "Historical Comments" on allocation of credit, dating the decision to embark on the EDVAC project to July 1944. That was before von Neumann arrived, and they credited him only with having "contributed to many discussions on the logical controls of the EDVAC … proposed certain instruction codes, and … tested those proposed systems by writing out the coded instructions for specific problems." The First Draft was described as a summary of the results of earlier discussions in which "the physical structures and devices proposed by Eckert and Mauchly" were "replaced by idealized elements to avoid raising engineering problems which might distract attention from the logical considerations under discussion."[51]

Eckert and Mauchly also sought to patent the design of EDVAC. Years later, Burks claimed that von Neumann had confided to him in early 1946 that Eckert and Mauchly were attempting to "steal his ideas."[52] In response, von Neumann submitted the First Draft to be considered for patentability by the Army lawyers. These rival patent bids caused alarm on all sides. The Moore School needed to use this intellectual property to build EDVAC. Eckert and Mauchly needed it in order to have a hope of succeeding with the computer company they founded after quitting the Moore School rather than comply with its demand to own their future inventions. In 1947 the Ordnance Department arranged talks among Eckert and Mauchly, the Moore School, and von Neumann to decide how to resolve the EDVAC patent issue.[53] The talks were curtailed when the Ordnance Department's lawyers concluded that the First Draft was an initial publication of the EDVAC design. Because that publication had taken place more than a year earlier, the inventions described therein could never be patented.

By 1945 the EDVAC collaborators had already begun to divide into rival camps with differing historical narratives. Their stories must be read in the light of the interest Eckert and Mauchly had in minimizing perceptions of von Neumann's inventive contribution to their joint work. Although Eckert and Mauchly's hopes of an EDVAC patent were soon dashed, establishing themselves as its inventors might still bring credibility, fame, and increased value to their other patents. Von Neumann never engaged as actively in the argument as Eckert and Mauchly, but, as several historians have observed, neither did he make any attempt to correct the misperception that the First Draft contained only his own ideas.[54] Even after the conclusion of patent proceedings in the 1970s and the death of the last of the participants in the 1990s, the dispute has remained central to many discussions of the First Draft.

The Giant Electronic Brain

We should take a moment to sketch the relationship of the First Draft, and indeed of ENIAC itself, to the cybernetics movement. ENIAC was famously reported as a "giant electronic brain" by many newspapers after the 1946 demonstrations. It is tempting to read such pronouncements as flights of fancy by journalists who had no idea what such a computer did. In a 1993 history paper titled "The Myth of the Awesome Thinking Machine," C. Dianne Martin did just that, tabulating references to ENIAC as a robot or a brain and contrasting those anthropomorphic fantasies with the much smaller number of "straightforward and unsensational" descriptions. According to Martin, computer designers quickly spoke out against this irresponsible hyperbole.[55] Edmund C. Berkeley's decision to title his 1949 introduction to automatic computing *Giant Brains, or Machines That Think* has likewise tended to be seen in retrospect as eccentric.[56]

The problem with this line of criticism is that many computing pioneers, including John von Neumann, did conceive of computers as artificial brains. Von Neumann had been interested in ways to conceptualize the brain as a system based on logical switches since 1939, if not longer.[57] On Norbert Wiener's recommendation, he read the seminal 1943 paper "A Logical Calculus of the Ideas Immanent in Nervous Activity" by Warren McCulloch and Walter Pitts.[58] McCulloch and Pitts presented an abstract model of neurons as switches, showing how networks of such neurons could be expressed as statements in a logical calculus, and asserting an equivalence between such networks and Alan Turing's abstract model of a computing machine. Von Neumann borrowed their notation for the First Draft. In January of 1945 he convened a two-day meeting on biological information processing at Princeton that was attended not only by McCulloch and Norbert Wiener (remembered as the founders of cybernetics) but also by such experts in automatic computing as Herman

Goldstine, Leland Cunningham, and Howard Aiken. Before the meeting, Warren Weaver had written to Brainerd asking for information on ENIAC that he could share with participants.[59]

The idea that brains and computers were functionally equivalent was promoted by Wiener in his 1948 book *Cybernetics, or Control and Communication in the Animal and the Machine.*[60] As that title indicated, cybernetics was an attempt to model both living creatures and complex machines as systems based on information flows. Cybernetics remained scientifically respectable for some years, winning the backing of elite scientists across a range of disciplines and financial support from the Macy Foundation.[61] Although cybernetics eventually drifted out of the scientific mainstream, its legacy remains clear in more specialized fields such as artificial intelligence and cognitive neuroscience.

Cybernetics was, in part, an attempt to broaden thought by changing vocabularies. Terms that had formerly been reserved for living things were now shared with machines. When reading the First Draft or *Giant Brains* today, one may stop short upon finding the words "brain" and "neuron" applied to the ordinary workings of a primitive computer carrying out a mathematical procedure. Yet a reference to the "memory" of that computer, based on the same metaphor, will slip past unnoticed merely because this linguistic usage was successfully disseminated. Cybernetics also spread the idea that a machine can store or process information (a term that had previously implied that a sentient being was informed of something). Stripped of its biological associations, the novel neuron notation used in the First Draft became a standard way of describing computer hardware at the level of "logic gates." The idea that the operations carried out by a computer were fundamentally equivalent to those underlying human thought was never universally accepted, particularly by people with more pragmatic engineering interests in the new machines or by companies hoping to clarify the machines' capabilities to potential customers. C. Dianne Martin was at least right that the idea of computers as brains was always controversial, and that most people professionally involved with the field had stepped away from it by the 1950s.

What the First Draft Described

Despite the First Draft's rough edges, its highly original and coherent cluster of ideas about computer architecture, hardware, and program formats exerted a direct and profound influence on the electronic computer projects launched over the next couple of years. Rather than reading the First Draft as the presentation of a single "stored program concept," we see in it three distinct clusters of ideas (or paradigms, to borrow a concept introduced by the historian and philosopher of science Thomas Kuhn in his classic book *The Structure of Scientific Revolutions*).[62] Each of these paradigms can be seen as a fairly direct response to ENIAC's shortcomings: its size and complexity, its small temporary storage capability, and the difficulty of setting it up for new problems. The early EDVAC design process was a systematic stripping away of the complexity that made ENIAC so large and therefore so expensive and unreliable. John von Neumann was no aesthete, but his intellectual response to ENIAC might be likened to that of a Calvinist zealot who, having taken charge of a gaudy cathedral, goes to work whitewashing frescos and lopping off ornamental flourishes.

We will take a moment to explain what we mean here by "paradigm," as that word lost favor within science studies decades ago, tainted by rampant overuse in the management literature and by Kuhn's own unruly tendency, later disavowed, to apply it to many different facets of a scientific community and its practices.[63] What attracts us to "paradigm" is its most fundamental meaning: an exemplary technical accomplishment based on a new approach. To Kuhn, this provided the core around which a scientific community grew. In its initial formulation a new paradigm might be clumsy or incomplete, but it held sufficient promise to attract other scientists to appropriate it, extend it, and apply it to new kinds of problems. The original paradigmatic accomplishment was thus "articulated" to become something almost unrecognizable. For example, later generations of scientists learned Newton's laws of motion in a form, and using a version of calculus, quite different from those written by Newton himself.

Focusing on the First Draft as a source of tangible paradigms thus helps us to understand the enormous power that it came to hold over the subsequent development of computing. Yet the First Draft became paradigmatic only retroactively, in a process in which some ideas contained within it were discarded, some were reformulated, and others were added. The treatment of its ideas in textbooks and papers has continued to evolve. Understanding what was originally so new and important about the First Draft requires us to strip away some of the later ideas and to ground our analysis in the realities of computer practice in the 1940s.

The "EDVAC Hardware Paradigm"

We will call the first major aspect of the First Draft the "EDVAC hardware paradigm." EDVAC appealed to early computer builders in large part as a model for designing a powerful, flexible machine using a relatively small number of components. Influential hardware ideas in the First Draft include a large high-speed delay-line or storage-tube memory, logic built entirely from electronic components, and the representation of numbers in binary. It is clear that the basic EDVAC hardware paradigm of an all-electronic computer with a large memory predated von Neumann's involvement and was made possible by Eckert's invention of the delay-line memory. These design choices constituted a bold commitment to new technologies at a time when the computing groups within Harvard University, Bell Labs, and IBM were still drawing up plans for new high-end machines based on relay storage and paper-tape control. Thus, we believe that the hardware choices specified for EDVAC in the First Draft functioned as a paradigm in Kuhn's most fundamental sense of a powerful and tangible exemplar.

Von Neumann's most substantial contribution in this area was probably to push the team toward what might have been considered an extravagantly large memory capacity. The First Draft specified a memory of 8,000 words, each 32 bits long, primarily intended for the storage of numbers rather than instructions. Conventional mathematical methods needed nothing like that capacity, but von Neumann's broad knowledge of science and exposure to the needs of the Manhattan Project had convinced him that other scientists would quickly turn their attention to problems they had hitherto ignored if a tool of this kind was developed. Over the next few years he continued to advocate large memories, suggesting in his lectures that with new machines "we should soon develop a justified desire to treat most [hydrodynamic] problems in two or three dimensions," creating such a demand for computing power that "acceleration by a factor of 100,000 is actually rather modest."[64]

In the First Draft von Neumann also showed creativity in finding ways to report the basic approach taken by the EDVAC team without mentioning the ENIAC project's underlying accomplishments. In abstracting away from specific components to idealized "neurons," he asserted the workability of machines having an unprecedented number of tubes and running at unfamiliar speeds without ever acknowledging the advances in electronic engineering that made this possible. ENIAC was still classified as "confidential," and these tactical omissions permitted the dissemination of the report beyond the immediate circle of those familiar with its details, further inflaming Eckert and Mauchly. Even Burks, who was far more charitably disposed to von Neumann, concluded that he "dissembled about what he knew of electronic digital computing."[65] In writing the First Draft, Burks asserted, "von Neumann was NOT starting from the current public state of 'radio engineering' and 'detailed radio frequency electromagnetic considerations,' as he pretended to be. He also failed to acknowledge credit for what he learned about digital electronic computing at the Moore School."

The "von Neumann Architectural Paradigm"

The second major aspect of the First Draft is the "von Neumann architectural paradigm." The idea of "von Neumann architecture" appears to this day in somewhat stylized form in computer architecture textbooks, though its definition has evolved. We include in this the basic structure of "organs" found in the report, including the separation of memory from control and arithmetic. Associated with this are the serialization of computation, with only one operation taking place at a time, the

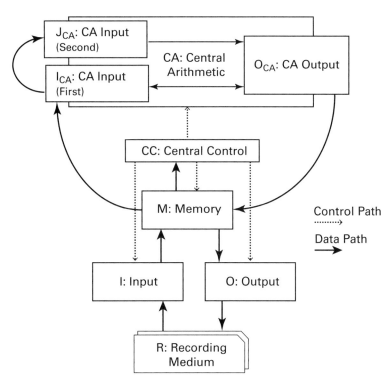

Figure 6.1
The EDVAC architecture as described in the First Draft provided a template that was used by computer designers around the world.

routing of all memory transfers through the central arithmetic unit, and a system of special-purpose registers to provide sources and destinations for arithmetic and logic instructions, and to provide a program counter and instruction register for control purposes.

The aesthetic of the machine described in the First Draft is one of radical minimalism, akin to high modernist architecture or design. Antoine de Saint-Exupéry had written a few years earlier that in design "perfection is finally attained, not when there is no longer anything to add, but when there is longer anything to take away, when a body has been stripped down to its nakedness."[66] By that standard, the EDVAC of the First Draft was approaching perfection; von Neumann had taken a great deal away. ENIAC was, in comparison, a gothic sprawl to which mechanism after mechanism had been added and from which little was ever removed. After reading the First Draft, Goldstine wrote to von Neumann praising the "complete logical framework for the machine" that he had provided and contrasting it with ENIAC, which was "chuck full of gadgets that have as their only raison d'etre that they appealed to John Mauchly."[67] This is rather harsh, but it captures a fundamental difference between the aesthetics guiding the two projects.

The drive for simplification brought some very real benefits. The vacuum tubes that made up the logic units of early electronic computers were bulky and unreliable and created a significant risk of fire. ENIAC had about 18,000 such tubes. EDVAC-type computers of significantly greater power reduced that number by an order of magnitude.[68] Thanks to the delay-line memory (a central feature of the EDVAC hardware paradigm), most of this reduction came from avoiding ENIAC's use of 11,000 vacuum tubes for its cramped high-speed memory. However, the elimination of hardware did not stop there. Each of ENIAC's accumulators included circuitry to perform additions. These were replaced by a single central adder. According to the First Draft, "The device should be as simple as possible, that is, contain as few elements as possible. This can be achieved by never performing two operations simultaneously … ."[69] Von Neumann admitted that "up to now all thinking about high speed digital computing devices has tended in the opposite direction," but felt that this justified applying his new "uncompromising solution … as completely as possible" until experience might show that compromise was necessary. His case for the collocation of code and data was subordinate to this drive for simplicity, introduced in strikingly tentative language: "While it appeared that various parts of this memory have to perform functions which differ somewhat in their nature and considerably in their purpose, it is nevertheless tempting to treat the entire memory as one organ, and to have its parts even as interchangeable as possible … ."[70]

Our best interpretation of the evidence is that, by editing, assembling, and extending ideas discussed at the joint meetings with the ENIAC team, von Neumann established, for the first time, the EDVAC architecture as a unified whole. Burks agreed. "I do not think any of us at the Moore School had an architectural model in mind for the EDVAC until we learned of Johnny's,"[71] he wrote after sifting through the surviving records. Some of the choices von Neumann made, particularly the decision to store programs and data in a single address space, were clearly related to the choices he made for the control system. His system of address modification relied on the ability to extract the address from an instruction, process it numerically in the arithmetic "organ," and then store the modified address back in the instruction. Although the different "organs" proposed in the First Draft had all been discussed in the joint meetings, the particular way in which they were connected was determined by design decisions made by von Neumann.

Later disputes reflect not only the personal interests of the participants and disagreements over details of fact but also a fundamental divergence in perspectives over what was really important in EDVAC. Eckert and Mauchly had designed ENIAC from the bottom up, paying great attention to circuits and tubes and to the design of individual adding mechanisms. Von Neumann began with EDVAC's overall structure of and its relationship to his system of logical control. This appealed greatly to Burks and Goldstine, whose doctorates were respectively in philosophy and mathematics rather than engineering.[72] They viewed the elegant way in which von Neumann arranged EDVAC's "organs" as a major accomplishment.

It seems equally plausible that Eckert and Mauchly's immediate and sincere reaction to the First Draft was that von Neumann had merely applied a pretentious and abstract variety of logic to restate the basic functioning of devices they had already begun to design in more detail. T. Kite Sharpless, who took over EDVAC's design after Eckert and Mauchly left, wrote in a 1947 affidavit that von Neumann's work, which he described as coming "from the point of view of a neurologist," was "of not much practical help" to him, as "all the organs ... already had an existing counterpart" in earlier work.[73] The significance of von Neumann's minimalism and the benefits for computer engineering of logical abstraction were not immediately apparent to Sharpless.

The "Modern Code Paradigm"

We will call the third crucial aspect of von Neumann's description of EDVAC "the modern code paradigm." We will use this new term to describe the program-related elements of the 1945 First Draft design that become standard features of 1950s computer design. Not all of those features were original to the First Draft, but their packaging together and their integration with the von Neumann architecture and with the new hardware technologies exerted a remarkable influence.[74]

• *The program is executed completely automatically.* To quote the First Draft, "Once these instructions are given to the device, it must be able to carry them out completely and without any need for further intelligent human intervention." This was essential for electronic machines, whereas human intervention at branch points had been workable with slower devices such as the Harvard Mark I. Of course operators still had to tend to input and output devices, and data might require preprocessing and post-processing either manually or with punched-card equipment.

• *The program is written as a single sequence of instructions, known as "orders" in the First Draft, which are stored in numbered memory locations along with data. These instructions control all aspects of the machine's operations. The same mechanisms are used to read code and data.* As was discussed earlier, the First Draft did specify the explicit demarcation of memory locations holding code from those holding data. It also pointed toward the idea of a program as a readable text: "it is usually convenient that the minor cycles expressing the successive steps in a sequence of logical instructions should follow each other automatically."

• *Each instruction within the program specifies one of a set of atomic operations made available to the programmer.* This was usually done by beginning the instruction with one of a small number of operation codes. Some operation codes are followed by argument fields specifying a memory location with which to work or other parameters. The First Draft specified only seven "types of orders," to be coded with three bits, although four of these instructions also included an additional four bits to select one of ten arithmetic and logic operations as a kind of parameter.[75] Several order types additionally incorporated thirteen-bit addresses. In all, instructions required between nine and 22 bits to express. Actual machines usually followed this pattern, typically merging the "order type" and "operation" fields from the First Draft so that each arithmetic or logical operation received its own numerical order code. The main exceptions, Alan Turing's Ace design and its derivatives, stuck close to the underlying hardware by coding all instructions as transfers of data between sources and destinations associated with specific circuits.

• *The program's instructions are usually executed in a predetermined sequence.* According to the First Draft, the machine "should be instructed, after each order, where to find the next order that it is to carry out." In EDVAC this was to be represented implicitly by the sequence in which they were stored, as in "normal routine" it "should obey the orders in the temporal sequence in which they naturally appear."[76]

• *However, a program can instruct the computer to depart from this ordinary sequence and jump to a different point in the program.* "There must, however, be orders available which may be used at the exceptional occasions referred to, to instruct CC [the central control organ] to transfer its connection [i.e. fetch the next instruction from] any other desired point" in memory.[77] This provided capabilities such as jumps and subroutine returns.

• *The address on which an instruction acts can change during the course of the program's execution.* That applies to the source or destination of data for calculations or the destination of a jump. This address modification capability was expressed rather cryptically in the First Draft, the final sentence of which noted that when a number was transferred to a memory location holding an instruction only the final thirteen digits, representing the address $\mu\rho$, should be overwritten. Actual computers achieved this instead through unrestricted code modification and/or indirect addressing mechanisms. EDVAC would have relied on address modification to make a conditional jump, for example to terminate a loop, but the designers of actual machines recognized the importance of this operation and gave it a special instruction.[78]

As a consequence of these capabilities, the logical complexity of the program was limited only by the memory space available to hold instructions and working data. This contrasted with the dependence of machines such as the original ENIAC or IBM's later Selective Sequence Electronic Calculator (SSEC) on other resources such as program lines, plugboard capacity, or tape readers as determinants of the maximum logical complexity of programs.

We see the reliance placed on address modification in the 1945 EDVAC design as an expression of a broader determination to replace ENIAC's many special-purpose mechanisms with a small number of general-purpose mechanisms. ENIAC, unlike most of the machines patterned after EDVAC, had special circuits to calculate square roots. In its original configuration, it relied on dedicated hardware in the master programmer to coordinate loops, repeat operations, and perform branching. In the new design, branching and looping were both accomplished with a simple control transfer instruction. Like many other early computers, ENIAC included dedicated hardware for table lookups. Its function tables returned the appropriate value of a function after being sent an "argument" stored in an accumulator. In the new paradigm, the same device was reinterpreted as a general-purpose read-only memory and the "argument" became an "address."

Some aspects of the modern code paradigm appeared in machines that von Neumann and the ENIAC team were familiar with, particularly the Harvard Mark I and the plans for the Bell Labs relay computer. However, we see no evidence that the key new ideas, particularly address modification, were discussed at the meetings of von Neumann and the Moore School staff, and contemporary sources support the idea that von Neumann was responsible for the design of a control system and instruction codes for EDVAC. Though it is possible that other discussions went unrecorded, it seems most likely that the modern code paradigm was created without significant input from the Moore School team.

We have discussed above the compelling practical reasons behind von Neumann's engagement with electronic computing. With his synthesis of the modern code paradigm, we see the expression of another side of his character, rooted in his profound early engagement with the axiomatic study of mathematical logic. As he put it a couple of years later, coding was "a logical problem and one that represents a new branch of formal logics."[79]

A Gradual Counter-Reformation

The EDVAC described in the First Draft was not, of course, the simplest possible computer. One might see it as balancing the conflicting impulses of von Neumann the logician, seeking a minimal set of operations, and von Neumann the champion of applied mathematics, building a practical tool to support researchers in the emerging world of militarized big science. These tendencies would later play out in different directions. Theoretical computer scientists looked for simpler models of computation to base their emerging discipline on, eventually settling on the universal Turing machine. Von Neumann, toward the end of his career, engaged in parallel work on cellular automata. On the other hand, computer designers found it expedient to add back into their designs some of the special-purpose mechanisms that had been left out of the First Draft. The first such change was made in EDVAC itself, to address the problem of having to wait for data to emerge from its delay lines. By September of 1945 it had been decided to provide the machine with a mixture of long and short lines.[80] Each of the short lines would hold a single number, enabling temporary rapid access to variables that were being intensively worked on. Keeping such variables in long lines would either make programming intolerably complicated or slow down performance unacceptably.

The changing treatment of conditional branching gives a clear sense of how these impulses were balanced over time. Each of the early computers provided some way to repeat a sequence of operations, but it took longer for their designers to accept the need to automatically finish looping after a fixed number of occurrences, or once a particular condition had been satisfied. ENIAC had a great deal of dedicated hardware to control branching and looping, but in the First Draft this capability was provided by a creative combination of several general-purpose mechanisms.

The EDVAC instruction set presented in the First Draft used a single, unconditional, control transfer instruction for all jumps. Von Neumann treated conditional branching as a combination of two more primitive operations: selecting the address to jump to and performing the jump itself. The former was handled by an arithmetic operation, s, which would select one of two numbers depending on whether the last value computed was positive or negative.

A conditional transfer involved (1) computing the branching condition in such a way that the desired outcome was determined by whether the result was positive or negative, (2) loading the two alternative target addresses into the arithmetic unit and executing the s operation, (3) transferring the resulting address into an unconditional transfer instruction, and (4) transferring control so that the unconditional transfer was the next instruction to be executed. There is an example of this technique in the code von Neumann wrote for a merge program for the modified EDVAC design with short delay lines. Von Neumann optimized the approach outlined above by storing a "template" unconditional jump instruction in a short line. When a conditional jump was to be performed, the address would be substituted into this instruction before executing it. As well as saving space by re-using the template, making it immediately available minimized the performance hit incurred every time a conditional branch was required.[81] Though ingenious, this was, even by the standards of machine-code programming, a cumbersome and fiddly approach.

Von Neumann's use of self-modifying code was a consequence of his minimalist design decisions rather than, as is sometimes implied, an essential feature of the universal computer appropriated from the work of Turing.[82] The vast majority of EDVAC-type computers added a conditional branch instruction, making it unnecessary to modify the destination address stored in memory.[83] This blurred the First Draft's clean separation of arithmetic and control by providing a single, highly convenient instruction consolidating the second, third, and fourth of the steps listed above. Even von Neumann's own computer at the Institute for Advanced Studies had acquired a conditional branch by the time its detailed design was documented in 1946. Its added features proved influential as an extension or (as Kuhn would put it) an articulation of the paradigms expressed in the First Draft.[84]

By the 1950s, computers generally did not rely on code modification to terminate loops or to traverse a data structure. A consensus emerged that self-modifying code was undesirable for most purposes, being hard to follow and to debug. However, users of actual EDVAC-type computers quickly discovered a different and enduring reason to permit programs to overwrite instructions held in memory. Early computers did not have room to keep anything akin to a modern operating system resident in memory, but their users quickly developed monitor programs, loaders (programs that loaded other programs, permitting batch execution or the integration of subroutines in memory), "load and go" compilers that built executable code directly into a computer's memory, and similar tools. These all involved storing executable instructions in memory, overwriting its existing content. As described in the First Draft, EDVAC would have been unable to do this. Each word of memory was flagged as either an instruction or a number. A program could entirely overwrite a number, but could overwrite only the address fields of an instruction. This would have prevented the development of anything akin to an operating system for this computer. The First Draft was, of course, not finished, and because Goldstine omitted the supplemental material that von Neumann had sent separately it never explained how a program got into memory in the first place. Perhaps von Neumann imagined a reset switch that cleared its memory so that new instructions could be loaded. The First Draft acknowledged in passing the need for a permanent storage medium, called R, but the machine's vocabulary included no special instructions for input and output.

The larger point is that we must be careful not to assume that the computer pioneers of the 1940s held the same perspectives or were driven by the same theoretical concerns as later generations of computer scientists. The EDVAC project received its initial funding to design a computer that would be cheaper, smaller, more powerful, and more flexible than ENIAC. During this first year of their work, the project's participants were spectacularly successful.

7

Converting ENIAC

ENIAC's relationship to the new ideas contained in the First Draft grew more complex over time. As we saw in the preceding chapter, the EDVAC design was partly based on work done by ENIAC's designers and reflected a reaction against some of its excesses and inefficiencies. However, the new ideas were soon applied to ENIAC itself, and after a year's concerted effort it became, in April of 1948, the first computer to run a program written in the new code paradigm. This approach was used for the rest of ENIAC's career, and thus for the bulk of its operational life ENIAC was experienced by programmers as a machine that employed the modern code paradigm first glimpsed in von Neumann's report rather than the original system of decentralized control pulses passed between largely autonomous units.

Rapid Acceptance of the EDVAC Design

In the first half of 1946, several projects were already underway to build computers based on the new ideas. While development of EDVAC itself continued at the Moore School, fission of the ENIAC team had led to two new projects. Arthur Burks and Herman Goldstine joined John von Neumann at the Institute for Advanced Studies in Princeton, while J. Presper Eckert and John Mauchly were now entrepreneurs planning the design of what would become Univac from their Philadelphia offices. These two teams developed the ideas contained in the First Draft in different ways. Both were influential—Univac set public impressions of what a commercial computer should be, and the design for von Neumann's new computer, described in the 1946 report *Preliminary Discussion of the Logical Design of an Electronic Computing Instrument*, directly shaped the next generation of American computers. IBM's first computer product, the model 701, was one of its descendants. In England, Alan Turing's design of a computer for the National Physical Laboratory took the First Draft as its starting point, and Max Newman (a mathematician and a veteran of the Colossus project) was writing to von Neumann about his plans to build a computer at the University of Manchester.

In July and August, a summer school on "Theory and Techniques for Design of Electronic Digital Computers" was held at the University of Pennsylvania, still home to ENIAC and to the EDVAC project. This event reunited the scattered ENIAC veterans and gave them a chance to present the new paradigms to a wider audience. Historians have credited the summer school, often called simply the "Moore School Lectures," as a crucial vector for the spread of the "stored program concept."[1] It inspired further computer projects, among them Maurice Wilkes' project at the University of Cambridge.

What made the EDVAC approach so immediately compelling to the would-be builders of electronic computers who had gathered at the Moore School? In one lecture, Eckert retraced for the audience the process he and his colleagues had gone through to design EDVAC as a reaction to the shortcomings of ENIAC. His argument for internal program storage was pragmatic. It would reduce set-up time, as "in the EDVAC there will be no cords, no plugs, and few switches. We are simply going to use the memory to hold the information electronically and to feed those pieces of information which relate to programming from the memory, into the control circuits in order to sequence the machine … ." He estimated that ENIAC's connecting cables, function tables, and switches effectively held the equivalent of about 7,000 digits of numerical and control information. But a larger, cheaper delay-line memory combining program and data storage, he asserted, "eliminates for the designer the problem of attempting to find the proper balance between the various types of the memory, and gives the problem to the user."[2] Memory technologies were, as these comments remind us, the biggest challenge to computer builders in the late 1940s. As various teams toiled to get their machines working, success or failure was determined in large part by their skill in disciplining unruly cathode-ray tubes and delay lines. In the first computing texts and conferences, a central place was therefore given to discussion of drums, electromagnetic delay lines, Selectrons, cathode-ray tubes, wire recorders, and phosphor discs.

Mauchly offered similar sentiments at a symposium held at Harvard University the next year, when he presented the modern code paradigm as one of the most important advantages of EDVAC-type computers. In a lecture titled "Preparation of Problems for EDVAC-Type Machines" he considered the "fundamental characteristics … which differ significantly from present machine design." Three of those fundamental characteristics, he said, "have a definite bearing on the handling of problems: (1) an extensive internal memory; (2) elementary instructions, few in number, to which the machine will respond; and (3) ability to store instructions as well as numerical quantities in the internal memory and modify instructions so stored in accordance with other instructions." Mauchly expanded on the final point as follows:

instructions are stored in the internal memory in the same manner as are numerical quantities, and one set of instructions can be used to modify another set of instructions ... . The total number of operations for which instructions must be provided will usually be exceedingly large, so that the instruction sequence would be far in excess of the internal memory capacity. However, such an instruction sequence is never a random sequence, and can usually be synthesized from subsequences which frequently recur.

By providing the necessary subsequences, which may be utilized as often as desired, together with a master sequence directing the use of these subsequences, compact and easily set up instructions for very complex programs can be achieved. Even greater powers are conferred, however, by the ability to use one instruction to modify another. ... [This] transfers to the machine a burden which would otherwise fall upon the operator—the burden of explicitly writing out and coding the successive variations which are to be used.[3]

Several early computing primers described the new breed of computer concisely and effectively by reproducing a small instruction set. In contrast, the descriptions of ENIAC's programming method that appeared in dozens of books and papers over the years included lengthy and conspicuously uninviting descriptions of panels, pulses, switches, buses, and other hardware. Consider the book *High Speed Computing Devices*, issued in 1950 by the staff of Engineering Research Associates, an early builder of computers. A chapter titled "A Functional Approach to Machine Design" presented a sample instruction set based on that designed by von Neumann's team at the Institute for Advanced Studies and went on to make this assertion:

A machine for which commands can be written in this way is clearly a versatile machine. Since the commands are numbers and since the machine must expect to have numbers introduced to it in some fashion, it certainly should not be difficult to enter these coded commands into the machine.... Since only a few different operations are required, the engineering structure of the machine may be expected to be attainable fairly simply.[4]

The chapter concluded that this would make for "convenient operation of a general-purpose machine," noting that the "requirement that a few written commands direct a long calculation is attained by (1) the inclusion of facilities permitting the reuse of commands with the operations unchanged and the address changed if desired; and (2) an operation permitting a departure from the normal sequence to a secondary one."[5]

In his 1949 book *Calculating Instruments and Machines*, Douglas Hartree used ENIAC as a baseline against which to identify two "main directions in which the first further developments are to be expected, namely the provision of a form of high-speed storage of much greater capacity without a corresponding increase in electronic equipment, and a means by which the machine can set up for itself the connections required for the sequence of computing operations, as in the Harvard Mark I calculator and various relay machines."[6]

Hartree described ENIAC, the Harvard Mark I, and the SSEC as "The First Phase of Development" of "Large Automatic Digital Machines." He concluded that "it seems very improbable that any of them will be duplicated," continuing:

The machines of the future will be considerably different in principle and appearance; smaller and simpler, with numbers of tubes or relays numbered in thousands rather than the tens of thousands of the machines considered in this chapter, faster, more versatile and easier to code for and to operate. Those at present projected or under construction are different enough to be regarded as forming a second stage of development … .[7]

Years later, Maurice Wilkes echoed these comments when he recalled that "the details of the ENIAC design … were of little interest" during the Moore School lectures to "the minute group of engineers (including myself) who were destined to build the first stored program computers."[8] The comment is a little brash, but there can be no doubt that the attention of machine designers, including ENIAC's creators, had moved on to the new paradigms even before ENIAC had become properly operational.

Boring as ENIAC may have appeared to Wilkes in 1946, it was then and for some years to come the fastest machine in existence, and therefore still of great interest to groups with complex computations to perform. Those making "pilgrimages"[9] to Aberdeen included John von Neumann. As a computer architect von Neumann had little left to learn from ENIAC, but as a computer user he was well aware of its power. Los Alamos had a backlog of large-scale computing needs to which the computer being built at the Institute of Advanced Study would be applied at the earliest possible date. However, in early 1947 even the most optimistic estimates assumed that that machine would not be operational for several years.

ENIAC was the only plausible short-term option when von Neumann and his collaborators at Los Alamos wanted to use an electronic computer to simulate nuclear chain reactions using the newly developed Monte Carlo method. By March of 1947, von Neumann had asked his close collaborators Herman and Adele Goldstine, both veterans of ENIAC's Moore School days, to investigate the "set-up" of ENIAC for Monte Carlo.[10] We will discuss the Monte Carlo project itself in the next two chapters; here we are interested in the intertwined effort it inspired to convert ENIAC into an EDVAC-style machine.

Launching the Conversion Project

W. Barkley Fritz, a member of the ENIAC team at the Ballistic Research Lab, later commented that the process of designing an ENIAC set-up in its original programming method "can best be described as analogous to the design and development of a special-purpose computer out of ENIAC component parts for each new application."[11]

In or around April of 1947, John von Neumann recognized that ENIAC's kit of parts could be used to build a computer very similar in its programming method to the forthcoming Institute for Advanced Studies machine. He and his collaborators, who were deeply immersed in the new design paradigms and the programming techniques required for an EDVAC-type computer, produced a series of reports proposing a programming methodology, a rich flow-diagramming technique, and methods for handling subroutines.[12] At that point they had probably thought more deeply about these matters than any other group in the world, so it is not entirely surprising that as they explored ENIAC's use for Monte Carlo they recognized that they could equip it with many of the advantages of the new code paradigm.

The goal of the conversion was to configure ENIAC's switches and wires so that it would decode and execute a fixed repertoire of basic EDVAC-type instructions. Programs would be stored as a sequence of numerically coded instructions on ENIAC's function tables, which then would be fetched and executed one at a time.

In ENIAC's original control mode, constraints on its programming capacity were embedded in many aspects of its design, and they interacted in unpredictable ways. For example, the twenty accumulators held 240 controls providing for numerical transfers, additions, and subtractions, and each of the twenty-four controls on the high-speed multiplier defined a single multiplication operation. The supply of controls placed an upper limit on how many operations of each type a program could contain. The master programmer contained only ten steppers, which further limited the overall logical complexity of a program. Setting up a conditional test not only tied up one of the master programmer's steppers but also monopolized one output terminal of an accumulator, limiting the usefulness of that accumulator for other purposes. As the machine's designers commented in 1945, "in planning a set-up of a problem for the ENIAC the inner economy of the machine must be considered in allocation [*sic*] program facilities to various parts of the program."[13] After conversion, the logical complexity of programs would be constrained only by the relatively generous 3,600 decimal digits of addressable high-speed storage available on the function tables.

Work on the Monte Carlo simulation program for Los Alamos took place in parallel with the design of the new programming system. Klara von Neumann and Adele Goldstine, the wives of the leaders of the Institute for Advanced Studies' computer project, were both hired by Los Alamos as consultants to assist with the project during the summer of 1947.[14] Though Adele Goldstine was only 26 years old, her qualifications were unmatched: she held a graduate degree in mathematics, and she had worked on documenting and programming ENIAC during its time at the Moore School. Thus, the team combined deep knowledge of the new programming concepts with an unparalleled understanding of ENIAC's capabilities.

We mentioned earlier that Adele Goldstine, in her 1946 ENIAC report, had written about "the storage of programming data by means of the function table" when describing a way to redirect pulses output by the function table to directly initiate up to fourteen subroutines.[15] The 1947 approach was quite different: numbers representing instructions were retrieved from the function table to be interpreted elsewhere in the machine. Still, that the tables had already been considered as repositories for programming data may have made the new system seem more natural.

Credit for the initial idea of converting ENIAC to an EDVAC-like control method was later claimed by Richard Clippinger, who was at that time a mathematician working at the BRL.[16] However, in a 1948 report Clippinger himself presented a different account:

In the Spring of 1947, J. von Neumann suggested to the author that it would be possible to run the ENIAC in a way very different from the way contemplated when it was designed … . His suggestion has been worked into a finished regime by J. von Neumann, [Adele] Goldstine, [Jean] Bartik, [Richard] Clippinger, and [Art] Gehring with contributions by A. Galbraith, [John] Giese, [Kay] McNulty, J. Holberton, [Betty] Snyder, [Ed] Schlain, [Kathe] Jacobi, [Frances] Bilas, and [Sally] Spear. The role of J. von Neumann in working out the details has been a central one.[17]

Clippinger's testimony in the ENIAC patent trial clarified the basis of his later push to be recognized as instigator of the conversion effort: he had originated the concept of using function-table pulses to sequence subroutines. The entire conversion process constituted "several evolutionary stages" in the refinement of this fundamental insight. The idea had come to him when he was working on a complex set of airflow calculations, sometime after Adele Goldstine explained the dummy program technique in "April or May" of 1946. She took it from him without credit.[18]

Clippinger struggled under cross-examination when presented with a January 1946 engineering diagram for the "F.T. Program Adapter" cable, which had somehow been designed long before he supposedly came up with the idea it implemented—indeed before Goldstine had taught him enough about ENIAC for him to understand what it did. Eckert later wrote that when designing ENIAC "we expected that at some time someone would want to do this, so we built the necessary cable … . Clippinger later 'rediscovered' these uses of the function tables, without knowing that they had already been provided for in the original hardware."[19] Chronology aside, it was rather misleading to conflate ENIAC's conversion to the modern code paradigm with the earlier concept of direct control by the function table.[20]

The 51 Order Code

By mid May of 1947, intensive planning work for ENIAC's conversion was underway. Richard Clippinger had previously arranged for Jean Bartik, who had not moved to Aberdeen with the machine, to lead a five-person group in Philadelphia doing work under a one-year contract to the Ballistic Research Lab.[21] Planning for ENIAC's conversion became the group's biggest project. Bartik recalls that a delegation from the BRL traveled up to Princeton with Clippinger for several visits of "two or three days" to work with Adele Goldstine, and that John von Neumann spent "maybe half an hour a day" with them.[22]

Detailed discussions with Clippinger began in mid May and continued until the end of that month. In mid June, John von Neumann wrote to the BRL's associate director, Robert Kent, that four weeks had passed "since I started to discuss with you, and in detail with Clippinger, the new method of setting-up and programming the ENIAC, and two weeks since we concluded these preliminary discussions," and mentioned that "several variants of this method have now been worked out by Clippinger and his group, on the one hand, and the Goldstines, on the other."[23] This led to the Goldstines' proposed "Princeton" configuration and to Bartik and Clippinger's proposed "Aberdeen" configuration. (Those were informal names for the two configurations.) The teams met repeatedly through the summer and the autumn of 1947, and Adele Goldstine made several trips to Philadelphia and at least one to Aberdeen.[24]

By July, Adele Goldstine had prepared a detailed preliminary conversion plan and an instruction set. Her report called the proposed method "central control," a name that nicely captures its consolidation of all application-specific programming in the function-table switches.[25] The report included a "51 order vocabulary" and set-up diagrams showing the wiring and the switch configurations that would be needed for ENIAC to decode and execute the instructions. Although the set-up was never implemented, its principles were followed throughout the rest of the conversion project.

ENIAC's accumulators exchanged control pulses with one another and with the machine's other units. These signals triggered whatever actions had been set up by the local program controls to occur when a pulse arrived on a wire attached to a particular input terminal. Thus, the "program pulses" did not directly encode arguments or instructions, but sent only one message: Go! It was not easy to centralize this distributed control system to support the modern code paradigm. The approach taken in Goldstine's proposal was to superimpose the abstract EDVAC organs discussed in the First Draft on ENIAC's twenty accumulators, partitioning them into three functional groups.

The proposal assigned eight accumulators to the "arithmetic system." Accumulator 15 became the machine's "accumulator" in the modern sense. Adele Goldstine called it a "central arithmetic and transfer organ." Accumulator 13 was an auxiliary arithmetic register. The six other accumulators placed within the arithmetic system were akin to special-purpose registers in later computer architectures and were attached to ENIAC's specialized hardware units to serve as fixed sources or destinations for the arguments and results of multiplication, division, and square-root operations. Accumulators 11 and 15 were also used as buffers to hold data read from the function table or from punched cards. The arithmetic operations provided were based on those John von Neumann's team was then refining for its computer at the Institute for Advanced Studies, with a few modifications made necessary by the properties of ENIAC's original arithmetic circuits.[26]

Three more accumulators were committed to a "control system" that provided the basic structure needed to fetch and decode instructions. Instructions were identified by a two-digit code, and as many as six instructions could be stored in each line of the read-only function tables. The control system included what would later be called an instruction register, though hardware changes made that unnecessary in later versions of the plan.

Each instruction was implemented through "local" programming using the traditional system of switches and wires to trigger basic ENIAC operations, such as clearing or incrementing accumulators and transferring numbers between units. This is reminiscent of the later practice of microprogramming. For example, the instruction "FTN" was described in subsequent documentation as a combination of six distinct actions. One was incrementing the address stored in the first three digits of accumulator 8; another was clearing accumulator 11.[27]

The master programmer mapped each instruction code to the program line initiating the corresponding sequence of operations. Nine of the sixty output terminals provided by its steppers were tied up decoding instruction numbers. Goldstine's proposal has therefore been remembered as "the 51 order code." In this context, "order" meant instruction and "code" meant instruction set.

The control system also held the addresses of several locations in the function tables. As we saw earlier, von Neumann's EDVAC instruction set relied on address modification to accomplish operations such as conditional jumps and data reads from calculated locations. Goldstine and her colleagues needed the same capability, but ENIAC programs could not modify data or instructions stored in the function tables. Instead they designed the control system to store the addresses used for these instructions in designated accumulators so that they could be manipulated programmatically.

One of the stored addresses, the "current control argument," indexed the current line of instructions. By default it was incremented each time the instructions in a line were completed, so instructions were executed sequentially. An "unconditional transfer" instruction overwrote the current control argument with a new address, changing the location from which the next instruction code would be read.

Another stored address, the "future control argument," was set with a "substitution order." The conditional transfer instruction implemented branching by checking the sign of the number in accumulator 15, overwriting the current control argument with the future control argument if it was positive. The same mechanism was later used to implement subroutine returns and to implement the "variable remote connections" used in von Neumann and Goldstine's flow-diagram notation to jump to a location determined and stored earlier in the computation.[28] The limitations of ENIAC's hardware had inspired a new mechanism that could directly implement what had formerly been an abstract capability.

A function-table address was also required by the "F.T.3 Numeric" instruction, which read numeric data from the third function table; as with the transfer instructions, the address required was stored within a designated accumulator location. These stored addresses gave ENIAC a simple form of indirect addressing. More elegant indirect addressing mechanisms, such as index registers, were widely relied on by later computers to limit the need to modify code. As we saw in the preceding chapter, John von Neumann had programmed conditional branches in the EDVAC code by modifying a template instruction stored separately from the main program.

In Goldstine's plan, nine accumulators remained after other needs were addressed. The set-up hid the arithmetic and programming capabilities of these accumulators so that they appeared to the programmer as simple storage devices. Together with the much larger expanse of read-only memory on the function tables, these accumulators constituted what von Neumann had called the "memory organ." Each received a distinct "talk" instruction that copied its data into accumulator 15 and a "listen" instruction that did the opposite. Similar provisions were made for the accumulators in the arithmetic system so that they could be used for general storage when not required for specific arithmetic operations.

Planning the 60 Order Code

The conversion plans went through several revisions. During the second half of 1947, efforts focused on the "60 order code." This was a refinement of the original conversion plan, and was developed primarily by the group of subcontractors in Philadelphia led by Jean Bartik. By then, Adele Goldstine's focus had shifted to programming a non-Monte Carlo nuclear simulation, code-named Hippo.

New hardware appeared in the plans supporting the expansion from 51 to 60 instructions. A counter known simply as the "10-stage stepper" was added to speed and simplify the decoding of instructions. Each of its outputs was connected to one of the master programmer's internal steppers. The new stepper advanced to the stage corresponding to the first digit of the instruction code, and each stepper in the master programmer advanced to the stage corresponding to the second digit. A program pulse sent to the new stepper was routed to one of the master programmer's steppers, and on to whichever of the 60 output terminals would initiate the appropriate operation. Two further steppers, the "function table selector" and the "order selector," provided dedicated hardware support for certain aspects of the decoding of operation codes. This redesign simplified the planned control system and freed a precious accumulator for storage of application data.[29]

The candidate 60 order codes maintained the basic structure of the earlier draft, diverging principally by incorporating more control instructions (to set up the current and future control addresses and the function-table argument) and more flexible shift instructions. None of the 1947 plans incorporated the "register" memory unit to which the BRL had committed in February. Presumably that was attributable to a well-grounded pessimism about the likelihood that it would work reliably in time for the initial conversion. By November, Bartik had produced a complete account of the implementation of the 60 order code, including all the details of configuration and wiring that were needed to set up ENIAC to run programs written in the code.[30] The document described both the "Princeton" instruction set and the "Aberdeen" instruction set.

Bartik and the four programmers she managed were employed under a one-year contract that had been granted to the Moore School on Richard Clippinger's instigation.[31] The concept of contracting for programming services was unprecedented, and to satisfy the federal government's procurement regulations the group was required to supply twelve ENIAC set-ups over the course of the contract. It was the formation of this group in March of 1947, rather than the original hiring of the operators in 1945, that truly established computer programming as a job in its own right.

Clippinger had been working for some time on a way of applying ENIAC to the simulation of supersonic airflow, a topic that dominated the contractual list of problems to be tackled by Bartik's team.[32] Not long after the beginning of that work, their energies were directed toward the conversion effort. In addition to detailed conversion plans, they developed a number of programs from the initial list, which now were delivered as instructions written in the 60 order code rather than as the originally anticipated set-up diagrams. They tackled ENIAC's original and most frequently recurring application, the calculation of ballistic trajectories, modeling the effect of projectile characteristics such as shape (one program was known as the "cone-cylinder" problem) and experimenting with a simplified version of the Heun method for numerical integration devised by the BRL mathematician L. S. Dederick. Flow charts and code listings for these programs have been preserved, each accompanied by a detailed step-by-step manual trace of its execution.[33] Because the 60 order code was never installed on ENIAC, this was the only form of testing available to Bartik's team. The group also worked on techniques for computing exponential and trigonometric functions, developing program segments that they explicitly described as "subroutines."[34]

Bartik's group also produced a suite of programs intended to test all of ENIAC's units. Bartik received feedback on those programs from Richard Clippinger and Adele Goldstine.[35] Because ENIAC continued to be unreliable, its operators would run test programs regularly to check that the machine was operating correctly before beginning a new job and to diagnose problems when it showed signs of trouble. The test programs were published in a 1948 report describing the 60 order code.[36] The same report included a lengthy discussion of Clippinger's supersonic airflow problem. Clippinger's report began with an extended description of the mathematical aspects of the problem, culminating in a flow diagram and a storage table showing how the variables to be stored were distributed among ENIAC's accumulators. Hewing to the methodology proposed by Herman Goldstine and John von Neumann, Clippinger commented "it is now a simple matter to … write the succession of orders that will cause the machine to carry out the computations described" and included a table showing the codes for the complete program (presumably coded by, or with much assistance from, Jean Bartik's team).[37]

The conversion plans were announced during a press conference at Aberdeen on December 12, 1947 and reported in the *New York Times* the next day. This coincided with Clippinger's initial presentation of the planned conversion to a technical audience at the 1947 meeting of the Association for Computing Machinery.[38] In a report that repeatedly referred to ENIAC as a "robot," the *Times* disclosed that these changes would give ENIAC "a substantial part of the efficiency which is being built into the Edvac."[39]

Implementing the Conversion

Planning for the conversion continued in parallel with work on the Monte Carlo program. One participant in that effort was Nicholas Metropolis, a veteran of Los Alamos and a confidant of John von Neumann who was then working at the University of Chicago's Institute of Nuclear Studies. He was scheduled to arrive at Aberdeen to begin preparations for the Monte Carlo program on February 20, 1948, by which time BRL staff members were expected to be "well on the way" to reconfiguring ENIAC after the anticipated completion of modifications by the Moore School team on February 9.[40] In fact reconfiguration for the 60 order code had not started when Metropolis and Klara von Neumann arrived. According to Metropolis, he and Klara von Neumann began their own work to expand the instruction set after coming across the new converter panel and deciding to use it to efficiently decode all possible two-digit codes.[41] The converter had been expected to arrive with the register, which would have been the centerpiece of an entirely new instruction set. The interim 60 order code had therefore relied on neither unit.[42] Changing that plan to immediately incorporate the converter allowed them to expand the available instruction set, speeded up operation of the code, and freed the master programmer. Treatment of shifts was modified significantly: two complex parameterized instructions were replaced by twenty simpler instructions, partially decoded by the master programmer, to perform specific shift operations.

The log book maintained by ENIAC's operators makes clear that, contrary to several previous accounts, the 60 order code was never installed.[43] The master programmer was not used with the 10-stage stepper for instruction decoding, having been replaced by the converter. It is not clear whether the 10-stage stepper was ever installed, but the new code did use the function table selector and the order selector in exactly the ways specified for the 60 order code.[44]

The converter unit was fitted to ENIAC on March 15, 1948. Two weeks later, on March 29, the log shows that "Nick [Metropolis] arrives about 4PM and started getting the background coding on for the A.E.C." In other words, Metropolis began to configure ENIAC with the new instruction set. The next day, "Nick got the basic sequence & 2 or 3 orders working." The day after that, ENIAC was "demonstrated for the first time using the new coding scheme." Various "troubles" slowed progress, and Richard Merwin was again summoned from the Moore School to fix the converter, but by April 6 implementation of the new coding method was complete.

A lengthy period of testing and debugging followed, full of "intermittents," "transients," and other "troubles." John and Klara von Neumann arrived during that period. John left soon afterward, but Klara stayed behind to work with Metropolis for the rest of his time there. According to the log, a demonstration to students of the Applied Physics Laboratory on April 12 "went off without hitches" and "was the first adequate demonstration using the new coding techniques"; thus, it was the first time that code written in the modern paradigm was successfully executed.

The "first production run" on the Monte Carlo problem followed on April 17, but "troubles of various kinds" returned immediately. By April 23, morale was flagging. The log recorded that "no progress [was] made for the day" and that "it looks like a major overhaul or something drastic is necessary to make the ENIAC work properly."

Metropolis salvaged the situation on April 28 with a more modest intervention: slowing ENIAC's clock from 100 to 60 kilohertz. Reliable operation suddenly became the norm rather than the exception. Monte Carlo simulation began in earnest, finishing on May 10, 1948. Stanislaw Ulam, one of several people who had been following the progress of the work with interest, wrote to John von Neumann "I heard from Nick on the telephone that the miracle of the ENIAC really took place."[45] All subsequent ENIAC operation was in the new mode.[46]

The Converter Code

Despite the extensive preparatory work done on the "60 order code," the first application run on ENIAC under central control used an extended instruction set, described in the operations log as a "79 order code," devised by Metropolis and Klara von Neumann to take advantage of the extra capacity provided by the converter.[47] Their success rendered the "60 order code" obsolete. On April 14, Clippinger came by to "discuss changes to be made in his code or in the current code" to prepare for running his problem once the Monte Carlo run was complete, and the machine was set up in mid May with an "83 order code."[48] From the programmer's point of view, the biggest difference between the instruction sets was the extended range of shift operations, so the changes required to Clippinger's existing programs would not have been too drastic.

A number of documents circulated in mid 1948 described slight variants of the new system. By the following year, it was referred to as the "converter code." It was officially documented by W. Barkley Fritz in BRL reports in 1949 and 1951.[49] Because this instruction set (or small variations on it) was used for the rest of ENIAC's working life, we will summarize the major features of its 1951 incarnation here.

Fritz began by describing the flow of data through ENIAC (see figure 7.1). Numbers were fed into ENIAC from punched cards or by setting switches on the function tables and the constant transmitter. The constant transmitter contained ten registers, from each of which a signed ten-digit number could be read. Eight of the registers were used as buffers to hold the contents of a punched card; the other two held constants that had been set manually before the program started. A function table provided 100 usable rows, each with twelve digits and two signs and each holding either six two-digit operation codes, a signed ten-digit number (read by the FTC instruction), or two signed six-digit numbers (read by the FTN instruction).[50] Read instructions transferred numbers from the constant transmitter and the function tables into accumulators 11 and 15. The print operation moved numbers from accumulators 1, 2, and 15–20 to buffers in the printer unit before asynchronously punching them onto a card.

In its use of ENIAC's memory, summarized in table 7.1, the "converter code" followed the model described by Adele Goldstine in 1947. Fritz listed thirteen accumulators that could be used "without storage restrictions." Accumulator 6 was the "control center of the code's operation," holding the address of the current instruction and also the new address to be used after a conditional branch operation. These replicated what Goldstine had called the current and future control arguments. Accumulator 15 was still the "arithmetic center of the code's operation." Accumulator 13 was involved in most operations, and was not generally available for storage.

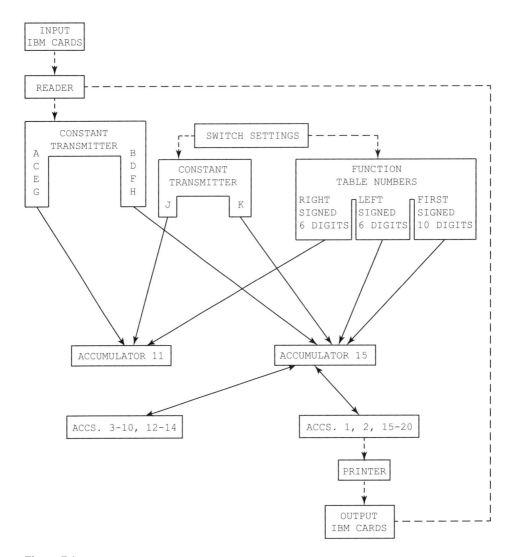

Figure 7.1
Data pathways through ENIAC as of 1951
(after figure 2 of Fritz, Description of the ENIAC Converter Code)

Table 7.1
Uses of memory in the 1951 "converter code."

Function	Accumulators or other memory used
Variable storage	1–5, 9, 10, 14, 16–20.
	6 (digits 7–10 and sign)
	7 (when not holding denominator for division)
	8 (when not used for function-table addressing)
Constant storage	Function tables, constant transmitter registers J, K
Data written to cards	1, 2, 15–20
Arithmetic system	7 (holds denominator)
	11 (holds multiplier)
	12 (receives multiplicand, remainders, and shift overflows)
	13 (working register, overwritten in most operations)
	15 ("the accumulator" in EDVAC sense. Adds numbers, holds arguments and results of multiplication, division and square-root operations)
Input from function tables	11, 15
Input from cards	Constant transmitter registers A–H
	11, 15 (receive data from constant transmitter).
Function-table address for FTN and FTC orders	8 (digits 1–4)
Current instruction address	6 (digits 1–3)
Future control address	6 (digits 4–6)
Instruction codes	Function tables (constant transmitter when card control used)

ENIAC's instruction set, summarized in table 7.2, is in general striking in its resemblance to the instructions available on other early machines using the modern code paradigm.

Strengths and Weaknesses

Even after ENIAC's conversion, staff members at the Ballistic Research Lab continued to see its new capabilities as comparable to those of their other calculating machines. A September 1949 report titled Preparation of Problems for the BRL Calculating Machines summarized two years of accumulated wisdom for users of the BRL Computing Laboratory's machines. Its authors included John Holberton, head of the ENIAC Branch, so we can assume that it was well grounded in practice. The opening chapter emphasized the fundamental similarity of ENIAC and the two varieties of Relay Calculator then in use at the BRL: all were controlled by programming units, all had input and output devices, and so on. The guide then cautioned

Table 7.2
The instruction set used in the 1951 version of the "converter code." Source: Fritz, *Description of the ENIAC Converter Code.*

Code	Mnemonic	Simplified definition
Storage instructions		
44	Rd	Read numbers from the next card in the IBM reader, and store them on the constant transmitter.
50	AB	Transfer numbers from two constant transmitter registers to accumulators 11 and 15.
51	CD	
54	EF	
55	GH	
56	JK	
72ab	N2D	Copy the next 2, 4 or 6 digits into accumulator 15. Used to write constants into the program code.
73abcd	N4D	
74abcdef	N6D	
47, 97	FTN, FTC	Read two six-digit numbers from the function table into accumulators 11 and 15 (FTN) or a ten-digit number into accumulator 15 (FTC), and increment the function-table address.
01, 02, 03, 04 05, 06, 07, 08 09, 10, 11 12, 13, 14, 16, 17, 18, 19, 20	1L, 2L, 3L, 4L, 5L, 6L, 7L 8L, 9L, 10L, 11L, 12L, 13, 1L, 16L, 17L, 18L, 19L, 20L	Accumulator α "listens to" (receives number from) accumulator 15, which then clears. All accumulators except 13 clear before listening.
15	CL	Clear accumulator 15.
92, 93	6_1, 6_2	Add digits from accumulator 15 into the general storage digits of accumulator 6.
91	S.C	Clear all accumulator memory except the current instruction address.
45	Pr	Send the contents of accumulators 1, 2, 15–20 to the printer for card punching.
Shift instructions		
32, 60	R1, L1	Shift the digits in accumulator 15 right or left. Digits shifted out are discarded.
43, 71	R2, L2	
42, 70	R3, L3	
53, 81	R4, L4	
52, 80	R5, L5	

Table 7.2 (continued)

Shift instructions

38, 66	R'1, L'1	Shift the digits in accumulator 15 right or
49, 77	R'2, L'2	left into accumulator 12, which is first
48, 76	R'3, L'3	cleared.
59, 87	R'4, L'4	
58, 86	R'5, L'5	

Arithmetic instructions

21, 22, 23, 24, 25, 26, 27, 28, 29, 30, 31, 62, 33, 34, 36, 37, 38, 39, 40	1T, 2T, 3T, 4T, 5T, 6T, 7T, 8T, 9T, 10T, 11T, 12T, 13T, 14T, 16T, 17T, 19T, 20T	Accumulator α "talks," i.e. its number is added to the number held in Accumulator 15.
41	M	Replace x in accumulator 15 by $-x$. Used as a precursor to a talk instruction to accomplish subtraction.
57	$\times$	Multiplication order. Form the product of accumulators 11 and 15 plus the contents of accumulator 13 in accumulator 15. (This use of accumulator 13 helps to calculate sums of products efficiently.)
63	$\div$	Divide accumulator 15 by accumulator 7, storing the quotient in accumulator 15 and remainder in accumulator 12.
64	$\sqrt{}$	Form the square root of accumulator 15 in accumulator 15, and the remainder in accumulator 12.
82	A.V.	Take absolute value of accumulator 15.
46	D.S.	"Drop sign": make accumulator 15 positive.

Control instructions

78, 830abc	6R3, N3D6a	Set the current instruction address from accumulator 15 (6R3) or 3 inline digits (N3D6) to execute an unconditional transfer (jump).
79, 89abc0	6_3, N3D6$_3$	Set the future control address from accumulator 15 (6_3) or 3 inline digits (N3D6$_3$).
84abcdef	N6D6	Set current and future control addresses from inline digits. Used to call a subroutine and set the return address in a single instruction.

Table 7.2 (continued)

Control instructions

69	C.T.	Conditional transfer. If accumulator 15 is negative then continue with the next instruction. Otherwise, set current instruction address from the future control address to jump.
94, 85, 96	i, di, cdi	Control the master programmer.[a]
75abcd	N3D8	Add 4 inline digits to the function-table address.
90, 99	D	Delay: go to next instruction.
00, 35	H	Halt the machine.

a. By 1951, these instructions had been added to allow loops to be set up on the master programmer (which was not fully utilized by the earlier converter codes) and controlled using the pre-conversion mechanisms.

users that "the machine does not solve a problem" but merely executes a "sequence of arithmetic operations designed by the problem preparer." In each case the challenge was to prepare a sequence without exceeding the limits of the machine.

ENIAC won praise for its unique electronic speed and its lack of arbitrary limits on the logical complexity of programs, but the guide warned that its speed advantage was largely sacrificed when punched cards were needed for short-term storage. As before, the Bell Labs relay calculators were praised for their reliability, their self-checking, their unattended operation, and their floating-point capabilities. The IBM relay calculators were still in use, and had been used to solve a "great many different types of problem," but were the most difficult machines to program. Programming them was a three-stage process: a "time chart of operations" was used to prepare a plugboard diagram, which was then used to wire the control board. The report warned that any schedule would have to anticipate "some unpredictably [*sic*] delays."[51]

ENIAC would be best suited for jobs otherwise requiring "several months of manual computation by a large staff of computers." "Methods requiring extremely lengthy schedules of operations" would go to the Bell Labs computers because of the unlimited length of their program tapes. So would tasks performed only occasionally (which didn't require lengthy set-up) and problems for which "the intermediate or final results of some computations may vary considerably in magnitude from cycle to cycle" because their floating-point hardware "obviates the necessity for extensive use of scale factors."[52] The other machines would require the programmer to fully understand the range of possible values each variable could take when designing the program. The Bell Labs machines were poorly suited to programs with large amounts of data, which the IBM relay calculators, with their punched-card capabilities, could handle admirably. Mathematical techniques could be tailored to the foibles of one or another of the machines, as Hartree had shown in 1946.[53]

The three computers were presented as idiosyncratic but roughly equivalent examples of the same kind of machinery, an interesting corrective to the present-day tendency to assume that ENIAC immediately rendered the relay calculators mere historical curiosities. Neither had hand calculation vanished from Aberdeen. A worked example for the tabulation of a sample function reduced the function to a suitable mathematical method before evaluating the time required to perform the calculations on each machine. It concluded that the calculations in question would best be tackled by hand, because they would require only a few weeks of human work and because they involved cube roots, which could still "be obtained much more simply by hand computer than by machine." Human computers could use more efficient methods and could offset some of their inherent slowness by looking up values in pre-calculated tables. By bringing their only tutorial example to such a conclusion, the Computing Laboratory's members were trying to ensure that their colleagues would not demand machine time for problems that could be tackled more effectively with traditional methods. (Their report did go on to show that some minor changes to the problem would render it more demanding, and thus suitable for machine solution.)

8

ENIAC Goes to Monte Carlo

Having told the story of ENIAC's conversion to the modern code paradigm, we will now jump back to 1947 to pick up the story of the development and execution of the Monte Carlo program that inspired the conversion and gave the modified machine its first task.

Inside the Trading Zone

Planning for the Monte Carlo computations was discussed in Peter Galison's classic essay "Computer Simulations and the Trading Zone," which depicted early computer simulation as the product of a heterogeneous community with "a new cluster of skills in common, a new mode of producing scientific knowledge" brought into existence by "common activity centered around the computer."[1] Different kinds of expertise were "traded" around this common object. Galison claimed that ENIAC's Monte Carlo calculations "ushered physics into a place paradoxically dislocated from the traditional reality that borrowed from both experimental and theoretical domains" by building within computers "an artificial world in which 'experiments' (their term) could take place."[2] The status of simulation as a new kind of scientific experimentation has since been a major concern for philosophers of science and for historians of computing.[3]

Galison's discussion is influential more because of the concepts and argument it introduced than because of its analysis of the specifics of early nuclear calculations on ENIAC, its central narrative thread, or its analysis of the other early simulations discussed. Galison first describes in some detail John von Neumann's 1944 work on numerical methods for the treatment of hydrodynamic shocks of the kind produced within exploding nuclear weapons. Although a greatly simplified model of the ignition of a fusion weapon provided ENIAC with its first actual problem, run in late 1945 and very early 1946, that was not a Monte Carlo simulation. Galison uses archival correspondence to explore the techniques that were used to produce pseudo-random numbers and sketches von Neumann's published 1947 plan for the

simulation of neutron propagation in a fission reaction. However, he does not follow, or even mention, the development of that plan into an evolving set of ENIAC
programs that were then used for at least four distinct batches of Monte Carlo fission simulations during 1948 and 1949. Instead his narrative jumps from von
Neumann's 1947 enthusiasm for the technique to efforts by Los Alamos scientists
in 1949 and 1950 to simulate an entirely separate physical system: Edward Teller's
design for a "Super" fusion bomb.[4] Anne Fitzpatrick has filled some of these gaps
from the Los Alamos perspective.[5]

Monte Carlo methods proved to be of great importance to scientific computing
and operations research after their computerized debut on ENIAC. The original
code's descendants, run on computers at Los Alamos and Livermore, were a central
tool in weapons design practice. They defined the needs of two of the world's most
important purchasers of high-performance computer systems, and so, according to
Donald MacKenzie, they exerted a direct influence on the development of supercomputer architecture.[6] Monte Carlo methods were among the most important and
widely adopted techniques in the transformation of scientific practices made possible
by computer simulation.

Beyond their established importance to the history of science, the Monte Carlo
programs that were run on ENIAC in 1948 are of considerable importance to the
history of software. The program run in April and May of 1948 was both the first
computerized Monte Carlo simulation and the first program written in the new
paradigm to be executed on any computer. We located several of the original flow
diagrams (among them the final version prepared for the spring 1948 calculations),
the second major version of the program code in its entirety, and a detailed document describing changes made between the first and second versions of the program.
We also consulted the ENIAC operations log book, which documents each day of
machine activity during the period and every step in the process by which ENIAC
was converted into a machine able to run code written in the modern paradigm.
We believe the ENIAC Monte Carlo programs to be the best-documented application programs run on any computer during the 1940s, making possible a detailed
reconstruction of the program as it was run.

The evolution we document—from a computing plan through a series of flow
diagrams and planning documents to several later revisions and extensions of the
code—allows us to observe the first full revolution of what would later be thought
of as the software development life cycle. Though scholarly historians of computing
have good reason to be leery of the hunt for "firsts" that dominated our field in its
infancy, all this does give the code undeniable historical interest.

The calculations also shed light on an underexplored aspect of the work on
John von Neumann and his Princeton-based collaborators. We can reconstruct
changes in the way they thought about the structure of the computation as they

began to absorb the implications of the modern code paradigm and the flexibility that its control structures of branches and loops offered in comparison with earlier control methods, in which computations were expressed either in the linear form of a sequential computing plan or instruction tape or as a physical loop in a control tape.

Origins of Monte Carlo Simulation

There is no single Monte Carlo method. Rather, the term "Monte Carlo" describes a broad approach encompassing many specific techniques. As the name light-heartedly suggests, the defining element is the application of the laws of chance. Physicists had traditionally sought to create elegant equations to describe the outcomes of processes involving the interactions of huge numbers of particles. For example, Einstein's equations for Brownian motion could be used to describe the expected diffusion of a gas cloud over time without a need to simulate the random progression of its individual molecules.

There remained many situations in which tractable equations predicting the behavior of the overall system were elusive even though the factors influencing the progress of an individual particle could be described with tolerable accuracy. One such situation, and one of great interest to Los Alamos, was the progress of free neutrons hurtling through a nuclear weapon. The mathematician Stanislaw Ulam, who joined Los Alamos during World War II and later helped to invent the hydrogen bomb, subsequently noted that "most of the physics at Los Alamos could be reduced to the study of assemblies of particles interacting with each other, hitting each other, scattering, sometimes giving rise to new particles."[7]

Given the speed, direction, and position of a neutron and some physical constants, physicists could fairly easily compute the probability that it would, during the next tiny fraction of a second, crash into the nucleus of an unstable atom with sufficient force to break it up and release more neutrons in a process known as fission. They could also estimate the likelihood that neutrons would fly out of the weapon entirely, change direction after a collision, or get stuck. But even in the very short time span of a nuclear explosion, these simple actions could be combined in an almost infinite number of different sequences, defying even the brilliant physicists and mathematicians who had gathered at Los Alamos to simplify the proliferating chains of probabilities sufficiently to reach a traditional analytical solution.

The arrival of electronic computers offered an alternative: simulate the progress over time of a series of virtual neutrons representing members of the population released by the bomb's neutron initiator when conventional explosives compressed the weapon's core to form a critical mass and trigger its detonation. Following these neutrons through thousands of random events would settle the question statistically, yielding a set of neutron histories that closely approximated the actual distribution implied by the parameters provided to the program. If the number of fissions increased, then a self-sustaining chain reaction was underway. The chain reaction would end after an instant as the core blew itself to pieces, so the rapid proliferation of free neutrons, measured by a parameter the weapon designers called "alpha," was crucial to the bomb's effectiveness in converting enriched uranium into destructive power.[8]

The weapon used on Hiroshima is estimated to have fissioned only about 1 percent of its 141 pounds of highly enriched uranium, leaving bomb designers with a great deal of scope for refinement. With the Monte Carlo approach, the explosive yield of various hypothetical weapon designs could be estimated after fewer test detonations, conserving America's precious stockpiles of weapons-grade uranium and plutonium. This was, in essence, an experimental method within a simulated and much simplified reality.

The origins of the Monte Carlo approach have been explored in a number of histories and memoirs, so we need not attempt an exhaustive account here. Stanislaw Ulam later recalled developing the basic ideas with John von Neumann during a long car ride from Los Alamos to Lamy in 1946.[9] Over the next few years both men, along with several of their Los Alamos colleagues, would actively promote the new approach within the scientific community. For example, von Neumann discussed its possible use in his August 13 contribution to the Moore School Lectures of 1946.[10]

Early Planning for Los Alamos Monte Carlo Simulations

The earliest surviving evidence of planning for what became the ENIAC Monte Carlo simulations is in a manuscript dispatched as a letter from John von Neumann to the Los Alamos physicist Robert Richtmyer on March 11, 1947. It included a detailed computing plan for simulating the diffusion of neutrons through various materials in an atomic bomb.[11] The physical model by von Neumann proposed in his initial letter was a set of concentric spherical zones each containing a specified mixture of three types of material: "active" material in which fission would take place, "tamper" to reflect neutrons back toward the core, and material intended to slow down the neutrons before a collision would occur.[12]

The spherical model simplified computation, as the only data that were needed to model a neutron's path were its distance from the center, its angle of motion relative to the radius, its velocity, and the elapsed time.[13] This established the physical model that would be used the following year on ENIAC. In a lecture delivered in 1959, Richtmyer gave a cogent explanation of the approach, noting that the calculations "were about as sophisticated as any ever performed, in that they simulated complete chain reactions in critical and supercritical systems, starting with an assumed neutron distribution, in space and velocity, at an initial instant of time and then following all details of the reaction as it develops subsequently" and continuing: "To get an impression of the kind of problem treated in that early work, let us consider a critical assembly consisting simply of a small sphere of some fissionable material like U^{235} surrounded by a concentric shell of scattering material … ."[14]

Von Neumann wrote of the plan: "It is, of course, neither an actual 'computing sheet' for a (human) computer group, nor a set-up for the ENIAC, but I think that it is well suited to serve as a basis for either." However, his preference for ENIAC was already clear from the detailed consideration he gave to its use and from his conclusion that "the problem … in its digital form, is well suited for the ENIAC."[15] He does not seem to have thought of changing ENIAC's programming method yet.

The maximum complexity of an ENIAC program, in its initial programming mode, was determined by a variety of constraints spread around the machine. Those constraints were complex, and their interplay depended on the particular program. Von Neumann thought it "likely that the instructions given on this 'computing sheet' do not exceed the 'logical' capacity of the ENIAC."[16] He intended to implement the plan as a single ENIAC set-up, using the function tables to hold all the numerical data characterizing a particular physical configuration so that different material assemblies could be tested, by entering new data on the function tables, without changing the programming of the Monte Carlo method set up on ENIAC's other units.

Von Neumann planned that each punched card would represent the state of a single neutron at a single moment in time. After reading a card, ENIAC would simulate the further progress of that neutron through the bomb and would then punch a new card representing its updated status. Random numbers were used to determine how far the neutron would travel before colliding with another particle. If the neutron entered a zone containing different material, it was said to have "escaped," and a card was punched recording the point at which it had moved from one zone to another. Otherwise, a further random choice was made to determine the type of the collision: the neutron could be absorbed by the particle it hit (in which case it ceased to participate in the simulation); or it could bounce off the particle and be scattered with a randomly assigned change in direction and velocity; or the collision could trigger fission, yielding up to four "daughter" neutrons whose directions would be random. Cards were punched describing the outcome of the collision. The output deck would then be fed back in for repeated processing to follow the progress of the chain reaction as far as was required.

Von Neumann's eagerness to harness external computing resources for Los Alamos was understandable. Until 1952, Los Alamos itself operated no computers more sophisticated than IBM punched-card machines. So great was the appetite for computer power that a team from the lab had taken control of ENIAC for several weeks from the end of 1945, before it had even been declared fully operational. Several years later, when word spread that the National Bureau of Standards' Eastern Automatic Computer (known as SEAC) was close to working, Nick Metropolis and Robert Richtmyer arrived from Los Alamos to commandeer it.[17] Code for Los Alamos was also run on IBM's showpiece SSEC (Selective Sequence Electronic Calculator) in the company's New York headquarters.

In a letter sent to Stanislaw Ulam in March of 1947, von Neumann reported that the "computational set-up" had been "investigated more carefully from the ENIAC point of view by H.H. and A.K. (Mrs.) Goldstine." He continued: "They will probably have a reasonably complete ENIAC set-up in a few days. It seems that the set-up, as I sent it to you (assuming third-order polynomial approximations for all empirical functions), will exhaust about 80–90 percent of the ENIAC's programming capacity."[18] It is not clear how close the Goldstines got to creating a conventional ENIAC set-up for Monte Carlo simulation before they abandoned that approach. Instead, as we discussed in the preceding chapter, their efforts were redirected, by mid May at the latest, to a major effort to reconfigure ENIAC to support the modern code paradigm. By lifting most of the arbitrary constraints that ENIAC's original design had imposed on its versatility as a general-purpose computer, this allowed for development of a Monte Carlo program considerably more ambitious than the one originally sketched by von Neumann, at the cost of deferring its execution until ENIAC had been converted to the new control mode. It also meant abandoning ENIAC's original style of programming, and the experience with that technique that had been accumulated during its 1945–46 operation at the Moore School, for the unfamiliar approach associated with EDVAC and with the machine being built at the Institute for Advanced Studies.

In the second half of 1947, most of the work on computerized Monte Carlo simulation for Los Alamos was done in a single office at the Institute for Advanced Study in Princeton. Its inhabitants included Adele Goldstine and Robert Richtmyer, who had been dispatched by Los Alamos to represent it in interactions with what was known informally as the laboratory's "Princeton Annex."[19] However, the focus of their work soon shifted from Monte Carlo simulation to Hippo, a different kind of atomic simulation. Adele Goldstine remained engaged through 1947 and into 1948 on ENIAC coding for Hippo, until the insurmountable constraints of ENIAC's accumulator memory forced her to switch to coding for IBM's SSEC.

Primary responsibility for diagramming and coding Monte Carlo simulations seems to have shifted to the third inhabitant of that busy office, Klara ("Klari") von Neumann. Klara Dan had met John von Neumann in 1937, during one of his regular visits to his hometown of Budapest. In 1938 they had divorced their previous spouses (von Neumann's wife had already left him) and married. It was his second

marriage, her third. As war began in Europe, the new Mrs. von Neumann was settling into the role of an academic wife in Princeton. As the war raged, her husband
grew ever busier, ever more famous, and ever more frequently absent. Their marriage
was strained.[20]

Klara von Neumann was 35 years old when she began to contribute officially to
ENIAC conversion planning and Monte Carlo programming, around June of 1947.[21]
Her family had been wealthy and well connected, and she had grown up in an intellectually stimulating environment, but her formal education in mathematics and
science had concluded at an English boarding school. She wrote later: "I had some
college algebra and some trig, just enough to pass my matriculation exams, but that
was some fifteen-odd years ago and, even then, I only passed the test because my
math teacher rather appreciated my frank admission that I really did not understand
a single word of what I had learned."[22] She loved the easy camaraderie between the
Eastern European scientists she encountered at Los Alamos on a visit at Christmas
1945. According to George Dyson, who profiled her in a book titled *Turing's
Cathedral,* "sparks between Klari and Johnny were rekindled and they began collaborating" on his computer work. She took to it with remarkable ease, despite her
later and characteristically insecure self-denigration as a "mathematical moron"
serving for John as an "experimental rabbit" in a Pygmalion-like attempt to create
a computer coder from unpromising materials. Programming, she found, was "just
like a very amusing and rather intricate jigsaw puzzle, with the added incentive that
it was doing something useful."[23]

From Computing Plan to Flow Diagram

As the team in Princeton worked to transform the original computing plan into
the design of a fully articulated program for ENIAC, it was guided by the systematic approach to programming that John von Neumann and Herman Goldstine
had developed. Their first report on "Planning and Coding Problems for an
Electronic Computing Instrument," issued in April of 1947, put flow diagrams at
the heart of a fairly rigorous approach for the translation of mathematical expressions into programs written in the new coding paradigm.[24] The technique was
far more nuanced and mathematically expressive than the simplified flow charts
used in the introductory computing texts of later decades to represent sequences of
operations.

In his letter to Richtmyer, John von Neumann had expressed the computation as
a single sequence of 81 simple steps, most of which involved the retrieval or calculation of a single value. Predicates describing certain properties of the current situation
were evaluated and then used to specify whether certain subsequent steps should
be executed or ignored.

Flow diagrams, in contrast, explicitly showed the splitting and merging of possible paths of control through a computation. They illustrated the behavior of programs written in the modern code paradigm, whose possible execution paths would diverge following conditional transfer instructions. In some situations (for example, when deciding whether a neutron was traveling inward or outward in the assembly) translating the computing plan into a flow diagram was fairly straightforward. In other cases significant changes to the structure of the original computation were required.

Two complete Monte Carlo flow diagrams from 1947, and a number of partial and summary diagrams, have been preserved, and with the aid of those diagrams it is possible to trace preparatory work for the first version of the program—which culminated in a complete diagram, dated December 9, 1947—in considerable detail.[25] The development seems to have followed the notation and the methodology laid down in the "Planning and Coding" reports fairly closely and, given the success of the effort, appears to have demonstrated its utility. The diagrams themselves remain relatively easy to follow, and squeeze a great deal of information on different aspects of the program onto a single (in the final version) piece of paper.

The earlier diagram is in John von Neumann's hand. Associated with it are plans for the storage of numerical data in ENIAC's third function table and an estimate of the running time of the program.[26] The estimate was obtained by multiplying the "repetition rate" of each box in the flow chart (the number of times it would be executed in a typical computation) by the time taken to execute the code for each box. This required knowing the durations of the various instructions in "add times" (an "add time" being the quantum of time measurement in ENIAC programs). The existence of these estimates implies that Monte Carlo coding was first carried out with a version of the "60 order" instruction set current in the fall of 1947, though we have only found fragments of this code, the most significant being a subroutine used to generate pseudo-random numbers.[27] The timing estimates were later refined with the aid of an overview flow diagram representing only the high-level structure of the computation.[28]

A complex program by the standards of the day, the December 1947 flow diagram included 79 operation boxes, many specifying multiple computational steps. That diagram was kept up to date as the design evolved and as changes were made to the algorithms in various parts of the calculation, as summarized in table 8.1. The program was carefully structured into largely independent functional regions, many of them single-entrance, single-exit blocks. This structure first appeared in von Neumann's diagram, which was divided into ten spatially distinct subdiagrams linked by connectors. Twelve regions were made explicit and labeled in the subsequent overview diagram; they are clearly visible in the December 1947 diagram, in

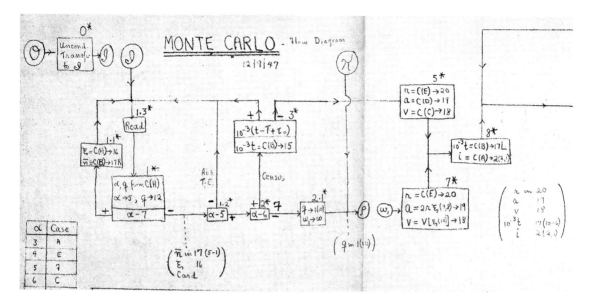

Figure 8.1
A detail from the December 1947 flow diagram showing 11 of the 79 operation boxes.
(reproduced from Library of Congress courtesy of Marina von Neumann Whitman)

which many of the boundaries between the regions are marked by annotations in the form of "storage tables" noting the variables calculated in the preceding region and the accumulator assigned to each.[29]

As table 8.1 indicates, the evolution of the program could also be tracked through the rather confusing conventions used to assign numbers to the operation boxes in the flow diagram. The basic sequence of boxes 0* to 54* implemented the functionality of the original computing plan along with some modifications to von Neumann's original proposals suggested by Los Alamos at the beginning of April. The switch from ENIAC's original programming method to its new implementation of the modern code paradigm allowed for a significant expansion of the program's scope and complexity. Thus, this original sequence accounted for little more than half of the eventual code. Changes made as development progressed from the original plan to the first Monte Carlo program went beyond elaborating storage mechanics or expressing processes in a different notation to altering the structure of the computational process itself. Among other things, these changes reduced the need for card operations, which were thousands of times slower than electronic processing, and enabled ENIAC to automate ever greater portions of the overall Monte Carlo process. In the subsections that follow, we summarize five important changes that were made in 1947.

Table 8.1
Regional structure and summary of the evolution of the Monte Carlo programs. Descriptions are ours, but the structure and letters assigned are from an original flow diagram. Numbers in cells are the box labels used on the various diagrams.

Region	Description	Von Neumann/Richtmyer plan, early 1947	Von Neumann's flow diagram, summer 1947	"First run" program (from Dec. 1947) flow diagram, spring 1948	"Second run" program, autumn 1948
A	Read card and store the neutron's characteristics. If the neutron is a fission product, calculate new values for its direction and velocity.	0	0*–8*	1*–8*	Restructured Virgin cards: 0–6 Output cards: 10–16
	Calculate parameter λ* the random parameter used in region E to determine the expected distance to a collision.	N/A (numbers produced externally)	9*–17*	New algorithm 1°–4°	40–45
B	Find neutron's velocity interval; this value is used in region D to find relevant cross-section values.		$\overline{1}$–$\overline{13}$	Simplified $\overline{1}$–$\overline{7}$	30–36
C	Calculate distance to zone boundary.	1–15	18*–23*	18*–23*	20–26
D	Calculate cross-section of material in zone.		$\overline{14}$–17.1	$\overline{14}$–17.1, 24*	46
E	Determine if terminal event on current trajectory is collision or escape.	16–47	24*–27*	25*–27*	47–49
	Determine if a census comes first.		28*–29*	28*–30*	50–54
F	Discriminate between terminal events. Update neutron characteristics as needed.	47	30*–35*	31*–35*	55–57
G	Refresh random number.		Inline code 6*	Subroutine ρ/ω	Subroutine ρ/ω
H	Determine collision type (absorption, scattering or fission).	48–53	$\overline{18}$–27	$\overline{18}$–27	65–69
J	Elastic scattering.	54–59, 61–68	51*–52*	51*–52*	74–76
K	Inelastic scattering.		53*–54*	53*–54*	75–78
L	Absorption/fission.	54–59, 65–81	36*–46*	Simplified 36*–39*, 46*	70–73
M	Print card and restart main loop.	No looping 51, 69, 73, 77, 81	47*–50*	37.1*, 47*–50*	58–64
N	Zonal escape.	48–50	Computation loops without printing	Computation loops without printing	New process 79–85

Change 1: Relaxation of Notation

A close look at the succession of draft flow diagrams illuminates the experience of using this technique to develop an actual program. John von Neumann's early diagram stuck closely to the notation published in the "Planning and Coding" reports: symbolic names were used for storage locations, and substitution and operation boxes were used systematically to keep the mathematical notation separate from the handling of storage. Von Neumann extended the notation slightly by including operations in the alternative boxes, and by using ad hoc notes within operation and storage boxes to document the effect of input and output operations.

The members of the team seem to have found the complete methodology defined in the report excessively cumbersome. By December their use of the flow-diagram notation had evolved visibly. For example, the symbolic labels for storage locations had been replaced by explicit references to ENIAC's accumulators. Decisions about data storage had been made, and evidently no benefit had been perceived in deferring their documentation to a later stage in the process. The careful distinctions made in the reports between the different types of boxes and their contents were becoming increasingly blurred: the substitution boxes that are meant to control loops had largely been replaced by operation boxes, and storage updates that officially should have been located in separate operation boxes were appearing in other boxes with increasing frequency.

Change 2: A Subroutine to Handle Random Numbers

At the heart of a Monte Carlo simulation is choosing among different possible outcomes on the basis of their probability. These choices were driven by random numbers, which in 1947 were therefore required by Los Alamos in unprecedented numbers. In von Neumann's original plan for the computation, each card fed into ENIAC included the random numbers used to determine a neutron's fate. Getting those numbers onto the cards would have required using an external process to produce cards holding random numbers, followed by a merge process using conventional punched-card machines to create a new card holding both the existing data on a particular neutron (read from one card) and the random numbers (read from another).

As planning continued, von Neumann figured out that ENIAC could itself produce pseudo-random numbers whenever they were needed. In various letters, he described a technique that involved squaring an eight-digit or a ten-digit number and then extracting the middle digits to serve as the next value.[30] Thanks to the new programming mode, the logical complexity of a program was limited only by the space available on the function table for its instructions. Thus, these numbers could be produced within the Monte Carlo program itself much more rapidly than they could be read from punched cards.

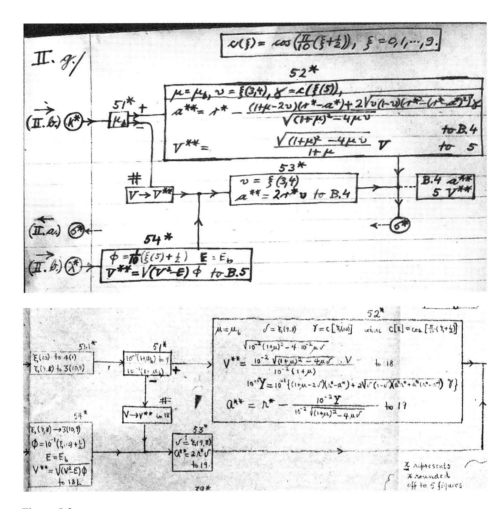

Figure 8.2
The structure and the mathematics of this part of the calculation were almost unchanged between drafts, but in John von Neumann's early draft (above) the flow diagram refers to symbolic storage locations (e.g., B.4). The December 1947 version (below) uses accumulator numbers directly for storage (e.g., 19). Note also the complex expressions accommodated within individual flow-diagram boxes such as 52*. (reproduced from the Library of Congress courtesy of Marina von Neumann Whitman)

In the earlier draft flow diagram, a cluster of three boxes representing this process (without providing much detail on the algorithm to be used) was simply duplicated at the four points in the computation at which a new random number was needed. The December 1947 version placed a detailed treatment of the process in a special box, entered from two separate places in the flow diagram. Newly-computed random digits were placed in one of ENIAC's accumulators, from which they could be retrieved when required.[31] This exploited the newly developed concept of a subroutine; it also demonstrated, apparently for the first time, the incorporation of a subroutine call into the Goldstine–von Neumann flow-diagram notation.[32] So far, the "Planning and Coding" series had not dealt with subroutines; they would be covered in the final installment issued in 1948. However, the April 1947 publication did introduce a "variable remote connection" notation that diagrammed code in which the destination of a jump was set dynamically. In the December 1947 flow diagram, a variable remote connection was used to control the return to the main sequence at the end of the subroutine box.

The invention of the "closed subroutine," defined by the historian Martin Campbell-Kelly as one that "appeared only once in a programme and was called by a special transfer-of-control sequence at each point in the programme where it was needed," is conventionally attributed to David Wheeler's work with EDSAC, which went into operation in 1949.[33] This is distinguished from the "open subroutine" in which a block of code is duplicated as needed, a technique that had been used on the Harvard Mark I some years earlier. We believe that this ENIAC Monte Carlo program was the first code with a closed subroutine to be executed.[34]

Change 3: Lookup of Cross-Section Data

The likelihood that a moving object will crash into an obstacle during a particular time period will change with its velocity, as will the likelihood of a destructive outcome. In nuclear physics, the probability that a neutron will interact with a nucleus to produce a particular result, such as absorption, fission, or scattering, is referred to as a *collision cross-section*. That probability depends on both the velocity of the neutron and the nature of the material it is traveling through. Von Neumann's original plan represented the cross-sections as functions of velocity, and he noted that these functions could be tabulated, interpolated, or approximated using polynomials. By the time the first flow diagram was produced, von Neumann had decided to use lookup tables. The range of possible neutron velocities was divided into ten intervals, giving 160 possible combinations of collision type, velocity interval, and material. A representative value of the cross-section function for each combination was stored in an array on the numeric function table, and von Neumann's flow diagram incorporated a new sequence of boxes labeled from $\overline{1}$ through $\overline{27}$ to handle the lookup procedure.[35]

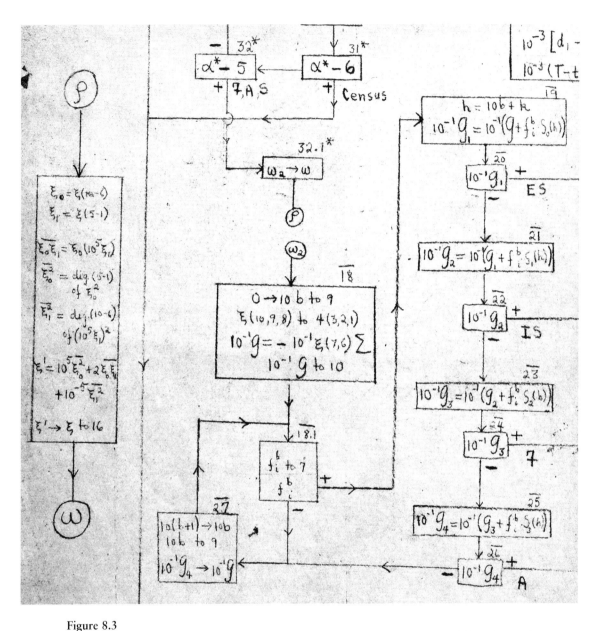

Figure 8.3
This detail from the December 1947 flow diagram shows both the subroutine (far left) and one of the points from which it is called (the connection ρ following box 32.1*, the box that sets the value of the variable remote connection ω to ω₂ so that the program will continue with box $\overline{18}$ on completion of the subroutine).
(reproduced from the Library of Congress courtesy of Marina von Neumann Whitman)

A neutron's velocity interval was found by searching through a table of interval boundaries. This search was coded as a loop, and that code provides an early example of an iterative procedure whose purpose was not simple calculation. Once the velocity interval had been located, the appropriate cross-section value could easily be retrieved from the function table by calculating the address corresponding to the current combination of parameters.

The design of the search went through a number of revisions. The correct interval for a neutron was found by comparing its velocity with the middle value in the table and then performing a linear search through the top or the bottom half of the table, as appropriate. That strategy can be seen in the initial branching in the diagrams shown in figure 8.4, which in each case is followed by two similarly structured loops. Originally, the address m of the current position in the table was used to control the loop, and the number of the interval k was then calculated from this in different ways, depending on how the loop had terminated (boxes $\overline{10}$ through $\overline{13}$). This was soon changed, however, so that the interval number itself was used to control the loop, which greatly simplified the termination conditions. These changes give a vivid impression of the team gradually acquiring a feel for idiomatic techniques of efficient programming in the modern code paradigm.

The introduction of velocity intervals also made it possible to simulate fission more realistically. In the initial plan, the "daughter" neutrons produced by fission all had the same velocity. After velocity intervals were introduced, a representative value known as the "center of gravity" was stored for each interval. This allowed different velocities to be easily generated for daughter neutrons by using a digit from the current random number to select a velocity interval.

Change 4: Census Times

The biggest change in scope from the initial computing plan to the program executed in the spring of 1948 was the change from following an individual neutron until it experienced its next "event" to managing a population of neutrons over time. Translating the computing plan into an ENIAC program made explicit, and partially automated, the work needed to manage multiple neutrons and multiple cycles of simulation. Code implementing the steps defined in the original plan to process one event for one neutron was wrapped in several levels of loops involving both automatic and manual processing steps.

The program was organized around the notion of "census times." That idea had been introduced when Richtmyer, in his response to von Neumann's original proposals, noted that it would generate output decks in which cards could represent snapshots of neutrons at widely different points in time. As a "remedy for this difficulty," Richtmyer suggested "follow[ing] the chains for a definite time rather than for a definite number of cycles of operation." He continued: "After each cycle, all cards

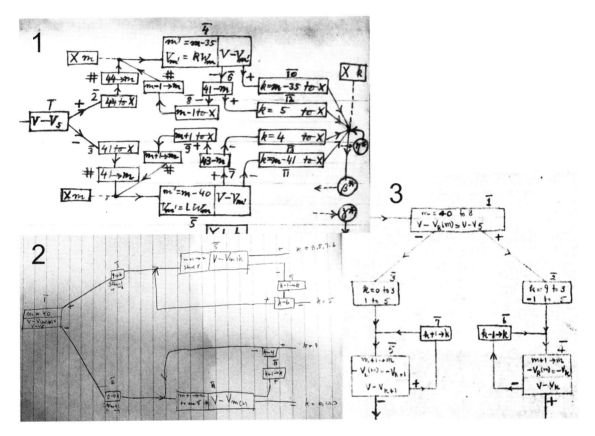

Figure 8.4
Three progressively more optimized versions of region B of the flow diagram, which finds a neutron's velocity interval. Image 1 is from von Neumann's original flow diagram; image 3 is from the December 1947 diagram; image 2 is an intermediate version.
(undated page containing handwritten flow diagram with nine boxes, JvN-LOC, box 11, folder 8; reproduced from the Library of Congress courtesy of Marina von Neumann Whitman)

having t[ime] greater than some preassigned value would be discarded, and the next cycle of calculation performed with those remaining. This would be repeated until the number of cards in the deck diminishes to zero."[36] These pre-assigned values were dubbed "census times."

A statistically valid snapshot of the overall neutron population at each census time would be produced, just as governments make measurements of the characteristics of their national populations at certain periodic dates. A census interval of one shake (ten nanoseconds) was chosen, this unit having been devised during the Manhattan Project as a convenient yardstick for the compressed timescale of a nuclear explosion.[37] The census concept was widely adopted for Monte Carlo simulations.[38]

Change 5: Simulating Multiple Events per Cycle

According to the original computing plan, each cycle of computation would track the progress of a neutron only as far as its next event (scattering, zonal escape, total escape, absorption, or fission). One or more new cards representing the consequences of the event would then be produced. The additional logical complexity afforded by the new programming mode made it possible for ENIAC to simulate more than one event in a neutron's career before printing a new card for it. If a neutron was scattered or moved into a new zone but had not yet reached the census time, the program branched back to an earlier region to follow its progress further rather than producing an output card immediately. This increased the complexity of the program, but reduced the amount of manual card processing required.

Figure 8.5 gives an overview of how these changes worked in practice. The initial stack of neutron cards was read one at a time from the input hopper. After reading each card, ENIAC punched one or more output cards. If a neutron reached the current census time without incident, it was followed no further for the moment and ENIAC output a "census" card with its updated information. When a free neutron was absorbed or escaped the weapon, the terminal event was logging on an output card for later analysis. If its terminal collision caused fission, the output card included the number of daughter neutrons unleashed as a "weight" field.

ENIAC's operators would then use a suitable configured sorter, a specialized kind of punched-card machine, to separate the output deck into three trays. One tray accumulated terminal event cards representing neutrons that did not have to be processed again after escaping or being absorbed. Another tray accumulated census cards representing neutrons that had reached the current census time without incident. The third tray held the cards representing simulated fission events. In an exploding weapon, each free neutron would, on average, trigger a fission every shake or so (and therefore each census time).[39] Because the neutron responsible had not reached the end of the current census period, the fission cards were carried over to ENIAC's input hopper, where they were read once but internally processed repeatedly. Each processing run followed the progress of a single daughter neutron generated by the fission up to the next census time or its terminal event. The output cards were sorted in case further fissions had occurred, and the process was repeated until ENIAC's output hopper held no fission cards.

Each neutron had now reached the census time, so the target census time was incremented and the next census period began. Operators manually duplicated or discarded census cards from the output deck, which represented neutrons still active at the end of the previous period, to create a new input deck of exactly 100 cards.

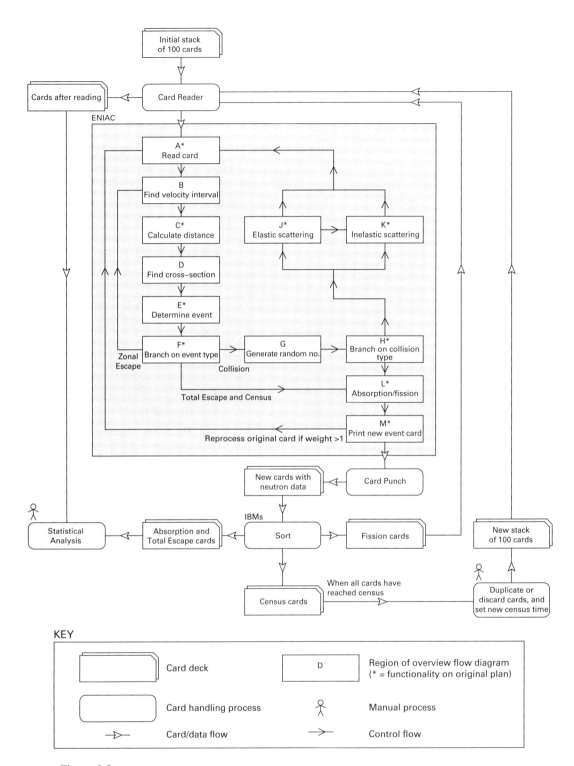

Figure 8.5
The shaded region in this diagram shows the structure of the "First Run" Monte Carlo program, including program regions. The unshaded region shows the card operations required outside ENIAC.

The team had decided to start each census period with the same number of neutron cards, even though the actual neutron population careening inside a bomb tends to rise precipitously after its detonator is triggered. Allowing the sample size to grow or shrink with the simulated population would sacrifice either accuracy or practicality. A larger sample population required punching more cards, taking more time, and doing more work. A smaller sample could be processed more easily but would be less statistically reliable as a representation of the larger population being simulated.

All the cards punched during the computation were retained. These could be analyzed to show the distribution of neutrons and fissions in time and space, something Richtmyer had mentioned as desirable. They would also reveal trends in neutron velocity, the relative frequency of events such as escape or fission at that instant, and the rate at which the population of free neutrons was increasing during each census period. Tracking the latter would allow Los Alamos to estimate the overall size of the population of free neutrons at each point in the simulation—something that ENIAC did not itself track.

Taken together, these five changes give a sense of how much work was needed to move from a computing plan—even one as careful and detailed as the one John von Neumann produced for the Monte Carlo simulation—to a practical and efficient implementation for a digital computer. In the process, the team overcame a range of practical and conceptual challenges to develop and apply techniques we would now recognize as indispensable idioms of programming practice, such as the use of a subroutine and the efficient coding of loops.

9

ENIAC Tries Its Luck

John and Klara von Neumann referred to the three main sets of Monte Carlo chain reaction calculations carried out for Los Alamos in 1948 and 1949 as the "first run," the "second run," and the "third run." Each run investigated a number of "problems" modeling different physical configurations, and the program code evolved between runs as experience was gained. The word "run" may echo the idea (later ubiquitous) of "running" a program or may refer instead to the physical movement of people and materials to Aberdeen and back, in the sense of a "bombing run" or a "school run." Von Neumann used the word "expedition" to refer to these trips, and to later trips made to Aberdeen to experiment with numerical weather predictions.[1] "Expedition" is a striking word, capturing a world in which computers were scare and exotic things by evoking the scientific tradition of mounting long, arduous, and painstakingly planned field expeditions to observe eclipses, uncover buried cities, or explore the polar regions. Explorers returned with knowledge that could never be obtained at home. Using ENIAC was an adventure, a journey to an unfamiliar place, and often something of an ordeal.

The "First Run" (April and May of 1948)

Anne Fitzpatrick, having had access to internal Los Alamos progress reports and to other classified documents, concluded that all of the ENIAC Monte Carlo work done for Los Alamos in 1948 and 1949 had focused on fission weapons, rather than relating directly to the fusion-powered hydrogen bomb. The initial seven calculations, done in the spring of 1948, were "primarily for the purpose of checking techniques, and according to Nick Metropolis, did not attempt to solve any type of weapons problem."[2] It is, however, clear that Los Alamos viewed the work on ENIAC as crucial to its own progress in designing new weapons. Fitzpatrick continued:

Throughout March and April Carson Mark [director of the lab's Theoretical Division] complained in his monthly reports about the delays encumbered by the fission program because of the slow pace of the ENIAC's conversion and "mechanical condition." The whole point of having fission problems run on ENIAC in the first place, Mark noted, was to speed up T Division's work by "mechanization" of calculations.[3]

Even a man as well connected as John von Neumann could not simply show up in Aberdeen and ask his friends for the keys to ENIAC. There were bureaucratic procedures to follow, and there was a chain of command to respect. On February 6, 1948, von Neumann wrote to Norris Bradbury, director of Los Alamos, asking him to make a formal request for time on ENIAC. Von Neumann, whose instincts for organizational politics were essential to his rise as a power broker in the emerging federal science bureaucracy, reminded Bradbury to "mention in your letter how much you appreciate all the courtesies that have been extended [to] your staff by the BRL and how extremely important the ENIAC is to your work, etc.," adding: "This will greatly help Colonel Simon politically and will also be good for our future relations with the BRL."[4]

The terms had already been worked out informally with Colonel Leslie Simon and his subordinates, but delays were imposed by the arrival of ceiling contractors, by testing, and by the delayed installation of some new hardware.[5] Bradbury sent the necessary official request, flattery included, to the Office of Chief of Ordnance. On March 13, von Neumann wrote to Carson Mark, leader of the Theoretical Division at Los Alamos, that the Monte Carlo problem was "set up and ready to go."[6] John and Klara von Neumann visited Aberdeen on April 8, 1948, and Klara remained behind for the next month to work with Metropolis, who had by then completed the initial reconfiguration of ENIAC to support the modern code paradigm. Adele Goldstine and Robert Richtmyer, for whom von Neumann had also requested clearance, did not come to Aberdeen. Perhaps they were too focused on Hippo.

The first successful "production run" made on Monte Carlo took place on April 17, 1948. However, the machine was still plagued by "troubles," and the calculation did not begin in earnest until April 28.[7] Progress seems to have been slowed far more by hardware glitches than by program bugs, which is interesting insofar as no one had previously attempted to debug a program written in the modern code paradigm. The small number of programming errors discovered is a tribute to the care with which the program had been planned, to the depth of thought the Princeton group had given to the new programming style, and perhaps also to ENIAC's relative friendliness to debugging.

We have not located the program code for the first run. However, triangulating from several sources gives a reliable sense of how the first Monte Carlo simulation worked. First, we have the series of flow diagrams discussed in the preceding chapter. Second, we have a complete program listing for the second run in late 1948. Third, we have a lengthy archival document, "Actual Running of the Monte Carlo Problems on the ENIAC," describing the programming techniques used in both versions. This explicitly highlights changes made between the two runs. Fourth, we have draft flow diagrams for the second run, which in many regions are identical to the diagram produced for the first run. Finally, archival materials for the first run document the allocation of data to ENIAC's accumulators, the layout of constant data on the third function table, the card format used, and the associated use of the constant transmitter.[8]

The calculations performed during the first run simulated seven different situations, each represented by changing some of the data stored on the third function table. Richtmyer wrote:

Certain experimentally determined nuclear data are obviously needed. One must know the so-called macroscopic cross-sections, that is, the probabilities, per unit distance travelled, of the various processes (absorption, elastic scattering, inelastic scattering) in each medium, as a function of the neutron's velocity. For scattering, one must know the angular distribution, that is, the relative probabilities of various angles of scattering; for inelastic scattering one must also know the energy distribution of the scattered neutrons; and, for fission, one must know the average number and energy distribution of the emitted neutrons.[9]

This data mentioned in that passage constituted the most militarily sensitive part of the entire operation. Documents retained in the archives record in triplicate the receipt of classified material by Klara von Neumann on various occasions, sometimes (as with "cross section data" on January 16, 1948) from her husband.[10]

We have already discussed several of the draft instruction sets that were created for ENIAC during the planning process. For the first run, ENIAC was set up to implement 79 rather than the planned 60 instructions.[11] Beyond updating the two-digit codes corresponding to the instruction mnemonics, the main challenge in updating the Monte Carlo program would have been to recode its shift operations in the new instruction set.

By May 10, 1948, the first Monte Carlo run was all over. John von Neumann wrote on May 11 to Ulam that "ENIAC ran for 10 days. It was producing 50% of these 10×16 hours, this includes two Sundays and all troubles … . It did 160 cycles ('censuses,' 100 input cards each) on 7 problems. All interesting ones are stationary at the end of this period. The results are very promising and the method is clearly a 100% success."[12] Three days later, he added: "There is now a total output of over 20,000 cards. We have started to analyze them, but … it will take some doing to interpret it."[13]

The ordeal had taken a toll on Klara von Neumann. According to her husband, she was "very run-down after the siege in Aberdeen, lost 15lbs" and had gone for a medical checkup.[14] Plans for a joint vacation with the Ulams were abandoned, and in June she wrote to Stanislaw that she was "just so furious" that her husband had "stopped" her from going to Europe, and that she felt "a little better but by no means well" and "was still being annoyed by various tests and treatments."[15] Her propensity to depression has been well documented elsewhere, though these letters describe no specific ailment.

She did, however, find the energy to document the techniques used in a manuscript cryptically headed "III: Actual Technique—The Use of the ENIAC."[16] It began with a discussion of the conversion of ENIAC to support the new code paradigm, then documented the data format used on the punched cards, and then outlined in reasonable detail the overall structure of the computation and the operations performed at each stage.

The Second Run (October and November of 1948)

The Monte Carlo approach had proved its worth for the simulation of neutron diffusion, and it was time to apply it to the actual weapon configurations under investigation at Los Alamos. According to Anne Fitzpatrick, this second series of problems "constituted actual weapons calculations," including "an investigation of the alpha for UH_3, "a 'hydride' core implosion configuration," and "a supercritical configuration known as the Zebra."[17] The calculations were run as one of three main problems tackled during a large block of ENIAC time that had been reserved for the Atomic Energy Commission (the body overseeing Los Alamos) from early October to late December of 1948. Klara von Neumann returned to Aberdeen on October 18, 1948, and was joined by Metropolis two days later. Production work began on October 22. On November 4, John von Neumann wrote to Ulam: "Things at Aberdeen have gone very well. The present segment of the Monte Carlo program is likely to be completed at the end of this week or early next week."[18]

Changes between the first and second versions of the Monte Carlo program were described in some detail in a report titled "Actual Running of the Monte Carlo Problems on the ENIAC." An expanded and updated version of the earlier "Actual Technique" report, it was written by Klara von Neumann and was edited in collaboration with Metropolis and John von Neumann during September of 1949. It contains a detailed description of the computations, highlighting changes in the flow diagram, in the program code, and in the manual procedures between the two versions.[19]

The physical model used and the calculations performed to follow the paths of individual neutrons were little changed. Representations of the zones of different materials and of the zonal escape of neutrons were modified. Most of the changes were operational optimizations. For example, some early sections of the program were reordered to marginally increase overall efficiency, and collision cross-section ratios for each zone were pre-computed and then stored on the function table instead of being calculating when needed.

The most important change was to further increase the level of automation in the overall Monte Carlo procedure. During the first run, the newly punched cards representing neutrons that had reached the current census time were sorted out into a separate pile. Not until all the fissions occurring before that time had been processed were the census cards read back in to simulate the next-period careers of their neutrons. Following the entire neutron population up to the end of one census period before proceeding to the next census period allowed von Neumann and Metropolis to intervene after each census time to adjust the population size, but it also introduced considerable inefficiency. Each deck of cards produced by ENIAC was passed through an IBM sorter to separate the neutrons according to what had happened to them, and at the end of a census period the input deck for the next period was assembled and adjusted by hand.

The second run eliminated both kinds of manual processing by including "in the logical sequence and coding of the program, an automatic way of handling the beginning and ending of a time cycle."[20] Now a neutron reaching the end of a census period was followed into the next period without waiting for all the other neutrons to catch up. There was thus no need to separate fission cards from census cards, or from other card types, and each deck of cards punched by ENIAC could be transferred immediately to its input hopper for further processing.[21]

Complete escape, absorption, or fission still ended a free neutron's career. The handling of zonal escape changed to limit the amount of time spent processing neutrons that were scattered in the outer zone of tamper material found in several second run problems. Each time a neutron escaped from one zone to another in the second run, a card was punched and the computation continued with the next neutron, whereas in the first run these "zonal escapes" had not been logged.

In the first run, manual procedures were employed to keep the population of simulated neutrons roughly constant by reestablishing an input deck of 100 cards at the beginning of each census period. In the second run, "no attempt was made to keep the input stack at a fixed number," according to Klara von Neumann's report. Instead, the "weighting" of each neutron surviving at the end of a census period was adjusted so that it gave rise to two neutrons in the next period. This ensured that the sample population increased even if the real-life population being simulated was decreasing, and that a larger sample of neutrons was available at the statistically more interesting end of the simulation.[22]

Even the production of the initial deck of neutrons was automated. A new section of code was introduced to read so-called virgin cards. Rather than specifying the properties of individual neutrons, these cards simply defined the times at which new neutrons would enter the simulation, and random velocities were then allocated automatically. Following these neutrons through one iteration of the simulation generated output cards in the normal format, which were fed back in to continue the simulation as normal.

The new operating procedures distinguished between subcritical reactions and near-critical or super-critical reactions. For subcritical systems, for which simply following the physics would lead to a declining neutron population, the "virgin" cards were punched with start times throughout the course of the simulation. The simulated injection of new neutrons increased to maximize the neutron proportion still active when the simulation finished, ensuring a sufficient sample size for final analysis. The program for the second run therefore contained two separate card-reading sequences. The appropriate one was selected by setting the target address of an unconditional transfer instruction on the function table before the computation was started. The same technique was also used to control certain aspects of the processing of zonal escape and to include special code sections that were required for particular problems.

ENIAC finished processing this series of problems by November 7, 1948. On November 18, John von Neumann wrote: "The whole second Monte Carlo seems to have been successful. The ENIAC functioned marvelously. About 10^5 cards were produced in three weeks, and while the material hasn't been analyzed as yet, there is reason to hope that it contains a considerable amount of valued and useful information."[23]

We uncovered two flow diagrams describing this run and a complete code listing that very closely matches one of them.[24] The two diagrams exhibit levels of formality similar to the first run diagram of December 1947, suggesting that a stable idiomatic usage of the flow diagram notation was emerging with experience. The code listing, in Klara von Neumann's handwriting, covers 28 pages. It is broken up into sequentially numbered six-line sections, each corresponding to a single row in the function tables holding the code. At many points, annotations provide a simulated trace of the progress of the program, checking the effect of the instructions on typical data values.

The code is faithful to the structure of the flow diagrams for the first and second runs. It includes a subroutine called from two places with a variable return address, and it implements the modular structure of the diagrams as code blocks with fairly disciplined entry and exit points.[25] Its main sequence filled rows –2, –1, and 12–97 of the first function table and rows –2 to 96 of the second function table. With about 100 digits in these rows unused, that amounted to about 2,220 digits of program code, representing about 840 instructions.[26] The first run was similarly complex—some aspects were simplified for the second run, but that was balanced by the addition of some new data fields and by the automation of some tasks that had required manual card sorting in the initial version.

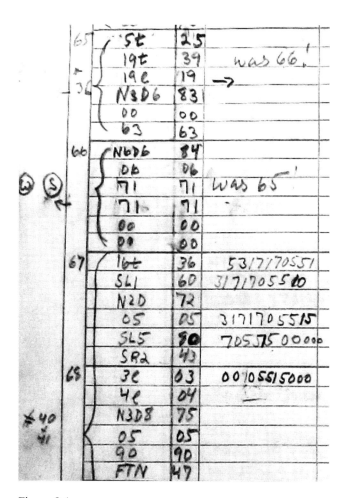

Figure 9.1

A detail from page 7 of the second run program code showing 13 of the 840 instructions in the program. The numbers 65–68 indicate positions on the function tables, and annotations in the left margin refer back to the corresponding boxes on the flow diagram. Each line gives the two decimal digits entered on the function table and, when those numbers code an operation rather than a data field, the corresponding mnemonic such as 3l or N3D8. Some corrections have been made in pencil, and blocks 65 and 66 of code have been erased and substituted for each other.

(reproduced from Library of Congress courtesy of Marina von Neumann Whitman)

The code for the second run included a number of variant paths and sections. It was configured for a specific problem by manually changing a few transfer addresses and constants before execution. The most significant variant section deals with the elastic scattering of neutrons in "light materials." This stemmed from interest at Los Alamos in the use of uranium hydride cores. The hydrogen separates from the uranium, acting as a moderator to slow neutrons and to reduce the critical mass of uranium needed to build a weapon. Edward Teller believed (wrongly, it turned out) that the opportunity to build more bombs from scarce weapons-grade uranium would justify the inevitable decline in explosive yield.[27]

Klara von Neumann left for Los Alamos around December 1, presumably to help interpret the results of the second run and to lay the groundwork for future calculations. She was followed by a letter from her husband expressing "dense confusion" after what seemed to be some kind of crisis as she prepared to provide "proof of [her] intellectual independence" via this solo trip.[28] In a second letter, written after finding Klara "catastrophically depressed" during a phone call, John von Neumann declared himself "scared out of my wits" that stress would leave his wife ruined "physically and emotionally." Even someone blessed with ample self-confidence and robust mental health would feel somewhat daunted at the prospect of defending her mathematical technique to Stanislaw Ulam, Edward Teller, and Enrico Fermi (the latter already a Nobel laureate). Seeking independence within her husband's shadow only added to the challenges facing Klara, despite his fervent attempts to allay her worries about aging ("your problems and dispositions are perennial, and age is the least of your troubles"), about her intelligence ("a bright girl"), and about her character ("and a very nice one").[29]

Klara von Neumann's worries could only have been compounded when an error was discovered in the hydride calculations. "It seems that one electronic computation is wrong in the Problem No. 4," Ulam wrote to John von Neumann on February 7. "Nick found out which it was. The problem has to be repeated."[30] Carson Mark complained in his regular Theory Division progress report that it was "evident that the ENIAC has not advanced beyond an experimental stage in doing serious computation for this project."[31]

The Argonne Monte Carlo Simulations (December 1948)

The second run Monte Carlo calculations for Los Alamos were followed immediately by a set of simulations performed by the Los Alamos physicist Jon Reitz, which was concluded by November 18. On November 29, Maria Mayer, Elmer Eisner, and James Alexander arrived from Argonne National Laboratory to run another Monte Carlo simulation.[32] Mayer's problem concerned neutron diffusion in a reactor and simulated eight different zones of material. It borrowed heavily from the work of the von Neumanns, which Klara described simply as "the usual Monte Carlo procedure" with some significant modifications including a shift of census intervals from fixed time to fixed distance (so that slow neutrons, important in reactors but not in bombs, could be modeled), a much more complex system of zones and movement, and special handling of the outer moderator zone to simplify the calculation.

A week later, John von Neumann wrote to his wife that "the problem was behaving quite unreasonably, presumably because of some logical or algebraical fault." A second letter spelled out the problems more clearly:

a) the Chicagoans had had the ENIAC since December 1. b) It had been in and out of trouble, and had worked a total of 3 days or so out of 6. It was improving, during the 36 hours immediately preceding it had run once for 24 hours uninterrupted. c) Maria stated that their code had been found to be "faultless" by "Pedaling" and by comparing with trial calculations: d) They were, however in bad logical (or geometrical?) trouble on December 6: the populations were increasing impossibly fast … . Neither the Chicagoans, nor I who spent two hours with them, had much of a diagnosis.[33]

The ENIAC log shows that, with round-the-clock operation, the calculation was concluded successfully on December 19 despite troubles with air conditioning, with one of the accumulators, and with the function tables.

The Third Run (May and June of 1949)

Carson Mark's griping about problems in the second run did not destroy enthusiasm for ENIAC-based Monte Carlo simulation, though surviving letters indicate that there was considerable tension among the collaborators. Klara von Neumann traveled to Chicago to work with Maria Mayer to investigate ideas for improving the weapon calculations for the pending third run, including the distance-based census method. In a letter dated March 27, 1949, John von Neumann argued against their adoption: "After all the nonsense that has taken place in the course of the last year—none of it through your fault, and some of the worst of it over your opposition—we have no longer the privilege of additional experimenting. At least not for the next run."[34]

By this point planning was underway for a third batch of calculations. Klara's role grew more prominent with each expedition. Ulam wrote that during her preparatory trip to Los Alamos she "impressed everyone very much by her knowledge of coding and flow diagramming."[35] Klara wrote to Harris Mayer (no relation to Maria) at Los Alamos that she had "looked a little more closely at both the available space on the numerical function table and also, with the help of Johnny, I have set-up a flow diagram for Maria's scheme of trying the tamper." From this Klara evaluated the time and space implications of coding this new method: "It will take approximately 35 lines of orders. It also looks as if it may take considerable time in computing it. (About 1/2 second per collision.)"[36]

Klara's relationship with Nick Metropolis seems to have been strained by that point, perhaps by recriminations in the wake of the errors that had been encountered in the second run. John consoled her: "For heaven's sake don't let your experience with Nick M. wreck your professional attitude and morale in the long run. This sort of thing happens again and again, but you came out if it with flying colors, and you can see that neither Edward [Teller] nor I think less of you for that … ." John's letters sought to bolster Klara against insecurity and depression, reassuring her of her talents and promising her that "explicit professional success" was within her grasp to the extent that she desired it rather than simply aspiring to "quiet and opportunity to work for yourself."[37]

Whatever inner turmoil Klara von Neumann felt was not evident in the crisp, confident notes she sent as she took the lead in arranging the logistics for a new round of calculations and assembling a Los Alamos delegation consisting of "Mr. and Mrs. Harris Mayer, Mr. and Mrs. Foster Evans, and myself" to work with ENIAC.[38] Monte Carlo work was again one segment of a larger block of ENIAC time procured by the Atomic Energy Commission. According to the ENIAC operations log, that group arrived on May 23. They took several days to configure the function tables with their program and their data, then began operating ENIAC three shifts a day, six days a week.[39]

After some "troubles" with ENIAC, the "first real progress" was made on June 1, 1949. By June 3, "the first of the 3 parts of the first A.E.C. problem" was completed, but problems with the machine, exacerbated by problems with air conditioning, continued to slow progress. On June 6, the log recorded the dry observation that "machine operating as usual for Monday" but also complained of "operator trouble," protesting that "it doesn't pay to turn machine over to strangers with no experience." Perhaps reflecting this, subsequent entries noted the assignment of staff operators to assist with each of the AEC problems.

The Monte Carlo work was interrupted on several occasions by other, shorter jobs for the Atomic Energy Commission, but the log book confirms that "A.E.C. #1 Problem 53 (Monte Carlo method) completed early in the afternoon" of June 24.[40] Klara von Neumann returned to Princeton, writing to Carson Mark to report on the success of the calculations (at least some of which indicated explosive potential). The nuclear cross-sections were again the most sensitive part of the data, so she had "brought with me to Princeton all secret documents" used during the calculations.[41] In contrast, "ten large boxes" of output cards (through which the progress of the simulations could be traced) and two smaller boxes with "the listing of all the problems" were being mailed directly to Los Alamos by staff members of the

Ballistic Research Lab. Klara von Neumann scheduled a flight to New Mexico for July 7 so that she would be able review the findings.

The next program that was run on ENIAC was also for Los Alamos, but it was for the "implosion group" and its specific purpose is not clear to us. It was beset by "troubles," but frantic calls back to Los Alamos to check figures and the arrival of additional laboratory staff eventually led to the location and correction of an error. The program began to run successfully on July 8, 1949 and work was completed on July 29.

Calculations for the "Super" (1950)

Accessible archival materials have relatively little to say about the details of the next set of Monte Carlo calculations that were conducted with ENIAC on behalf of Los Alamos. Discussions sent though unclassified channels were deliberately vague about the purpose of proposed calculations, referring for example to "certain problems" of vital interest and to possible application of ENIAC to the "category of problems ... which have been and are the main program of the IBM group at Los Alamos."[42]

Although ENIAC's very first application had been to a set of (non-Monte Carlo) hydrogen-bomb calculations for Los Alamos, designed to address the feasibility of Edward Teller's "Super" bomb, it was only after three full sets of Monte Carlo calculations on fission weapons that ENIAC was again applied to the hydrogen bomb. According to Anne Fitzpatrick, John von Neumann had been working since late 1948 on a Monte Carlo simulation of the Super.[43] The Evanses, the von Neumanns, Metropolis, and Teller were all involved. In mid 1949, von Neumann dispatched several letters to Ulam concerning plans for "hydrodynamical Monte Carlo" and "S." He concluded ENIAC could not handle the latter, but it would be a "24–30 hour problem for our future machine."[44] Like the 1945–46 calculations, those calculations attempted to determine how much tritium would be needed to ignite a self-sustaining fusion process. Ulam and a colleague ran a version of the simulation by hand in early 1950, with disappointing results; the "Evanses, the von Neumanns and others" then used ENIAC to simulate the ignition of the fusion reaction in the "spring and summer of 1950."[45] Delays in the completion of the Institute for Advanced Studies' machine and their urgent need for an answer forced them to simplify the simulation.

John von Neumann wrote to Teller in April of 1950 to update him on "the digital calculation we are now planning for the ENIAC." Work on "the details of this scheme" was "considerably past the 50 per cent point," and von Neumann was "now satisfied that the calculations we are planning can be fitted on the ENIAC."

He had "received informal assurances from the Aberdeen authorities that the ENIAC will be available essentially any time in May when we ask for it."[46] Klara von Neumann continued to play a central role—John wrote to Carson Mark that she would go to Aberdeen a week ahead to help prepare ENIAC, and that "Klari will mail the last part of the code to Foster and Cerda Evans today."[47]

The results of the new ENIAC simulations supported the findings of the hand calculations, and the Super design was abandoned. The hydrogen-bomb designs tested from 1952 onward used a quite different approach that had been formulated by Teller and Ulam in 1951 in response to the Super's loss of credibility.

Soon the Los Alamos laboratory's contract for machine time was allowed to expire. By the summer of 1951, the Institute for Advanced Studies' computer was at last becoming operational, and at Los Alamos Metropolis' own MANIAC was nearing completion. Some of Klara von Neumann's code made the transition to the new machine—Cerda Evans wrote to her in early 1952, just before the MANIAC first ran successfully:

I assume that you will be part of the group that finally runs the problem when the fatal day arrives … . The hydrodynamics is essentially your original code so there doesn't seem to be much point in your going through it again. Transition I you have also examined if I remember correctly, but there have been some changes which you will observe when the new sheets are sent. Would you look carefully to see that we haven't done anything completely outrageous? The neutron-proton section and the photon-transition II are probably new to you and we would appreciate a systematic checking, since we have made various changes at various times and are not sure that the thing really hangs together properly.[48]

Despite this evidence that her expertise was still valued by Los Alamos, Klara von Neumann's involvement with computing was coming to an end. As major labs acquired their own computers, they increasingly relied on full-time staff programmers and operators rather than on outside consultants and contractors. Her bouts of crippling depression and insecurity had always made this work stressful for her, and her husband fell terminally ill in 1955. After his death in 1957 she remarried and moved to California. Despite having seemingly found peace, she committed suicide in 1963.

The Monte Carlo Simulations in Retrospect

The ENIAC Monte Carlo simulations executed from the spring of 1948 on stand out among the programs executed during the 1940s for their complexity and for the fidelity of their diagramming and coding style to the ideas of John von Neumann and his collaborators. Our detailed analysis of the first and second runs illuminates the evolution of the program over a two-year period from an initial plan of computation through a series of flow diagrams to an initial ENIAC program and then through a major cycle of revision and improvement. This gives a uniquely detailed and richly substantiated look at a landmark program.

Our analysis challenges a common characterization of early scientific computer problems as having placed a premium on computational speed and having had little need for input and only modest volumes of output, in contrast with administrative data-processing jobs in which effectiveness depended primarily on the speed at which data could be pushed in and out of the machine from card or tape units. ENIAC's original task of calculating trajectory tables certainly fits this model, as do the celebrated "first programs" run on Manchester University's "Baby" computer and on EDSAC, both of which performed long series of calculations with no input data and a tiny output consisting of solutions.[49] In contrast, the first program run on ENIAC after its conversion to the new code paradigm was a complex simulation system that might take days to complete its tasks, depending primarily on the speed at which data could be fed through the machine.

The program included several features of the modern code paradigm. It was composed of instructions written using a small number of operation codes, some of which were followed by additional arguments. Conditional and unconditional jumps were used to transfer control between different parts of the program. Instructions and data shared a single address space, and loops were combined with index variables to iterate through values stored in tables. A subroutine was called from more than one point in the program. The return address was stored and then used to jump back to the appropriate place on completion. Although earlier programs, such as those run on the Harvard Mark I, had been written as series of instructions and had been coded numerically, this was the first program ever executed to have incorporated those other defining features of the modern code paradigm.

Our investigation has also shed new light on the human dimensions of early computing. Klara von Neumann's central contribution to the Monte Carlo work has, with the exception of previously cited comments by Nick Metropolis and recent coverage by George Dyson, barely been mentioned.[50] The story told here fits, in its broad outline, with Galison's famous depiction of the first Monte Carlo simulations as a trading zone, yet it looks more closely than Galison did at the details of the computations, and it deepens our understanding of what is being traded and by whom. According to Galison, Monte Carlo simulation led physics to a "netherland that was at once nowhere and everywhere."[51] That description of Monte Carlo simulation's intellectual legacy also describes the unconventional social structure of the project, creating shadowy opportunities in unexpected places. Monte Carlo simulation engaged not only the great men who populate Galison's story, who were from diverse disciplinary backgrounds, but also a broader cast of characters lacking elite scientific credentials.

Klara von Neumann, mentioned by Galison only as one of a list of early female computer programmers, emerges as a surprisingly central participant in these exchanges. Entering the trading zone with her natural talent and with some social capital borrowed from her husband, but with no scientific credentials, she was soon running a successful stall of her own. Looking back at early computing work on ENIAC from the vantage point of more than six decades, one is struck by the prevalence of husband-and-wife teams in every aspect of the machine's operation.[52] For Klara von Neumann and Adele Goldstine, marriage to brilliant men opened doors to spectacularly successful collaborations on projects of great importance while also ensuring that their contributions to that work would be forever viewed as peripheral. The von Neumanns and the Goldstines collaborated closely on their Los Alamos work with two other couples: the Mayers and the Evanses. Though the daughters and granddaughters of that generation would enjoy much more freedom to build independent careers, rather than channeling their creativity into work with their husbands, we admire the success of these unions in building intellectual collaborations as well as domestic partnerships.

10

ENIAC Settles Down to Work

In early 1948 ENIAC was still not working well. Immediately before Nick Metropolis arrived in March to begin the conversion, it struggled to complete one day's computational work over a full month. It successfully ran the Monte Carlo program only after Metropolis set its cycling unit to 60 KHz rather than the intended speed of 100 KHz. This helped a great deal, but ENIAC required a lot more attention over the coming months and years to improve its reliability and standardize its configuration. Modifications to its power supply and electrical connections, improvements in procedures, and more experienced operators greatly increased the time it spent carrying out useful work. By the early 1950s, attention had shifted to a series of hardware additions to increase performance and capabilities. This chapter explores those changes and their implications for ENIAC as a workhorse of the Ballistic Research Lab's computer laboratory until 1955.

Stabilizing ENIAC

Preparations for the next problems to be run on ENIAC were well underway as the first Monte Carlo run neared completion. On May 6, 1948, Richard Clippinger visited to give the ENIAC group "a good lesson on his problem," and two men from the United Aircraft Company "left … their turbojet problem," the problem that was to be "put on" ENIAC next. Metropolis left Aberdeen on May 11. The operations team first tweaked the configuration that Metropolis had left behind to implement an "83 order code" and revised the "enumeration of lines" for consistency with those originally planned.[1] After a week of testing and tuning, authorization for the turbojet problem had not arrived. Clippinger arrived early, on May 17, with Jean Bartik and one of the other Philadelphia-based contractors, to start work on his long-planned calculations of supersonic wind flow.

Over the next three months, work progressed on both problems as the new configuration was stabilized. Attempts to run Clippinger's program proceeded much as before, with frequent public demonstrations of the machine and even more frequent losses of entire shifts to troubleshooting. By July 6 a definitive-looking set of "orders for coding ENIAC problems" defining 84 different instructions had been typed up.[2] On July 12, Clippinger was bumped off the machine, and the "new orders," two control instructions originally proposed in the Princeton dialect, were set up before "putting on the turbo-jet problem." This code ran for a couple of "quite successful" days, after which efforts shifted back to Clippinger.[3] When his calculations were finished, the operators again "set [the] switches" for the turbojet problem, which was completed in early August.[4]

Further tweaking of ENIAC's configuration and instruction set continued through the summer of 1948. A switch that could be toggled between function-table control and punched-card control was fitted on August 6. We believe its primary purpose was to run decks of diagnostic cards without disrupting programs set up on the function tables. In September, a complete description of the set-up for the "converter code," now containing 91 orders, was circulated.[5]

Despite intensive work during May of 1948 to get the machine functioning at its full 100 KHz, not until October was the happy news "Machine running OK @ 100KC except for square-rooter" logged.[6] Full-speed electronic operation did little to justify the more frequent errors and machine failures it produced because throughput on most jobs was limited by the speed of ENIAC's punched-card equipment. According to Harry Reed, who programmed ENIAC in the 1950s, "we only ran it at 100 kHz early in the week to see if everything was working all right, because it would develop more errors if we kept operating it that way."[7] That practice eventually developed into "repetitive operational tests at higher than normal operating frequencies and oscilloscope inspection of pulse shapes to locate and remove tubes of only marginal reliability."[8]

The Register Code

After the initial tweaking, the instruction set barely changed for five years. The enduring stability of the 1948 configuration was not planned. Clippinger had expected that initial conversion work would be quickly superseded by the installation of the register, the delay-line memory that the BRL had ordered from the Moore School in early 1947. At the end of July 1948, he noted that it was not worthwhile to "describe [the code then in use] in detail since there will be a better code available by the time this report is available [in September of 1948]."[9] Since April of 1948, and perhaps longer than that, he had been working on an entirely different instruction set intended to exploit the new hardware—an instruction set he presented at the 1949 meeting of the Association for Computing Machinery.[10]

Computers with delay-line storage, such as EDVAC or those based on Alan Turing's ACE design, typically included a mix of longer and shorter lines.[11] The short lines provided faster access times but held fewer numbers. The "register code" used ten of the existing accumulators in lieu of short lines. Data would have been transferred from the register into an accumulator for processing, using an indirect addressing mechanism similar to that employed with the function table. Instructions held in the register could be executed directly, with "programming capacity being increased indefinitely." Arithmetic instructions used a three-address format, specifying two source accumulators and one destination accumulator. A major increase in overall speed was promised, partly by speeding up the basic instruction cycle itself, but also because the three-address instruction set meant that one instruction could often take the place of three.

As we discussed in chapter 5, the Ballistic Research Lab awarded the contract for construction of the register to the Moore School, where it was constructed under the supervision of Richard Merwin. If the register had been delivered as promised, ENIAC would have become the first computer to have a large high-speed electronic memory. But the register progressed no more smoothly than EDVAC's delay-line memory, also being built at the Moore School, or the units for Univac and the one-off BINAC being built across town by the Eckert and Mauchly Computer Company.[12] Its scheduled delivery date slipped repeatedly.

In early 1949, weekly meetings began for the BRL "Eniac Group to discuss various aspects of the art."[13] The register code was discussed in several of the early meetings. On May 27 the register finally arrived at Aberdeen. Hooked up a few days later, it never worked properly. After a high-level meeting on June 29, "the Moore School went home to consider either putting more money in to make it work or to sell it to Aberdeen at a considerably reduced price."[14] The actual decision seems to have been to give up on the whole thing, as the register was never mentioned again in the log book.

An effort had already been made to decouple the "register code" from the uncertain fate of the register itself. Arguing that the new set-up was faster than the current "converter code," and its programs more compact, George Reitwiesner, one of the new ENIAC specialists, suggested that installing it would be worthwhile even in the absence of the delay-line memory. He planned for the construction of a "block of [vacuum tube] memory cells" to compensate for the two additional accumulators that the register code would have needed for control purposes.[15] The idea does not seem to have gained much traction. Instead, the instruction set implemented by Nick Metropolis and Klara von Neumann, which had been preemptively dismissed by Richard Clippinger as already obsolete, served as the basis for coding over the machine's entire productive life at Aberdeen.

Improved Reliability

Statistics gathered by the Ballistic Research Laboratory illuminate ENIAC's performance over the period from early 1948 to early 1952. During the second quarter

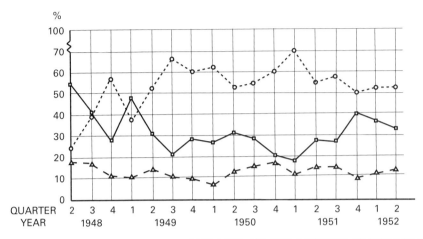

1. o----o CORRECTLY   OPERATING ON THE SOLUTION OF REGULAR PROBLEMS.
2. □———□ LOCATING AND CORRECTING MACHINE TROUBLE
   IN THE ENIAC, NON DUPLICATION TIME, AND DOWN TIME ON SPECIAL
   PREVENTIVE MAINTENANCE.
3. ▲– – ▲ PLACING NEW PROBLEMS ON THE ENIAC, CHECKING
   PROGRAMMING, DATA ANALYSIS, AND DOWN TIME DUE TO HUMAN
   OPERATING ERROR.

Figure 10.1
ENIAC's time spent solving problems, being fixed, and being prepared in the years 1948–1952.
(W. Barkley Fritz, BRL Memorandum Report No 617: A Survey of ENIAC Operations and Problems:
1946–52, Ballistic Research Laboratory, 1952)

of 1948, it spent more than half its time being fixed and only about a quarter of
the time doing production work. Six months later, it was "correctly operating on
the solution of regular problems" about 57 percent of the time. A corner had been
turned, though ENIAC remained less reliable than the Bell Labs relay computer
owing to the inherent unreliability of vacuum tubes. According to figures compiled
by Homer Spence, approximately 19,000 failed tubes were removed from ENIAC
during 1952 alone.[16]

After 1948, only once did the percentage of time ENIAC was operating on problems dip below 50, and a peak of 70 percent was approached in early 1951 as the
hardware team continued to tinker with circuits and the operations team gained
experience with the machine's foibles. For most of ENIAC's productive career, it lost
about 30 percent of a typical week to time spent "locating and correcting machine
trouble." That was enough to cause frustration, but it did not stop the machine from
handling an impressive workload.

By August of 1952, ENIAC had tackled about 75 distinct programs in its new
control mode, many of them recurring jobs such as the generation of firing tables

and the analysis of missile telemetry.[17] Its increasing productivity depended on ongoing improvements in many aspects of its hardware.

BRL sources attributed much of the improvement in reliability to a "tube surveillance program" initiated "at the beginning of 1950" so that "tubes were life-tested and statistical data on the failures were compiled." That program led, it was claimed, to "unique" methods of tube testing and to "many improvements in vacuum tubes themselves."[18] Historians have since documented a similarly elaborate and comprehensive investigation and testing of vacuum tubes launched by Eckert during ENIAC's infancy at the Moore School, so it is not clear if the later measures were entirely new or were merely a re-introduction of the techniques that had originally made ENIAC tolerably reliable.[19] Some of the improvement may simply have come from installing newer tubes, as electronics firms were constantly improving their products and had begun to optimize them for digital applications. For example, Sylvania introduced the 7AK7, dubbed a "computer tube," in 1948.[20]

Although historians have focused on vacuum tubes as the main reason for ENIAC's limited reliability, improvements to less exotic technologies such as power supplies were just as important. As we noted in discussing their procurement, power supplies were sensitive, custom-built devices. "Cleaning" the incoming power enough to eliminate voltage fluctuations as a source of errors and of tube failures was a constant struggle. In 1950 the BRL sidestepped the problem of cleaning the incoming power by powering ENIAC with a dynamo connected to a flywheel spun by an electric motor. This severed the direct electrical connection between ENIAC and the power grid.

Another prosaic reason for the improvement of ENIAC's reliability was the elimination of minor defects in its circuits. During the frenzied night shifts of 1945, the soldering done by the "wiremen" had not always been done to the highest standards. Shaken by the move to Aberdeen, weak connections contributed to the intermittent errors that crippled ENIAC's first eighteen months at the BRL. In his testimony in the ENIAC patent trial, Clippinger later recalled that Spence had "detected so many cold solder joints that he simply went through and resoldered every joint in the machine."[21] Week after week, year after year, Spence's soldering iron moved throughout ENIAC's panels, replacing the tiny blobs of solder left by the less skilled wiremen. The fate of the world's most complex electronic device depended on such craft work.

The BRL sometimes reported the number of different jobs ENIAC completed. Those reports gives us a good sense of how improvements in operating techniques and in hardware and the growing experience of its program developers and operators came together to dramatically improve ENIAC's effectiveness. Between November 1950 and March 1951, for example, the following problems were completed:

(a) an investigation of some of the properties of interior ballistics, (b) an evaluation of error in axially symmetric supersonic airflow, (c) two additional programs for the determination of the equilibrium composition of a four component system of fuel elements, (d) two complete bombing tables, (e) the reduction of data for 9,950 points of guided missile data, and (f) two programs involving normal trajectory computations.

This is a diverse list, but it represents an average of only three programs a month.[22] By the next quarter, the group seems to have got into the swing of faster changeovers. ENIAC had "completed computations for 24 different problems (which involved 53 changes of program)," or almost eighteen changeovers a month.[23] Further improvements were reported in the next few years.

Daily Life with ENIAC

ENIAC is often discussed as if it were a distinct event, celebrated on anniversaries ending with the digit 0, during which humanity entered the digital age. Yet it was also, for almost nine years, a suite of rooms in Aberdeen, Maryland. Dozens of people spent significant portions of their careers there tending to ENIAC's needs by writing programs, operating the computer and its gaggle of punched-card machines, re-soldering joints and replacing vacuum tubes, servicing troublesome power and air conditioning units, or simply mopping the floor at its center. By the end of 1948 the ENIAC group had grown sufficiently that 22 people attended the "first ENIAC Christmas party and dinner."[24] ENIAC was already somewhat famous and undeniably exotic, but, as the saying goes, no man is a hero to his valet. As those men and women worked with the machine year after year, they experienced the humdrum satisfaction and frustration of daily routine rather than the heroic thrill of legend.

ENIAC's 80 feet of panels formed the walls of a fairly large inner room, leaving space in the middle for a sizable delegation of visitors. For Harry Reed, it was a site of public spectacle—an idea that is supported by the mentions of visitors, some humble and some powerful, recorded in the operations log. The following is from a "record of a symposium and celebration" held at Aberdeen Proving Ground in 1996:

Every year at springtime, the West Point graduating class would come down … . Among the things they came to see was the ENIAC … when you had large groups of people wandering through … things always went wrong. People always bumped cables and so forth … . So we would usually take out a deck of punched cards that contained some special diagnostic tests … . It was a great display, because these tests were constructed so that you could watch the numbers sort of flow through the registers … . It reminded you of Times Square in New York … . Then this escort officer … briefed ahead of time … would say, "Over there, you can see in this register that this is the velocity of a bullet, and you can see how it is moving … ." None of this was true … . But we got away with it, and it did look good.[25]

The fire-prevention changes made to ENIAC during its relocation from the Moore School seem to have worked, as there is no record of another fire after the one that

Figure 10.2
ENIAC as set up in Aberdeen. Betty Holberton stands in the foreground and Glen Beck (about whom we know nothing) at the rear. After April 1948, the wires and the switches on the wall panels were rarely modified, and only the switches on the three portable function tables (seen here at right, now arranged neatly together) were routinely moved. The suspended ceiling and the custom-built space made ENIAC look its best for streams of visitors.
(U.S. Army photo)

occurred in October of 1946. Neither was the flooding that had occurred at the Moore School repeated in Aberdeen. The log book does record failures of the power and cooling systems, but the machine's carefully constructed new environment was significantly better suited to its needs. However, it remained vulnerable to less dramatic threats, such as unintended changes to the permanent configuration of wires implementing the modern code paradigm. According to Homé McAllister Reitwiesner, who was on the ENIAC operations team at the BRL, the cleaning staff posed a constant threat to the machine's stability:

We would come in the morning, and look all the way around the bottom of the ENIAC. If a plug was sitting in a place that didn't have the same kind of dirt pattern as the others, we would know that a cleaning person had knocked it out and just put it near a nearby plug. We spent hours trying to find out what was wrong one day and we discovered that cleaning personnel had moved one of the plugs. After that we checked every morning.[26]

Reed noted that the effects of moisture on punched cards were "one of the biggest problems" during the sweltering mid-Atlantic summers. The "only rooms at the BRL that were air-conditioned were those that were used for the handling and storage of IBM cards ... because the IBM cards had a nasty habit of soaking up moisture, and the readers and printers that we had in those days were extremely intolerant of changes in the size of the cards."[27] The log book for July 28, 1949 noted that ENIAC was giving its operators trouble on "another record hot day" and that Bernard Dimsdale had suggested moving card-storage cabinets to the room that held ENIAC's auxiliary punched-card equipment.[28] (Late in ENIAC's career, the staff of the BRL found an additional use for its space. As one of the most intensive users of scientific computers, the BRL was a central node in the informal networks of information exchange. In the 1950s, this activity was formalized with the publication of a series of reports giving detailed technical information on every working electronic digital computer known to be in operation. For a while, the project's leader Martin H. Weik and his "Special Systems Section" kept their desks inside ENIAC, sheltered from the summer heat and humidity.[29])

The Weather Simulations

Among historians of science, the best-known ENIAC calculations run at BRL are the numerical weather simulations of 1950. Those calculations, which have many parallels with the Monte Carlo simulations, provide the best documentary evidence of ENIAC practice during the 1950s.

Like the Monte Carlo "runs," they were arranged by John von Neumann to use ENIAC to tackle work that had been slated for the computer slowly taking shape at the Institute for Advanced Studies. The weather simulations were likewise run by "expeditionary" parties heading down from Princeton to spend a few weeks punching, shuffling, and reintroducing to ENIAC vast quantities of punched cards. Like the Monte Carlo simulations, this work used ENIAC to demonstrate the feasibility of what later would become a hugely important area of scientific practice. In later decades, research centers for weather and climate research, such as the National Center for Atmospheric Research, vied with the atomic research laboratories and their huge Monte Carlo simulations to be the initial and most influential purchasers of each new model of record-breaking supercomputer.[30]

Von Neumann had been promoting the potential of the forthcoming Institute for Advanced Studies computer to the meteorological community since 1946.[31] According to William Aspray, he selected the hydrodynamics of the atmosphere as "a prime example of those complex, nonlinear phenomena previously inaccessible to mathematical investigation."[32] The Navy's Office of Research and Inventions supported the work of five professionals and associated support staff in the Institute for Advance Studies' Numerical Meteorology Project from May of 1946 on. Researchers with expertise at the intersection of meteorology and numerical analysis proved hard to find and retain until the arrival in 1948 of Jule Charney. Work then began to focus on the creation of a mathematical model of atmospheric flow, balancing the huge complexity of real weather against the computational power of early computers and the lack of accurate and evenly spaced weather observations. Charney had produced a promising two-dimensional model by 1949. Unfortunately there was little opportunity to test it, as the Institute for Advanced Studies' computer project failed to make a corresponding leap forward.

On September 29, 1949, the Ordnance Department approved a request via the Weather Bureau to provide two weeks' use of ENIAC, then still the only computer in the United States to have implemented the modern code paradigm.[33] Work immediately shifted to designing and coding a suitably simplified model. Klara von Neumann was thanked in the resulting report for "instruction in the technique of coding for the ENIAC and for checking the final code."[34] According to Kristine Harper's history of numerical meteorology, John von Neumann handled "the numerical-analysis-related parts of the computer program" and Jule Charney was deeply involved in the conversion of his model to computer code.[35]

Richard Clippinger requested that "flow diagrams in detailed code for the ENIAC operations" be sent at least a month ahead "in order that our operators may check the coding."[36] Checking was very thorough to ensure efficient use of machine time and detect errors that might render results useless. John Holberton sent Charney a long list of queries, ambiguities, and suspected mistakes that his staff had detected.[37]

Plans for an "expedition" of meteorologists to Aberdeen in February of 1950 were scuttled by what Holberton called "more than the normal amount of machine trouble and slower progress than expected" with the trajectory calculations ENIAC had to complete first.[38] In March a team of five meteorologists from the Institute for Advanced Studies, the University of Chicago, and the U.S. Weather Bureau arrived in Aberdeen to use ENIAC for what was supposed to be a two-week period. Each of them had to receive security clearance before being allowed to enter the proving ground. The "expedition" model was something of a throwback to ENIAC's earlier days. By 1950 the BRL was running in a more conventional way—jobs were usually handled by internal staff members and completed within hours or a few days rather than in weeks.

The meteorologists' time on the machine began at midnight on Sunday, March 5, and they relinquished it 33 days later, having run it around the clock "with only brief interruptions."[39] Following normal practice, the first two days were spent "pedaling" the program—that is, stepping slowly through to verify its correct operation.[40]

Figure 10.3
Participants in the 1950 meteorological expedition to Aberdeen pose in front of ENIAC. Jule Charney
is on the right; John von Neumann is second from the left.
(courtesy of MIT Museum)

The party found ENIAC more reliable than it had been in 1948, but still by no
means trouble free. Homé McAllister and Clyde Hauff were among the operators
assigned to help, working closely with the Institute for Advanced Studies group to
check the code in advance and follow up after the end of the calculations to mail
tabulated results and to check whether output cards were still needed.[41] ENIAC
failed on a number of occasions, and some of the failures were caught only by checks
that showed errors creeping into the results. Hardware problems were dealt with
by members of the regular staff, which caused delays of several hours.[42] Despite the
advance checking, early runs produced erroneous results or took too long, leading
to many last-minute changes to blocks of code and the values of constants after
they had been set up on the function tables. Charney estimated that 41 percent of
their scheduled machine time was spent on useful work, 19 percent was squandered

by "errors in programming, i.e. our own foolishness," and the remaining 40 percent was lost to machine problems.[43]

ENIAC lacked some of the refinements planned for the Institute for Advanced Studies' machine—particularly floating-point arithmetic, which, as Aspray noted, meant that "large blocks of time prior to calculation were consumed in trial-and-error attempts to scale the variables" manually.[44] ENIAC's limited accumulator memory was another obvious limitation; Charney complained that "the lack of an external memory gives us no end of headaches," although the size of the model would have likewise overwhelmed the memory capacity of any computer under construction at the time.[45] Simulation remained highly dependent on input and output. Unusually, a diagram of the various punched-card operations required and their relationship to the different stages of the model has survived. These computations were among the most complex ever attempted on ENIAC. A single 20-hour forecast required 36 hours of uninterrupted work.

Charney and his colleagues had split the weather simulation into many distinct processes, each of which was simple enough to be practicable with the equipment available. Each deck of cards fed to ENIAC was disposed of relatively quickly. Operation 5, one of the longest, took 23 minutes to run through its full input deck.[46] That is far from instant, but it was measured in minutes rather than hours. However, operation 5 was only one of sixteen operations that went into one simulated weather cycle, and at least six cycles were necessary to produce a 20-hour forecast. Generating a forecast thus involved shuffling many intermediate decks of cards through many distinct processes, most of which were conducted manually. The log book's references to duplication of test runs makes it clear that the machine's reliability was still uneven enough to justify running steps twice and comparing the results.[47]

Much of the time was spent handling decks of punched cards rather than waiting for ENIAC itself to finish processing a deck of cards. The punched-card operations required for this application were much more complicated than those for the "first run" of the Monte Carlo problem in 1948. Like the Monte Carlo simulations, the weather forecasts were based on applying the same steps repeatedly to simulate the progression of the system in question through a sequence of time intervals. In a weather simulation, each complete cycle represented the passage of at least one hour.[48] The diagram reproduced here as figure 10.4 reveals that each cycle would generate seven intermediate decks of punched cards, each forming the input for the next stage of processing. Fortunately, ENIAC's function-table memory was large enough to hold the program code and the constants for all the steps (shown in the leftmost column), so there was little need to adjust its switches between steps. Not all the operations required to run a forecast could be handled by ENIAC, as six of

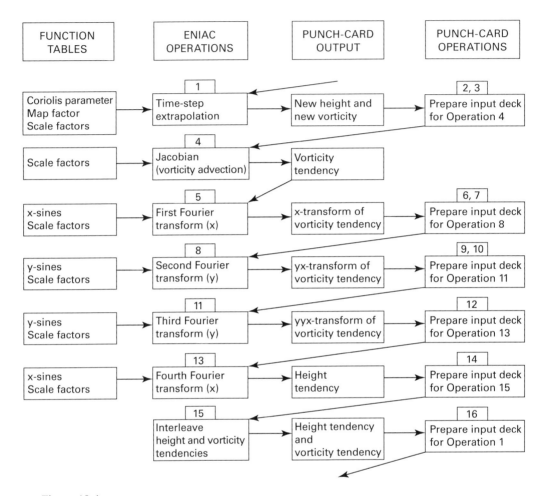

Figure 10.4
Procedures for the first numerical meteorology simulations, run in 1950, showing ENIAC procedures and manual punched-card processing. (courtesy of American Meteorological Society; redrawn, thanks to Paul Edwards, from Platzman, "The ENIAC Computations of 1950—Gateway to Numerical Weather Prediction")

these seven kinds of intermediate card decks had to be processed manually before they could be fed back into ENIAC. For example, operations 2 and 3 were performed on the first intermediate deck to provide the input for operation 4, the second phase of ENIAC processing. In those operations the deck was "first duplicated, then altered manually, then triplicated, and then altered manually again" before being "subject[ed] to two interfiling procedures on the collator."[49]

Output was checked in a number of ways. Early results were compared with hand-computed results, and the comparison revealed errors in both sets of results. Errors were found in the code itself, in the constant values for scaling set on the function tables, and in the approach taken to rounding. Mistakes were a constant possibility—particularly in punched-card operations, "each fraught with the peril of human error."[50] About 25,000 cards were punched in the course of each 24-hour forecast, most of which were processed manually after being produced.[51] Work progressed in three shifts, the participants sleeping in turns.

The need to split the job into small steps, each achievable with ENIAC's limited memory size, also influenced the choice of a mathematical method. According to one of the participants, ENIAC's "nontrivial" contributions came in steps 5, 8, 11, and 13, in which "the Laplacian was inverted to solve Poisson's equation." Von Neumann chose a direct method for that task, providing an exact solution in a set number of steps. Models run on the Institute for Advanced Studies' computer instead used iterative methods, which were faster but less predictable in the number of steps required and so harder to compartmentalize to meet the constraints of a very small memory.[52]

The expedition was recognized immediately as "the beginning of a new era in weather forecasting."[53] There was a second "expedition" in 1951, though ENIAC's limitations seem to have prevented it from throwing much more light on the techniques involved. By the summer of 1952 the Weather Bureau and military weather forecasting groups were already beginning to make arrangements to adopt the new computerized techniques.[54] At that point the Institute for Advanced Studies' computer was finally operational and available for further experimentation. The model used on ENIAC was re-implemented as a test. The new machine ran in 90 minutes the forecast that had taken 36 hours with ENIAC.[55] The IAS computer was significantly faster than ENIAC in its core electronic logic, but the biggest performance boost came from its larger writable internal memory and from its magnetic drum, which greatly reduced its reliance on card storage and external card processing.[56] ENIAC had an initial performance edge when it was necessary to push data out to external storage, as the IAS machine was using paper tape and slow teletype readers whereas ENIAC was using IBM punched-card units. But once the IAS computer had been upgraded with its own punched-card equipment, a forecast took only ten minutes.[57] The meteorology group was also able to incorporate the results of its experimentation with ENIAC into the first three-dimensional models of weather flow.

ENIAC Evolves in Use

ENIAC's new control mode challenged some of the tradeoffs that had been made during the original design. In particular, the modern code paradigm involved constantly fetching instructions from the function table. The increased complexity of programs made possible by the relatively generous size of the function tables, in conjunction with the loss of some formerly usable accumulator space, made ENIAC's limited memory more of a constraint than ever before. From 1951 to 1954 a series of modifications were made to the hardware to address all these shortcomings and to better support the new patterns of use. The modifications greatly improved the speed of instruction retrieval and shift operations, allowed programs to be stored on plugboards that could be mounted or dismounted as needed, and gave the machine a pioneering core memory that increased its high-speed writable storage by a factor of 5.

Some parts of ENIAC were used much more intensively than had been anticipated; others were used little or not at all. The master programmer was barely used, and treating most accumulators simply as storage devices meant that the circuitry and program controls that controlled more complex functionality were no longer needed for their original purposes.

More and Faster Function Tables

In ENIAC terminology, a "function table" was a fixed unit consisting of two panels containing the circuitry and program controls that provided access to numbers set on the switches of a free-standing unit known as a "portable function table." This arrangement was intended to provide flexibility—for example, by allowing a portable unit to be set up offline and then plugged into the function table when it was needed. The portable tables had been designed so that data tables and program parameters could be changed easily. They were less suitable for data with a longer life span, such as tables of standard functions, or for program code that might be run on many occasions.

ENIAC's creators had considered several different designs for the function tables. In May of 1944, John Brainerd had been enthusiastic about Leland Cunningham's suggestion that two of the three tables should be "set by a teletype mechanism" rather than by hand, so that data could be reloaded automatically.[58] Adele Goldstine's 1946 report mentioned a different possibility: constructing "fixed" portable function tables—read-only memories that could be hooked up whenever a particular function was needed.[59] It does not appear that any such function tables were built, but in

December of 1948 a similar plan was mooted for storing standard program code. John von Neumann wrote to Klara soon afterward that, because "making one more, 'fixed', function table is so little work," the BRL engineers had "decided that they will build one" with some of her code "soldered in."[60]

A variation on the latter idea was finally implemented in 1951 with the addition of a fourth function table. Most of its values were set by clipping plugboards into place rather than by turning knobs. The plugboards stored numbers as patterns of wires threaded into little holes, a control method used on IBM punched-card machines. Storing data was tedious and produced boards festooned with tangled wires, but it proved advantageous when a program, a subroutine, or a table of constants was needed frequently. Instead of resetting thousands of switches, a pre-wired plugboard was taken from a rack and mounted. This was akin to burning a program onto a ROM cartridge that could then be snapped into place when needed. The new function table used several plugboards of different sizes, presumably to increase flexibility in the recombination of subroutines and data tables. "2 triple panel and 4 single panel IBM plugboards" held a total of 1,152 digits.[61] The remaining 48 digits were set with switches, which made it easy to change parameters.

The developments recounted above illustrate how ENIAC's hardware continued to evolve in response to the needs and practices of its users—in this case, the need to make it easy to switch between recurring jobs quickly, or the need to run an urgent recurring job without disrupting a special project that had been set up on regular function tables. The new table also increased the overall size of the memory available for storing programs and constant data. A side effect was to make a little more of ENIAC's original hardware obsolete. The first three function tables had 104 rows, originally selected by a two-digit "argument." To make the full range of rows accessible, an offset switch specified a value between 2 and –2 that was automatically added to each argument received. The initial conversion maintained this offset capability, originally intended to help in program interpolation, by coding the offset as part of the address. The introduction of the fourth function table, which had only 100 rows, was accompanied by a change in the code so that only 100 rows could be accessed on each table; that rendered the additional rows on the original tables, and the switches that provided access to them, redundant.

Early in 1952, the machine was modified with "high speed function tables." Changes were made to the fixed function table units. (It is not clear from the archival record whether they were replaced or simply modified.) Retrieval speed had not been a priority for the original designers, as function-table accesses, which took five addition times, occurred only when it was necessary to retrieve a parameter or a value from a lookup table. After conversion, however, each instruction executed was first read from a function table. This slowed ENIAC considerably. Addition (which, as an astute reader might guess, originally took ENIAC only one add time) required six after the initial conversion to the modern code paradigm.[62] The high-speed function tables retrieved data in only one add time, accelerating the instruction cycle. For example, ENIAC could then add in only three add times or multiply in seventeen add times rather than twenty.[63]

Optimizing the Shift Instructions

After its conversion to the modern code paradigm ENIAC spent much of its time shifting numbers. Accumulators were designed to hold a single signed number of up to ten decimal digits. In practice, many of the numbers stored were smaller: single-digit codes, counters known never to exceed 100, and so on. Devoting a whole accumulator to storing one of these numbers was highly wasteful in view of the tight limits on storage. In the original ENIAC, devices known as "adapters" were inserted into input and output terminals to re-route incoming digits. Because ENIAC carried each digit on a separate wire, this was easy to accomplish. Shifters moved them a certain number of places to the left or to the right to provide instantaneous multiplication or division by a power of 10, while "deleters" replaced certain digits with zeroes.

After conversion, programmers accomplished these operations and others with shift instructions. The additional complexity afforded by the modern code paradigm made it easier to use the precious storage space more efficiently by packing several variables (for example a five-digit number, a three-digit number, and two one-digit codes) into a single accumulator. Working with these variables imposed considerable overhead. Five instructions would be necessary to extract a number held in digits 6–8 of accumulator 18, as follows: copy the contents of accumulator 18 into accumulator 15, use a shift instruction "R5" to shift accumulator 15 to the right to get rid of digits 1–5, do a "shift prime" instruction "R'3" to move the three digits of interest to accumulator 12 (which served as temporary working space), clear accumulator 15, and then copy the contents of accumulator 12 into it. If the variable was updated, a similarly convoluted process would be needed to overwrite the relevant three digits of accumulator 18 with the new quantity. Optimization of the instruction set during planning reduced the amount of shifting required—for example, an instruction in the 51 order code to retrieve two digits of data from the function table was joined in later codes by variants acting on four and six digits, eliminating the need for multiple read and shift operations.

Approximately 18 percent of the instructions in the Monte Carlo second run program were shifts. Each shift now incurred the full overhead of the basic "fetch and decode" sequence, whereas in ENIAC's original design shifters did not slow down computation at all. The Monte Carlo team had been acutely conscious of the amount of computer time consumed by these instructions. Their analysis of an early design for the first run program had suggested that 32.2 percent of the total computation time would be spent shifting. In the planned 60 order code, each shift instruction was followed by two digits indicating direction and size. Shifts took twenty add times, most spent processing these arguments. This probably motivated the switch to simpler and faster shift instructions in the expanded instruction set implemented for Monte Carlo. Each of its twenty argument-free shift instructions took only nine add times to run.

Recognizing that shifts were very common and still disproportionately slow, the BRL designed a new set of circuits for ENIAC; collectively they were known as the "electronic shifter" or the "high speed shifter."[64] The shifter used a matrix of diodes to create direct mappings of inputs to outputs for each possible shift, removing the need to shuffle numbers between accumulators during the shift. This reconfiguration meant that shifts added no overhead to the three add times taken by the basic sequence.[65] The most frequent operation was now the fastest. The new shifter was also reported to have "eliminated numerous tubes and program units" after its installation in early 1952.[66]

Core Memory

After the failure of the register in 1949, ENIAC's internal writable memory remained tiny until July 1953, when a completely different unit—an early magnetic core memory constructed by the Burroughs Corporation—was installed. The new memory provided ENIAC with the storage capacity of 100 additional accumulators, and the *New York Times* explained that it would "enable the machine to deal with bigger problems without consulting its notes."[67]

With core memory, ENIAC skipped an entire generation of memory technologies and marched straight to the technological frontier. Core memory had been in use since 1951, most notably in MIT's ultra-fast Whirlwind computer. Compact, simple, and reliable, it allowed rapid access to any desired memory location. Once perfected, it rendered the leading computer memory technologies of the early 1950s—delay lines and cathode-ray-tube storage—obsolete. They were bulky, complex, and unreliable. Delay lines required much effort on the part of programmers to synchronize the computer's data needs with the signals emerging from the memory tanks. The device fitted to ENIAC was one of the first core memories to be procured from a supplier rather than constructed in-house, having been custom built in Burroughs' Philadelphia research lab.

Interfacing the new memory technology with the idiosyncratic old machine created its own challenges. ENIAC worked with decimal numbers, each communicated as a series of pulses. For example, eight would be transmitted as a succession of eight pulses. Extra hardware was needed to translate between the memory's internal representation of each decimal digit as a four-bit binary sequence and ENIAC's trains of pulses.[68] A total of 48 signal wires ran between the new memory and the rest of ENIAC. The addition of this relatively large writable random-access memory required the addition of four new instructions to ENIAC's code. All versions of the code had allocated two distinct instruction codes to code for data transfer to and from a general-purpose accumulator and accumulator 15. Clearly this approach would not scale up to handle the 100 new locations provided by the core memory. Instead, the revised set-up handled the core memory unit as a fifth function table. The new "store" and "extract" instructions extended the indirect addressing approach used with the function tables, operating on an address specified in a designated subfield of accumulator 8.[69] Again, we are struck by the flexibility provided by ENIAC's modular architecture.

The installation of the new memory caused sudden increases in both "scheduled" and "unscheduled" engineering time. The increases were blamed on the need for "further training of the service personnel in circuitry and machine logic," on the slow accumulation of "actual trouble-shooting experience" with the new hardware, and on "unfamiliar error symptoms and test procedures which had become inadequate." After seven new tests had been "evolved from examination of the difficulties encountered during memory breakdowns," the machine's usable time began to recover.[70] This gives us an insight into the importance of the maintenance staff to early computer installations and the importance of the process by which engineering expertise was applied to problems encountered with unfamiliar new devices, such as the core memory, and then translated into new sets of procedures for routine use.

ENIAC and the Next Generation

At the start of 1950, more than four years after it began to carry out useful work, ENIAC retained its heavyweight title as the most powerful all-electronic computer operational in the United States. When a computation was infeasibly complex for conventional punched-card machines or for any of the few relay computers in use at Harvard and at Columbia, one could either visit New York City to run it on the SSEC or Aberdeen to run it on ENIAC. ENIAC time had a list price of $800 a day, and by that point "a day" meant 24 hours of computer time. Two days with ENIAC cost about the same as the average new car. Programming for outside users was generally done by members of the BRL staff, and approval had to be obtained from the Office of the Chief of Ordnance in Washington.[71]

In 1950 ENIAC surrendered its title to SEAC, a computer that had been built at the National Bureau of Standards in Washington. SEAC had originally been called the "interim computer," as it was intended to be large enough to be useful but small enough to be built quickly. Although finished well behind schedule (as most early computers were), it was nevertheless completed more rapidly than any of the other machines patterned after the IAS computer. SEAC was a little faster than ENIAC and had a much larger writable high-speed memory. It immediately replaced ENIAC and the SSEC as the machine of choice for Los Alamos work.

A number of other groups succeeded in getting computers working over the next eighteen months. Among these machines were SWAC (built for the National Bureau for Standards at the University of California at Los Angeles), Whirlwind (at MIT), two computers built by Engineering Research Associates in Minnesota, and John von Neumann's computer at the Institute for Advanced Studies in Princeton. The first Univac computer was accepted by its customer, the United States Census Bureau, in 1951, though it was not actually delivered until the following year. As 1952 dawned, ENIAC was still among the dozen or so most powerful computers in regular production use across the United States. By the end of that year it was no longer the most powerful or even the second most powerful computer solving problems in its own building. The Ballistic Research Lab had added EDVAC and ORDVAC to its collection of computers.

EDVAC is a name more often associated with words "First Draft of a Report On" than with an actual computer. We have already discussed the early progress of the EDVAC project and the contested relationship between the highly influential First Draft and the work carried out by the Moore School team. Those with a less than obsessive knowledge of computer history may not be aware that EDVAC was ever actually delivered to the BRL.

The design produced under the guidance of J. Presper Eckert and John Mauchly and discussed at the Moore School lectures of 1946 was abandoned shortly thereafter. John von Neumann and Herman Goldstine were by then immersed in their own computer project at the Institute for Advanced Studies, and Eckert, Mauchly, and Arthur Burks had also moved on from the Moore School. Some experienced members of the ENIAC design team (among them T. Kite Sharpless) remained at the Moore School for another year or two, and by 1947 they had produced a highly modified design.[72] Several other EDVAC project leaders came and went as it was constructed over the next few years, and the final product suffered enormously from the exodus of talent.

EDVAC's design gradually moved away from the radical simplicity of the First Draft. For example, its instruction set, like ENIAC's proposed "register code," defined arithmetic operations in a single instruction with three address fields, and in common with other delay-line machines (such as the Pilot ACE) it added another address specifying where the next instruction was to be taken from. Its complexity and its number of vacuum tubes increased considerably during its gestation.

EDVAC was shipped to the BRL in 1949 and was installed in a room barely large enough to hold it. For several years it produced nothing but frustration. Its delay-line memory system was hopelessly unstable, and it did not have functioning peripherals for input or output. A decision to go with magnetic-wire recording, which in the mid 1940s had seemed a plausible alternative to the equally unproven technology of magnetic tape, had led the Moore School team into a technological dead end. EDVAC was delivered without a storage system. It lacked even the special registers, and physical interfaces needed to connect conventional paper-tape or punched-card equipment.

EDVAC's construction was shoddy, and not until 1952, three years after its arrival at Aberdeen, did it begin working well enough to be assigned any work. An official history noted, tactfully, that it "had more than its share of marginal circuits which had to be modified before it could become operational."[73] Michael Williams was less tactful in his account, documenting numerous defects before concluding as follows: "The EDVAC … is no more, and many who worked on her would say, 'Just as well.'"[74]

EDVAC continued to evolve and to become more robust as marginal Moore School hardware (such as an unreliable power supply) was replaced and new input and output devices were added.[75] Eventually stabilized, it gave the BRL ten years of increasingly dependable service before its retirement in 1962.[76]

ORDVAC, the other computer to join the BRL's workforce in 1952, was based, like many American computers of the early 1950s, on the design created by von Neumann's team at the Institute for Advanced Studies. That design was widely distributed and exerted considerably more influence than the machine itself. To call these machines that were based on it "clones" would be an exaggeration, however. Their designs diverged in a number of important respects, their instruction sets usually were not compatible, and they employed a range of different storage and memory technologies. Still, there was a distinct family resemblance in their architecture.

The problems that the BRL had experienced with equipment built at the Moore School after 1945, including the ENIAC "register" memory and EDVAC, may have convinced the BRL to send its next contract elsewhere. ORDVAC was built by the University of Illinois, and was delivered in February of 1952.[77] By the standards of early computer projects, this one went quickly and smoothly, as did the relocation of the machine to Aberdeen and its initial troubleshooting there. The university built two of each part, retaining the spares to build a copy of ORDVAC for its own Digital Computer Laboratory. The copy, dubbed ILLIAC, became the centerpiece of one of the most important computing research groups of its era, establishing Illinois as a leading center for what later became computer science.

At the end of 1952, the BRL tallied the figures for ENIAC's performance alongside those of EDVAC and ORDVAC. Thanks to experience gained over years of operation, ENIAC had averaged only 48.1 hours a week of "engineering time" (meaning downtime for repairs)—less than half as much time as EDVAC lost to repairs. ENIAC managed 67.1 hours of production work, versus 21.7 for EDVAC and 29.4 for ORDVAC. Of course, each of the early computers faced a lengthy period of troubleshooting and shakedown before its hardware became fully reliable.[78]

A final comparison gives a less expected result. Loading a new program onto ENIAC meant setting hundreds of switches by hand. The newer machines loaded their programs automatically from paper tape in a fraction of the time. However, ENIAC lost only 20.4 hours a week to "problem set up and code checking," while EDVAC lost 23.3 and ORDVAC 39.1. ENIAC's efficiency in getting jobs running may have been attributable to the experience that programmers at the BRL had gained with the older computer, to its library of tested programs, to the simplicity of its instruction set, and to the ease with which its code could be debugged.[79]

Tinkering with the new machines persisted into 1953, particularly in the case of EDVAC, and they received several new pieces of hardware that further reduced their time spent on running programs. But ENIAC remained unchallenged as the laboratory's workhorse.[80]

ENIAC Is Overtaken

Like ENIAC, the new machines at the Ballistic Research Lab evolved to better suit the needs of their users. For example, a paper-tape interface was added to EDVAC in a stop-gap solution devised after the machine was delivered without any storage mechanism for data or programs. Paper tape was a familiar technology that could be used with standard punches and readers. It was also slower than punched cards and difficult to use with large volumes of data. In 1953 a punched-card interface was added. A magnetic-drum memory entered regular use in 1955, a floating-point arithmetic unit in 1958, and a magnetic-tape unit in 1960.[81]

The BRL guided the evolution of its computers to maximize the interchangeability of skills and data between them. ENIAC had been run by the staff of a special "ENIAC Section." Parallel sections were later created to handle the programming and operations needs of EDVAC and ORDVAC. Soon, however, the laboratory's leaders recognized that programmers would be more effective if they were trained on all three computers so that they could specialize in problem areas rather than in particular machines. That put a premium on finding ways to make the three computers appear more alike to their users—for example, adding punched-card input to EDVAC and ORDVAC so that they could read and write data in the same medium used by ENIAC. ORDVAC had originally taken 38 minutes to fill its 1,000-word memory via paper tape, which seemed too long to those with experience of the relatively fast and flexible punched-card system.[82] ENIAC would never be able to read binary or textual cards, but some tweaks to its card interface made it compatible with numerical cards punched on the other machines.[83]

The old machine could not stay competitive forever, and the amount of time it spent in the hands of its support engineers rose after its core memory was installed. During the summer of 1954, it lost more time than EDVAC or ORDVAC to unscheduled maintenance but still managed more hours on production jobs (an average of 84 a week) and was left idle for only 2 hours. Yet however many hours ENIAC worked it could never match the productivity of its younger co-workers. In an average week it ran only five distinct programs, with fourteen "problem changes" between them. An average job required 1.2 hours of set-up and instruction-set checking and 5.4 hours of processing. ENIAC was now getting more done in a typical week than it had accomplished in an entire month five years earlier, but its pace was now judged against the new generation. ORDVAC ran an average of 31 programs in a week, with 252 reported changeovers. A typical job took it less than an hour to check and run, so it would have finished calculating while ENIAC's operators were still checking switch settings. EDVAC, still underused five years after its arrival at the BRL, spent only 24 hours a week running production problems. Nonetheless, the perpetual slacker finally managed to out-produce ENIAC that summer, executing 24 different programs with 119 problem changes.[84]

The new core memory eventually allowed an increase in ENIAC's clock speed from the 60 Hz at which Nick Metropolis had discovered it to be most stable. A 1954 report claimed that "ENIAC is now normally operated with pulses generated in the 90-100 kc range as the [new core] memory operates with greater reliability at this frequency."[85] Unfortunately the core memory also undermined ENIAC's reliability. Between December of 1954 and May of 1955 it spent 60.8 hours a week being serviced and only 44.6 hours running production jobs. Despite cheerful claims that the increase in clock speed had offset the increased repair time and made ENIAC "overall a faster computer," it was now spending 51.8 hours a week idling for want of work. Its recurring jobs were being shifted to other machines, and its long career was drawing to a close.[86]

ENIAC's Exit

ENIAC's launch had been marked with national press coverage, a button pushed ceremonially by a general, and a lavish dinner. Those high-profile events continued to provide grist for legal arguments and personal grumbling decades later. In contrast, its final shutdown went almost unnoticed by the world, and we have not found any description of the occurrence in memoirs, oral histories, or archival materials. Only the date and the time (October 2, 1955, 11:45 p.m.) have been preserved.

Digital Computer Newsletter, which had faithfully recorded ENIAC's accomplishments and upgrades, mentioned its passing only in a footnote to the latest quarterly summary of computer uptime at the BRL: "ENIAC figures are given for an eight week average." During this last eight weeks of life it had spent an average of 49 hours being serviced, 33 hours idling, and only 2.3 hours running jobs.

Some sources suggest that ENIAC was abandoned after being damaged in a lightning strike.[87] That would have been a dramatic end: ENIAC destroyed by the very force which had flowed through its tubes to power a transformation of computational practice. Yet the strike, if it took place, could have hastened the inevitable by only a few weeks. The old machine had little work left to do but was just as expensive to staff and maintain as ever. Its remains were removed from the Computing Laboratory and spent the next decade or so slowly decaying elsewhere at the Aberdeen Proving Ground.

11

ENIAC and Its Contemporaries Meet the "Stored Program Concept"

In this chapter we broaden our perspective to compare ENIAC with the other computers operating during the prime of its working life and to consider it in the context of the "stored program concept" that is ubiquitous in historical discussion of early computing. Historians have agreed that development and adoption of this concept during the 1940s constitute the most important dividing line in computer history, separating modern computers from their less evolved predecessors. Yet, as Doron Swade recently noted, historians do not agree on why this should be the case. For years Swade had "assumed that the significance of the stored program must be self-evident" and attributed his own confusion to "deficiency of understanding" or to "some lack" in his computer science education. When he "became bold" and "began asking" computer historians and pioneers, their answers were "all different," and whether "the primary benefit was one of principle or practice" was "frustratingly blurred." Swade concluded that "there was one feature of all the responses about which there was complete agreement: no one challenged the status of the stored program as the defining feature of the modern digital electronic computer." "While the reasons given for this were different," he continued, "none discounted its seminal significance. But it seems that we struggle when required to articulate its significance in simple terms and the apparent mix of principle and practice frustrates clarity."[1]

The "stored program concept" is almost universally agreed to have been present in von Neumann's "First Draft of a Report on the EDVAC," defined (often implicitly) as some combination of the features we separated in chapter 6 into the modern code paradigm, von Neumann architecture paradigm, and EDVAC hardware paradigm. Authors have disputed whether the First Draft was the first or the most influential statement of the concept. Some favor either Alan Turing or J. Presper Eckert and John Mauchly as its true originator or originators. Though ENIAC has conventionally been seen merely as having inspired the concept by providing an inefficient model on which to improve, the actual relationship between ENIAC and new paradigms was more complex. As we have seen, ENIAC was reconfigured in the middle of its career to run programs written in the modern code paradigm, remaking it as the first operational computer directly shaped by the First Draft. If one thinks of that design as a progeny of ENIAC, then ENIAC became, in a sense, its own grandchild, alongside cousins such as EDVAC, the Institute for Advanced Studies' machine and its derivatives, Univac, EDSAC, the ACE family, and the Manchester machines.

In this chapter we explore the historical questions of how and why historians came to define modern computers in terms of their adherence to the "stored program concept," examine the existing historical discussion of the relationship between that concept and the post-1948 ENIAC, and then present a broader and more practice-oriented analysis of ENIAC's capabilities as a general-purpose computer against those of other machines of its generation—including those that did not follow the EDVAC template, such as IBM's SSEC.

First, however, we will look in detail at something that has often been taken to be the first statement of the "stored program concept": Eckert's January 1944 description of a new kind of calculating machine.

Eckert's Magnetic Calculating Machine

Eckert and Mauchly later claimed to have fully developed the "stored program" breakthrough, including instruction modification, by early 1944. Eckert deployed the rhetoric of obviousness:

My best computer idea, today briefly called "stored program," became to us an "obvious idea," and one that we started to take for granted. It was obvious that computer instructions could be conveyed in a numerical code … . It was also obvious that the functions supplied by the Master Programmer in controlling loops and counting iterations, etc., would be achieved very naturally by allowing instructions to be subject to alterations within the calculator.[2]

Toward the end of his life, Mauchly wrote that, because "naturally, 'architecture' or 'logical organization' was the first thing to attend to" in designing EDVAC, by early 1944 they had settled on a single storage device, a single arithmetic unit, and full centralization of control.[3] However, the Moore School's records show that the possibility of giving EDVAC multiple arithmetic units was still on the table a year later, which suggests that the transition from ENIAC approaches toward the eventual EDVAC architecture proceeded more slowly and incrementally than Eckert and Mauchly suggested in retrospect.[4]

Eckert's January 1944 "Disclosure of Magnetic Calculating Machine" has often been cited in support of their claims. It sketched the idea of a computer memory based on metal disks or drums attached to rotating shafts. The crucial passage reads, in its cryptic entirety, as follows:

If multiple shaft systems are used a great increase in the available facilities for allowing automatic programming of the facilities and processes involved may be made, since longer time scales are provided. This greatly extends the usefulness and attractiveness of such a machine. This programming may be of the temporary type set up on alloy discs or of the permanent type on etched discs.[5]

Some have claimed that this passage proves that Eckert already planned to store instructions and data interchangeably in ENIAC's successor. In an important early history, Nancy Stern concluded that "months before von Neumann knew of the Moore School the stored-program concept had been conceived, if not developed."[6] Others alleged that von Neumann misappropriated a breakthrough by Eckert and Mauchly. The journalist Scott McCartney has perhaps been the most vigorous advocate of that position, marshaling an array of quotations from Eckert, Mauchly, and other Moore School veterans to question von Neumann's ethics and honesty. McCartney concluded that "many of von Neumann's actions ... appear to be calculated moves to claim credit for the birth of the computer."[7]

We disagree with the idea that the disclosure quoted from above represents an early statement of any "stored program concept," whether considered in the narrow sense of the interchangeable storage of program instructions and data within a single writable and addressable storage medium or in a broad sense encompassing other major ideas of the First Draft. One assumption that makes such conclusions plausible is that Eckert was describing a general-purpose machine with the scope and generality of ENIAC—a kind of proto-EDVAC. However, the disclosure introduces the invention as "a simplified method of constructing a numerical calculating machine" in which "some of the mechanical features of an ordinary mechanical calculating machine are retained and combined with certain electronic and magnetic devices to produce a speedier, simpler machine." In the concluding paragraph Eckert returned to this theme, noting that the machine "should be cheaper to build, because the precision of the electric parts is much smaller than the equivalent mechanical parts. Maintenance should be reduced because of the reliability and long life of the electric parts, the residual mechanical parts having only very simple bearing surfaces capable of giving long life."

Although the words "calculator" and "computer" did not refer in any systematic way to different kinds of machines during the period in question, the descriptions given in his disclosure suggest that Eckert was proposing an improved, electronic version of a desk calculator. Calculators such as those produced by the Marchant Calculating Machine Company were among the most intricate mechanical devices of the era. Controlled by means of keyboards, they displayed output on dials. Complex configurations of gears, drive shafts, and levers were crammed into boxes small enough to sit on desks to deliver the basic arithmetic operations of addition, subtraction, multiplication, and division. Manufacturing tolerances were extremely

precise, assembly was challenging, and the calculators required regular servicing by
an expert. These machines were widely used in science, engineering, and business.
A clear commercial market therefore existed for a superior alternative, whereas the
commercial prospects for a huge automatic computer costing hundreds of thousands
of dollars were extremely hazy.

One thing Eckert retained from the conventional calculator was its "continuously
rotating shaft called a time shaft, driven by an electric motor." Mechanical calculators stored numbers as cog positions. Eckert proposed instead to store them on
"discs or drums which have at least their outer edge made of a magnetic alloy
capable of being magnetized and demagnetized repeatedly and at high speed." Data
would be stored in "sectors," a term still used today. Eckert was describing for the
first time the hard-disk drive (widely used from the 1960s on) and the magnetic-
drum memory (a leading storage technology of the 1950s). Driving a conventional
mechanical indicator dial with electronic logic would have been difficult, so Eckert
also proposed a special class of indicator "discs or drums carrying characters, usually the digits 0 to 9." As the disks rotated, these digits would be illuminated by
neon lights flashing according to a "stroboscope principle" to display the results.

John Atanasoff's computer had used a rotating drum to store working data, but
it had used capacitance rather than magnetism to represent numbers. Timing the
operation of electronic logic against the much lower rate at which data could be
read from the drum greatly slowed its computation speed (something for which
Mauchly later criticized it severely), but also dramatically reduced its cost.[8] Indeed,
Mauchly's now-famous June 1941 drive to Iowa to inspect the device was prompted
by Atanasoff's claim to have hit on a very inexpensive method of data storage. The
tradeoff of reduced speed against lower cost and increased capacity might be undesirable for a high-end computer such as ENIAC, but it was extremely attractive for
a desk calculator. The prototype Atanasoff-Berry Computer (ABC) cost less than
$7,000 to build.[9] Perhaps Eckert therefore assumed that a substantially simpler
mass-produced calculator could be sold for about $1,000, a cost competitive with
that of a high-end mechanical calculator. By the optimistic standards used to estimate the cost and duration of electronic computing projects of the 1940s that would
not seem absurd.

Historical discussion has focused on Eckert's reference to the setting up of "automatic programming" on the rotating disks of his machine. However, we should not
jump to the conclusion that Eckert was using the word "programming" in its current
sense. Throughout ENIAC's development, "program" referred primarily to the
action of a "program control" to direct a single operation—not, as it would later,
to the complete set of instructions required to solve a particular problem.[10] In
the ENIAC project's first progress report, issued in early 1944 just as Eckert was
preparing his disclosure, "programming" typically appears in references to the

"programming circuits" in each unit that sequenced actions according to that unit's external switch settings, only occasionally coming closer to today's sense of the word by referring more loosely to the activity of setting those switches. The "joining of these [basic operations] for carrying out a problem" is described as "setting up a problem," not as programming it, and the word "program" does not occur in the chapter of the report dealing with the "setup of problems on the ENIAC." Elsewhere, the report noted that the design, the construction, and the testing of ENIAC were speeded up by avoiding "the necessity of devising and constructing separate equipment for automatically setting up the interconnections and programs."[11]

The phrase "automatically programmed" first appeared in ENIAC documentation in connection with the multiplier. Numbers to be multiplied had to be placed in accumulators connected directly to the multiplier. The June 1944 progress report proposed that "when a program pulse is sent to any particular program control of the multiplier, the multiplier and multiplicand accumulators will be automatically programmed to receive the multiplier and the multiplicand."[12] Here it is the multiplier unit that is said to be "programming" the accumulators, not the human operator.

Eckert's discussion of "automatic programming" should be understood in the light of these contemporaneous usages: rather than the instructions for a complete problem, it refers to the process whereby a command signal received by a control unit to perform a complex operation, such as multiplication, would automatically trigger a series of more basic operations in the machine's arithmetic units. High-speed multiplication and division capabilities made mechanical calculators far more expensive than mere adding machines and pushed the limits of what could be engineered into a reasonably compact unit. Eckert's disclosure proposed to simplify this greatly by making addition the only basic operation. In his calculator, "subtraction, multiplication, and division" would be "carried out by processes of successive addition," which would have to be sequenced somehow. Eckert introduced the idea of automatic control by discussing "discs or drums having edges or surfaces engraved" so that as they rotated they would "generate such pulses or other electric signals as were required to time, control, and initiate the operations required in the calculations." This, he noted, "is similar to the tone generating mechanism used in some electric organs," in which bumps on the rim of a rotating disc were read magnetically to determine the combination of frequencies generated when a key was pressed.

The procedure proposed by Eckert is akin to the later concept of microcoding. A single mathematical function requested by the user (such as a multiplication) would trigger the execution of a series of operations (such as additions and data transfers) according to the control sequence etched onto the disk. This allows us to make sense of Eckert's puzzling comment that "multiple shaft systems" would yield "a great increase in the available facilities for allowing automatic programming" because "longer time scales are provided."[13] Eckert expected programs and data to be stored on separate disks, and indeed on disks of different kinds. He had mentioned that disks might be magnetized only on the outer edges, providing only one data track per disk. The maximum complexity of a programmed operation (for example, multiplication) might thus be limited by the time a program disk would take to rotate once. Rotating the shaft more slowly would provide a "longer time scale" for the operation. Because separate shafts were needed so that data disks could rotate more rapidly than program disks, the calculator would have time to complete a coded action involving the retrieval or updating of a number from the faster-rotating data disk before the slower-rotating program disk delivered a new code to trigger the next action. The idea of using different rotational speeds within a single machine was certainly familiar to Eckert and Mauchly—Atanasoff's computer had used a small drum, mounted on a shaft rotating sixteen times as fast as its main storage drums, to temporarily store carries between digits.

The idea of building sequences of operations into hardware to be executed on demand was also familiar. We have already mentioned ENIAC's own multiplier and divider units. In late 1943, a "function generator," which would store certain values of a function and would implement an interpolation algorithm to generate intermediate values, was planned for ENIAC.[14] The Harvard Mark I took a similar approach, hard-wiring what have in retrospect sometimes been called "subroutines" into its specialist units for multiplication, division, logarithmic, exponential, and sine functions, and interpolation so that a call for one of these operations would trigger an elaborate series of steps across the machine. A single operation could take a full minute to complete.[15] Eckert's "automatic programming" mechanism might easily have been used to implement these functions and others.

As we read Eckert's disclosure, then, he was proposing a calculator designed for interactive, individual use—a calculator that would occupy a place in the computational ecosystem similar to that occupied by the most advanced mechanical calculators of the day. He suggested that "numbers might be put into the machine by means of the usual keyboards." In contrast, the experimental electronic and electromechanical computers of the 1940s read numbers and output results on punched cards or paper tape. Those media were expensive—particularly punched cards, on which IBM enjoyed high profit margins. In his disclosure, a preliminary statement of a possibly patentable invention, Eckert expressed its potential in the broadest possible terms so as to maximize the scope of any resulting patent. He mentioned the possibility of using paper media for input and output, but his conclusion reiterated his assumption of keyboard control, stating that his calculator achieved "an economy over card and tape machines" because "no materials are normally used in the operation of the machine, only electric power is consumed."

The general goal of building an electronic desk calculator may even have predated the ENIAC project. Mauchly testified during the ENIAC patent trial that as early as January of 1941 he was beginning to design "rather simple" machines, "essentially desk calculators capable of storing enough information so that you would not have to repeatedly reenter numbers which were to be used again and again … . But working from a keyboard, not from a punched card necessarily."[16] It seems that by 1944 Eckert, whose engineering abilities were far superior to his partner's, was returning to this idea.

The proposed calculator would have been much simpler and cheaper than ENIAC, and far less capable than the successor to ENIAC that was promised to the BRL in the summer of 1944. However, one can identify some parallels between the ideas Eckert explored in his disclosure and what we have called the EDVAC hardware paradigm. The calculator's logic would be simplified by using binary rather than decimal number representations. Its aggressive target cost placed a premium on simplicity, which pushed Eckert toward minimizing the logic circuitry by transmitting digits serially rather than in parallel.

Eckert did not mention the possibility of reading instruction sequences from a control tape, or that of copying such instructions onto disks or drums for internal storage.[17] Certainly it is not reasonable to conclude from the disclosure that Eckert had already settled on the EDVAC approach of fetching and executing coded instructions, one at a time, from an addressable storage medium where they were stored interchangeably with data.[18] Surviving material discussing ENIAC upgrades and successors before the First Draft includes no discussion of instruction formats or of addressing systems. Even in early 1945, what little time Eckert and Mauchly could devote to EDVAC appears, from the various surviving disclosures of potentially patentable ideas, to have been spent primarily on storage technologies, including delay lines and magnetic disks. A patent was, in fact, granted to them on delay-line memory.[19]

Pulling back from the specifics of the disclosure, we conclude that the attachment of historians to a singular "stored program concept" has obscured more than it has revealed by forcing Eckert's admirers to make the case for his contribution to EDVAC on the basis of a few rather ambiguous words. Eckert's contributions to the modern computer are undervalued by such an approach. In early 1944, Eckert's idea of using delay lines to build a large, high-speed, rewritable memory was far more important in driving the EDVAC project forward than his rather inchoate ideas about control. Before Eckert's breakthrough, there was no high-speed writable memory technology large enough to store a program of any usefulness. A suggestion to use ENIAC-style accumulators for program instructions as well as for data would reveal its originator to have been an idiot rather than a genius. Eckert's impulse to focus on memory technologies and his identification of delay lines and rotating magnetic media as promising alternatives to ENIAC's accumulators confirm his greatness as an engineer.

The "Stored Program Concept"

In this book we have avoided using the undifferentiated term "stored program," preferring to define the contributions of the First Draft in terms of the modern code paradigm, the von Neumann architecture paradigm, and the EDVAC hardware paradigm. This avoids the implication, implicit in discussion of "the stored program concept," that the development of modern computing is merely a working through of the implications of a single brilliant idea.

We will now justify this choice by historicizing the term "stored program." We saw earlier that discussion of "EDVAC-type" machines during the late 1940s identified a number of distinct advances. In conjunction with new memory technologies, the von Neumann architecture allowed construction of computers that were smaller, cheaper, and more reliable than their immediate predecessors. Two intertwined histories are of interest here. The first is the process by which the many ideas explored in the First Draft and in related documents were eventually reduced to a consensus that the single crucial characteristic setting the computers of the late 1940s apart from their predecessors was the storage of instructions and data in a shared memory. The second is the process by which the specific term "stored program" was attached to that concept.

The Earliest Uses of the Term "Stored Program"

The First Draft does not, despite the role it has been assigned in later historical work, define the meaning of "stored program." Indeed, the word "program" never appears in it. John von Neumann consistently favored "code" over "program" and "memory" over "storage." "Memorized code" would be a more natural summary of its vision of instruction storage than "stored program." Thus, the current attachment to the term "stored program" as a description for computers built along these lines requires some historical explanation. Read literally, the term conveys very little. Any program that can be executed by a computer must be stored in some form. The First Draft itself observed that "instructions must be given in some form which the device can sense: Punched into a system of punchcards or on teletype tape, magnetically impressed on steel tape or wire, photographically impressed on motion picture film, wired into one or more fixed or exchangeable plugboards—this list being by no means necessarily complete."[20]

"Stored program" took several years to appear. The proceedings of the Moore School lectures, issued in 1948, did not include the phrase.[21] Neither could we find it in the proceedings of a conference held at Harvard University in 1947, in the introductory books published by Douglas Hartree in 1947 and 1949, in the proceedings of the 1949 Cambridge University computer conference, or in the primer *High-Speed Computing Devices*, published in 1950 by Engineering Research Associates.[22] In fact, we have been unable to locate it in any publication of the 1940s.

In the 1940s, authors used a variety of other terms to describe the new breed of computers. The most common was "digital automatic computer." "Digital" separated them from analog machines, such as differential analyzers. "Automatic" indicated that machines, rather than people, were being referred to. "Electronic," another popular adjective, set the high-speed machines apart from their electromechanical ancestors. With this vocabulary, the distinction between ENIAC or IBM's SSEC and computers patterned after EDVAC was not always apparent. *High-Speed Computing Devices* grouped machines such as ENIAC and EDVAC together as "large scale digital computer systems."[23] A similar implicit taxonomy presented at the 1951 joint AIEE-IRE conference lumped computers such as the Harvard Mark III and even IBM's humble Card Programmed Calculator together with the new EDVAC-style machines in its treatment of "operating high-speed digital computers."[24]

Where did the term "stored program" actually come from, and why did it eventually replace alternatives such as "EDVAC-type machine" as a description of the new kind of computer? The earliest use we have been able to establish is in 1949, within the small team at IBM's Poughkeepsie facility that, under the direction of Nathaniel Rochester, produced IBM's first EDVAC-type computer, usually called the "Test Assembly." That experimental system deployed IBM's first electronic calculator, the 604 Electronic Calculating Punch, as the arithmetic unit of a cobbled-together computer. It was joined to a new control unit, a cathode-ray-tube memory, and a magnetic drum.

The resulting machine had two potential programming mechanisms, as the 604 already included a plugboard able to hold a program of up to 60 instructions. To distinguish between that wired program and the more complex and flexible sequence of instructions held in the 250-word electronic memory or on the drum, the team began to call the latter the "stored program." A proposal written by Rochester in 1949 noted that the cost of the plugboard and the work required to program made it impractical once a certain level of complexity had been reached. Thus, he asserted, "the best solution to this difficulty is to introduce the calculating program into the machine on a deck of tabulating cards and to retain it, along with the numerical data, in the storage section of the calculator." The report was titled "A Calculator Using Electrostatic Storage and a Stored Program."[25]

The earliest appearance of "stored program" in print we have so far come across is a 1950 description of the Northrop Aircraft Corporation's Magnetic Drum Digital Differential Analyzer (MADDIDA) as "controlled by a novel form of stored program."[26] Today, MADDIDA is not considered a stored-program computer or even a programmable computer, though its control information was stored internally on a magnetic drum. In this instance the term seems to have attached itself to drum control rather than to use of the modern code paradigm.

The Term "Stored Program" Spreads in the 1950s

Nathaniel Rochester and his IBM collaborators took the term "stored program" with them as they progressed from the Test Assembly to its experimental successor, the Tape Processing Machine, and eventually to the 701 (IBM's first computer product). For example, Clarence Frizzell, a veteran of the Test Assembly project, noted that the 701 was "controlled by means of a stored program."[27]

In later usage, references to digital computers controlled by stored programs were condensed into references to "stored program computers." In a paper presented at the 1951 AIEE-IRE Computer Conference, two employees of IBM described that company's Card Programmed Calculator, which coupled a 604 Electronic Calculating Punch with a card-driven control unit. The authors praised the flexibility and speed of that configuration, contrasting it with a "stored program machine," for which, they said, "it is usually necessary to economize on the length of sequences [of instructions], on account of the limited storage available."[28]

In a 1953 paper titled "Fundamentals of Digital Computer Programming," another IBM employee, Walker Thomas, asserted that "all stored-program digital computers have four basic elements: the memory or storage element, the arithmetic element, the control element, and the terminal equipment or input-output element," and that because the "coded form in which an instruction appears in memory is a number, there is no distinction between a number representing data for calculations and a number representing an instruction." An instruction could therefore "be acted upon by other instructions to change its meaning."[29] Here "stored-program" had evolved beyond its literal meaning to encompass two important characteristics of the modern code paradigm: the use of the same internal memory for both programs and data, and the ability of the computer to modify the stored program by means of the same instructions and techniques used to modify numerical data.

By 1953, "stored program" was sufficiently well established within the small world of electronic computer users that Willis Ware of the Rand Corporation could refer to "what we know now as the 'stored program machine.'"[30] The phrase was not enormously common in the 1950s, but it occurred in conference proceedings with reasonable frequency—particularly in presentations by employees of IBM. A promise that the IBM 650 would be "a vital factor in familiarizing business and industry with the stored program principles fundamental to electronic data processing" made its way into the 1953 announcement of that computer.[31] The phrase does not seem to have entered IBM's carefully controlled official vocabulary for documentation and advertisements, however.

"Stored Program Computer" Becomes a Historiographical Term

"Stored program" was no more common in the 1960s than in the 1950s, probably because all mainstream digital computers of the era executed their programs from addressable memory rather than directly from paper tape, plugboards, or external switches. In the title of a book or an article, "digital computer" was understood to imply stored-program control. Only with the rise of interest in the history of computing did it again become necessary to distinguish stored-program computers from other kinds of digital computers. "Stored program" enjoyed a renaissance in the 1970s after its prominent use by the computer pioneer Herman Goldstine in a book titled *The Computer from Pascal to von Neumann.*[32] Goldstine, then an IBM fellow, helped to establish the relatively obscure technical term at the center of the growing historical discourse.

ENIAC has generally been considered by historians to be a "general purpose" computer but not a "stored program computer," although the idea that these two things could be separated has sometimes been disputed. Arthur and Alice Burks, in a substantial 1981 article documenting ENIAC, had attempted to precisely define the capabilities of a general-purpose computer.[33] In response, Brian Randell, an early leader of historical efforts in the field, suggested that ENIAC could not be considered general purpose because it lacked the crucial feature of being able "to select among items held in its read-write memory, based on results so far computed," which was "one of the most significant and distinct characteristics of so-called stored-program computers."[34] In other words, to Randell only an EDVAC-type computer could be considered general purpose. That was rather a revisionist position, given that ENIAC had been called "general purpose" back in the 1940s. For example, a 1946 article by John Brainerd had been subtitled "Mathematical robot is the first all-electronic general purpose computer ever to be developed."[35]

After historians resolved the debates of the 1970s over the "first computer" by collectively withdrawing that metaphorical prize without having settled on a winner, the most dazzling of the remaining accolades for early computers was that for the "first stored-program computer." That prize was split between two British machines: Cambridge University's EDSAC and Manchester University's Small Scale Experimental Machine (nicknamed the Baby), which ran its first program on June 21, 1948.

Manchester University's tiny prototype was built to test a novel method of using a cathode-ray tube for data storage. It was assembled quickly in the most modest configuration possible—a code of only eight instructions (not including add) and a single memory tube holding 32 words of memory. The Baby ran several test programs to prove the reliability of the memory but never tackled a program of any practical use before its parts were redeployed to build a full-sized computer.

In contrast, EDSAC was, by the standards of its day, a powerful computer. It ran its first programs on May 6, 1949, and it remained in service until 1958. Its creators built an extensive subroutine library, wrote the first textbook on programming, and pioneered several ideas that would become fundamental to systems programming, including that of the assembler.[36] EDSAC, like ENIAC, was applied to numerous scientific and mathematical problems. In their authoritative overview of the history of computing, Martin Campbell-Kelly and William Aspray wrote that, with the first successful run of EDSAC in May of 1949, "the world's first practical stored-program computer had come to life, and with it the dawn of the computer age."[37] That consensus put ENIAC (which was programmed with wires and switches) and the Harvard Mark I (which read its instructions from a paper tape) on the wrong side of the historical divide.

"Stored Program" Becomes a "Concept"
The emergence of the "stored program concept" was a third stage in the evolution of the term "stored program." That term originally and literally described a type of program, but soon it was used to denote a class of "stored program computers." Historical discussion extended this further with the implication that a "stored program concept" was the dividing line between the first true computers and their predecessors. With so few machines to distinguish among, one could agree that (for example) the Harvard Mark I was not a stored-program computer but EDSAC was a stored-program computer without having to determine what permutation of the many differences between them was necessary and sufficient to establish this. The new consensus did imply that the dividing line involved the ability to load a data sequence into memory and execute it as a program; however, as Doron Swade discovered, the extent to which this was seen as the only significant difference or as one aspect of a much broader shift could and did vary wildly.

Agreement on a "stored program concept" as the defining characteristic of the modern computer has inspired attempts to cram more features into its definition. In a report titled "The Origin of the Stored Program Concept", Allan G. Bromley demarcated ten "sub concepts" with separate inventors. According to Bromley, the "stages" of invention began well before the First Draft with the invention of electronic digital arithmetic and finished some years later with the invention of microprogramming and assemblers.[38] Others have suggested that Turing's work on the design for the ACE, carried out a few months after he read the First Draft, added crucial aspects of the concept that von Neumann had either missed or failed to develop fully.[39] We have some sympathy with efforts to separate and clarify distinct aspects of the modern computer, and we acknowledge the continued articulation of the various paradigms disseminated in the First Draft over the months and years that followed. However, labeling all these aspects with the monolithic term "the stored program concept" rather undermines the whole enterprise.

Historians have also tended to treat "stored program concept" and "von Neumann architecture" as synonymous, further blurring their meanings. For example, Campbell-Kelly and Aspray noted with distress that "computer scientists routinely speak of the 'von Neumann architecture' in preference to the more prosaic 'stored program concept'; this has done an injustice to von Neumann's co-inventors."[40]

In recent years, "stored program concept" has increasingly been conflated with the more formal concept of a computer's being "Turing complete" or "universal" if equipped with a memory of sufficient size. There are few references to Turing's theoretical work among the discussions of those who were building computers in the 1940s.[41] In more recent discussion, however, the advantages of stored-program machines have often been argued for by appealing to the theoretical concerns of later generations of academic computer scientists rather than to the pragmatic issues of primary importance to their designers.[42]

Here we will cite three of many recent examples of this now conventional wisdom: As of this writing, the Wikipedia page on "stored-program computer" defines it as "one which stores program instructions in electronic memory," adds that "often the definition is extended with the requirement that the treatment of programs and data in memory be interchangeable," and then says that "the stored program computer idea can be traced back to the 1936 theoretical concept of a universal Turing machine."[43] In *Computing: A Concise History*, Paul Ceruzzi defined stored-program computers as storing "both their instructions—the programs—and the data on which those instructions operate in the same physical memory device" and suggested that this "extended Turing's ideas into the design of practical machinery."[44] Doron Swade eventually retreated from the endearingly bold confession of confusion we quoted earlier in this chapter to conclude that "the internal stored program" was "the practical realization of Turing universality" and thus conferred "plasticity of function, which in large part accounts for the remarkable proliferation of computers and computer-like artefacts."[45] Some have even claimed that Alan Turing was the true inventor of the stored-program computer.[46]

ENIAC as a "Stored Program Computer"

The current literature gives a contradictory picture of the post-1948 ENIAC as a stored-program computer, reflecting the inherent ambiguity of the concept. Many of those involved in the discussion of early computers have a deep attachment to the claims of one machine or another. For example, one peer reviewer of an earlier paper of ours took exception to discussion of the ways in which ENIAC did and did not implement ideas from the First Draft, decrying our "attempt to equate the converted ENIAC with a true general-purpose stored-program computer. To fellow computer historians this will seem like playing with words. ENIAC was an extremely significant machine in its own right but it was not a true general-purpose stored-program computer." Our challenge to the conventional structuring of history by agreed "firsts," in which the "stored program concept" is in effect defined as the line dividing ENIAC from the next generation of computers, was so self-evidently heretical that the reviewer recommended rejection without documenting any specific flaws in evidence or reasoning.

In contrast, some of those involved in the conversion itself did consider ENIAC to be a stored-program computer. At the end of her life, Jean Bartik wrote: "ENIAC was the world's first stored-program computer and I should know, because I led the team that turned the ENIAC into a stored-program computer."[47] Richard Clippinger, who had likewise claimed primary credit for the conversion, was more nuanced in a 1970 oral history, calling ENIAC a "microprogrammed machine which had a stored program in the sense that it was stored in the function table, but not in the sense that it was stored in the same memory, and could be operated upon by the instructions themselves."[48]

These claims can be, and have been, attacked in two ways. The first is by arguing that ENIAC never became a stored-program computer. The second is by arguing that it became one only after a purpose-built stored-program computer, the Manchester "Baby," ran its first program on June 21, 1948.

The second objection, that of timing, is unequivocally refuted by the primary sources we cited in our discussion of the conversion. In his influential book *The Computer from Pascal to von Neumann*, published in 1972, Herman Goldstine devoted several paragraphs to ENIAC's conversion and stated with apparent exactitude, though without any cited source, that "on 16 September 1948 the new system ran on the ENIAC."[49] Coming several months after the Manchester milestone, this appeared to leave little point to debating the status of ENIAC's read-only system. Later authors (among them Hans Neukom, author of a detailed published treatment of ENIAC's conversion) have generally accepted Goldstine's date.[50]

The first objection—that the post-conversion ENIAC was not truly a stored-program computer—cannot be dealt with so conclusively. Less partisan experts who have looked closely at ENIAC in its mature configuration have generally described it as a stored-program computer but qualified that with an adjective or two.

Nicholas Metropolis, in one of the earliest articles on computer history, credited ENIAC with a third step ("internal control of calculations," in 1946) and a fourth step ("storage control of a computer," in 1948) toward the stored-program computer, but not with the final step of "read write memories for stored programs." Thus, one should "credit the ENIAC as the first computer to be run with a *read-only* stored program" but the "BINAC and the EDSAC as being the first computers to be run with a *dynamically modifiable* stored program."[51] Goldstine called ENIAC "a somewhat primitive stored program computer."[52] Aspray, in his definitive treatment of von Neumann's computing work, called ENIAC "a (read only) stored program computer" that was "used in the stored-program mode" and was "modified for stored-program operation."[53] Attaching "primitive" to "stored program computer" nevertheless acknowledges ENIAC as a kind of stored-program computer. Yet Aspray and Goldstine backed away from the implications of their own descriptions, which would logically make ENIAC the first operational stored-program computer. Perhaps confused by the issue of timing, they elsewhere endorsed EDSAC as the first useful stored-program computer, and SEAC as the first useful stored-program computer in the United States.

Arthur Burks, researching ENIAC's conversion during the 1970s, noted this contradiction. He concluded that the "program language of the ENIAC had the same instructional ability as the program language of the von Neumann computer, except that the latter also had the revolutionary address substitution instructions."[54] Burks insisted that these substitution instructions were essential to the "stored program concept." In 1990 he reviewed Aspray's one-page article "The Stored Program Concept" for *IEEE Spectrum*. His comments filled four pages. Aspray's draft had given ENIAC a significant role, calling it "the first full-scale working model of a stored program computer." Burks insisted that "the stored program must be read-write" and that therefore ENIAC remained "a programmable, but not a stored program computer, by the universally accepted definition of the stored program concept." He warned that Aspray's language, if read logically, implicitly credited the ENIAC of 1948 as the first true computer. Aspray's published paper followed Burks' advice to "remove all mention of the 1948 ENIAC."[55]

Neither position seems satisfactory to us, and that provides further evidence of the inadequacy of "stored program concept" as an analytical category. We have some sympathy with the graduated definitions proposed by Metropolis 40 years ago, but the community of historians of computing took a different direction. The phrases chosen by Aspray and Goldstine likewise capture the reality that the 1948 ENIAC implemented some but not all aspects of the EDVAC design, but within the discourse of the "stored program concept" this truth can be expressed only fuzzily by attaching adjectives to acknowledge ENIAC's subaltern role. Burks set up a crisp definition of "stored program computer" that ENIAC did not meet. Yet this arbitrarily denied the real and direct connections between the First Draft and the converted ENIAC. In particular, Burks did not acknowledge that ENIAC, by storing jump destinations in writable accumulator memory (a form of indirect addressing), gained the same address-modification capabilities that von Neumann's EDVAC gained by allowing direct manipulation of an instruction's address field.

These battles to define "stored program" remind us of the earnest moral of the movie *WarGames*: the only winning move is not to play. Its complex career in the hands of pioneers and historians has left the term hopelessly overloaded with contradictory meanings. The 1948 ENIAC aligns with some of those meanings but not with others. Our definition of the "modern code paradigm" characterizes the new kind of program that was introduced with the First Draft in 1945. The ENIAC code and flow diagrams preserved from the 1948 Monte Carlo computations have an unmistakable kinship with those described by von Neumann's team in their publications.

On the other hand, in the 1940s the significance of "EDVAC-type" machines was often understood in terms of the simplicity and flexibility of the new von Neumann architecture, which, in combination with new memory technologies central to the EDVAC hardware paradigm, promised a radical reduction in the number of expensive and unreliable tubes needed. ENIAC remained just as bulky and full of tubes after its conversion, and thus stayed off the mental radar of other computing groups. We know of no direct influence from its 1948 conversion to the design of any other computer. In contrast, the Manchester Baby's demonstration that cathode-ray-tube storage worked was treated as sensational news.[56]

ENIAC and Its Peers

Rather than pursue this semantic game any further, we will now compare the 1948 ENIAC with other machines of the late 1940s as a practical tool and as an embodiment of the new ideas about computer design and programming introduced by von Neumann and his collaborators in the First Draft and in subsequent publications. Only by privileging certain aspects of EDVAC as described therein, and ignoring others, can one draw a clear line separating the Manchester Baby, EDSAC, and the Pilot ACE (which are invariably described as "stored program computers") from the 1948 ENIAC.

This is particularly striking in the case of the Manchester Baby, as the 1948 ENIAC came much closer to many aspects of the EDVAC vision. For example, von Neumann insisted on a large memory capacity, favoring 8,192 32-bit words. Yet the Baby had only 32 words of memory in which to squeeze both programs and data and could run only programs of trivial scope. ENIAC's writable memory was similarly tiny, but its read-only memory was much closer to the size suggested by von Neumann and could be partitioned between program code and numerical data as the needs of particular problems demanded, as he had recommended. Both the 1948 ENIAC and the Baby were usually programmed by moving switches, but ENIAC treated its large arrays of switches as addressable memory whereas the Baby copied the input into writable memory one location at a time. The First Draft was explicit about the need to be able to store results on an external medium and feed them back into the machine. Unlike the Baby, ENIAC, with its card punch and reader, could do that, and could even execute programs directly from punched cards.[57]

The SSEC and the "Stored Program Concept"

One of ENIAC's more neglected contemporaries, IBM's quirky Selective Sequence Electronic Calculator, provides a particularly interesting comparison with ENIAC. Both were one-of-a-kind machines, and the SSEC falls outside the well-documented story of 1940s computing as a succession of "firsts" leading inexorably to the modern computer. Installed for a few years as a street-level showpiece in IBM's New York City headquarters, the SSEC was operational in January of 1948, before any other machine of comparable versatility. Like ENIAC, it was much sought after by groups with serious computational requirements, and some of the Los Alamos computations originally slated for ENIAC were found to exceed ENIAC's storage capacity and promptly transferred to the SSEC.

The SSEC's design was not perceptibly influenced by the ideas expressed in the First Draft. It has nevertheless occasionally been advocated for as the first stored-program computer, because instructions could be fetched and executed from its relatively spacious electromechanical relay memory or its rather cramped electronic memory.[58] The SSEC could hold specific instructions in memory alongside data and could modify them under programmatic control, satisfying one widely used definition of the "stored program concept." Yet when looking at the machine as a whole, one is struck instead by the fact that a group with so many resources at its disposal produced something more complex than an EDVAC-type computer but considerably less capable.

The SSEC soon seemed spectacularly idiosyncratic. It was equipped with a large number of high-speed punched-card readers and tape readers, many of the latter based on an unusual 80-column design in which the "tape" was essentially a roll of punched-card stock. Each instruction included a two-digit code to specify the source (usually one of the paper-tape drives) from which the next instruction was to be fetched. Portions of code that were to be executed repeatedly, such as subroutines and the inner portions of loops, were stuck end to end with a glue gun to form a physical loop. Conditional branching was accomplished by transferring control to a different tape held on a separate drive, not by jumping to a different location number within the same program sequence.[59]

The use of a two-digit code for the source of the next instruction severely limited the SSEC's ability to execute programs from memory. Because it possessed 150 relay memory locations, dozens of tape readers, and eight electronic memory locations, three digits were needed to specify an actual memory location. The two-digit codes were mapped to physical locations by re-wiring a plugboard that linked the codes to specific paper-tape drives, card readers, card punches, printers, or memory locations. Repeated reads from the same tape source via "read with move" address codes would trigger automatic advances so that instructions or data were read sequentially.[60] Because the SSEC did not provide a similar feature for its random-access

Table 11.1
Comparison of pre- and post-conversion ENIAC with von Neumann's 1945 plan for EDVAC and three other computers of the late 1940s.

	1945 EDVAC	1945 ENIAC	IBM SSEC	1948 ENIAC	Manchester "Baby" SSEM	EDSAC
Operational (specs as of)	Not applicable	December 1945–Jan 1946	January 1948	April 12, 1948	June 21, 1948	May 6, 1949
Programs loaded via	Mechanism not specified. Storage was "organ R."	Re-wired from "set up diagrams"	Run directly from card or tape	Turning switches	Flipping switches	Five-channel paper tape; 31 words of memory wired onto terminals for "Initial Orders"
Programs usually executed from	Mercury delay lines	Distributed system of switches, plugboards and ad hoc buses	High-speed paper tape	Banks of switches	Williams tubes	Mercury delay lines
Programs can also be executed from	Not applicable	Not applicable	Relay memory; electronic memory	Direct from punched card	Not applicable	Not applicable
Readable, addressable memory size	8,192 32-bit words	4,000 decimal digits (data only)	Up to 100 19-digit words (only 8 electronic; others relay)[a]	4,000 decimal digits	32 words	512 17-bit words[b]
Approximately equivalent size in bits	262,000	12,800	7,700[c]	12,800[d]	1,024	8,704
Writable high-speed memory size	Same as readable	200 decimal digits	Same as readable	200 decimal digits (many double as special-purpose registers)	Same as readable	Same as readable

Approximate equivalent size in bits	262,000	640	7,700	640	1,024	8,704
Add time	Not applicable	200 microseconds[e]	285 microseconds[f]	1,200 microseconds[g]	2,880 microseconds[83]	1,500 microseconds
Input/Output	Various options discussed	Punched-card machines (one at 133 cps for output, one at 133 cps for input).[j]	Many card readers and high-speed 80-track tape readers.	Punched-card machines (one at 133 cps for output, one at 133 cps for input).[j]	Results read from tube. Numbers entered via switches.	5 channel paper tape at 6.23 cps,[k] Teleprinter
Conditional Branch Mechanism	Via instruction modification	Adapter and "null program" turns data output from comparison into control input.	Transfer control to device specified by two-digit code, mapped via plugboard.	N3D6 loads three-digit argument into accumulator 6; CT jumps to that address if accumulator 15 is positive[j]	Jumps made to location number specified by the contents of a memory location specified in the instruction.	Conditional branch to location specified in instruction based on sign of accumulator, or via instruction modification.
Indirect Addressing Mechanism	Via instruction modification	Not applicable	Instructions taken from electronic or relay memory could be modified programmatically.	Transfers/jumps made from location number specified by value placed in a fixed memory location.	Via memory indirect method—a transfer instruction includes the address from which to fetch either the address to jump to or the amount by which to increment the program counter.	Via instruction modification

Table 11.1 (continued)

	1945 EDVAC	1945 ENIAC	IBM SSEC	1948 ENIAC	Manchester "Baby" SSEM	EDSAC
Instruction format	1 address	Not applicable	4 address	0 and 1 address mix[1]	1 address	1 address
Instruction word length	32-bit	Not applicable	19 decimal digits	2 to 8 decimal digits	16-bit	17-bit
Instruction set	8 operations, mostly load and store for different registers with one arithmetic instruction performing a choice of ten operations on a stack-like configuration of three registers.	Not applicable	Two instructions per word. Three digits for operation code. Two digits each for addresses, incl. next instruction source. Have not located full instruction set.	79 instructions, of which 40 are store or load variants, 20 are shifts.	Subtract; Negate; Transfer; Conditional skip; Conditional jump; Unconditional jump; Halt.	Add; Subtract; Copy to multiply register; multiply (x2); Transfer (x2); Collate; Shift (x2); conditional jump (x2); read tape; print; verify output; no operation; round; halt.
Maximum Program Length	8,192 instructions, less space needed for data.	Not applicable (multiple constraints distributed around machine).	Effectively unlimited, as a large program can span many paper tapes. Each subroutine on a different tape. Number of jumps limited by two-digit address coding scheme.	1460 instructions (assumes average 2.6 digits per instruction) less space needed for constants.	32 instructions, less space needed for data.	512 instructions, less space needed for data (and initial orders).

a. The SSEC had 150 words of relay memory and 8 words of electronic memory, but each location from which an instruction was to be read had to be given its own two-digit code. These codes were mapped to actual memory locations via a plugboard. In practice only instructions requiring modification were read from relay or electronic memory. Branches were accomplished by transferring control to a different paper-tape drive, from which instructions could be read sequentially without the need for multiple plugboard entries. Each subroutine or inner loop was stored on a different drive.

b. The original memory size of EDSAC is sometimes given as 256 36-bit words, reflecting its ability to handle 35-bit data words as well as 17-bit instruction words. Because of timing issues with its delay-line memory the last bit in either size of word was always wasted.

c. The SSEC stored words of 19 digits in binary coded decimal format as 76 number bits plus sign and parity, so we are treating each word as 77 data bits here.

d. Conversion assumes that one twenty-digit decimal word is equivalent to one 64-bit word. Use of binary coded decimal would require 4 bits per digit, or 80 bits per twenty-digit word.

e. 1945 ENIAC is hard to compare here, since several additions could be performed simultaneously.

f. However, the SSEC would usually spend a much longer time waiting for its next instruction to load from high-speed paper tape, an issue only partly addressed by a complex system of loading instructions two at a time. Even reads from relay memory could not take place at electronic speeds as relays had to move to access the location needed.

g. Confusingly, after conversion ENIAC needed six "add times," each of 200 microseconds, to execute one addition. Subtraction took eight, multiplication twenty, and shifts nine. We are assuming here 100-KHz operation. Later improvements reduced these times.

h. Adding required two operations as it was performed via subtraction and negation.

i. According to Goldstine, *A Report on the ENIAC*, VII-1 "The rate is 160 cards per minute when the reader reads continuously without stopping and may be either 120 or 160 cards per minute when the reader stops between readings." For output, Goldstine notes (IX-1) that "Cards may be punched at the rate of approximately 100 per minute."

j. Instructions to punch (Pr) or read (Rd) a card each took 3,000 add times, i.e., 600,000 microseconds or 0.6 seconds. Each card held 80 characters, hence throughput of 133 characters per second.

k. As of 1949, "input was on 5-track teleprinter paper tape via an electromechanical tape reader running at 6⅔ characters per second" and "output was delivered via a teleprinter at 6⅔ char/sec" (http://www.cl.cam.ac.uk/conference/EDSAC99/statistics.html).

l. As was discussed in chapter 7, ENIAC had different operation codes to store data in and retrieve from each accumulator. Reads from the function table used an address previously stored in the function table, as did jump instructions. The instructions storing those numbers were the only ones that literally included an address, though several others were followed by arguments.

memory, each location from which an instruction would be read required its own entry in the plugboard.

The SSEC's designers scaled up the tape-controlled relay calculator model used by several earlier computers well past the point of diminishing returns. Kuhn called this the "functional failure" of the old paradigm, as it stumbles when pushed beyond the problems to which it was well adapted. One telling detail will suffice: The SSEC provided a relatively fast, high-capacity tape loop for table lookup. Operators pushed 400-pound rolls of card stock up purpose-built ramp to a custom machine that produced tape strips so bulky that a chain hoist was used to lift them and so wide that another machine was engineered just to glue their ends together securely. No other computer ever used this approach on so large a scale. After computer designers understood the ideas of the First Draft, it became obvious that adding a program counter to fetch instructions sequentially from relay memory would greatly reduce the need to glue tapes together or the need to build massive numbers of bulky and expensive input devices to support loops and branches. The SSEC shows us that what was to become obvious after computer builders had fully assimilated the lessons of the First Draft was much less obvious a year or two earlier, even to a skilled and creative design team.

ENIAC and EDSAC

The question of utility has played a somewhat inconsistent role in the historical literature on early stored-program computers, perhaps because it has been used instrumentally to grant both Manchester and Cambridge the right to celebrate the first modern computer. EDSAC is generally called the first "useful," "practical," or "full-scale" stored-program computer and thus credited with a more significant historical role than that credited to the Baby.[61] EDSAC became operational in 1949 and soon established a role, similar to that of ENIAC, as a machine that was widely used by scientists with demanding computational needs. Yet the 1948 ENIAC was, for problems of many kinds, more useful, more practical, and larger in scale than either the Baby or EDSAC.

The instruction set of the 1948 ENIAC was comparable in scope to that of EDSAC and far more complete than that of the Manchester Baby. Because most of ENIAC's instructions were stored in only two digits, it had the potential to store more complex programs than EDSAC, which had to commit the entirety of one of its 512 seventeen-bit words to store even the simplest instruction. The compact two-digit instruction format of the 1948 ENIAC included some unusually powerful instructions, including square root, a range of decimal shift options, and transfer of an entire punched card's worth of information to or from electronic memory.

But the 1948 ENIAC could not store variables in its large read-only memory, which held program code and constants. Instead, variables were squeezed into the vacuum-tube memory that was spread around ENIAC's twenty accumulators. The ENIAC Monte Carlo code illuminates its abilities as it was actually used. Some accumulators were used to hold specific physical quantities accessed at many points in the program, akin to global variables; others were re-used at various points for temporary storage. In the conversion design as it was implemented, 131 decimal digits of accumulator memory were entirely safe from the threat of being overwritten and so could be used to store global data without any special precautions. Another 30 digits could be used cautiously to store temporary data as their special roles were connected with less frequent operations, such as square root.

Our analysis of the Monte Carlo program suggests that ENIAC's practical capabilities for this application were little diminished by its dual memory system. When running a short program EDSAC had more writable memory available for variables than ENIAC, but it is far from certain that, as configured in 1949, it could have accommodated 800 instructions of the Monte Carlo code. If the program and the numerical constants had somehow been streamlined to fit, EDSAC would have been left with no more memory for working data than ENIAC.

Only ENIAC's relatively robust input and output capabilities made Monte Carlo feasible at all. Any data-intensive simulation would soon have exhausted the internal memory of either computer, leaving overall throughput bound by input-output performance. ENIAC could read and write punched cards using high-performance IBM units, and the Monte Carlo cards were sorted and processed between computer runs on conventional punched-card equipment. EDSAC, like many other early computers, used standard five-channel paper tape, which was slower than punched cards, cumbersome in large volumes, and impossible to sort. One of EDSAC's early users recalled "the incredible difficulty we had ever to produce a single correct piece of paper tape with the crude and unreliable home-made punching, printing and verifying gear" then available.[62] It is not clear that this storage medium would have met the needs of Los Alamos even if the Monte Carlo program could have been shoehorned in.

ENIAC's restriction to a single card reader and a single punch may have been a bigger practical limitation than its limited writable memory. Many problems still relied on preparatory work with sorters, mergers, and duplicating punches to combine the required information into a single deck of cards. These manual operations were a traditional part of punched-card work. For example, in administrative use of punched cards it was common to cross-reference an employee master file with a set of time clock cards to produce weekly payroll stubs. And, as has been noted, many different manual punched-card operations were needed for the 1950 weather simulations on ENIAC. Many such chores could have been automated if ENIAC had had two punched-card readers.

Usability is another aspect of practicality. For a machine of its era, the 1948 ENIAC was, when working reliably, exceptionally easy to program and to debug. ENIAC had always offered single-step debugging and a variable clock so that the machine could operate slowly enough for its operator to follow the progress of a computation. Neon lights in each accumulator displayed the entire contents of the electronic memory. After the conversion to the modern code paradigm, the entire program was visible on the function tables and could be altered at any time by turning switches. This made it easy to set a break point or to debug interactively.

Another limitation of ENIAC in comparison with the next generation of computers was that programs had to be placed in its memory manually, by turning switches. Loader programs and other kinds of systems software, which had not been anticipated by von Neumann in the First Draft, entered computing practice with the earliest computers inspired by EDVAC. Most notably, EDSAC introduced a system of "initial orders" encoded in read-only memory to read symbolic instruction codes from paper tape, loading them into memory and translating them into binary as it went.[63] This also allowed for the automatic loading and relocation of subroutines within its main memory, something that could never have been accomplished with ENIAC's function table storage.

Theoretical Limitations on ENIAC

Discussion of the computational legacies of early computers can easily veer into the counterfactual. What if the Atanasoff-Berry Computer had worked properly, Konrad Zuse's Z3 had not been bombed, Charles Babbage had been better funded, or the Colossus had not been secret? Historical significance has been asserted as much on the basis of what might have been as on the basis of what was. This is particularly true whenever discussion relates to the universality or the Turing completeness of a machine architecture, since any discussion that begins with the assumption of unlimited time and storage space has already departed irrevocably from the realities of an era in which the overwhelming challenge was to develop reliable and capacious storage. In this sense, the search for the logical foundations of computing and the search for its historical foundations may pull us in opposing directions. It was purity and abstraction from the messy details of actual hardware that earned the Turing Machine its iconic place within computer science. The idea of universality served to decouple theoretical computer science from the material world of computing platforms and architectures.[64] The intellectual utility of that approach is clear, as is its strategic benefit to the early computer-science community at a time when that community was struggling to separate itself intellectually from mathematics, electronic engineering, and service work for other disciplines.

Michael Mahoney struggled for many years to encapsulate the history of theoretical computer science.[65] His great theme was the need of scientific communities to construct their own historical narratives. Mahoney saw theoretical computer science as an assemblage of mathematical tools originally developed in quite separate contexts, from group theory and lambda calculus to Chomsky's hierarchy of grammars. On a still larger scale, work on mathematical logic and work on the engineering of calculating machines both had long and largely distinct histories. Yet from within the discipline of computer science and from the present-day viewpoint the connections between these things came to seem obvious, and history is often written as if work over the centuries had been directed toward the development of the computer or as if the computing pioneers of the 1940s had been inspired primarily by the work of Turing.

As Mahoney wrote, the interest of computing practitioners in "finding a history" has "its real dangers" because, although scholarly historians and practitioners "both seek a history," it is "not for the same purpose and not from the same standpoint."[66] Abstraction is the soul of computer science, but we historians lose something vital if we abstract away from the historical grubbiness of early computer projects, their focus on engineering challenges, and their specific goals and roots in the thinking of the 1940s. For example, Raul Rojas' argument that Konrad Zuse's 1943 Z3 computer was universal was an impressive party trick, but diverged entirely from the way the machine was designed, how it was actually used, or indeed from anything that would have made sense in the 1940s.[67] The programming method Rojas described required the construction of an impossibly long paper tape and a massive loss of computational performance. Calculation would have been quicker by hand. To us, the real lesson of his analysis is that the Z3 could have been Turing complete with only minor design changes, but that it wasn't because the concept and its benefits were not yet widely understood. Indeed, Zuse later claimed to have considered and rejected treating program instructions as data while working on its design.[68] The past really is a foreign country.

The Turing machine has provided computer scientists with the dominant theoretical model of a minimal universal computer. ENIAC, even before its conversion, is generally thought to have been Turing complete even though, as far as we know, no formal proof of that has ever been attempted.[69] Insofar as the 1948 ENIAC followed the modern code paradigm, it is instructive to compare it with the smaller but still significant body of work on minimal universal models for computation derived by simplifying real-world architectures. These models include the Random Access Machine and the Random Access Stored Program machine.[70] As Rojas summarized this work, the "minimal structure of a universal computing machine" requires no more than the combination of either indirect addressing or the capability to modify addresses stored in memory with a single accumulator, instructions to clear and increment that accumulator, a conditional branch operation, and instructions to load and store the contents of the accumulator against an addressable memory.[71]

From this theoretical viewpoint, the architecture of the 1948 ENIAC did have one apparently serious weakness: its writable electronic memory was not addressable. Its read-only function-table memory was addressable, because operations on instructions or on data worked with the contents of a numerically specified address. Its writable electronic memory, in contrast, was held in accumulators, each of which was assigned a unique two-digit instruction to load it with data and another two-digit instruction to retrieve its contents.

The lack of addressability imposed some potential constraints. One might wish to write code to process the content of a data structure (for example, a matrix in need of inversion) whose size and position in memory are not fixed in advance. A subroutine written on a computer with addressable writable memory could accept as parameters the length and the start location of the data structure.

ENIAC's standard instructions would work only on fixed locations in its writable memory.[72] This was a limitation more in theory than in practice. ENIAC's tiny memory could not accommodate a list worth sorting or a matrix worth inverting. The smallness of the accumulator memory, rather than its lack of addressability, provided the real constraint. If the lack of an addressing mechanism for the accumulators had posed a real problem, the "converter code" set-up would have been changed. The "register code" designed in 1948 treated the new delay-line memory itself and ten of the accumulators as addressable. Years later, when the core memory unit was installed, at last giving ENIAC a large writable electronic memory, the team again turned to the indirect addressing method that had been used with the function tables.[73] Even if such changes were, for some reason, ruled out, then, accumulator memory could have been made addressable by writing parameterized storage subroutines.[74]

Our exploration of the "stored program concept," its history, and its relationship to ENIAC has reinforced our sense that it is more revealing to approach the history of early machines by documenting their use (that is, on the basis of what they actually did and how it was accomplished) than by speculating on what inherent limitations would have been if they had been provided with effectively unlimited quantities of time and storage. Attempts by historians to appropriate from theoretical computer scientists the concept of universality and a determination to treat the "stored program concept" as if it were a single, precisely definable feature of a computer have pushed the dominant discourse of early electronic computing into a swamp of pointless bickering and misunderstandings.[75] We have shown that the "stored program concept" was never proposed as a specific feature in its agreed source, the First Draft, and was only retroactively adopted to pick out certain features of the EDVAC design. Its meaning has continued to shift over time as various authors have tried to cram various theoretical and practical developments into an ostensibly singular concept as "stages" or "sub concepts."

After ENIAC's conversion, its capabilities and its coding method had some very fundamental similarities to and some striking differences from the other leading computers of the late 1940s. It is neither possible nor desirable to compress these similarities and differences into a single yes/no answer in order to contest the ownership of an imaginary trophy for the "first stored-program computer." A cynic might conclude that the traditional argument has been about which university building most deserves to have a new historical marker affixed to its exterior wall. We believe that the work done within the building to shape and apply the first computers is of greater historical interest.

12

Remembering ENIAC

Since 1955, when ENIAC punched its last card, its prominence has only grown. Its reach always extended far beyond those who worked directly with it, or on whose behalf it labored. ENIAC was as much symbol as machine, producing cultural meanings as well as numbers. Even before it was finished, representatives of various companies, universities, and government agencies visited the Moore School to marvel. In its own small way, ENIAC has become a historical figure that, like Winston Churchill or Teddy Roosevelt, has returned frequently to the forefront of public awareness over the decades as a symbol of a variety of virtues and vices.

ENIAC as Textbook Computer

In February of 1946, when it was unveiled, ENIAC was a technological triumph, leaping far ahead of other known computers in performance and flexibility. Yet a few months later the organizers of the Moore School Lectures already viewed ENIAC as outmoded and were focusing on the potential of EDVAC-type designs.

To the rest of the world, including scientists and engineers who had computations to perform, ENIAC conveyed the idea of what an electronic digital computer was and what it could do. John von Neumann's "First Draft of a Report on EDVAC," for all its intellectual power, was an unfinished speculative essay of interest to a narrow audience. In contrast, ENIAC was a physical spectacle of impressive size and speed. Douglas Hartree played an important role in spreading awareness of the machine with two articles in *Nature*, a short book based on his 1946 inaugural lecture at Cambridge, and a detailed discussion in a longer book published in 1949.[1]

In the United States the most important of the early popular guides to computing was Edmund Berkeley's *Giant Brains*, in which ENIAC was characterized as the most powerful "mechanical brain" in operation. Berkeley gave ENIAC an entire chapter, calling it "the first giant brain to use electronic tubes" and commenting that

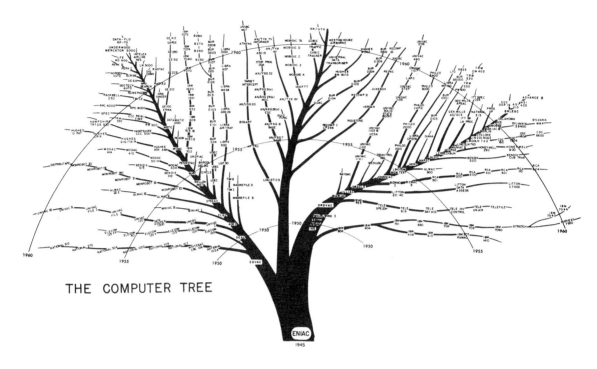

THE COMPUTER TREE

Figure 12.1
This 1961 "computer tree" was originally published in Kempf's *Electronic Computers Within the Ordnance Corps*, an official history of computing at the Ballistic Research Laboratory. It was widely reproduced in other contexts, which spread the idea of ENIAC as the trunk from which all other digital computers had grown. EDSAC and ORDVAC, two other BRL computers, also fill strategic positions. (U.S. Army diagram)

"as soon as ENIAC started thinking, he promptly made relay calculators obsolete."[2] (As we have seen, that was not the case.) As many subsequent authors would do, Berkeley went into considerable detail on the machine's structure, programming method, and various electronic units. Like Hartree, Berkeley used ENIAC as a baseline against which to compare the advantages of the newer electronic machines that were under construction.

The descriptions produced by Hartree, Berkeley, and others benefitted from the very thorough documentation of ENIAC's hardware and programming methods carried out as part of the Moore School's contract. The widespread textbook descriptions of ENIAC's original programming mode contrast with the much lower profile of its post-1948 programming method. This has helped to keep historical attention on the earlier programming method, even though ENIAC did the vast majority of its work in the latter configuration.

ENIAC as Iconic Yardstick

ENIAC's career as a functioning computer spanned a little less than ten years, from its awakening to fitful life at the end of 1945 to its eventual decommissioning in 1955. By 1955 it had outlived most of its contemporaries and some of its successors. IBM's enormous SSEC had been disassembled in 1952. John von Neumann's computer at the Institute for Advanced Studies had had a functional life of only six years. The successors of these one-of-a-kind machines were not only smaller, faster, and more powerful; they were, for the most part, commercial products, not yet mass produced but no longer unique devices built around unproven technologies to satisfy the needs of a specific user. A computer-industry joke captures the transition: An early computer salesman calls on a potential customer, whose newly established computer team is attracted to the idea of building its own machine. "Well," says the salesman, "it seems that you face very much the same choice as Noah when he discovered the urgent need for an ark. Do you buy one or build it yourself?" "But sir," replies a rash member of his audience, "Noah did build his own." "Yes," answers the salesman in triumph, "and if you have 60 years and God on your side you should do the same." Once computer suppliers such as Univac, IBM, and ERA had proved that they could actually deliver working computers, that line of argument became increasingly convincing.

Yet the idiosyncratic ENIAC, with its forty panels enclosing a space large enough to hold operators, peripheral units, and miscellaneous items of furniture, did more than any other machine to propagate the idea that early computers were covered in blinking lights, filled entire rooms (if not buildings), and consumed vast amounts of power. One urban myth held that lights dimmed across Philadelphia when the machine was turned on. Science-fiction authors perpetuated that image, often assuming that increasing computing power demanded increasing size. Isaac Asimov wrote stories about Multivac, a computer with people and rooms inside it that grew to fill an entire city and run the world. This trope proved strangely resistant to personal experience. David H. Ahl's *Colossal Computer Cartoon Book*,[3] published in 1977 and marketed to early users of personal computers, continued to depict computers as monumental and oracular.

ENIAC has frequently been used as a source of standard measures against which the cost, size, price, weight, and performance of later machines could be flatteringly compared. ENIAC has sustained sufficient name recognition to make such comparisons meaningful. (Boasting that an early microprocessor was more powerful than ORDVAC or SEAC would not communicate much.) To illustrate the special character of computer technology, its boosters also like to point out that if other technologies (most commonly automobiles) had shown similar proportional

Figure 12.2
Members of the BRL staff in 1962 with the circuits used by a succession of computers to store a single decimal digit. ENIAC's massive plug-in decade (left, held by Patsy Simmers) already seemed absurdly large.
(U.S. Army photo)

improvement since 1945 they would now be absurdly inexpensive, cruise at speeds better suited to interstellar travel, or run forever on a single tank of fuel. The usual rejoinder is that they would explode often and for no discernible reason.[4]

ENIAC as an Information Age Relic

ENIAC has had a very public afterlife. After it was dismembered, its parts were scattered widely, like those of the saints of antiquity. Four of its panels are on display at its birthplace, the Moore School at the University of Philadelphia. Other relics can be found at the Computer History Museum in Mountain View, California, at the Heinz Nixdorf Museums Forum in Paderborn, Germany, in the lobby of the computer science department of the University of Michigan, stashed in asbestos-contaminated crates at some of the Smithsonian Institution's off-site storage locations, arranged blinking in the lobby of Perot Systems in Plano, Texas, and piled in a corner of the Peirce Edition Project's office at Indiana University–Purdue University Indianapolis.

The paths by which ENIAC made its way from Aberdeen to these various places are not entirely clear, as is normal for relics, though in many cases their paths ran through the Smithsonian Institution, which accessioned much of the machine in 1965. A museum curator at the University of Pennsylvania reported seeing signs of rust and water damage while cleaning the panels on display in the Moore School, which she tied to reports that "the pieces were rescued from the dump at the Aberdeen Proving Ground."[5]

Parts for one exhibit were indeed taken directly from Aberdeen. Arthur Burks went on to become a professor at the University of Michigan. His efforts to track down parts of ENIAC began in 1960 when, according to John H. Giese, who was by then head of the BRL's Computing Laboratory, one accumulator was operating in a display at the U.S. Military Academy at West Point and the National Science Foundation was showing a single digit of storage in a roaming exhibit. According to Geise, "all the remainder," including portions earmarked for the Smithsonian, had "been corroding in an Aberdeen Proving Ground warehouse since 1957." It had not yet been declared "excess to requirements," and the Historical Properties Branch of the Army Office of Military History wasn't willing to designate it "historical property" and assume the consequent storage responsibilities.[6]

In 1965 Burks organized a campaign to obtain some of ENIAC, eventually winning the four panels he requested and a generous assortment of plug-in units and cables. He had the parts shipped to Ann Arbor and arranged for their restoration. "After much difficulty," he later wrote, "we found a shop man who took an interest in refurbishing our part of the machine. He put the plug-ins through a car wash and a sand-blast, enameled them, and then baked them … . After the treatment the plug-ins still worked!"[7] Burks also commissioned "two small accumulators of three decimal digits and a sign each" to demonstrate the principles of ENIAC in action. The four panels were displayed in the lobby of the university's Institute of Science and Technology after plans for a grander exhibit fell through.

Just as a knuckle bone attributed to a biblical figure was once a source of local pride, today even a single digit of ENIAC storage can be given pride of place in a small museum such as Northwest Missouri State University's shrine to Jean Bartik.[8] When an accumulator was operated at the Smithsonian, giving visitors a glimpse of glowing tubes and blinking lights, its burned-out tubes were reportedly saved in a box, having themselves been sanctified as relics by this service.

Although no museum was able to offer enough space to showcase the entire machine, ENIAC could be, and was, divided into several clumps, each of which gave

Table 12.1
The most recent known locations of surviving ENIAC panels. Collections owned by the Smithsonian Institution are indicated by asterisks.

Location	Parts
Moore School display, Philadelphia (*)	Accumulator 18 Constant Transmitter, Panel 2 Cycling Unit Function Table 3, Panel 1 Portable Function Table B Master Programmer, Panel 2
Computer History Museum display, Mountain View, California (*)	Accumulator 12 Function Table 2, Panel 2 Printer, Panel 3 Portable Function Table C
Field Artillery Museum display, Fort Sill, Lawton, OK (until Oct 2014 in the lobby of Perot Systems, Plano, Texas)	Accumulators 7, 8, 13 and 17 Function table 1, Panels 1 and 2
University of Michigan, Computer Science building lobby display, Ann Arbor	Two accumulators High Speed Multiplier, Panel 3 Master Programmer, Panel 2
Heinz Nixdorf Museums Forum display, Paderborn, Germany (*)	Printer, Panel 2 High Speed Function Table
Smithsonian Institution storage, Washington DC area (*)	Accumulators 2, 19 and 20 Constant Transmitter, Panels 1 and 3 Divider and Square Rooter Function Table 2, Panel 1 Function Table 3, Panel 2 High Speed Multiplier, Panels 1 and 2 Initiating Unit Printer, Panel 1

a sense of how the computer looked. Fragments of the machine are therefore indispensable for any exhibition aimed at giving a comprehensive sense of computing history. At the Computer History Museum in Mountain View, a fragment was long stationed near a Univac and the neatly engineered cabinets of an early IBM computer. For those other machines, one large box is identifiable as "the computer." The ENIAC display appears, in comparison, as something built in the basement lair of a mad scientist—a sprawling, baffling, incomplete cluster of cabinets and wires.

ENIAC provided the literal and metaphorical centerpiece to the long-running (1990–2006) Information Age exhibit at the Smithsonian's National Museum of American History. A smaller ENIAC configuration was featured in the permanent exhibit of the Computer Museum in Boston until it closed in 2000. Those panels were displayed in visible storage in its Silicon Valley successor, the Computer History Museum, until 2012, when a new comprehensive exhibit was ready. In 1996, during anniversary celebrations, the University of Pennsylvania built an ENIAC display for the Moore School's old building. The four panels held by the university are now a characterful backdrop for a student computer lab.

The biggest surviving ENIAC assemblage, consisting of four accumulators, a power supply, and set of function-table units, was displayed from 2007 to 2014 in an unexpected location: the lobby of the headquarters of Perot Systems in Plano, Texas. After a museum at Aberdeen Proving Ground closed, Ross Perot, the memorably unconventional presidential candidate and computer-services entrepreneur, obtained them on long-term loan. A piece in the magazine *Wired* fancifully credited Perot's team with having "rescued" the "world's first computer from the scrap heap." The panels were worked on by "Dan Gleason, a video-conferencing engineer at Perot Systems who had zero experience with fixing vintage computers." Gleason sandblasted and repainted them, then stripped out the original neon indicators and their wiring and replaced them with modern circuits that would flash at random when a motion detector fired. *Wired* described this as "fixing" ENIAC, though one online commentator was less impressed, suggesting that Gleason and his collaborators "destroyed them just so the boss could see lights."[9] In October of 2014 the installation was transferred to the Field Artillery Museum at Fort Sill in Oklahoma.[10]

ENIAC as Valuable Intellectual Property

We have already shown how the ENIAC patent and the ensuing lawsuits shaped the historical stories that the project's participants told. From the 1950s to the 1970s, lawyers did far more than historians to keep ENIAC in the public eye. The narratives they constructed for an audience of judges and patent officials would determine the fate of millions of dollars in licensing fees. This focused a great deal of money and ingenious argumentation on the question of "who invented the computer," igniting a debate that would otherwise surely have been shorter and less vituperative.

The trial's 135 days of courtroom testimony, a record for the federal court system, were the culmination of a still larger battle, waged with dozens of depositions, thousands upon thousands of legal exhibits, and decades of preparatory maneuvering. Legal strategies and patent law interacted in subtle ways to turn some obscure historical points into major legal issues to which hundreds or thousands of pages of court testimony and affidavits were directed. As we saw previously, the patent was filed on June 26, 1947, establishing a June 1946 cutoff date for many kinds of evidence. This played an important role in establishing 1943–1946 as the most significant and the best-documented years of ENIAC's life.

When it took place the case was seen as a potential turning point for the computer industry. IBM, by far the largest computer firm, had agreed to pay a license fee as part of an exchange of patent rights with Univac's parent corporation, Sperry. The Sperry Corporation had recently acquired RCA's computer business and was the second largest firm in the industry. Sperry planned to use the ENIAC patent to squeeze hefty royalties out of its smaller competitors, which were already struggling to compete against IBM's increasingly dominant line of mainframe computers.

The ENIAC patent case has loomed less large in historical work, perhaps because the judge left the industry's status quo unchanged by eliminating the threat of a patent duopoly. Historians looking at the 1970s have focused on minicomputers, software, and personal computers, conveying a sense that the mainframe competitors such as Univac and Honeywell were already fading from relevance.

U.S. District Court Judge Earl R. Larson's judgment in the trial contained a variety of findings that were devastating to Sperry. Many were phrased in such a way as to independently invalidate the patent or to greatly limit its enforceability even if other parts of the judgment were to be reversed on appeal. The judge found that ENIAC had been in "non-experimental use" since December of 1945 for a series of applications, beginning with the Los Alamos hydrogen-bomb calculations run by Stanley Frankel and Nicholas Metropolis. However, the two-accumulator test configuration of ENIAC, operational in July 1944, was itself deemed an automatic digital electronic computer, the invention claimed in the patent. ENIAC had been displayed to the public during the press events at the Moore School in February of 1946, a conclusion that seems hard to dismiss in view of front-page treatment by the *New York Times* and newsreel film showing it in action. ENIAC, Larson ruled, had been delivered in completed form to the Army as of December 31, 1945. The "First Draft of a Report on the EDVAC," circulated well before the crucial date, was also judged to have disclosed the ideas needed to construct an automatic digital electronic computer.[11]

Section 11 of the judgment reflected particularly badly on Sperry. Before being granted in 1964, the patent lingered an exceptionally long time at the patent office while Sperry made numerous changes to its claims and to the supporting text to increase their relevance to modern computers. Because the computer industry was growing constantly, delaying the start of the patent's seventeen-year term increased the volume of potential license payments. Judge Larson determined that Sperry had dragged its feet by employing only token legal representation for years at a time. Its lawyers had devoted as many billable hours to a single patent amendment over a six-month period as to the entire lawsuit over a six-year period as it had crawled toward a trial. Although this "unnecessary and unreasonable delay" did not invalidate the patent (a conclusion the judge said he had reached "with reluctance"), the "various derelictions of Eckert and Mauchly and their counsel before the Patent Office" were in themselves sufficient to "render the ENIAC patent unenforceable" even if it was otherwise valid.[12]

The 26 distinct sections of Larson's judgment fill several hundred pages, but the judgment is remembered primarily for section 3, in which Larson rather unexpectedly ruled the patent invalid because the claimed invention, the automatic electronic digital computer, was not novel, having been created in 1939 by John V. Atanasoff. This did not bring Atanasoff, whose computer was little known before the trial, any rights to the invention, but it was a proud day for Iowa, and Atanasoff's flame has been kept burning there ever since.[13] Scott McCartney, in his book on ENIAC, argues that those who see Larson's ruling primarily as a statement about Atanasoff's work are missing his true motivation. According to McCartney, Larson was less interested in settling vexing questions in computer history than in safeguarding competition in the computer industry. He sought grounds to invalidate the patent that would be hard to appeal.[14] This complements an observation by Alice Burks that Sperry's team adopted a bold but unwise enforcement strategy by seeking license payment for the automatic digital electronic computer as a whole rather than on specific features defined in the patent's claims. Had the patent been limited to the general-purpose computer, it could have sidestepped Atanasoff as prior art.[15] Alice Burks' assertion that Sperry was aggressively enforcing an overly broad patent is entirely consistent with the idea that Larsen was motivated primarily to avoid the formation of a patent cartel in the computer industry. Sperry didn't appeal, and ENIAC's career as a money tree was over before it had ever really begun.

ENIAC and the Historians

Larsen's judgment of October 19, 1973 reduced ENIAC's value as a piece of intellectual property from tens or even hundreds of millions of dollars to zero. Identifying the first computer and determining its inventors abruptly ceased to be activities with anything tangible riding on their outcomes. The lawyers moved on, but surprisingly little changed in the way ENIAC was discussed. During the 1970s and the early 1980s, much history of computing work was effectively a continuation of the lawsuit by other means, written by veterans of the trial proceedings who often based their historical work on documents gathered as expert witnesses. As we have noted, Herman Goldstine's book *The Computer from Pascal to von Neumann* was shaped by Goldstine's previous involvement in proceedings having to do with the patent. Its story ran from differential analyzers and relay calculators to ENIAC and then to von Neumann, the First Draft, and the various real machines patterned after that report. Goldstine's endured for decades as the central story of the invention of the computer, against whose narrative arc other stories were judged and into which they were integrated.

The emerging community of historians of computing was dominated by pioneers who had worked on the machines of the 1940s and by slightly younger computer specialists who had entered computing during the 1950s. In 1976, an International Research Conference on the History of Computing held at Los Alamos brought them together. Nick Metropolis and Jack Worlton were the main hosts, and the cost was underwritten by the National Science Foundation. The invitation promised that the conference would "encourage research of high quality into the history of computing," would "record 'living history' in the context of discussions among the pioneers in the origins of electronic computing," and would "provide computer scientists—especially those who are pursuing historical interests—with an insight into the discipline of historiography." The format was designed to "provide an uncrowded program while allowing for leisurely discussion."[16] The initial list of 51 participants included only three credentialed historians.[17]

ENIAC was well represented. Eckert and Mauchly gave separate addresses, each titled simply "The ENIAC." Arthur Burks spoke on ENIAC and its relationship to the emergence of the stored-program computer. Stanislaw Ulam discussed John von Neumann's work on computing. Nicholas Metropolis, while setting out the history of Los Alamos' work on computing, briefly discussed ENIAC's use for Monte Carlo simulation and its conversion to the modern code paradigm.

At the conference, disputes that lingered from the trial led to heated discussion during the formal sessions and in private griping sessions. The influence of Atanasoff on ENIAC was a burning question for Burks, as were the assignment of credit for ideas in the First Draft and the classification of particular computers. Burks continued to collect papers related to ENIAC and to swap memories with other participants after the conference.

Questions of character were prominent in the private exchanges of the early participant historians, giving us an insight into the beliefs shaping their more carefully presented public accounts. Burks, for example, summed up his opinions on his former bosses in a personal note dated September 1976: "Pres was … highly creative, original, systematic, responsible, hard working … . John was knowledgeable, bright … not very original, not very responsible, erratic. … His performance ranked well below Pres. Johnny v N was a full genius level above Pres."[18] Goldstine too harbored strong private opinions beneath his more considered public statements. "If any single person is responsible for the ENIAC," he wrote in 1959, "it is Eckert. Mauchly was nothing but a drain on our energies from the beginning. He is a dilettante and is totally undisciplined."[19]

The exchange of views and information at the Los Alamos conference did lead to a certain amount of convergence of historical accounts around new evidence.

Most notably, the British computer scientist Brian Randell had been working hard to make information about the British Colossus machines available.[20] Historians eventually accepted that ENIAC had not been the first operational electronic digital computer, but no real consensus was ever reached on many of the other issues. The revised papers published in the carefully edited proceedings volume, *A History of Computing in the Twentieth Century*, continued to disagree on many points of fact and interpretation.

The historical status of ENIAC was still being debated in the early 1980s in early volumes of *Annals of the History of Computing*. The most substantial description of ENIAC and its capabilities came in "The ENIAC: The First General-Purpose Electronic Computer," a 1981 article by Arthur and Alice Burks. Among other things, they attempted to precisely define the capabilities of a "general purpose computer" so as to make that fuzzily defined term more useful for the purposes of historical analysis.[21]

The first historians to write PhD dissertations on the history of computing were now entering the field, and neither they nor the few established historians who had begun to take an interest in computer history were interested in enlisting as combatants in a never-ending battle over the identity of the first computer. Paul Ceruzzi's dissertation, later the basis of his book *Reckoners*, surveyed the histories of several early computers and provided a narrative of incremental advance to tie them together.[22] A truce was effectively brokered.

The question of whether ENIAC was a "computer" or a "calculator," raised repeatedly during the 1970s and the early 1980s continues to recur with some regularity in public forums. "Calculator," in this context, was taken to mean something that could perform mathematical operations automatically but was not truly programmable. Some argued that "computer" should be reserved for machines modeled on EDVAC. This debate had more to do with the emergence of small electronic calculators in the 1970s, and with efforts to distinguish them from true computers, than it did with any consistent pattern of distinct usage during the 1940s.[23] It is true, for example, that the Harvard Mark I, which had no branching mechanism, was officially called the Automatic Sequence Controlled Calculator. However, the IBM 701, undisputedly a computer, was initially called the Defense Calculator, and the C in the name EDSAC stood for "calculator." Conversely, the C in the name ENIAC stood for "computer." The purported distinction simply did not exist during the 1940s.[24]

ENIAC as Civic and National Heritage

ENIAC's public profile peaked as its fiftieth anniversary approached. The many history sessions organized for a meeting of the Association for Computing Machinery in Philadelphia during 1996 were overshadowed by the presence of Vice President Al Gore at the university's own "birthday party" for ENIAC on February 14. Gore and President Bill Clinton were engaged in their campaign for reelection. As a senator, Gore had long supported the development of network infrastructure. Now enthusiasm was building across the United States for the transformative power of the Internet and the newly invented World Wide Web. ENIAC provided a powerful example of an earlier success by the federal government in supporting the development of information technology.[25]

In November of 1996, the Army, unwilling to let Philadelphia and the Moore School get all the credit, held its own celebration of "50 Years of Army Computing" in Aberdeen at what was by then called the U.S. Army Research Laboratory. About half of the event was devoted to ENIAC. Herman Goldstine, the star speaker, was presented with a medal. Panels featured many survivors of ENIAC's time there, including several of its female operators. The past, unavoidably, is commemorated to the extent that it serves the needs of the present. The anniversary was used to speculate on the future of computing and, according to the event's sponsor, to "celebrate a new beginning with the dedication of the DoD-sponsored ARL Major Shared Resource Center."[26] Around the same time, a separate ceremony was held in Aberdeen to mark the issue of a commemorative postage stamp.

A team at the University of Pennsylvania developed a custom chip to instantiate the familiar claim that ENIAC, if constructed with modern technology, would be orders of magnitude smaller, lighter, and less power hungry. Intended to reproduce ENIAC's basic arrangement, including the separate units and the pulses transmitted between them, the chip was announced as "a teaching tool that dramatically illustrates the performance improvements brought about by semiconductor technology." Diving into the details yields instead a lesson on the incommensurability of old and new technologies. The chip imposed much stricter limits on the paths by which units could be interconnected than the original machine did. Unlike the real ENIAC, it could never have been configured to work in the new programming mode.[27] Various simulator projects were also launched, though as far as we are aware none of them emulated the full range of ENIAC's hardware units or its functionality.[28]

Despite these festivities and memorials, ENIAC never made it into the first rank of beloved symbols of Philadelphia. This contrasts with the place of some other early computers in the popular memory of their home cities. As Jon Agar noted when discussing Manchester's commemoration of its "Baby" computer, "History was being mobilized by the city's institutional elite in a deliberate act of connection: building on school history knowledge of industrialization and then associating it with today's computer-based developments, the city attempts to justify Manchester's claims to having been one of the places, even *the* place, where the machine that pervades our lives today was first developed."[29] Creating such memories takes work and money. Perhaps any city has only enough space in its collective memory and enough money in its coffers to elevate a few local accomplishments as emblems of civic pride. Philadelphia already has the Liberty Bell, the Declaration of Independence, the Constitution, Ben Franklin, William Penn, an outstanding art museum with stairs once ascended by Rocky Balboa, a full complement of professional sports teams, an Ivy League university, mummers, and a beloved vernacular cuisine of pretzels, cheesesteaks, and hoagies.

ENIAC as Team Mascot

John von Neumann died in 1957. The other men with a plausible claim to be the inventor (or at least a principal creator) of the modern computer lived longer. John William Mauchly, whose health had long been poor, died in 1980. After that things progressed much as the actuarial tables would predict. In 1995 J. Presper Eckert Jr. fell to leukemia, John V. Atanasoff to a stroke, and Conrad Zuse to heart failure. Tommy Flowers had the longest lease on life, but his tenancy finally ran out in 1998 at the age of 92. Herman Goldstine, who has never been accused of inventing the computer but certainly played an important supporting role, survived until 2004. What of the next cohort, the men who left the Moore School lectures in 1946 with clear purpose and went on to lead the teams that built the first computers patterned after the EDVAC design? Maurice Wilkes left us in 2010, but Harry Huskey, a participant in the creation of ENIAC and several other early computers, lives as of this writing.[30]

Thus is "historical distance" achieved from the squabbles and debates of an era, leaving historians free to tell their own stories about what happened without having to yell over the objections and the cheers of those who were alive at the time and who will always and forever trust the authority of their own memories over that of historians and archival documents.

Have the battles over the identity of the true inventor of the computer died down now that all potential claimants, their close colleagues, and those they initially influenced have been laid to rest? The answer is "no." Those disputes still shape the ways in which ENIAC is remembered. If one were to gather everything that has been written about ENIAC in the past two decades and then discard everything primarily concerned with celebrating pioneering female programmers into a somewhat smaller heap nearby, most of what remained would be marked by an obsession with ENIAC's status, or lack thereof, as the first computer. The boosters of the early machines have come to resemble the fans of professional sports teams, continuing to chant long-established arguments at their opponents.

This has kept alive the closely examined question of Mauchly's relationship with Atanasoff. Alice Burks makes the case for Atanasoff as the single true inventor of the computer with explicitly prosecutorial zeal in *Who Invented the Computer?* She convicts Mauchly of having stolen crucial ideas from Atanasoff and misrepresented the historical record during the legal battles that followed. She also argues that historians of computing have been negligent in their "effective widespread *rejection* of its verdict," placing various unscrupulous historians of computing and the editorial practices of *Annals of the History of Computing* in the dock alongside Mauchly.[31]

Jane Smiley is a highly respected novelist and a former professor at Iowa State University. Her sole foray into history came with *The Man Who Invented the Computer: The Biography of John Atanasoff, Digital Pioneer*, the writing of which was sponsored by the Alfred P. Sloan Foundation.[32] As a trade publication by a major author this book was one of the few works on the history of computing given enough of a marketing push to impinge on popular consciousness. Title notwithstanding, it is a popular retelling of the history of electronic computing in the 1940s rather than a biography. Thus, a significant portion of the book is devoted to ENIAC. Smiley takes a partisan jaunt through the 1940s and the ENIAC litigation of the 1960s and the 1970s, arranging facts and claims plucked from other books to build a case for her outsider hero and against the well-financed East Coast villains who stole his ideas. But Smiley's narrative, despite being lively by the standards of academic history, was savaged by specialists for inaccuracies and misunderstandings.[33]

The ENIAC of Women

Since the anniversaries of 1996, ENIAC has remained in the public eye, or at least has received occasional glances, chiefly because it was operated, and often programmed by, women. This phase of its posthumous career has given what may be the most dramatic twist to its memory. Most of the six original operators were still alive in the 1990s, and their voices were heard increasingly loudly after decades of obscurity. When they had been interviewed in the 1970s for legal proceedings or for oral histories, it had been as witnesses to momentous events rather than as participants in those events. But after Herman Goldstine and the other ENIAC principals were beyond the reach of microphones, they had the stage to themselves until Jean Bartik, the longest-surviving operator, died in 2011.

Their rediscovery owes a great deal to W. Barkley Fritz, who worked with ENIAC for years at the Ballistic Research Lab and who during the 1990s published two important articles on how the machine was used.[34] While researching those articles, he contacted other surviving participants. The articles that he then wrote included lengthy passages from their letters. Fritz's second article, "The Women of ENIAC," focused explicitly on the operators. It included information on each member of the original cohort and reflections and fragments of memoir from most of them. Being profiled in *IEEE Annals of the History of Computing* does not normally get one a ticket out of obscurity, but their story was featured by Tom Petzinger, a columnist for the *Wall Street Journal*, in a 1996 piece titled "History of Software Begins with Some Brainy Women."[35] Explaining that the first computer programmers had been unjustly excluded from computer history, Petzinger's column established the women as public figures and highlighted the efforts of Kathryn Kleiman, a lawyer specializing in computer issues, to produce a documentary film about them. A separate film featuring the women, LeAnn Erickson's *Top Secret Rosies*, premiered in 2010. Kleiman's project eventually produced a rather anticlimactic 20-minute film in 2014. The funding appeals and the publicity campaigns of both aspiring documentarians brought further attention to the work of the operators.

The years had taken the operators in different directions. Betty Holberton had the highest profile career, holding senior programming positions and contributing to the development of standards for the COBOL and FORTRAN programming languages. Others had left technical work for marriage or motherhood, though Jean Bartik returned later to computing as an editor for trade publications. At the end of their lives they found their identities unexpectedly reconstructed around a brief period five decades earlier.

The historian Jennifer S. Light brought the story of the women of ENIAC to a broad audience of historians of technology with her 1999 paper "When Computers Were Women," which focused on the symbolic exclusion of the women from contemporary reporting of ENIAC and its launch. Light argued that "programming was a woman's job" because "software, a secondary, clerical task, did not match the importance of constructing the ENIAC and getting it to work."[36] She grounded the story in the broader contexts of the Moore School's human computers and in historical scholarship on women's wartime work. One of the most widely cited papers ever written on the history of technology, Light's paper brought ENIAC status as a machine that had been programmed by women to a broad academic audience.[37]

The persistent shortage of women in its classrooms has given computer science a great hunger for female role models. Ada Lovelace's imaginative and insightful commentary on Charles Babbage's Analytical Engine has led to her canonization as "computer pioneer" and "first programmer," and a major programming language has been named after her.[38] Grace Hopper has been granted awards, has had her name attached to a major conference for women in computing, and has received other honors in commemoration of her contributions. Similarly, the story of the ENIAC women included an inspiring claim that the first people hired as programmers had been female. More recent underrepresentation of women in programming or in computer science was thus framed as an unfortunate but reversible fall from grace. Computing organizations rushed to symbolically remedy the situation. The women were inducted collectively into the Women in Technology International Hall of Fame. Jean Bartik lived long enough to be made a Fellow of the Computer History Museum and a winner of the IEEE Computer Pioneer Award. Her death was reported around the world.

Despite Jean Bartik's many awards, she still felt neglected, saying in 2008 that "in history afterward nobody ever mentions us. And of course Goldstine in his book lied." Her opinions of the ethics of John von Neumann and Arthur Burks were hardly more flattering. "Computer history can't seem to bring these guys to justice," she complained, "I'm still angry today."[39] Of Herman Goldstine's book, she asked "How on earth could you ... tell lies like that?"[40] Bartik and her fellows had their own wounded pride and followed their own agendas when bearing witness to history. Of a 1996 reunion and celebration at Aberdeen, Bartik complained "they never even mentioned Pres[per Eckert] and John [Mauchly] ... . It was all Goldstine and von Neumann. It was unbelievable." In her opinion, during the entire two-day event "the only thing they had that amounted to anything was they had the ENIAC Women, a seminar on us ... . The rest of it was trash."[41] Those angry words remind us that these women were not saints who forgave all offenses against them, and they were not, in the end, mere passive victims of historical sexism.[42] Nor should we expect them to be. The prevalent desire to beatify them says more about today's hunger for female role models in computing than it does about the women themselves.

In 2014, the journalist Walter Isaacson followed up his biography of Apple Computer's co-founder Steve Jobs with *The Innovators: How a Group of Hackers, Geniuses, and Geeks Created the Digital Revolution*. Its earlier chapters gave a surprisingly detailed retelling of technical stories from the early history of computing literature, in particular the tales of Ada Lovelace and of ENIAC. One of Isaacson's twists was to emphasize the advantages that teams held over the romantic figure of the lone genius. The other was to focus on the contributions of "forgotten" women. Isaacson's long passage on the initial cohort of operators, sourced largely from the memoir of Jean Bartik, was reprinted in *Fortune*. Isaacson even inserted Bartik into the spring 1945 Moore School meeting between John von Neumann and ENIAC's designers by mischaracterizing her descriptions of 1947 meetings held in Princeton to plan ENIAC's conversion to the modern code paradigm. "One day," Isaacson writes, "she disputed one of his points, and the men in the room stared at her incredulously. But von Neumann paused, tilted his head, and then accepted her point."[43]

In what is almost certainly the most widely read history of computing yet to have been published, Jean Bartik and her colleagues are lauded not only as the true creators of ENIAC but also as contributors to the instruction set that John von Neumann described in the "First Draft of a Report on the EDVAC." In two decades we have gone from "the women of ENIAC" as neglected historical footnotes to "the ENIAC of women" as the primary way in which the machine is remembered.

Conclusion

ENIAC is probably the most written about of the early computers and, thanks to various legal proceedings, undoubtedly the best documented. When we began this project, we knew that considerable archival material on its computing career had yet to be exploited, but we imagined that the volume of material written on its construction and on its initial use at the Moore School rendered further original research pointless. When we began to dig more deeply, however, the surprising inconsistencies of the existing treatments, and their incompleteness, drew us back to the archives for a more fundamental reassessment of ENIAC's entire trajectory.

Some of the inconsistencies are relatively trivial errors of fact. For example, the oft-quoted statistic that ENIAC had 5 million electrical joints turned out to be wrong by a factor of 10 or so. In many cases, original errors in more scholarly sources have been reproduced in popular books, online articles, and reference sources. ENIAC became operational in its new programming mode in April of 1948, but the September date given in Goldstine's influential book has been cited far more often than the correct date.

These errors can be corrected in passing, but other errors have the potential to significantly distort our understanding of the development of computing practice. The need for a conditional branching capability, recognized early in ENIAC's design, became a central design requirement for its master programmer unit. It was not, as was once believed, an afterthought. Likewise, the question of how to set the machine up to tackle particular problems had not, as often suggested by historians, been entirely neglected, in favor of the more serious task of designing and building hardware, until mid 1945, when the first operators were selected. In fact, it had been planned for in detail since the beginning of the project, and it had informed many aspects of the computer's design.[1]

These inconsistencies, omissions, and errors brought us back to the primary sources. However, we did not return to well-trodden ground merely to correct details. New questions guided us to reposition ENIAC within broader stories about the development of computer simulation as a new kind of experimentation, about

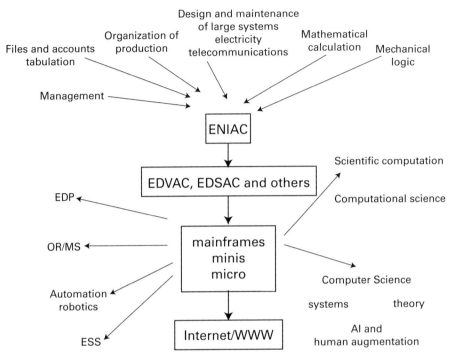

Figure C.1
Michael Mahoney was critical of this traditional hardware-oriented view of history, in which ENIAC formed a narrow thread connecting pre-World War II scientific and administrative practices to the worlds of modern computing.

the work of women in mathematics, the invention of the modern computer, and about the evolution of programming practice.

ENIAC and the Communities of Computing

To speak of "the history of the computer" is to assume both a single object and a singular story. Michael S. Mahoney rejected both in his influential essay "The Histories of Computing(s)." His sketch of the received "machine centered view" of history, reproduced here as figure C.1, exposed the assumed and often unearned centrality given to ENIAC. Its hourglass shape resembles that of the diagram by Arthur and Alice Burks presented as figure I.1 in the introduction to this volume, but it shows application areas rather than technologies. Historians, Mahoney

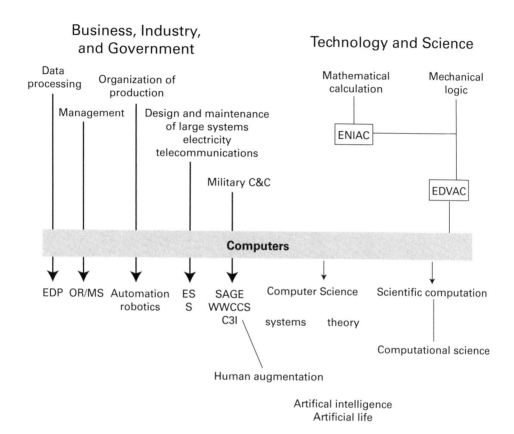

Figure C.2
Mahoney's preferred "community oriented" conceptualization of computing history emphasized continuities of practice within particular application areas.

believed, had skewed things by assuming that a variety of previous technologies and their users had somehow converged in the creation of ENIAC and the invention of the computer, and that computer technology, as it grew more and more powerful, spawned ever more complex and diverse areas of application ("Its progress is inevitable and unstoppable, its effects revolutionary").[2]

Mahoney argues instead for the "community view" of history that he captured in the diagram reproduced here as figure C.2, which confines ENIAC's direct influence on later practice to the specific area of scientific computation. We share Mahoney's belief that the use of computer technology in particular areas, such as military command and control or business data processing, usually involved profound continuity with the specific technologies and practices previously used in that area. In this book, we situate ENIAC within particular traditions of mathematical labor and conclude that its direct influence on later practice (for example, on the selection and work of programmers) was felt far more strongly within scientific programming than in other application areas.

This community view presents postwar computing as a set of evolutionary developments within different areas of society, from management to military command and communication. The accompanying shift of focus toward the applications of computers, in which hardware is combined with software, institutions, and practices, leads us away from a single story about a revolutionary moment whose impact radiates outward and toward a set of connected but largely distinct stories about how users, applications, and institutions evolved in particular social spaces.

Despite the focus on communities of use, Mahoney largely retained the traditional view of ENIAC as a machine that was important because of its location on the main flow of development through EDVAC to the historical rupture represented by the cross-cutting bar that Mahoney titled simply "computers." The currents of history flow through ENIAC, eventually carrying computer technology downstream from its spawning ground in "technology and science" to reach other kinds of users. We deepen and nuance this perspective with archival evidence, demonstrating that the EDVAC design itself emerged partly as a response to perceived shortcomings in ENIAC and partly in response to the demands of a new mathematical application: the solution of partial differential equations. This new project led not only to the expected development of a new machine but also, and more importantly, to the articulation of a set of new paradigms of computing. This is one of the senses, alluded to in our subtitle, in which the ENIAC project both made and remade the modern computer.

In the same spirit, we have moved away from a simple story of innovation and of ENIAC as a "wonder" of the early history of computers. ENIAC was, as Galison noted, a trading zone. Whereas tourists might view Stonehenge, say, simply as an awe-inspiring monument, archeologists have studied its development and constructed accounts of how the site mattered to and was used by the inhabitants of its region over thousands of years. We have similarly treated ENIAC as a site at which technological innovation, conceptual development, and computational practice came together over a period of more than ten years.

Following Mahoney's suggestion to look at continuities in use, we warn against automatically situating ENIAC as the starting point of every story to be told about the history of the modern computer unless a case can be made for a direct continuity of practice and influence. Like most other automatic computers of the 1940s, ENIAC was a one-off machine in the sense that it was designed to a unique set of plans and hand-built in a production run of one. But ENIAC was more idiosyncratic than most other early computers, and therefore some of its practices were particularly difficult to transfer. Many later machines adapted their architectures and instruction sets from a few models, such as the 1945 EDVAC design, Turing's plans for the ACE, or von Neumann's design for the Institute for Advanced Studies computer. The results, varied as they were, were variations on a theme.

Everything about ENIAC was distinctive, from its decimal ring counters to its decentralized control mechanism and modular architecture. ENIAC became even less representative during the 1950s, as corporations overtook universities and research centers as the primary users of computers. The custom building of computers was replaced almost entirely by the procurement of standard commercial models. When Harvard pulled the plug on its Mark I (the only wartime machine to have outlasted ENIAC), its place was taken by a Univac 1, the machine that first proved a market existed for commercially built computers.[3] The SSEC's prime place on Madison Avenue was taken by another commercial machine, the IBM 701, which quickly won favor among aerospace firms funded by lavish government contracts. It is striking how foreign many aspects of ENIAC practice were to the dominant modes of computer use even a decade later.

ENIAC and the Origins of Programming

ENIAC's initial operators have often been called the "first computer programmers." This is not entirely accurate, given that ENIAC set-ups had previously been developed by Arthur Burks and others, and all who were involved agreed that the set-up used for ENIAC's inaugural work on the Los Alamos problem was created primarily by Nicholas Metropolis and Stanley Frankel. Earlier documents produced by others, such as Ada Lovelace and John von Neumann, are often said to contain "programs" that were never executed, and the users of other computers such as the Harvard Mark I (among them Grace Hopper) were coding and running sequences of instructions before the ENIAC operators were hired.

The historian Nathan Ensmenger has claimed that "the history of vocational computer programming begins, in the United States at least, with the construction of the ENIAC in summer 1945."[4] This is a much more nuanced assertion, explicitly confined to programming as a distinct occupation rather than an activity. This specificity prompts a different concern: the people in question were hired as operators, and their contributions to tasks later seen as the domain of specialist "programmers" were deeply entwined with their other responsibilities. Throughout ENIAC's time at the Moore School, programming occurred collaboratively at the intersection of machine operation and mathematics, with input from both sides. As we mentioned earlier, not until March of 1947 did the group led by Jean Bartik became the first group employed specifically to program ENIAC.

We have shown that the work practices associated with ENIAC evolved from practices that had already been established within applied mathematics to manage large-scale computations. The mathematical analysis of problems and the creation of detailed plans to carry out computations had long ago been separated from the laborious execution of step-by-step plans by human computers. Adding desk calculators to the process increased the productivity of the human computers but did not change the division of work. In contrast, the introduction of the differential analyzer during the 1930s transferred large parts of the computation process to a machine, creating the new role of operator. Operators mediated between mathematics and machine, working in hands-on fashion to trace input data and to configure the analyzer with wrenches but also developing craft skills that were important in the effective transformation of a mathematical equation into a form suitable to the machine. In this respect, ENIAC followed the model of the differential analyzer. But, as a digital computer, it could automate a much broader range of computational procedures. In complex calculations, some work was still carried out manually, typically by sorting and processing punched cards between runs, but most of what had formerly been carried out by a human computer was now performed by the automatic computer. As early as 1943 the project team had recognized that preparing ENIAC to tackle a particular problem involved new kinds of labor, proposing a three-phase division of the work into mathematical analysis, preparation of set-up forms, and physical configuration of ENIAC according to those forms.[5] ENIAC's operators were always expected to carry out the last of these tasks, in addition to their core responsibility of working the machine and its ancillary punched card equipment. In the event, they contributed significantly to the development of many of the set-ups—something that may not have been anticipated when they were hired. This recalls Stephen Barley's characterization of the work of technicians as a "buffer" between professionals and technologies.[6] A neat separation of expertise between the two is always challenging to maintain, a tension that may explain the evidence of close collaboration on many problems between mathematicians and operators.

Several of ENIAC's operators left wonderfully vivid accounts of the process by which they discovered how to set up ENIAC to sequence mathematical operations. These are sometimes quoted in support of claims that they discovered radical new uses of ENIAC's hardware that its creators had not anticipated, for example with Kay McNulty's recognition that the master programmer could repeat sequences of operations for trajectory calculations.[7] In fact the operators were grasping the precise application around which the unit was designed, just as millions of students since them have experienced sudden flashes of understanding into how loops can be used to structure computer programs.

It was hard to devise a mathematical treatment without good knowledge of the processes of mechanical computation, and it was hard to turn a computational plan into a set-up without hands-on knowledge of how ENIAC ran. For example, using ENIAC involved a great deal of careful attention to the scaling of quantities, because, unlike later machines intended for scientific work, it lacked floating-point capabilities. In its original programming mode, this scaling was carried out not in ENIAC's circuits but by special plugs called "shifters" that the operators manually inserted into its data terminals. It was also hard to operate ENIAC without understanding something about the mathematical task it was undertaking. In her 1946 report, Adele Goldstine mentioned a broad range of responsibilities for the operators, including the need for "the operator to first break down the equations into a form" that ENIAC could handle, the "scheduling of parallel operations when planning the set-up of a problem," and providing "for the deletion of non-significant figures by placing a deleter at the output terminal" from which a number would be transmitted. Operators were also urged to "pay particular attention to the interlock coincidence flip-flop neon … before starting a computation." She seems to have seen these duties, from analyzing equations to placing plugs and starting the computer, as natural parts of a single role.[8] Scientific programming, as a distinct job, evolved as a set of intermediate tasks between the longer-established and better-understood jobs of mathematical analysis of a computation and the computation's execution (with or without mechanical aids).

Historians have tended to see the "planning and coding" model that was presented in 1947 by Herman Goldstine and John von Neumann, which distinguished the mathematical analysis of a problem from the work of coding the resulting computational plan, as the basis of a rigid, unworkable, and patently sexist division of labor.[9] One problem is that their approach seems to divorce understanding of computing from understanding of the system being modeled. We did, however, find a broadly similar and successful division of labor in the contemporaneous preparations for the Monte Carlo computations, in which John von Neumann drew an early draft flow diagram but Klara von Neumann developed later versions and translated the diagram into computer code. We are not sure how well the division of labor would have worked with a mathematician less talented and less interested in the intricacies of machine computation than John von Neumann driving the process—though Richard Clippinger's partnership with Jean Bartik and her fellow contractors to code his supersonic air flow problem was also successful. Neither is it clear that coders without the natural gifts of Adele Goldstine, Jean Bartik, or Klara von Neumann would have taken so readily to the task.

Practices that developed around early computers such as ENIAC and the Harvard Mark I did, as several historians have noted, have a direct influence on computer companies' production of hardware and software.[10] The experience gained at the Moore School in the construction of ENIAC and the preparatory work for EDVAC had an obvious and profound effect on the hardware designs and engineering practices Eckert and Mauchly applied at their own company. Even after its assimilation as the Univac division of Sperry Rand, this business unit continued to employ many other ENIAC veterans—among them Betty Holberton, who worked under Grace Hopper to develop automatic programming tools in the 1950s. ENIAC also exerted a definite influence on computing practice in many areas of science. For example, the Monte Carlo code run on ENIAC had a clear and direct influence, through the involvement of Nick Metropolis and other Los Alamos staff members, on later Monte Carlo simulations. Other ENIAC applications discussed above, including the 1950 numerical meteorology simulations and the statistical tables produced by Frank Grubbs, also pioneered techniques that were then widely used with later generations of computer hardware.

The perception of ENIAC's operators as "the first computer programmers" has led some historians to tell a story in which the development of software was originally seen as women's work but, through some unfortunate or nefarious process, was transformed into a boys' club. This has sometimes been tied to an argument that programming work was originally conceptualized in terms that made it seem particularly suited for women. In her celebrated paper, Jennifer Light suggested that "engineers originally conceived of the task of programming as merely clerical," and therefore suitable for women, who were later excluded once the skilled nature of the work was recognized.[11] Nathan Ensmenger drew on Light's analysis to provide the departure point for a history of programming work in which the "first computer programmers were not scientists or mathematicians, they were low-status female clerical workers and desktop calculator operators."[12]

The specific and to a large extent local association of women with particular kinds of mathematical labor seems to us more important than a general association of women with work seen as clerical, particularly since there was nothing obviously clerical about operating ENIAC. Ensmenger suggested that the ENIAC women were hired as "coders" whose primary role was to develop plans of computation, and that coding work was seen as low-status activity akin to transcription.[13] We believe, echoing Janet Abbate, that it is more accurate to say that the project's leaders did not originally recognize "programmer" or "coder" as an occupation separate from "operator."[14] Some of the work later seen as part of programming was expected to be undertaken by the mathematician who analyzed the problem, while other aspects were conflated with machine operation.

As we have shown in this book, the selection of women as operators, though in part a function of wartime labor conditions, also reflected a long tradition of female participation in applied mathematics within the institutional settings of universities and research laboratories. Women had been carrying out firing-table computations manually, using desk calculators, and had been working the differential analyzer. The tradition continued with the introduction of new technology such as ENIAC, which was seen as a new and faster way to accomplish the same work. There was, in any event, no obvious alternative source of operators for ENIAC. (The Harvard

Mark I, interestingly, was operated by a team of uniformed enlisted men on the naval system of "watches," because the computing center, though on Harvard's campus, was officially a Navy facility.[15])

During the early 1950s all of the automatic computers at the Ballistic Research Lab (ENIAC, two other electronic computers, and the relay calculators) were operated by a predominantly female workforce. Women were also hired in large numbers for computer work at other institutions (such as Bell Labs), which had a strong tradition of scientific computing work. In contrast, the computerization of clerical work was approached within the mental frame of "electronic data processing" and within the institutional context of the corporation. Women were present in large numbers as typists, and after computerization they continued to do similar labor as key-punch workers. There were three kinds of staff performing work relevant to administrative programming, from which most firms selected the employees to be seconded to the data processing group and re-trained for computer work: punched-card-machine workers, corporate "systems men" (responsible for redesigning business processes), and junior professional or supervisory employees in the department concerned (typically accountants, as computers were usually applied first to accounting or payroll tasks). Because all these groups were predominantly male, the story of male domination of administrative programming work was likewise a story of continuity within a particular institutional context.

Thus, we see the history of programming labor not as the creation of a new occupation in which women were first welcomed and then excluded, but rather as a set of parallel stories in which the influence of ENIAC and other early machines remained strong in centers of scientific computation but was negligible in corporate data-processing work.[16]

Practice and Place

One interesting feature of early ENIAC practice is the machine's ability, until about 1952, to attract what participants called "expeditions" or "pilgrimages" by scientists eager to apply its unique talents to their problems. This mirrored the growing importance of other rare and expensive experimental devices, such as particle accelerators in the emerging world of "big science."[17] The concept of a "center of calculation" has entered the vocabulary of science studies thanks to Bruno Latour, although he used it to describe the ability of those at the center to control events elsewhere by gathering remote data on impersonal paper forms ("immutable mobiles") and processing it.[18] In our story, scientists moved along with their data. ENIAC itself was immobile, but its configuration was surprisingly mutable in response to scientists' needs. As computers proliferated during the 1950s, the need for journeys from Los Alamos faded, as the lab there consistently housed several of the world's fastest computers. Still, scientists in more marginal institutions continued to trek to powerful computers. Even after minicomputers became a standard laboratory fixture, scientists needing supercomputer time typically had to work to arrange access and then had to make a long trip. Several of the under-pinnings of today's Internet, including the original development of the ARPANET and the development of the Mosaic Web browser, were motivated by the need to make powerful computers available to researchers without the need to physically visit them.

We are not the first to consider ENIAC in these broader contexts. Atsushi Akera used the metaphor of "ecologies of knowledge" to explore its roots in a specific and short-lived alignment of institutions, artifacts, people, occupations, and knowl-edge.[19] We argue, similarly, that ENIAC should be understood, in its local context, as a machine intended to perform a particular kind of computation, exemplified by the calculation of trajectories. That requirement brought a sharp focus to Mauchly's inchoate ideas about electronic computation, and, when aligned with the organiza-tional capabilities and technological expertise of the Moore School, it formed the matrix that brought ENIAC into existence.

We have gone beyond Akera's analysis to explain how initial conceptions of ENIAC and the structure of the computations it would carry out were changed in unforeseen ways during the detailed design and construction of the machine. That process evokes what Andrew Pickering called "the mangle of practice," a concept that scholars of science have found useful when considering the role of material objects in science and the ways in which they transform and are trans-formed by people, ideas, and institutions in the practice of modern science.[20] His phrase captures the messy heterogeneity of scientific practice, standing as a rebuke to pristine worlds of theory, ideas, and data and the assumption of a single culture of science found in traditional philosophy of science. Like Mahoney, Pickering insists on the specificity of time and place. In history, as in politics, all stories are local. Rather than trying to capture ENIAC in a neat and tidy retrospective historical schema, we have charted the process of its emergence in a specific and contingent set of circumstances.

We have also documented how the mangling of ENIAC continued long after its initial construction. To an extent that has not previously been fully appreciated, ENIAC's users remade the way in which it was programmed, turning it from a device that had to be re-wired for each problem into a machine that could execute pro-grams written in a repertoire of standard instructions and stored as a sequence of numbers. The modern code paradigm itself thus became a significant agent in ENIAC's ongoing transformations. Further changes during the 1950s continued its co-evolution with changing practices, including modifications and additions to its hardware to optimize its performance within the new programming paradigm. The most striking of these was the addition of the new core memory unit.

Remaking Scientific Practice

In our introduction, we began with Douglas Hartree's comments that ENIAC promised scientists a thousandfold increase in the complexity of calculations they could undertake. Hartree asserted that scientists could "do quite a lot with ten million multiplications." How did scientific practice change as people engaged with ENIAC's tantalizing possibilities? We will conclude the book by teasing out three broader lessons.

Doing Quite a Lot with Ten Million Multiplications

One crucial development was a surge of interest in numerical methods to approximate the solution of equations. Numerical methods had been around for hundreds of years, and their application was already beginning to emerge as an area of research in mathematics. Hartree's chair was in "mathematical physics," though "numerical analysis" was the term that stuck as the field developed during the 1950s. Even in 1943, the ENIAC team was able to find a suitable expert, Hans Rademacher, elsewhere within the University of Pennsylvania, and his work helped to shape the design of ENIAC's accumulators. However, the adoption of digital electronic computers gave the area a degree of visibility and intellectual excitement it had never before experienced.

Existing methods had been optimized for laborious hand calculation with, at most, thousands of multiplications for each data point. They had also, as we saw with Hartree's 1946 analysis of the laminar boundary problem, been optimized for the capabilities of humans rather than machines. Humans would perform better if directed to calculate a smaller number of data points using relatively complex methods requiring them to look up previously calculated intermediate results. ENIAC could calculate with lightning speed but had no space in its memory for storing previous results. Later machines could accommodate much more complex methods, leading to the development of new approaches that would have been entirely infeasible without electronic computer power. Nevertheless, their architectures had their own distinctive strengths and weaknesses to which methods were tweaked, from cache memories to vector processing units. Numerical analysis involved plenty of theorems and proofs, and the development of some enormously creative algorithms, but it was also an experimental discipline to an extent that was unusual in the history of mathematical practice.

Algorithmic Simulation

Another development was the rise of simulation. As we discussed earlier, this topic is receiving an increasing amount of attention from historians and philosophers of science. The basic shift was from analytical descriptions of a situation, in which an equation explained the relationship between different quantities, to an algorithmic approach in which the relationship was described only by a series of steps necessary to transform input into output.[21] In that sense, simulation is a characteristically digital practice, and the ENIAC Monte Carlo calculations may plausibly be described as the first computerized simulations. Analog computers gave physical reality to quantities, implementing the equations connecting them as adjustable rotator arms or configurable water pumps. In contrast, ENIAC could be set up to carry out whatever steps were needed to implement the algorithm, particularly after its 1948 conversion to the modern code paradigm enabled it to use its function tables to store arbitrarily complex sequences of instructions.

Simulation provided a fundamentally experimental way of discovering the properties of the system described. One set initial parameters, ran the program, and waited to see what happened. As Mahoney observed, by relying on simulation over traditional mathematical analysis scientists have run into the main conceptual challenge of theoretical computer science. Computer scientists would like to be able to reason analytically about the behavior of a computer program by examining its code, rather than having to run it repeatedly with different input data and see what happens. Similarly, scientists would like to have a deeper understanding of why simulations produce the results they do. Computer scientists learned from Turing's classic 1936 paper that some questions about computer programs are inherently impossible to answer, placing fundamental limits on the completeness of such analysis. Mahoney noted that "we confront the question of whether the computer, the newest and leading medium of scientific thought, can be comprehended mathematically, i.e., in some way algebraically or analytically. If so, then it will be viewed as the newest chapter of a history that began in the seventeenth century with the beginning of algebraic thought. If not, then perhaps fifty years from now someone will be giving a lecture on the topic of 'The End of Algebraic Thought in the Twentieth Century.'"[22]

Loving the Machine

A third discovery was that programming a computer to carry out a scientific computation was a craft skill in its own right, and that computers exerted their own fascination as objects of scientific curiosity. One sees around ENIAC the origins of what became a common set of experiences and choices within the world of science during the 1950s and the 1960s. In the 1940s there was no such thing as a computer scientist or a computer programmer. Everyone who approached ENIAC did so from the vantage point of another socially recognized, and self-perceived, role. The women now remembered as programmers had been hired as machine operators. Similarly, the men who designed ENIAC were electronic engineers, and the men and women who used the machine to tackle their mathematical problems were mathematicians, statisticians, physicists, aeronautical engineers, or members of other established disciplines.

Not everyone exposed to ENIAC reacted the same way. As with quintessential 1960s experiments such as taking LSD, some continued on much the same path as before but others rebuilt their lives around the new experience. Richard Clippinger, for example, first approached ENIAC as a potential scientific consumer of its services. He later transferred to the computing group and made the rest of his career around computers, eventually becoming a programming language expert at Honeywell. Frank Grubbs, a statistician, likewise approached ENIAC as someone with a complicated problem to solve. But after obtaining the necessary results from ENIAC, and from the BRL's relay computers, he continued in his existing career trajectory. Today he is remembered as a great statistician and an important contributor to the Ordnance Department.

The same pattern repeated itself more broadly in later decades. The first members of computer-science faculties had all received PhDs in established disciplines, and many had already held faculty positions in such disciplines. At some point, often as graduate students, they had encountered computers and had come to recognize that they identified more strongly with those machines than with the concerns of the disciplines to which they were apprenticed. This may have been attributable to a fascination with the process of programming, accompanied by a shift from application code to the world of system tools or subroutine libraries. Yet for many scientific users the computer remained merely a tool, a means to an end. Most engineers, mathematicians, and physicists who relied on computers to obtain results did not become computer scientists. Many faculty members relied on their graduate students to do their programming and to run their problems on computers, and most of those graduate students repeated the pattern if and when they became successful enough to be in a position to hand the work over to others.

The Future of ENIAC

Anyone drawn to read or write about a historical topic is driven, in one way or another, by some present-day motivating factor. We have tried to dispel misconceptions and to illuminate forgotten aspects of ENIAC's story so as to depict it more faithfully in its original context. Yet no subject of genuine historical interest will ever receive a definitive treatment. Although we have worked to ground our story in the exceptionally rich archival material, there is much more to be said about ENIAC, and still more to be said about other early computers and their use.

As we noted in the preceding chapter, ENIAC has been remembered in many different ways in the past 70 years. It remains sufficiently central to narratives about the history of computing, both popular and scholarly, that it is easier to advance an agenda by reinterpreting ENIAC than by ignoring it. ENIAC's recent fame as a computer programmed by women, for example, stems from a broad concern among computer scientists and technology workers about the representation of women in computing. Anchoring this inspirational narrative on ENIAC simultaneously exploits and perpetuates the machine's renown as the origin point of modern computing. ENIAC will find new tales in which to perform as members of future generations looking to make a point about the essential nature of some or another aspect of computing turn to it.

Notes

Introduction

1. Douglas R. Hartree, *Calculating Machines: Recent and Prospective Developments and Their Impact on Mathematical Physics* (Cambridge University Press, 1947), 24 and 27.

2. Bruno Latour, *Science in Action: How to Follow Scientists and Engineers through Society* (Harvard University Press, 1987).

3. Peter Galison and Bruce Hevly, *Big Science: The Growth of Large-Scale Research* (Stanford University Press, 1992).

4. See, e.g., Nancy Beth Stern, *From ENIAC to Univac: An Appraisal of the Eckert-Mauchly Computers* (Digital Press, 1981), 16–23; Atsushi Akera, *Calculating a Natural World: Scientists, Engineers, and Computers During the Rise of U.S. Cold War Research* (MIT Press, 2007), chapters 1 and 2.

5. This perspective is sympathetic to that of Akera's book *Calculating a Natural World*, which situates ENIAC within an "ecology of knowledge."

6. During its most productive period, the early 1950s, ENIAC still had "25 per cent of its computing time devoted to artillery and bomb ballistics computation" (Harry L. Reed Jr., "Firing Table Computations on the Eniac," in *Proceedings of the 1952 ACM National Meeting (Pittsburgh)*, Association for Computing Machinery, 1952).

7. H. R. Keith, letter to R. E. Clement, October 27, 1952, Cuthbert C. Hurd Papers (CBI 95), Charles Babbage Institute.

8. Peter Galison, "Computer Simulation and the Trading Zone," in *The Disunity of Science: Boundaries, Contexts, and Power*, ed. Peter Galison and David J. Stump (Stanford University Press, 1996); Anne Fitzpatrick, *Igniting the Light Elements: The Los Alamos Thermonuclear Weapon Project, 1942–1952* (Los Alamos National Laboratory, 1999).

9. Recently, for example, in Alice Burks, *Who Invented the Computer? The Legal Battle That Changed Computing* (Prometheus Books, 2003) and Jane Smiley, *The Man Who Invented the Computer: The Biography of John Atanasoff, Digital Pioneer* (Doubleday, 2010).

10. Alice R. Burks and Arthur W. Burks, *The First Electronic Computer: The Atanasoff Story* (University of Michigan Press, 1989).

11. This distinction was introduced in an influential early description of Colossus as a "special-purpose program-controlled electronic digital computer" (Brian Randell, "The

Colossus," in *A History of Computing in the Twentieth Century*, ed. Nicholas Metropolis, Jack Howlett, and Gian-Carlo Rota, Academic Press, 1980). For more complete information on the machines in their use, see Jack Copeland, *Colossus: The First Electronic Computer* (Oxford University Press, 2006).

12. Michael R. Williams, "A Preview of Things to Come: Some Remarks on the First Generation of Computers," in *The First Computers: History and Architectures*, ed. Raúl Rojas and Ulf Hashagen (MIT Press, 2000).

13. Ibid.

14. George Dyson, *Turing's Cathedral: The Origins of the Digital Universe* (Pantheon Books, 2012); Martin Campbell-Kelly and William Aspray, *Computer: A History of the Information Machine* (Basic Books, 1996).

15. Michel Callon, "Some Elements of a Sociology of Translation: Domestication of the Scallops and the Fishermen of St Brieuc Bay," in *Power, Action and Belief: A New Sociology of Knowledge?*, ed. John Law (Routledge, 1986).

16. Trevor Pinch and Richard Swedberg, eds., *Living in a Material World* (MIT Press, 2008).

17. In part because the advancement of computer technology soon came to be associated with miniaturization, the use of computers as showpieces of scientific modernity has received less attention than more obviously monumental structures, such as the radio telescope. See Jon Agar, *Science and Spectacle: The Work of Jodrell Bank in Post-War British Culture* (Routledge, 1998).

18. Walter Isaacson, "Walter Isaacson on the Women of ENIAC," *Fortune*, October 6, 2014. Elsewhere in *The Innovators* (Simon & Schuster, 2014) Isaacson does discuss the work of Eckert, Mauchly, and Goldstine, so these remarks are more an odd rhetorical flourish than a systematic erasure of the role of ENIAC's actual designers, engineers, and builders.

19. Wendy Hui Kyong Chun, *Programmed Visions: Software and Memory* (MIT Press, 2011), 34.

20. Borrowing a term from electronic engineering, scholars characterized the inner workings of technological devices or scientific theories as "black boxes." In the original sense of that expression, "black boxing" a subsystem allowed engineers to focus on its documented inputs and outputs without having to worry about what was going on within.

21. Langdon Winner, "Upon Opening the Black Box and Finding It Empty: Social Constructivism and the Philosophy of Technology," *Science, Technology, & Human Values* 18, no. 3 (1993): 362–378.

22. Martin Campbell-Kelly, "The History of the History of Software," *IEEE Annals of the History of Computing* 29, no. 4 (2007): 40–51.

23. Maarten Bullynck and Liesbeth De Mol, "Setting-Up Early Computer Programs: D. H. Lehmer's ENIAC Computation," *Archive of Mathematical Logic* 49 (2010): 123–146; Liesbeth De Mol, Martin Carle, and Maarten Bullynck, "Haskell before Haskell: An Alternative Lesson in Practical Logics of the ENIAC," *Journal of Logic and Computation*, online preprint, 2013. The details of ENIAC set-ups are also explored in Brian J. Shelburne, "The ENIAC's 1949 Determination of π," *IEEE Annals of the History of Computing* 34, no. 3 (2012): 44–54.

24. Paul Edwards, *A Vast Machine: Computer Models, Climate Data, and the Politics of Global Warming* (MIT Press, 2010); Kristine C. Harper, *Weather by the Numbers: The Genesis of Modern Meteorology* (MIT Press, 2008).

25. Galison, "Computer Simulation and the Trading Zone."

26. The "platform studies" approach, championed in Nick Montfort and Ian Bogost, *Racing the Beam: The Atari Video Computer System* (MIT Press, 2009), is the approach most directly related to our work here. The "software studies" approach is explored in *Software Studies: A Lexicon*, ed. Matthew Fuller (MIT Press, 2008).

27. Herman H. Goldstine, *The Computer from Pascal to von Neumann* (Princeton University Press, 1972); Jean Jennings Bartik, *Pioneer Programmer: Jean Jennings Bartik and the Computer That Changed the World* (Truman State University Press, 2013); Arthur W. Burks and Alice R. Burks, "The ENIAC: First General-Purpose Electronic Computer," *Annals of the History of Computing* 3, no. 4 (1981): 310–399.

28. Burks' involvement in the ENIAC patent litigation of the 1960s and the 1970s is well documented in AWB-IUPUI. That collection includes probability trees in which he gamed out the financial payoff he expected to gain from his attempt to win recognition as a co-inventor of ENIAC.

29. Burks and Burks, "The ENIAC"; Burks and Burks, *The First Electronic Computer*.

30. Burks, *Who Invented the Computer?*

31. It is not altogether clear why this is the case, as it has long been known that ENIAC ran a highly complex calculation for Los Alamos weeks before the public launch.

Chapter 1

1. Earl R. Larson, Findings of Fact, Conclusions of Law, and Order for Judgment in *Honeywell Inc. v. Sperry Rand Corporation et al.* 180 USPQ 673, 1973 (available at ushistory.org).

2. Akera, *Calculating a Natural World*, 81.

3. Eckert's story is not as well documented as Mauchly's, but he comes vividly to life in Scott McCartney's book *ENIAC: The Triumphs and Tragedies of the World's First Computer* (Walker, 1999).

4. "1296. Eckert. T.I. (carbon) to Robert P. Mulhauf," in Diana H. Hook and Jeremy M. Norman, *Origins of Cyberspace: A Library on the History of Computing and Computer-Related Telecommunications* (Norman, 2002), 601.

5. McCartney, *ENIAC*, 43–45.

6. John W. Mauchly, "Amending the ENIAC Story," *Datamation* 25, no. 11 (1979): 217–219.

7. Goldstine, *The Computer*, 202.

8. According to Application for Federal Employment, July 1945 (in JWM-UP), Mauchly was appointed an assistant professor in September of 1941; however, Akera implies in *Calculating a Natural World* that there was an initial short-term contract.

9. David Alan Grier, *When Computers Were Human* (Princeton University Press, 2006), 134.

10. See table extracts reproduced in Harry Polachek, "Before the ENIAC," *IEEE Annals of the History of Computing* 19, no. 2 (1997): 25–30.

11. For contemporary treatments of exterior ballistics, see, for example, Ernest E. Herrmann, *Exterior Ballistics* (U.S. Naval Institute, 1935) or Gilbert Ames Bliss, *Mathematics for Exterior Ballistics* (Wiley, 1944). Interior ballistics, in contrast, studies the behavior of shells inside gun barrels.

12. Herrmann, *Exterior Ballistics*, v–vi; L. S. Dederick, "The Mathematics of Exterior Ballistic Computations," *American Mathematical Monthly* 47, no. 9 (1940): 628–634.

13. Vannevar Bush, "The Differential Analyzer: A New Machine for Solving Differential Equations," *Journal of the Franklin Institute* 212, no. 4 (1931): 447–488.

14. Irven Travis, OH 36: Oral History Interview by Nancy B. Stern, Charles Babbage Institute, October 21, 1977, 3.

15. J. G. Brainerd, "Genesis of the ENIAC," *Technology and Culture* 17, no. 3 (1976): 482–488.

16. Travis, OH 36: Oral History Interview by Nancy B. Stern, 3–4.

17. Gordon Barber, *Ballisticians in War and Peace, Volume 1: A History of the United States Army Ballistics Research Laboratories, 1914–1956* (Aberdeen Proving Ground), 17.

18. Travis, OH 36: Oral History Interview by Nancy B. Stern; Brainerd, "Genesis of the ENIAC," 484.

19. Barber, *Ballisticians in War and Peace*, 12–13.

20. Irven Travis, "Automatic Numerical Solution of Differential Equations," March 28, 1940, MSOD-UP, box 51; Burks and Burks, *The First Electronic Computer*, 182–184.

21. Goldstine, *The Computer*, 133.

22. Polachek, "Before the ENIAC."

23. Brainerd, "Genesis of the ENIAC," 484.

24. Polachek ("Before the ENIAC," 28) describes finding in one table errors of about 10 percent, caused by failure to convert between yards and meters.

25. Jonathan B. A. Bailey, "Mortars," in *The Oxford Companion to Military History*, ed. Richard Holmes et al. (Oxford University Press, 2001).

26. Whether the promised boost would be delivered is another question. According to Mitchell P. Marcus and Atsushi Akera ("Exploring the Architecture of an Early Machine: The Historical Relevance of the ENIAC Machine Architecture," *IEEE Annals of the History of Computing* 18, no. 1, 1996: 17–24), "military tacticians have debated the value of printed ballistics tables especially as they were used in World War II. Field conditions rarely match the formal settings of a laboratory environment, and given the general patterns of combat during World War II, ballistics tables had a limited tactical value at best." Marcus and Akera attribute the production of the tables more to the efforts of mathematicians within the BRL to promote their relevance than to any particular demand from soldiers in combat.

27. Polachek, "Before the ENIAC."

28. Burks and Burks, *The First Electronic Computer*, 186–190.

29. John Mauchly, "The Use of High Speed Vacuum Tube Devices for Calculating," MSOD-UP, box 51 (PX-Electronic Computation (Mauchly)).

30. Goldstine, *The Computer*, 149.

31. Moore School of Electrical Engineering. "Report on an Electronic Difference* Analyzer," April 8, 1943, AWB-IUPUI. A footnote to the title explained the motivation for the new terminology. An April 2, 1943 version of this document marked as a "first draft" with the title "Report on an Electronic Diff.* Analyzer" is archived in MSOD-UP b51 (PX—Electronic Computation (Mauchly), 1942–1943).

32. Stern, *From ENIAC to Univac*, 18.

33. Section II.3 of the proposal explicitly compares the new machine with the differential analyzer.

34. Brainerd to Pender, April 26, 1943, MSOD-UP, box 51 (PX—Electronic Computation (Mauchly), 1942–1943).

35. Brainerd to Johnson, April 12, 1943, MSOD-UP, box 49 (PX-1 General).

36. Stern, *From ENIAC to Univac*, 18–23.

37. John Mauchly, "The Use of High Speed Vacuum Tube Devices for Calculating," MSOD-UP, box 51 (PX-Electronic Computation (Mauchly)). Akera (*Calculating a Natural World*, 86) interprets "step-by-step" as meaning "strictly sequential." However, the 1943 proposal made it clear that each step could contain many individual operations, some of which could be performed in parallel.

38. Travis, "Automatic Numerical Solution of Differential Equations." For a strong argument that Mauchly and Eckert were aware of Travis' earlier work, see Burks and Burks, *The First Electronic Computer*, 182–184.

39. John Mauchly, "The Use of High Speed Vacuum Tube Devices for Calculating," MSOD-UP, box 51 (PX-Electronic Computation (Mauchly)).

40. Moore School of Electrical Engineering. "Report on an Electronic Difference Analyzer," April 8, 1943, AWB-IUPUI.

41. Ibid., appendix C. As if to emphasize the general-purpose nature of the machine, appendix D contained a similar example of a program for a pair of rather different equations from interior ballistics.

42. Pender to MacLean, November 5, 1943, MSOD-UP, box 48 (PX-1).

43. "List of supplies and equipment needed for PX-1," May 6, 1943, MSOD-UP, box 48 (PX—drawings, pamphlets, estimates, misc.); Fetterolf to Brainerd, May 26, 1943; Fleitas to Brainerd, May 29, 1943, MSOD-UP, box 29 (PX-1 General).

44. Pender to Musser, June 7, 1943, MSOD-UP, box 51 (PX—Electronic Computation (Mauchly), 1942–1943).

45. Brainerd to MacLean, June 21, 1943, MSOD-UP, box 49 (PX-1 General).

46. Goldstine appears to have covered for Gillon himself at one point (Goldstine to Gillon, May 26, 1944, ETE-UP).

47. "War Research in the Moore School of Electrical Engineering," February 18, 1943, MSOD-UP, box 45 (Projects General, 1943).

48. Budget documents in MSOD-UP, box 48 (PX—Budgets, 1943).

49. "Check List for Things to be Done: Project PX," July 26, 1943, MSOD-UP, box 57 (Parts Lists, 1943–1944).

50. Fleitas to Brainerd, May 29, 1943, MSOD-UP, box 49 (PX-1 General, 1943).

51. John G. Brainerd, "Project PX—The ENIAC," *Pennsylvania Gazette* 44, no. 7 (1946): 16–17, at 32.

52. "Laboratory Notebook #4, Project PX #1. Issued to T. K. Sharpless by Isabelle Jay. 7/4/43", MSOBM-UP, box 2, serial no. 14 (Z14), p. 3.

53. Unlike the majority of later computers, ENIAC used the decimal rather than the binary number system.

54. "Report for Project PX: Positive Action Ring Counter (August 19, 1943)" and "Report for Project PX: The NCR Thyratron Counter," both in Arthur W. Burks, Laboratory Notebook, No. 1 (MSOBM-UP, box 1, serial no. 16).

55. "ENIAC Progress Report 31 December 1943," volume 1, MSOD-UP, box 1.

56. John Mauchly, "The Use of High Speed Vacuum Tube Devices for Calculating," MSOD-UP, box 51 (PX-Electronic Computation (Mauchly)).

57. "Report for Project PX, September 30, 1943, Accumulators and Transmitters," MSOD-UP, box 3 (Reports on Project PX).

58. Five handwritten pages numbered 1–5 pasted in as pages 94, 96, 88, 90, 92 of "PX Laboratory Notebook #1. Issued June 17, 1943 to Dr. A. W. Burks by Isabelle Jay," MSOBM-UP, box 2, serial no. 16 (Z16).

59. Kurt W. Beyer, *Grace Hopper and the Invention of the Information Age* (MIT Press, 2009), 55.

60. Hans Rademacher, "Mathematical Topics of Interest in PX: Part One—General Considerations" and "PX Report Number 14: Mathematical Topics of Interest in PX, Part Two: Summary of Articles Dealing with Rounding Off Errors," November 30, 1943, MSOD-UP, box 48 (PX-Computations, Rademacher, Etc.).

61. "Report for Project PX: Accumulators and Transmitters," September 30, 1943, MSOD-UP, box 3 (Reports on Project PX). For the manual calculations, see, for example, the 1943 calculation sheets preserved in MSOD-UP, box 48 (PX-Computations, Rademacher, Etc., 1943–1946), which recorded a maximum of eight significant figures.

62. "ENIAC Progress Report 31 December 1943," III, (3), (4).

63. Hans Rademacher, "On the Precision of a Certain Procedure of Numerical Integration," April 1944, MSOD-UP, box 48 (PX-Computations, Rademacher, Etc.).

64. "ENIAC Progress Report 31 December 1944," volume 1, MSOD-UP, box 1, III (3).

Chapter 2

1. Burks and Burks, "The ENIAC," 343.

2. For example, Eckert wrote of constraints imposed by "the limited time that conditions of war demanded" and suggested that use of "distributed control was dictated by the ease of building and getting it done in good time." J. Presper Eckert, "The ENIAC," in *A History of Computing in the Twentieth Century*, ed. N. Metropolis, J. Howlett, and Gian-Carlo Rota (Academic Press, 1980).

3. "Report for Project PX, September 30, 1943, Accumulators and Transmitters," 3. Bound in "Reports on Project PX, Electronic Differential Analyzer, Moore School of Electrical Engineering, T. K. Sharpless," MSOD-UP, box 3.

4. Sharpless, Z14 Notebook, p. 19.

5. Ibid., p. 24; Burks, Z16 Notebook, pp. 144–147.

6. Stern, *From ENIAC to Univac*, 47.

7. Burks, Notebook Z16. The diagram is pasted over p. 135. The next page holds notes of a meeting held on October 17, 1943.

8. Arthur W. Burks, unfinished book manuscript, chapter 5.

9. David Alan Grier, "The ENIAC, the Verb "to program" and the Emergence of Digital Computers," *IEEE Annals of the History of Computing* 18, no. 1 (1996): 51–55.

10. In fact this idea of a computer as something that carries out a "sequence" of operations automatically is prevalent in early computing terminology, "sequence" having a meaning similar to that later given to "program." IBM called the giant relay computer it built for Harvard University, often referred to as the Mark I, the "Automatic Sequence Controlled Calculator," thus highlighting its ability to automatically execute a sequence of calculating operations. After falling out with Harvard, IBM built a bigger, better, and much more flexible rival to display at street level in its flagship New York building. The name of this "Selective Sequence Electronic Calculator" trumpeted another advance: the new machine could be configured to automatically select the appropriate sequence on the basis of the current state of its computation.

11. John Mauchly, "The Use of High Speed Vacuum Tube Devices for Calculating," MSOD-UP, box 51 (PX-Electronic Computation (Mauchly)). Mauchly also uses the slight variant "programming device," apparently with the same meaning. As we discussed in chapter 1, this device was to have a central coordinating role.

12. "Report on an Electronic Difference Analyzer," April 8, 1943, appendixes A, C, and D.

13. Sharpless, Notebook Z14, p. 19, dated "11-6-43" and headed "Desc. of Program Unit."

14. Sharpless, Notebook Z14, p. 144, dated "Nov. 20, 1943," has the heading "Programming" for a block diagram of the circuits in the program unit of an accumulator.

15. The act of configuring what became ENIAC was already being called "set up" in the 1943 proposals, and this would appear to have evolved into the later usage of "set-up" as a noun to describe a particular configuration.

16. For example, "ENIAC Progress Report 31 December 1943" mentions the "24 different multiplication programs" that can be set up on the multiplication unit. This remained the basic sense of "program" in the literature on ENIAC: in 1946, Adele K. Goldstine, *A Report on the ENIAC Part I: Technical Description of the ENIAC, Volume I* (Moore School, University of Pennsylvania, 1946), p. I-21, stated that "the instructions given to a single program control are referred to as a 'program'." The title of appendix B of J. Presper Eckert et al., *Description of the ENIAC and Comments on Electronic Digital Machines. AMP Report 171.2R. Distributed by the Applied Mathematics Panel, National Defense Research Committee, November 30* (Moore School of Electrical Engineering, 1945), "Programming the ENIAC," is one of the earliest uses of the word with something like its present meaning.

17. "ENIAC Progress Report 31 December 1943," XIV (1–3).

18. These parameters, and the anti-aircraft application, are very similar to those chosen for the first known use of ENIAC to generate actual firing tables, in August of 1946. See "Deposition of Mrs. Genevieve Brown Hatch", October 18, 1960, in GRS-DC, box 35 (Civil Action No, 105-146. Sperry Rand vs. Bell Labs. Deposition of Mrs. Genevieve Brown Hatch).

19. "PX-1-81: Setup of Exterior Ballistic Equations" in volume II of "ENIAC Progress Report 31 December 1943."

20. The transfers shown between accumulators 2 and 3 in operation 2 in figure 2.2 take place in parallel with a multiplication (not visible in this excerpt) that takes nine addition times to complete, as is noted in the third column. Each row in the table corresponds to a mathematical operation, and parallelized operations have to be squeezed into the available space. By the end of 1944, the format had been tweaked so that each row represented one addition time, making the detailed timing considerations in the set-up easier to read.

21. "ENIAC Progress Report 31 December 1943," IV (9).

22. "PX-1-82: Panel Diagram of the Electronic Numerical Integrator and Computer (Showing the Exterior Ballistics Equations Setup—Heun Method," in volume II of "ENIAC Progress Report 31 December 1943," GRS-DC.

23. Donald F. Hunt to Burks, November 16, 1970, AWB-IUPUI.

24. This reverses the layout used on the original sketch, and reflects the physical layout of ENIAC's panels.

25. The most significant difference is that the setup form does not show which data lines are used to transfer numbers between units.

26. "ENIAC Progress Report 31 December 1943," XIV (8).

27. "ENIAC Progress Report 30 June 1944," MSOD-UP, box 1, p. 2 of preface.

28. This became standard practice in subsequent ENIAC programming, reflecting the importance that the team gave to checking the reliability of the machine.

29. "ENIAC Progress Report 31 December 1943," IV (18).

30. "Meeting of April 21," Z16 notebook, MSOBM-UP, box 1, serial no.16, pp. 244–255; also see Z14 notebook, MSOBM-UP, box 3, serial no. 14, pp. 60–61.

31. Z16 notebook, MSOBM-UP, box 1, serial no.16, p. 252. The register was introduced in the context of discussions about input and output capabilities, and its eighty-digit capacity precisely matched that of a punched card.

32. Arthur W. Burks, "Exhibit A: Contributions of Arthur W. Burks, Thomas Kite Sharpless, and Robert F. Shaw to the Design and Construction of the ENIAC," paragraph A6, part of *Exhibits of Arthur W. Burks* in *Honeywell Inc. vs. Sperry Rand et al.*, AWB-IUPUI.

33. Notebook headed "Arthur W. Burks, PX April 28, 1944," MSOBM-UP, box 2, serial no, 17 (Z17), pp. 15–16; "ENIAC Progress Report 30 June 1944," IV-1. As finally constructed, ENIAC also included an initiating unit and comprised 30 units and 40 panels.

34. Marcus and Akera, "Exploring the Architecture of an Early Machine," 21.

35. Howard A. Aiken and Grace M. Hopper, "The Automatic Sequence Controlled Calculator—I," *Electrical Engineering* 65 (August–September 1946): 390.

36. Richard Bloch, "Programming Mark I," in *Makin' Numbers: Howard Aiken and the Computer*, ed. I. Bernard Cohen and Gregory W. Welch (MIT Press, 1999), 107.

37. "ENIAC Progress Report 31 December 1943," XIV (8–9).

38. Ibid., XIV (9).

39. Ibid.

40. "ENIAC Progress Report 31 December 1943," XII (2–3).

41. Ibid., XII (3).

42. Burks, unfinished book manuscript, chapter 5.

43. Undated manuscript pages in John Mauchly's handwriting, HLU, box 7 (ENIAC: 1944 Notes Programmer). These documents make reference to Burks' set-up, and also describe features of the master programmer. They can therefore be dated with confidence to the first half of 1944. The mid-year report noted (on p. IV-33) that some of the work described in the section on the master programmer had been done after the report's date of June 30, 1944.

44. "ENIAC Progress Report 30 June 1944," p. IV (40).

45. In fact, this diagram would not repeat the whole calculation as Mauchly claimed, because the stepper is not set back to its first stage after printing.

46. "ENIAC Progress Report 30 June 1944," IV (40).

47. Mauchly's plans also describe a rather mysterious "program coupling unit," whose function remains obscure.

48. ENIAC Progress Report 30 June 1944, IV (33).

49. Ibid., IV (41).

50. This technique was documented in Goldstine, *A Report on the ENIAC.*

51. "ENIAC Progress Report 30 June 1944," IV (40).

52. "ENIAC Progress Report 31 December 1944," chapter 2 (11–13).

53. Goldstine, *A Report on the ENIAC,* (IV) 30.

54. "ENIAC Progress Report 30 June 1944," IV (41).

55. Eckert et al., *Description of the ENIAC (AMP Report),* appendix B.

56. Burks, unfinished book manuscript, appendix B.

Chapter 3

1. "Project PX #1, Notebook #8, issued Sept 30, 1943 to J. H. Davis," MOSBM-UP, box 12, serial no. 2 (Z2), pp. 12–57.

2. "ENIAC Progress Report 30 June 1944," I-5.

3. Brainerd to Goldstine, May 17, 1944, MSOD-UP, box 48 (PX-2 General Jan-Jun 1944).

4. "ENIAC Progress Report 30 June 1944," II-1. See Davis' notebook for accumulator tests.

5. Pender to Goldstine, July 3, 1944, GRS-DC, box 19 (PX—Project 1943–1946).

6. Burks and Burks, "The ENIAC," 343 explain the mathematics of the two-accumulator test and highlight similarities between it and the set-up of a differential analyzer to solve the harmonic equation.

7. Sharpless, Z14 notebook, pp. 71–72 (June 27, 1944) and 73–75 (July 10, 1944).

8. Ibid., pp. 76–77 (July 18, 1944).

9. Arthur W. Burks, "Exhibit A: Contributions of Arthur W. Burks, Thomas Kite Sharpless, and Robert F. Shaw to the Design and Construction of the ENIAC," paragraph S15, part of *Exhibits of Arthur W. Burks* in *Honeywell Inc. vs. Sperry Rand et al.* in AWB-IUPUI.

10. McCartney, *ENIAC*, 79.

11. Numbers quoted for the number of joints in ENIAC vary by a factor of 50. The widely quoted figure of 5 million is currently endorsed by Wikipedia but, insofar as the total number of tubes, resistors, switches, and capacitors in ENIAC was approximately 105,000, implies that there were several dozen joints on each component. One witness in ENIAC patent trial stated that ENIAC had "in the order of one hundred thousand joints," which implies fewer joints than components. (Richard F. Clippinger, ENIAC Trial Testimony, September 22, 1971, ETR-UP, 8888.) The most plausible figure we found was an estimate of half a million joints given in one of the press releases for ENIAC's launch, "Physical Aspects, Operations of ENIAC are Described," War Department Bureau of Public Relations, HHG-APS, series 10, box 3, early February 1946, and later endorsed by Eckert himself in "Remarks by J. Presper Eckert, Dinner Marking 15th Anniversary of ENIAC," University of Pennsylvania, October 12, 1961, SRUV-HML, box 381 (Whitpain Dedication and ENIAC Dinner).

12. "PX-Project Laboratory Organization," May 4, 1944, MSOD-UP, box 48 (PX-2 General Jan-Jun 1944).

13. Arthur W. Burks, "Exhibit A: Contributions of Arthur W. Burks, Thomas Kite Sharpless, and Robert F. Shaw to the Design and Construction of the ENIAC, part of Exhibits of Arthur W. Burks in *Honeywell Inc. vs. Sperry Rand et al*," 1972, AWB-IUPUI, S7.

14. "Estimate of cost of six months (January 1 to June 30, 1944) continuation … ," December 7, 1943 and "Estimation of Cost: Completion of the ENIAC (Jun 1 to June 30, 1945)," both in MSOD-UP, box 49 (PX—Estimates).

15. We found the names of ENIAC workers in the detailed, tabulated accounting statements for "Project PX-2" in MSOD-UP, box 48 (MS-112). These list the full names of most employees, as do some of the monthly tabulations in "PX-2 Payrolls, 1944-1945" in the same archival box. By mid-1944, women made up a clear majority of those being paid to create ENIAC. Personnel records in MSOD, box 48 (MS-104) record earlier employment; pay rises and changes of status are logged in MSOD, box 49 (PX-2 Accounts 1944). Unlike ENIAC's operators, hired by the BRL the next year, these women have not been remembered by history, with the exception of Adele Goldstine ("Project Mathematician"). We can do little more than remember them here, as literal footnotes to the project's history. Let the record show that among the women who helped to design and build ENIAC during 1944 were Viola Andreoni, Martha Bobe, Lydia R. Bell, Vava Callison, Nellie T. Collett, O'Bera Darling, Helen Anna De Lacy, Jeanette M. Edelsack (draftswoman), Theresa Fraley, Gertrude E. Gilbert, Ann Gintis, Rita Golden, Margaret Henshaw, Jane Hodes, Virginia Humprey, Mary Ann Isreall, Dorothy F. Keller, Mary Knos, Alice T. Larsen, Alma Markward (assembler), Mary Martin, Anne D. McBride, Cathrine J. McCann (draftswoman), Rose McDonough, Mary E. McGrath, Mary McNetchell, Gertrude Moriarty, Anna Munson, Ann O'Neill, Violet Paige, Jane L. Pepper (draftswoman), Alice Pritchett, Ruth Ruch, Marjorie Santa Maria (draftswoman), Nancy Sellers, Eleanor Simone (technician), Carolyn Shearman, Dorothy K. Shisler, Frances Spurrier, Grace M. Warner, Evangeline E. Werley, Charlotte Widcamp, Sally Wilson, Diana Wrenn, and Isabelle Jay (secretary).

16. "List of supplies for beginning PX-1, April 24, 1943" and "List of supplies and equipment needed for PX-1, May 6, 1943." In MSOD-UP, box 48 (PX—Drawings, Pamphlets, Estimates, Misc.).

17. Goldstine to Strachen, September 14, 1945, ETE-UP. In June of 1941 Signal Corps procurement centers in Chicago and San Francisco were merged into the Philadelphia operation, making it a national center for electronic supplies. By April of 1942, the Philadelphia depot handled more than 14 million pounds of incoming supplies each month and stockpiled more than 100,000 distinct items, according to George Raynor Thompson et al., *The Signal Corps: The Test (December 1941 to July 1943)* (Government Printing Office, 1957), 182.

18. Goldstine to Bennie, March 30, 1945, ETE-UP.

19. Brainerd to Bernbach Radio Corp, August 12, 1943, MSOD-UP, box 48 (PX-Manufacturers 1943). Two small strands of wire remain stapled to the file copy.

20. Various letters in MSOD-UP, box 48 (PX-2 General Jan-Jun 1944).

21. According to Eckert, ENIAC contained 70,000 of these, mostly "small one-half watt composition resistors." J. Presper Eckert Jr., "Reliability of Parts," in *The Moore School Lectures: Theory and Techniques for the Design of Electronic Digital Computers*, ed. Martin Campbell-Kelly and Michael R. Williams (MIT Press, 1985).

22. Goldstine to Gillon, August 21, 1944, ETE-UP. Pender's relationship to IRC is discussed on page 20 of Travis, OH 36: Oral History Interview by Nancy B. Stern.

23. Goldstine to Bogert, July 9, 1945, ETE-UP.

24. Travis to Warshaw, MSOD-UP, box 52 (ENIAC Moving to Aberdeen).

25. Eckert, "Reliability of Parts."

26. Akera, *Calculating a Natural World*, 100–101.

27. Ibid., 100. Randolph to Brainerd, August 5, 1944, MSOD-UP, box 48 (PX Tubes Manual).

28. A sketch of the test table can be found in Dais, Z2 Notebook, p. 100. For tests on individual tubes, see for example Sharpless Z14 Notebook, 86–95, recording work done in October of 1944.

29. Goldstine to Stibitz, August 12, 1944, ETE-UP.

30. Goldstine to Power, June 9, 1945, ETE-UP.

31. Goldstine to Pender, June 26, 1945, ETE-UP.

32. DuBarry to Greathread, September 15, 1945, GRS-DC, box 3 (Material Related to PX-Project) gives permission for Chandler and Flowers to visit in September and October of that year.

33. Stibitz to Weaver, November 6, 1943, MSOD-UP, box 49 (PX-1 General, 1943).

34. "Discussion of a Proposal by Dr. Stibitz for the Development of a Relay Differential Analyzer for Ballistics," circa October 1943, MSOD-UP, box 49 (PX-1 General, 1943).

35. Stibitz to Weaver, November 6, 1943, MSOD-UP, box 49 (PX-1 General, 1943).

36. Goldstine to Stibitz, January 4, 1944, ETE-UP.

37. "Report of a Conference on Computing Devices," February 1, 1944, ETE-UP.

38. Gillon to Brainerd, February 21, 1948, GRS-DC, box 3 (Material Related to PX-Project).

39. Goldstine to Stibitz, August 12, 1944, ETE-UP.

40. Von Neumann was also an important voice in these discussions. Von Neumann to Oppenheimer, August 1, 1944 (declassified Los Alamos document in possession of authors). Both he and Goldstine later helped the BRL define its requirements for the machine. Curry to Goldstine, September 12, 1945 and Goldstine to von Neumann, September 13, 1945, both in ETE-UP.

41. Goldstine to Gillon, September 2, 1944, ETE-UP.

42. Goldstine to Brainerd, February 1, 1944, ETE-UP.

43. William Aspray, *John von Neumann and the Origins of Modern Computing* (MIT Press, 1990), 30.

44. Goldstine to Brainerd, April 21, 1944, ETE-UP.

45. Goldstine to Quaintance, May 27, 1944, ETE-UP.

46. Stern, *From ENIAC to Univac*, 30.

47. Barnes to Pender, February 1, 1944, MSOD-UP, box 48 (PX-2 General Jan-Jun 1944).

48. Goldstine to Gillon, May 26, 1944, ETE-UP.

49. Ingersoll to Brainerd, June 8, 1944, MSOD-UP, box 48 (PX-2 General Jan-Jun 1944).

50. Goldstine to Pender, July 28, 1944, ETE-UP.

51. Goldstine to Gillon, September 2, 1944, ETE-UP.

52. Goldstine to Simon, August 11, 1944, ETE-UP.

53. Goldstine to Gillon, December 14, 1944, ETE-UP.

54. Campbell to Pender, February 20, 1945, MSOD-UP, box 49 (PX—Estimates).

55. Goldstine to von Neumann, May 15, 1945, ETE-UP.

56. Burks, "Contribution of Arthur W. Burks," S16. Burks had written the specifications for these units. Total power consumption is taken from War Department Bureau of Public Relations, "Physical Aspects, Operations of ENIAC."

57. Goldstine to Smith, February 12, 1945, MSOD-UP, box 48 (PX-Maguire Power Supplies).

58. Bill Yenne, *Tommy Gun: How General Thompson's Submachine Gun Wrote History* (Thomas Dunne Books, 2009).

59. Burks to Sarbacher, February 27, 1945, MSOD-UP, box 48 (PX-Maguire Power Supplies).

60. "Memorandum Concerning Meeting Between the Representatives of the University of Pennsylvania and Representatives of Maguire Industries, Inc.," April 7, 1945, MSOD-UP, box 48 (PX-Maguire Power Supplies). Maguire Industries' shift into radios and consumer products was eventually overshadowed by the political activity of its owner, Russell Maguire, who bankrolled the anti-Semitic tract *Iron Curtain Over America*.

61. Goldstine to Bogert, July 9, 1945, ETE-UP.

62. Burks, Z17 Notebook, pp. 57–62.

63. Brainerd to Goldstine et al., September 8, 1945, MSOD-UP, box 48 (PX-2 General Jul-Dec 1945).

64. Congress had defined ahead of time the procedure to be used when exercising the government's "convenience clause" at the end of the war, passing the Contract Settlement Act of 1944, Pub.L.No.78–395, 58 Stat. 649.

65. "Summary of W-670-ORD-4962," MSOD-UP, box 55a (ENIAC General, 1944–1945).

66. This is based on cost-of-living inflation measures, as determined by the Bureau of Labor Statistics CPI Inflation Calculator at http://www.bls.gov/data/inflation_calculator.htm. Since the economy was much smaller in the 1940s than it is today, this understates the importance of the investment even after adjusting for inflation.

67. Campbell to Pender, February 20, 1945, MSOD-UP, box 49 (PX—Estimates).

68. Lisa Todd is quoted discussing Holberton's responsibilities on page 15 of W. Barkley Fritz, "The Women of ENIAC," *IEEE Annals of the History of Computing* 18, no. 3 (1996): 13–28.

69. Jennings recalled that in late 1945 she and Snyder were assigned to work out a set-up to calculate a trajectory while Lichterman and Wescoff hand-computed exactly what ENIAC would compute. The results were used to verify the set-up and also later to help in debugging the physical set-up. Bartik, *Pioneer Programmer*, 85.

70. Fritz, "The Women of ENIAC." The work and training of the computers is reconstructed in Jennifer S. Light, "When Computers Were Women," *Technology and Culture* 40, no. 3 (1999): 455–483.

71. Bartik, *Pioneer Programmer*.

72. Fritz, "The Women of ENIAC," 15.

73. Ibid., 15–16. Herman Goldstine later claimed to have persuaded the Moore School to terminate its "arrangements with the elderly instructors" then training the computers, replacing them with three women including his own wife. Light ("When Computers Were Women," 467) showed that the three wives were in fact members of a larger group of three male and nine female instructors.

74. Grier, *When Computers Were Human*, 260.

75. She discussed her arrival in Philadelphia in Adele K. Goldstine, "Affidavit in Public Use Proceedings by IBM against the 1947 ENIAC Patent Application," 1956, HHG-APS, series 10, box 3.

76. Akera, *Calculating a Natural World*, 82.

77. Judy Green and Jeanne LaDuke, *Pioneering Women in American Mathematics: The Pre-1940s PhDs* (American Mathematical Society, 2008).

78. Herbert R. J. Grosch, *Computer: Bit Slices from a Life* (Third Millennium Books, 1991), 81.

79. Judy Green, "Film Review: Top Secret Rosies," *Notices of the AMS* 59, no. 2 (2012): 308–311.

80. David Alan Grier, "The Math Tables Project of the Work Projects Administration: The Reluctant Start of the Computing Era," *IEEE Annals of the History of Computing* 20, no. 3 (1998): 33–50. Much of the same material can be found in Grier, *When Computers Were Human*. The number of workers is taken from page 242 of the latter.

81. Janet Abbate, *Recoding Gender: Women's Changing Participation in Computing* (MIT Press, 2012), 18–19.

82. Bartik, *Pioneer Programmer*, 66–74.

83. JoAnne Yates, *Structuring the Information Age* (Johns Hopkins University Press, 2005). Lars Heide, *Punched-Card Systems and the Early Information Explosion, 1880–1945* (Johns Hopkins University Press, 2009).

84. L. J. Comrie, *The Hollerith and Powers Tabulating Machines* (Scientific Computing Service, 1933).

85. Wallace J. Eckert, *Punched Card Methods in Scientific Computation* (Thomas J. Watson Astronomical Computing Bureau, Columbia University, 1940).

86. Fritz, "The Women of ENIAC."

87. Goldstine, *The Computer*, 229–230. As well as enraging the women concerned, this statement also seems to discount the work of Burks, who figures more prominently than either of the Goldstines in archival materials concerning the design of ENIAC's control method and early work on the firing tables problem.

88. Goldstine, *A Report on the ENIAC*.

89. These affidavits, sworn in February of 1962, are preserved among the legal materials in HHG-APS, series 10, box 3.

90. Block diagrams were produced of all of ENIAC's units, giving a schematic view of their circuits. These are the diagrams the operators are usually assumed to be talking about, but the phrase was sometimes also applied to diagram formats specifically designed to representing ENIAC program structures, which would have had obvious relevance as programming tutorials. For example, Adele Goldstine wrote of the master programmer configuration diagrams as "block diagrams designed to summarize the way in which various program sequences of a problem are tied together." Goldstine, *A Report on the ENIAC*. Lehmer characterized what would later have been called a flow chart, showing decision points within a program, as "a block diagram of the ENIAC set up." D. H. Lehmer, "On the Converse of Fermat's Theorem II," *The American Mathematical Monthly* 56, no. 5 (1949): 300–309, at 302.

91. Bromberg to Goldstine, "Comments in Regard to Proposed Changes in Your Book Manuscript," April 5, 1971, HHG-HC box 1 (Correspondence, Apr 2, 1960–Apr 6, 1971).

92. Bartik, *Pioneer Programmer*, 75–76.

93. Fritz, "The Women of ENIAC."

94. Ibid., 21.

95. W. Barkley Fritz, "ENIAC—A Problem Solver," *IEEE Annals of the History of Computing* 16, no. 1 (1994): 25–45, at 28.

96. The United States tested a fission bomb, Ivy King, with a yield of about 0.5 megatons in 1952, but no further efforts were made in this direction as the first hydrogen bomb had already been successfully tested. Jeremy Bernstein, *Oppenheimer: Portrait of an Enigma* (Ivan R. Dee, 2004), 118.

97. Fitzpatrick, *Igniting the Light Elements*, 104.

98. Ibid., 175.

99. Ibid., 114.

100. Goldstine to Gillon, February 19, 1945, ETE-UP.

101. Fitzpatrick, *Igniting the Light Elements*, 115.

102. Goldstine to Metropolis and Frankel, August 23, 1945, ETE-UP.

103. Nicholas C. Metropolis, ENIAC Trial Testimony, December 13, 1971, ETR-UP, p. 14,454.

104. Jean J. Bartik and Frances E. (Betty) Snyder Holberton, "Oral History Interview with Henry S. Tropp, April 27, 1973," National Museum of American History, 1973 (http://amhistory.si.edu/archives/AC0196_bart730427.pdf), pp. 41–47 and 89.

105. Bartik, *Pioneer Programmer*, 84. Bartik implies an October date for the beginning of calculations on the Los Alamos problem, which is not consistent with primary sources.

106. Goldstine, *The Computer*, 226.

107. "ENIAC Service Log (1944-48)," AWB-IUPUI, January 1, 1946.

108. Ibid., December 9, 1945.

109. Ibid., December 26, 1945. The entry is signed "JWM."

110. Brainerd to Pender, November 14, 1945, MSOD-UP, box 48 (PX-2 General Jul-Dec 1945).

111. Brainerd to Pender, November 15, 1945, MSOD-UP, box 47 (Overhead Third Floor).

112. "ENIAC Service Log (1944-48)," February 7, 1946.

113. Bradbury to Barnes and Gillon, March 18, 1946, MSOD-UP, box 55a (Parts Supplies).

114. Nicholas C. Metropolis, Affidavit in *Sperry Rand et al. vs. Bell Telephone Laboratories*, January 3, 1962, HHG-APS, series 10, box 3.

115. Fitzpatrick, *Igniting the Light Elements*, 122–124.

116. Goldstine, *The Computer*, 231.

117. "Item 22904: Reclassification of the Project for Development of the Electronic Numerical Integrator and Computer," GRS-DC, box 3 (Material Related to PX-Project).

Chapter 4

1. Goldstine to Simon, December 12, 1945, ETE-UP.

2. "Press Arrangements for University of Pennsylvania E.N.I.A.C. Press Demonstration, 1 February 1946," HHG-APS, series 10, box 3.

3. "ENIAC Guide for Press Day, Feb 1, 1946," JWM-UP (Notes and Datasets: ENIAC Functions in Comparison to Other Computers, 1944–45).

4. "Dinner and Ceremonies Dedicating the Electronic Numerical Integrator and Computer," HHG-APS, series 10, box 3.

5. "Seating chart, ENIAC Dinner, Houston Hall, February 15, 1946," HHG-APS, series 10, box 3.

6. In fact the invitation, which gave a start time of 6:30 p.m., also noted that "informal demonstration and technical discussion" of ENIAC would take place throughout the preceding morning and afternoon, so that those interested could arrive "at whatever time on February 15 might be most convenient." "University of Pennsylvania Announcement re

Dinner and Ceremonies," HHG-APS, series 10, box 3. Eckert and Mauchly were asked to spend the day with ENIAC to answer any questions.

7. Goldstine, *The Computer*, 225–226.

8. Bartik, *Pioneer Programmer*, 98.

9. T. R Kennedy Jr., "Electronic Computer Flashes Answers, May Speed Engineering," *New York Times,* February 15, 1946.

10. The Moore School's concerns with Mauchly's slow progress on patent work are documented in Warren to Mauchly, November 2, 1945, AWB-IUPUI. The patent process was of understandable later interest to those involved, and many of the surviving collections of ENIAC material were formed from documents gathered in support of its litigation. We pay relatively little attention here to the reasons for the slow processing of the patent and the disputes between Eckert and Mauchly and the Moore School administrators. These issues have been argued in depth by others, and add little to the story of ENIAC's development and use.

11. Travis to Kessenich, November 18, 1946, MSOD-UP box 49 (Letters regarding reduction to practice).

12. This date for the acceptance of ENIAC by the U.S. government has been challenged by Goldstine, who argues that ENIAC was formally accepted by the Philadelphia Ordnance District on June 30, 1946. Goldstine, *The Computer*, 234.

13. "Affidavit of Adele K. Goldstine," May 1, 1956, HHG-APS, series 10, box 3.

14. "Affidavit of Mrs. Jean J. Bartik," February 17, 1962, HHG-APS, series 10, box 3, p. 3.

15. "Affidavit of Homer W. Spence," February 15, 1962, HHG-APS, series 10, box 3, p. 1.

16. John W. Mauchly, "The ENIAC," in *A History of Computing in the Twentieth Century*, ed. N. Metropolis, J. Howlett, and Gian-Carlo Rota (Academic Press, 1980), 541–550, 451–452.

17. Bartik, *Pioneer Programmer*, 90.

18. "Affidavit of Adele K. Goldstine," May 15, 1956, HHG-APS, series 10, box 3.

19. Goldstine, *The Computer*, 229–230. The other set-ups used at the demonstrations did not attract such passion. Even Bartik conceded that "the ENIAC women had nothing to do with the [press lunch on the] 1st, but I understand from people that were there that it was very unimpressive … they just had sines and cosines and things like that." Jean Bartik, "Oral History Interview with Gardner Hendrie, Oaklyn, New Jersey, July 1," Computer History Museum, 2008, accessed July 25, 2012 (http://archive.computerhistory.org/resources/text/Oral_History/Bartik_Jean/102658322.05.01.acc.pdf).

20. "Affidavit of Mrs. Jean J. Bartik."

21. Bartik, *Pioneer Programmer*, 80–81, 84–85, 91–92.

22. Bartik, "Hendrie Oral History, 2008," 28; Bartik, *Pioneer Programmer*, 95.

23. Bartik, "Hendrie Oral History, 2008," 30.

24. Thomas Haigh, "The Chromium-Plated Tabulator: Institutionalizing an Electronic Revolution, 1954–1958," *IEEE Annals of the History of Computing* 23, no. 4 (2001): 75–104.

25. "PX-1-82: Panel Diagram."

26. Program cards are first mentioned on page XIV (8) of "ENIAC Progress Report 31 December 1943." For the templates, see "ENIAC Progress Report 31 December 1944," page 23 and figure 4.

27. For example, Mauchly's comment on page 50 of "ENIAC Service Log (1944-48)" (December 18, 1945).

28. "PX-1-81: Setup of Exterior Ballistics Equations."

29. "ENIAC Progress Report 31 December 1944," 21–23. This example became a familiar tutorial resource, reappearing in several later reports and publications.

30. Ibid., 22.

31. Bartik, *Pioneer Programmer*, 91. Bartik claimed that the women had developed this diagramming technique, but archival evidence makes it clear that it predates their involvement with ENIAC.

32. Eckert et al., *Description of the ENIAC (AMP Report)*.

33. Goldstine, *A Report on the ENIAC*.

34. Jennings later insisted that Goldstine had no experience of ENIAC programming until after she had finished work on the manual, and claimed to have taught her how to program ENIAC when working with Taub in September of 1946. Bartik, *Pioneer Programmer*, 105. On page 11 she wrote: "*I taught Adele to program the ENIAC. She knew the ENIAC technology because she had written the operator's manual, but she had not done a real program before I took her under my wing.*"

35. Three sheets provided to us by the Jean Jennings Bartik Museum headed "Compressible Laminar Boundary Layer. Zero-order Equations. Set up for integration procedure." We believe the handwriting to be Hartree's.

36. See, for example, Derrick Lehmer's set-up for the Riemann Zeta function, dating from 1947, which was documented using a hand-written flow diagram and two set-up tables preserved in MSOD-UP, box 9 (Riemann Zeta Fctn).

37. Eckert et al., *Description of the ENIAC (AMP Report)*, appendix B.

38. For example, Herman H. Goldstine and Adele K. Goldstine, "The Electronic Numerical Integrator and Computer (ENIAC)," *Mathematical Tables and Other Aids to Computation* 2, no. 15 (1946): 97–110.

39. "List of Problems That the ENIAC Has Been Used to Solve," in "Sperry Rand v. Bell Telephone Laboratories Civil Action No. 105-146: Defendant's Goldstine Exhibits," HHG-APS, series 10, box 3.

40. Charlotte Froese Fischer, *Douglas Rayner Hartree—His Life in Science and Computing* (World Scientific Publishing, 2003), 14.

41. Douglas R. Hartree, "Ballistic Calculations," *Nature* 106 (1920), September: 152–154. A broader overview of the British firing-table calculating effort of World War I, focused on the leading role of statistician Karl Pearson, can be found on pp. 126–133 of Grier, *When Computers Were Human*.

42. Fischer, *Douglas Rayner Hartree—His Life in Science and Computing*, 11–15.

43. Goldstine, *The Computer*, 246.

44. Hartree to Goldstine, January 19, 1946.

45. Goldstine, *The Computer*, 246.

46. Goldstine to Gillon, April 13, 1946. HHG-APS series 10, box 3.

47. Fischer, *Douglas Rayner Hartree—His Life in Science and Computing*, 109–113.

48. Cope and Hartree, "The Laminar Boundary Layer in Compressible Flow," plate 1, facing p. 4.

49. Douglas R. Hartree, *Calculating Instruments and Machines* (University of Illinois Press, 1949), 90.

50. Cope and Hartree, "The Laminar Boundary Layer in Compressible Flow," 56–63.

51. Cope and Hartree, "The Laminar Boundary Layer in Compressible Flow," 69.

52. "Compressible Laminary Boundary Layer: Calculation of Inputs for the Higher Order Equations," ENIAC-NARA, box 5, folder 2 (Hartree's Original Notes).

53. The entire equation, impressively complex, can be found on pp. 25–26 of Cope and Hartree, "The Laminar Boundary Layer in Compressible Flow."

54. Hartree, *Calculating Instruments and Machines*, 91.

55. Hartree, *Calculating Machines*.

56. J. Brillhart, "Derrick Henry Lehmer," *Acta Arithmetica* 62 (1992): 207–220; Bartik and Holberton, Oral History Interview with Henry S. Tropp, 68–69.

57. During 1946, Lehmer was recorded working with ENIAC only on April 22 and 23 (but probably continuing to April 26) and on May 13 and 14.

58. Lehmer, "On the Converse of Fermat's Theorem II," 301; Lehmer, "A History of the Sieve Process," in *A History of Computing in the Twentieth Century*, ed. N. Metropolis, J. Howlett, and Gian-Carlo Rota (Academic Press, 1980). This event is not recorded in the service log, but an archival list of applications run on ENIAC does note "computations completed during several holiday week ends," and it seems plausible that these might be less consistently logged. Hartree was using ENIAC around this time, so if Lehmer remembered the timing correctly then it must have been Hartree's set-up that was disrupted.

59. Bullynck and De Mol, "Setting-up early computer programs: D. H. Lehmer's ENIAC computation."

60. We have completed their set-up and verified it experimentally using an ENIAC simulator. With minor modifications, it works as intended and computes the results reported by Lehmer.

61. Lehmer, "A History of the Sieve Process," quotation on p. 451.

62. D. H. Lehmer, "On the Roots of the Riemann Zeta-function," *Acta Mathematica* 95 (1956): 291–298. We discuss the modifications in chapter 6.

63. Goldstine to Gillon, December 14, 1944, ETE-UP.

64. "Letter Order W 18-001 Ord 355 (P.O. 5-6016)" to Moore School from Ordnance Department, January 26, 1945, MSOD-UP, box 51 (Summary of Status of ENIAC Moving).

65. "Notes on Design and Construction for the AB-Installation," MSOD-UP, box 51 (AB—Installation—Dr. Brainerd, 1945).

66. Goldstine to Pender, April 13, 1945, MSOD-UP, box 51 (Summary of Status …).

67. The contract was "Contract W 18-001 Ord 335 (816)." An initial version was sent on May 8, but the Moore School objected to some terms and received a revised version on June

22 according to documents in MSOD-UP, box 51 (Summary of Status ...). The value is taken from "Summary of Status MS111," dated March 14, 1947.

68. Pender to Dubarry, February 5, 1945, MSOD-UP, box 51 (Summary of Status ...). This created "a necessity for the Moore School to operate in a conservative manner even though this may result in higher costs to the Army" according to "Moore School Project AB Principles of Operation" in the same folder.

69. Sharpless to Research Division, October 26, 1946, MSOD-UP, box 51 (ENIAC Alterations, Repair of Fire Damage).

70. Travis to Murray, November 21, 1946 and Travis to Murray, January 21, 1947, both in MSOD-UP, box 51 (ENIAC Alterations, Repair of Fire Damage).

71. Lubkin to Simon, October 28, 1946, MSOD-UP, box 55a (ENIAC General, 1944–45).

72. Mauchly later faulted the Army for its rule that "any unattended hot electrical device required a guard for fire precautions, and this expense was not authorized. Whatever the reason for this rule, it was applied to the ENIAC, as a matter of routine it would seem. Whoever made such a rule probably made it for some good reason, but without knowing a thing about the ENIAC ... . Here seems a clear case not only of stupid rules stupidly applied, but failing somewhere to transmit information vital" to ENIAC's proper use. Mauchly, "The ENIAC," 542–543.

73. "Government's Order and Contractor's Advice," issued to the University of Pennsylvania by Aberdeen Proving Ground, December 5, 1946, MSOD-UP, box 51 (ENIAC Alterations, Repair of Fire Damage).

74. "Schedule ENIAC Move MS-111," MSOD-UP, box 51 (ENIAC and EDVAC Progress Reports, 1946–1949).

75. Travis to Murray, November 8, 1946, MSOD-UP, box 51 (Summary of Status of ENIAC Moving).

76. Universal Insurance Company, "Special Floater Policy NO. V.S. 4098," MSOD-UP, box 51 (Summary of Status ...).

77. Scott Brothers to Trustees of the University of Pennsylvania, September 13, 1946, MSOD-UP, box 52 (ENIAC Moving (Frank T. Wilson Co., Scott Brothers)).

78. Stern, *From ENIAC to Univac*, 52.

79. Bartik, *Pioneer Programmer*, 88–89.

80. Ibid., 111.

Chapter 5

1. Goldstine, *The Computer*, 149.

2. Leslie E. Simon, Frank E. Grubbs, and Serge J. Zaroodny, *Robert Harrington Kent, 1886–1961: Biographical Memoir* (National Academy of Sciences, 1971).

3. Franz L. Alt, "Archaeology of Computers," *Communications of the ACM* 15, no. 7 (1972): 693–694.

4. Barber, *Ballisticians in War and Peace*, 60.

5. Bartik, *Pioneer Programmer*, 79.

6. Barber, *Ballisticians in War and Peace*, 64.

7. Travis to Murray, "Modification of ENIAC Moving Contract," November 8, 1946, MSOD-UP, box 51 (Summary of Status of ENIAC Moving, 1944–1948).

8. Simon to Travis, December 18, 1946, MSOD-UP, box 51 (Summary of Status of ENIAC Moving, 1944–1948).

9. Simon to Pender, February 18, 1947, MSOD-UP, box 51 (Summary of Status of ENIAC Moving, 1944–1948).

10. "All panels are mounted in position allowing for change order of 27 February 1947 to permit the insertion of 2 extra panels for automatic program selector. This change order has been charged at $10,000 which will be added to moving contract." T. Kite Sharpless, "MS 111 Moving ENIAC: Progress Report 1 March 1947," MSOD-UP, box 51 (ENIAC and EDVAC Progress Reports). Eckert and Mauchly had proposed a "program selector" device in 1943—see chapter 1 above.

11. John Mauchly, "Card Control of Programming," August 11, 1945, UV-HML, box 7 (ENIAC 1944 Notes Programmer).

12. A. Goldstine, *Report on the ENIAC*, VII-22. Section 8.7 of the manual described an actual computation in which a similar situation arose.

13. If each of the twelve numerical switches on a row was set to 0 or 9, and the sign digits to P or M, then each of the fourteen switches would emit either 0 or 9 pulses when the row was stimulated by a program pulse.

14. Transcript of conversation among Travis, Dederick, and Lubkin, "late-March," 1947, MSOD-UP, box 51 (Summary of Status of ENIAC Moving, 1944–1948).

15. Reeves specialized in military electronics, and soon after the war was over it entered the market for analog computers with military contracts and commercial models. After arguing for Reeves a as reliable subcontractor, Lubkin briefly worked for the firm. James S. Small, *The Analogue Alternative: The Electronic Analogue Computer in Britain and the USA, 1930–1975* (Routledge, 2001), 110.

16. Fritz, "ENIAC—A Problem Solver," 29.

17. Ibid., 37–38. "ENIAC Log Book. Friday November 21, 1947," UV-HML, box 10 (Operations Log After 1947).

18. These details are taken largely from Fritz, "The Women of ENIAC."

19. Paul Ceruzzi, "Crossing the Divide: Architectural Issues and the Emergence of the Stored Program Computer, 1935–1955," *IEEE Annals of the History of Computing* 19, no. 1 (1997): 5–12. For an overview of the relay calculators of the 1940s, see Ceruzzi, "Relay Calculators," in *Computing Before Computers* (Iowa State University Press, 1990).

20. Wallace J. Eckert, "The IBM Pluggable Sequence Relay Calculator," *Mathematical Tables and Other Aids to Computation* 3, no. 23 (1948): 149–161.

21. Karl Kempf, *Electronic Computers Within the Ordnance Corps* (U.S. Army Ordnance Corps, 1961).

22. W. G. Andrews, "A Review of the Bell Laboratories' Digital Computer Developments," in *Review of Electronic Digital Computers: Joint AIEE-IRE Computer Conference (Dec. 10–12, 1951)* (American Institute of Electrical Engineers, 1952).

23. Fragments of program code could be split into tapes loaded onto different readers, giving a limited subroutine capability by transferring control from one to another at different points in the computation. Paper-tape drives could also be used for table lookup.

24. "Aberdeen Proving Ground Computers," *Digital Computer Newsletter* 7, no. 3 (1955): 1.

25. All quotations in this paragraph are from J. O. Harrison, John V. Holberton, and M. Lotkin, *Technical Note 104: Preparation of Problems for the BRL Calculating Machines* (Ballistic Research Laboratories, 1949).

26. Dorrit Hoffleit, "A Comparison of Various Computing Machines Used in the Reduction of Doppler Observations," *Mathematical Tables and Other Aids to Computation* 3, no. 25 (1949): 373–377, quotations from pp. 374 and 375.

27. Dorrit Hoffleit, "Oral History Interview with David DeVorkin, August 4, 1979," Niels Bohr Library and Archives, American Institute of Physics, College Park, Maryland.

28. Dorrit Hoffleit, *Misfortunes as Blessings in Disguise: The Story of My Life* (American Association of Variable Star Astronomers, 2002), 44–45.

29. Hoffleit, "Oral History Interview with David DeVorkin, August 4, 1979."

30. Hoffleit, "A Comparison of Various Computing Machines Used in the Reduction of Doppler Observations," 375.

31. Ibid., 376.

32. Andrews, "A Review of the Bell Laboratories' Digital Computer Developments."

33. Hoffleit, "A Comparison of Various Computing Machines Used in the Reduction of Doppler Observations," 376.

34. Fritz, "ENIAC—A Problem Solver." The BRL also used ENIAC to analyze visual data from camera stations, which likewise could be cross-referenced from several observation points to determine the actual position for the rocket being fired. Fritz cites several reports on this topic in section 1.2.22 of the appendix to the aforementioned article.

35. Barber, *Ballisticians in War and Peace*, 65–66, Boris Garfinkel, *BRL Technical Report 797: Least Square Determination of Position from Radio Doppler Data* (Aberdeen Proving Ground).

36. "ENIAC Service Log (1944–1948)", p. 163, entry dated "7/29/47".

37. Will Lissner, "Mechanical 'Brain' Has Its Troubles," *New York Times*, December 14, 1947. Lissner noted that the "balance" of the time (18 percent) was "believed to be wasted."

38. Mauchly, "The ENIAC," 542. Mauchly also claimed that Merwin and others from the Moore School "never reported that they had any difficulty getting similar performance" after the move to the BRL, which is hard to square with evidence in the operations log that Merwin was called to Aberdeen frequently to deal with intractable problems.

39. "Dr. Frank E. Grubbs," Ordnance Corps Hall of Fame, 2002, http://www.goordnance .army.mil/hof/2000/2002/grubbs.html.

40. Frank E. Grubbs, "A Quarter Century of Army Design of Experiments Conferences," Armyconference.org, 1980, http://www.armyconference.org/50YEARS/Documents/Typed %20Papers/DOE25Grubbs.pdf, 3.

41. Ibid., 4.

42. "Operations Log." Bierstein is mentioned as a newly arrived trainee on January 26, 1948. The assignment of personnel is noted in an entry dated March 15.

43. Ibid., February 25–27, 1948.

44. Ibid., March 1, 1948.

45. Ibid., March 2–3, 1948.

46. Ibid., March 4–12, 1948.

47. Ibid., March 15–17, 1948.

48. Ibid., March 18, 1948.

49. Ibid., March 19–22, 1948.

50. Hartree, *Calculating Instruments and Machines*, 119.

51. "Operations Log," March 23, 1948.

52. Ibid., March 23–24, 1948.

53. Frank E. Grubbs, "Sample Criteria for Testing Outlying Observations," *Annals of Mathematical Statistics* 21, no. 1 (1950): 27–58.

54. Frank E. Grubbs, "Procedures for Detecting Outlying Observations in Samples," *Technometrics* 11, no. 1 (1969): 1–21.

Chapter 6

1. See, for example, Ceruzzi, "Crossing the Divide: Architectural Issues and the Emergence of the Stored Program Computer, 1935–1955."

2. Modifying relay memory was slow because storing a number required movement of a physical switch. However, reads from relay memory could also be slow if (as on the IBM SSEC, which combined electronic logic with a fairly large relay memory) selecting the location from which to read itself involved the movement of relay switches.

3. The term "electronic speed" was used to describe the new pace of computation associated with ENIAC in various early reports, including Allen Rose, "Lightning Strikes Mathematics: Equations That Spell Progress Are Solved by Electronics," *Popular Science*, April 1946.

4. The 6SN7 devices used in the ring counter integrated two triodes into a single glass "envelope." This whole assemblage was usually considered to be one "tube," so the count of 28 given here is actually for envelopes. Sometimes the individual triodes within the envelope were considered "tubes" in their own right, which would yield a higher tube count.

5. In 1943 Eckert built the first successful delay line after introducing the idea of using mercury. See Eckert and Sharpless, "Final Report Under Contract OEMar 387," November 14, 1945, MSOD-UP, box 50 (Patent Correspondence, 1943–46). An earlier attempt to build a delay line using water and ethylene glycol had been made by William Shockley at MIT. See Peter Galison, *Image and Logic: A Material History of Microphysics* (University of Chicago Press, 1997), 505.

6. The delay-line memory was subsequently patented by Eckert and Mauchly. An early description appears in "Applications of the Transmission Line Register," circa August 1944, GRS-DC, box 3 (Material Related to PY Project).

7. Alice and Arthur Burks credited John Atanasoff with coming up with the basic idea of a regenerative memory and believed that this was one of the ideas Mauchly borrowed from him. The Atanasoff-Berry Computer used capacitors for its memory. See Burks and Burks, *The First Electronic Computer*.

8. "ENIAC Progress Report dated 31 December 1943," preface.

9. The canonical form of the anecdote is told by Goldstine on pp. 182–183 of *The Computer*.

10. For a general and surprisingly jovial account of von Neumann's life, see Norman McRae, *John von Neumann: The Scientific Genius Who Pioneered the Modern Computer, Game Theory, Nuclear Deterrence, and Much More* (Pantheon Books, 1992).

11. Aspray, *John von Neumann and the Origins of Modern Computing*, 26.

12. Ibid., 28–34.

13. When Warren Weaver received von Neumann's request for information on computing projects in January of 1944, he did not mention ENIAC. This is usually attributed to the unproven technology used, the experimental nature of the project, the low standing of the Moore School among the scientific elite, and the obscurity of Eckert and Mauchly within the mathematical community. See Aspray, *John von Neumann and the Origins of Modern Computing*, 35.

14. Goldstine to Gillon, August 21, 1944, ETE-UP.

15. Goldstine to Pender, July 28, 1944, ETE-UP.

16. Goldstine to Simon, August 11, 1944, ETE-UP.

17. On p. 185 of *The Computer*, Goldstine says that he showed von Neumann around ENIAC on August 7.

18. During the war von Neumann served as a consultant to numerous government organizations, "moving almost constantly from one project to the next." This included involvement with several divisions of the National Defense Research Committee and its successor, the Office of Scientific Research and Development, with Los Alamos, and with the Navy Bureau of Ordnance. However, his longest-standing consulting activity was with the Ballistic Research Laboratory, and insofar as he had been a founding member of its Scientific Advisor Committee one might expect him to have had a very good idea of how to frame a project to win support there. See Aspray, *John von Neumann and the Origins of Modern Computing*, 26–27.

19. Aspray, *John von Neumann and the Origins of Modern Computing*, 37.

20. Morrey to Simon, August 30, 1944, AWB-IUPUI.

21. Brainerd to Philadelphia Ordnance District, September 13, 1944, AWB-IUPUI.

22. Goldstine to Gillon, September 2, 1944, ETE-UP.

23. Ibid.

24. Brainerd to Gillon, September 13, 1944, ETE-UP.

25. Goldstine to Gillon, September 2, 1944, ETE-UP.

26. Goldstine to Gillon, August 21, 1944, ETE-UP.

27. Ibid.

28. Goldstine to Gillon, September 2, 1944, ETE-UP.

29. Goldstine to Gillon, December 14, 1944. Von Neumann's immersion in these circuits has often been overlooked by later commentators. For example, according to Scott McCartney (*ENIAC*, 128) "engineering structures ... were outside von Neumann's area of expertise. The notion that von Neumann figured out better ways to wire up devices to manage electrical pulses is hard to figure."

30. Brainerd to Bogert, September 13, 1944, AWB-IUPUI. Only "Experimental work ... on a small scale ... in free time" was planned for 1944.

31. J. Presper Eckert, John W. Mauchly, and S. Reid Warren, PY Summary Report No. 1, March 31, 1945, GRS-DC, box 30 (Notebook Z-18, Harold Pender).

32. Goldstine to Power, February 19, 1945, and telegram from Goldstine to Gillon, December 14, 1944, both in ETE-UP.

33. "Notes of Meeting with Dr. von Neumann, March 14, 1945," "Notes on Meeting with Dr. von Neumann, March 23, 1945," "Notes on the First April Meeting with Dr. von Neumann (rough draft)," and "Notes on the Second April Meeting with Dr. von Neumann (rough draft)," all in AWB-IUPUI.

34. "The trunk system to connect the registers to the central equipment was discussed. At least three wires would be required, one for the input, one for the output, and one for control (i.e. the wire from the switch). This last wire could be dispensed with by using a recognition system, but the latter arrangement is more complicated than the former. The possibility of being able to connect both the control unit and the computor to tanks was discussed." "Notes of Meeting with Dr. von Neumann, March 14, 1945," AWB-IUPUI. According to later analysis by Burks, segregation was believed to have performance advantages. It would have been accomplished by setting controls to connect certain lines to a data "trunk" and the rest to a program trunk, rather than by physically separating tanks. Burks, unfinished book manuscript, appendix C.

35. Burks, unfinished book manuscript, chapter 7.

36. John von Neumann, "First Draft of a Report on the EDVAC," *IEEE Annals of the History of Computing* 15, no. 4 (1993): 27–75. Hereafter referred to as the First Draft.

37. Von Neumann to Curry, August 20, 1945, ETE-UP.

38. Von Neumann to Goldstine, February 12, 1945, AWB-IUPUI.

39. S. Reid Warren, "Notes on the Preparation of 'First Draft of a Report on the EDVAC' by John von Neumann. Prepared April 2, 1947," GRS-DC, box 3 (Material Related to the PY Project ...).

40. J. Presper Eckert, John W. Mauchly, and S. Reid Warren, PY Summary Report No. 1, March 31, 1945, GRS-DC, box 30 (Notebook Z-18, Harold Pender).

41. Von Neumann to Goldstine, May 8, 1945, ETE-UP.

42. Goldstine to von Neumann, May 15, 1945, ETE-UP.

43. Burks' original carbon copy of the initial, internal version of the First Draft is preserved in AWB-IUPUI.

44. "Copies of von Neumann's report on Logical Analysis of EDVAC," June 24, 1945, GRS-DC, box 3 (Material Related to the PY Project ...).

45. Curry to von Neumann, August 10, 1945, ETE-UP. Interestingly, Curry saw the arrangement of memory in temporal terms rather than spatial terms. He therefore proposed musical

metaphors, favoring "beat" as the "fundamental unit of time" and arguing for "measure" and "bar" rather than von Neumann's "minor cycle" and "major cycle" to describe what would later be called "bits" and "words." In view of the functioning of a delay-line memory, Curry's might be a more intuitive metaphor than the idea that a datum is stored in a particular memory location.

46. Hartree to Goldstine, August 24, 1945, ETE-UP.

47. J. Presper Eckert, John W. Mauchly, and S. Reid Warren, PY Summary Report No. 1, March 31, 1945, GRS-DC, box 30 (Notebook Z-18, Harold Pender).

48. Burks, unfinished book manuscript, appendix C.

49. J. Presper Eckert Jr., John W. Mauchly, S. Reid Warren, PY Summary Report No. 2, July 10, 1945, GRS-DC, box 30 (Notebook Z-18, Harold Pender).

50. J. Presper Eckert and John W. Mauchly, Automatic High-Speed Computing: A Progress Report on the EDVAC (University of Pennsylvania, September 30, 1945).

51. Ibid., 3.

52. Burks, unfinished book manuscript, appendix C.

53. "Minutes of 1947 Patent Conference, Moore School of Electrical Engineering, University of Pennsylvania," *Annals of the History of Computing* 7, no. 2 (1985): 100–116.

54. This critique is made, for example, by Stern (*From ENIAC to Univac: An Appraisal of the Eckert-Mauchly Computers*, 77-78) and by Campbell-Kelly and Aspray (*Computer*, 95).

55. C. Dianne Martin, "The Myth of the Awesome Thinking Machine," *Communications of the ACM* 36, no. 4 (1993): 120–133.

56. Edmund C. Berkeley, *Giant Brains or Machines That Think* (Wiley, 1949).

57. Aspray, *John von Neumann and the Origins of Modern Computing*, 178–189.

58. Warren S. McCulloch and Walter Pitts, "A Logical Calculus of the Ideas Immanent in Nervous Activity," *Bulletin of Mathematical Biophysics* 5 (1943): 115–133. For a useful discussion of this paper, see Gualtiero Piccinini, "The First Computational Theory of Mind and Brain: A Close Look at McCulloch and Pitts's 'Logical Calculus of Ideas Immanent in Nervous Activity,'" *Synthese* 141, no. 2, 2004: 175–215. We thank David Nofre for drawing our attention to Piccinini's work.

59. Weaver to Brainerd, Dec 19, 1944, MSOD-UP, box 48 (PX-2 General Jul-Dec 1944).

60. Norbert Wiener, *Cybernetics, or Control and Communication in the Animal and the Machine* (Technology Press, 1948).

61. Steve Joshua Heims, *The Cybernetics Group* (MIT Press, 1991).

62. Thomas S. Kuhn, *The Structure of Scientific Revolutions*, second edition (University of Chicago Press, 1969).

63. Thomas S. Kuhn, "Second Thoughts on Paradigms," in *The Essential Tension: Selected Studies in Scientific Tradition and Change* (University of Chicago Press, 1979).

64. John von Neumann, "The Principles of Large Scale Computing Machines (with an introduction by Michael R. Williams and a foreword by Nancy Stern)," *Annals of the History of Computing* 10, no. 4 (1988): 243–256, at 249.

65. Burks, unfinished book manuscript, chapter 7.

66. Antoine de Saint-Exupéry, *Wind, Sand and Stars* (Reynal and Hitchcock, 1939).

67. Goldstine to von Neumann, May 15, 1945, ETE-UP.

68. One can find quite different tube numbers quoted for many early computers, and in fact the exact number would have fluctuated over their operating lives as hardware was added and removed. According to Martin H. Weik (*BRL Report 971: A Survey of Domestic Digital Computing Systems*, Ballistic Research Laboratory, 1955), ENIAC then had 17,468 tubes, the IAS computer about 3,000, and SEAC 1,424. Simon Lavington, in *Early British Computers* (Digital Press, 1980), reports "800 thermionic valves" for the Pilot Ace (p. 44), 3,000 for EDSAC and, as of April 1949, 1,300 for the Manchester Mark 1 (p. 118). So effective was the new architecture in eliminating vacuum tubes that ENIAC's total was only ever exceeded by the immense AN/FSQ-7 computers that pushed the limits of 1950s computing technology for the military SAGE project.

69. Von Neumann, "First Draft of a Report on the EDVAC," section 5.6.

70. Ibid., section 2.5.

71. Burks, unfinished book manuscript, appendix C, section 1.

72. Burks later recalled Eckert objecting to his use of logic to describe part of the multiplier, and asking instead for practical diagrams of its actual circuits.

73. T. Kite Sharpless, "Von Neumann's Report on EDVAC—July 1945," April 2, 1947, GRS-DC, box 3 (Material Related to the PY Project …).

74. The list below has some overlap with the characteristics attributed to the "stored program concept" in Ceruzzi, "Crossing the Divide: Architectural Issues and the Emergence of the Stored Program Computer, 1935–1955," which shows that historians have invested "stored program" with a great deal more than the literal ability to store a program.

75. The order code specified in the report has been presented most clearly in M. D. Godfrey and D. F. Hendry, "The Computer as von Neumann Planned It," *IEEE Annals of the History of Computing* 15, no. 1 (1993): 11–21.

76. Von Neumann, "First Draft of a Report on the EDVAC," 37.

77. Ibid.

78. One of the ten arithmetic operations, *s*, would take a number from one or the other of the machine's arithmetic source registers, depending on the sign bit of the results of a previous arithmetic operation. Among other conditional operations, this could be used to set the address stored within an instruction to one of two possible values according to whether a particular condition was true or false. Von Neumann, "First Draft of a Report on the EDVAC," section 11.3.

79. Herman H. Goldstine and John von Neumann, "Planning and Coding Problems for an Electronic Computing Instrument. Part II, Volume 1," in *Papers of John von Neumann on Computing and Computer Theory*, ed. William Aspray and Arthur Burks (MIT Press, 1987), 154.

80. Eckert and Mauchly, Automatic High Speed Computing. This design choice was also made by Turing in his later plans for the ACE.

81. J. von Neumann, untitled manuscript 510.78/V89p, HHG-APS, series 5, box 1. This code is discussed in Donald E. Knuth, "Von Neumann's First Computer Program," *ACM Computing Surveys* 2, no. 4 (1970): 247–260.

82. For a logic-centered version of the story see Martin Davis, *Engines of Logic: Mathematicians and the Origin of the Computer* (Norton, 2001), 185.

83. An exception is the ACE, in which Turing followed von Neumann's original approach and implemented conditional branching by computing the desired unconditional branch instruction. Alan M. Turing, "Proposed Electronic Calculator (1945)," in *Alan Turing's Electronic Brain*, ed. B. Jack Copeland (Oxford University Press, 2012).

84. Arthur W. Burks, Herman Heine Goldstine, and John von Neumann, *Preliminary Discussion of the Logical Design of an Electronic Computing Instrument* (Institute for Advanced Studies, 1946).

Chapter 7

1. Martin Campbell-Kelly and Michael R. Williams, eds., *The Moore School Lectures: Theory and Techniques for Design of Electronic Digital Computers* (MIT Press, 1985).

2. Eckert, "A Preview of a Digital Computing Machine," in Ibid., quotations from pages 114 and 112.

3. John W. Mauchly, "Preparation of Problems for EDVAC-Type Machines," in *Proceedings of a Symposium on Large-Scale Digital Calculating Machinery, 7–10 January 1947*, ed. William Aspray (MIT Press, 1985) quotations from pages 203 and 204.

4. Engineering Research Associates, *High-Speed Computing Devices* (McGraw-Hill, 1950), 65.

5. Ibid., 62, 72.

6. Hartree, *Calculating Instruments and Machines*, 94. Hartree thus conceptualized the earliest EDVAC-type machines as a combination of the Harvard Mark I approach of programming via a machine-readable input medium with the new electronic logic units and a fast and large electronic memory. He did not, as later analysts would, see the external program storage of the Mark I as antithetical to the internal program storage of the new machines.

7. Hartree, *Calculating Instruments and Machines*, 88.

8. Maurice Wilkes, "What I Remember of the ENIAC," *IEEE Annals of the History of Computing* 28, no. 2 (2006): 30–31.

9. Nick Metropolis wrote that after his successful ENIAC runs in early 1948 "other Laboratory staff members made their pilgrimages to ENIAC to run Monte Carlo problems." Metropolis, "The Beginning of the Monte Carlo Method," *Los Alamos Science* 15 (1987): 122–130, at 128–129.

10. John von Neumann to Stanislaw Ulam, March 27, 1947, Stanislaw M. Ulam Papers, American Philosophical Society, Philadelphia (Series 1, von Neumann, John, #2).

11. Fritz, "ENIAC—A Problem Solver," 31.

12. The report on "Planning and Coding Problems for an Electronic Computing Instrument" was issued in installments during 1947 and 1948 and is reprinted in *Papers of John von Neumann on Computing and Computing Theory*, ed. William Aspray and Arthur Burks (MIT Press, 1987).

13. Eckert et al., *Description of the ENIAC (AMP Report)*, B-4.

14. A date of June 7 is given for Adele Goldstine's hiring in Goldstine, *The Computer*, 270. However one of his letters dated July 28 notes "Adele just received a duly signed and executed contract from Los Alamos. So she is now officially in business." Herman Goldstine to John von Neumann, July 28, 1947, JvN-LOC, box 4, folder 1. Klara von Neumann shifted from salary to hourly compensation at the end of August 1947, but it is not clear exactly when she was first hired. Kelly to Richtmyer, 28 Aug 1947, JvN-LOC, box 19, folder 7.

15. Goldstine, *A Report on the ENIAC*, section 7.4.

16. Richard F. Clippinger, "Oral History Interview with Richard R. Mertz, December 1, 1970," in Computer Oral Histories Collection. His claim has been repeated elsewhere, including Bartik, *Pioneer Programmer*.

17. Richard F. Clippinger, *A Logical Coding System Applied to the ENIAC (BRL Report No. 673)* (Aberdeen Proving Ground, 1948), 4.

18. Clippinger Trial Testimony, September 22, 1971, 8952–8968.

19. Eckert, "The ENIAC," 529.

20. Perhaps Clippinger contributed to some planned elaboration of the function-table control technique that led to or involved the still mysterious decision taken by the BRL very early in 1947 to order this new device.

21. The other members were Arthur Gehring, Ed Schlain, Kathe Jacobi, and Sally Spear. See Bartik, *Pioneer Programmer*, 115–116.

22. Bartik, "Hendrie Oral History, 2008."

23. JvN to R. H. Kent (BRL), June 13, 1947, JvN-LOC, box 4, folder 13.

24. Goldstine's travel records confirm visits to Aberdeen on August 29, 1947 and to the Moore School to visit Bartik's group on October 7 and October 17. A. Goldstine, "Travel Expense Bill," December 17, 1947, HHG-APS, series 7, box 1.

25. "Control Code for ENIAC," July 10, 1947, HHG-APS, series 10, box 3. We have made an electronic reproduction available at www.EniacInAction.com.

26. The design for the IAS computer was described in Burks, Goldstine, and von Neumann's highly influential technical report *Preliminary Discussion of the Logical Design of an Electronic Computing Instrument*.

27. Ballistic Research Laboratories, *Technical Note 141: Description and Use of the ENIAC Converter Code* (Aberdeen Proving Ground, 1949), 9. We have made an electronic reproduction available at www.EniacInAction.com. FTN stood for several different things in different revisions of the documentation. In this version it stood for "Function Table Numeric."

28. Herman H. Goldstine and John von Neumann, *Planning and Coding Problems for an Electronic Computing Instrument*, part II, volume I, section 7.

29. These steppers were among several new pieces of ENIAC hardware commissioned by the BRL. Design work was well advanced by summer 1947, as evidenced by blueprints PX-4–122 (June 10), PX-4–212 (July 2) and PX-4–215 (July 16)—all in UV-HML, box 17 (VII-5-4).

30. "60 Order Code, Nov 21—1947," HHG-HC, box 1, folder 5.

31. Bartik, *Pioneer Programmer*, 113–120.

32. "Problems 1947–1948," MSOD-UP, box 13 (Programming Group). Bartik, in *Pioneer Programmer*, can be read as claiming that the group was chartered explicitly to assist

Clippinger with the conversion work, but that is not consistent with archival evidence or with the timing of other developments.

33. An extensive collection of flow diagrams and programs written in the 60 order code can be found in MSOD-UP, box 9.

34. "Computation of an Exponential or Trigonometric Function on the ENIAC," MSOD-UP, box 9 (Set-up Sheets). Although the intention was presumably to write re-usable routines, program listings placed the code at a fixed position in the function tables. The subroutines would have been relocated by hand to include them within particular application, a chore aided somewhat by the use of symbolic addresses for the numerical data used within the subroutines.

35. "Testing ENIAC—60 Order Code," HHG-HC, box 1, folder 8.

36. Clippinger, *A Logical Coding System.*

37. Ibid. The flow diagram and the code tabulations are dated, respectively, March 2 and March 1, 1948.

38. Richard F. Clippinger, "Adaption of ENIAC to von Neumann's Coding Technique (Summary of Paper Delivered at the Meeting of the Association for Computing Machinery, Aberdeen, MD, Dec 11-12 1947)—Plaintiff's Trial Exhibit Number 6341," 1948, in ENIAC Trial Exhibits Master Collection (CBI 145), Charles Babbage Institute, University of Minnesota.

39. Will Lissner, "'Brain' Speeded Up, For War Problems! Electronic Computer Will Aid in Clearing Large Backlog in Weapon Research," *New York Times,* December 12, 1947. Before the current project, the most detailed discussion in recent decades of ENIAC's conversion, focusing particularly on the 60 order code, was in Hans Neukom, "The Second Life of ENIAC," *IEEE Annals of the History of Computing* 28, no. 2 (2006): 4–16, particularly its "Web extras" online technical supplement.

40. Von Neumann to Simon, February 5, 1948, HHG-APS, series 1, box 3.

41. Nick Metropolis and J. Worlton, "A Trilogy on Errors in the History of Computing," *Annals of the History of Computing* 2, no. 1 (1980): 49–59. Metropolis recalls having originated the idea of using the "converter" for decoding when "on a preliminary visit to the Aberdeen Proving Ground in Maryland" he "noticed a complete many-to-one decoder network nearing completion; it was intended to increase the capability of executing iterative loops in a program." We dated this trip to February 20 on the basis of the "Operations Log."

42. BRL staff members continued to work on the "60 order code" into March, so the decision by Metropolis and von Neumann to use the converter to enable the full range of two-digit codes unquestionably diverged from the BRL's established plans. However their idea may not have been as original as he later suggested. The concept of using the full range of two-digit codes predated their February 20 visit, as is shown by occasional log-book references from January 19, 1948 on to projected development of a "99 order code," apparently intended for use with the register memory. This would also have required use of the converter for decoding. Thus, although Metropolis was responsible for reworking plans for the initial reconfiguration to use the converter, he probably built upon existing plans to exploit the register (then expected to arrive around May of 1948).

43. Previous accounts have suggested that ENIAC was operated with the 60 order code for some time before the addition of the converter and the shift to the full 100 order code.

See, for example, Neukom, "The Second Life of ENIAC" and Fritz, "ENIAC—A Problem Solver."

44. See the set-ups for the basic sequence in "ENIAC—Details of code (16 Sep, 1948)" and "Detailed Programming of Orders" in ENIAC-NARA. These were the original binders documenting the ENIAC set-ups used during portions of its career at the BRL.

45. Ulam to von Neumann, May 12, 1948, JvN-LOC, box 7, folder 7.

46. Accounts differ on whether ENIAC was ever temporarily "reconverted" to run the ballistics calculations already programmed using its native mode. Clippinger ("Oral History Interview with Richard R. Mertz, December 1, 1970") later said that it was. However, we found no evidence of this in the log book during the period covered (through August 1949), and a February 1949 reconversion order from the BRL official Bernard Dimsdale was ignored by ENIAC staff after protests from John von Neumann that ENIAC's unique capabilities were crucial to the Atomic Energy Commission and would be jeopardized by a "double-changeover [that] can and probably will consume a great deal more time than one may optimistically estimate" (von Neumann to Kent, March 16, 1949, JvN-LOC, box 12, folder 3).

47. E.g. "Operations Log," April 2, 1948. The Monte Carlo programs used a "count" instruction for an application-specific purpose. This instruction did not appear in any of the order codes described in detail, providing evidence for the malleability of ENIAC's instruction set.

48. "Operations Log," April 14 and May 17, 1948.

49. Ballistic Research Laboratories, *Technical Note 141: Description and Use of the ENIAC Converter Code*; W. Barkley Fritz, *BRL Memorandum Report No 582: Description of the ENIAC Converter Code* (Ballistic Research Laboratory, 1951).

50. A twelve-digit number would not fit into a single accumulator. The three original function tables had 104 rows, but by 1951 ENIAC had acquired a fourth "high-speed function table," and the later converter codes allowed programmatic access to only 100 rows on each table.

51. J. O. Harrison, John V. Holberton, and M. Lotkin, Technical Note 104: Preparation of Problems for the BRL Calculating Machines (Ballistic Research Laboratories, 1949).

52. ENIAC worked with decimal numbers, which made the factors influencing the accuracy of its arithmetic easier for programmers to understand than with many of the binary machines that followed. However, it lacked floating-point capabilities, so called because they would delegate to the computer's hardware the task of tracking the implied position of the decimal point. For example, the gravitational constant is 667384 when expressed in metric units. The initial string of zeroes would fill all ten digits of an ENIAC accumulator. So the programmer would store the number as 667384 and make a note explaining that the results of any calculation involving it would need to be corrected appropriately. This helps to explain the importance of equipping the converter codes with an adequate supply of efficient shift instructions. A computer with floating-point capabilities would use its hardware to track the number of zeros following or preceding the digits actually stored, relieving the programmer of this chore.

53. "Since the ENIAC has relatively small sequencing and storage capacity but high speed of operation, it is usually desirable to carry out stepwise approximations on this machine by using low order approximations, small intervals, and many steps." Harrison, Holberton, and Lotkin, *TN104: Preparation of Problems*, 22.

Chapter 8

1. Galison, "Computer Simulation and the Trading Zone," 119.

2. Ibid., 120.

3. Michael S. Mahoney, "Software as Science—Science as Software," in *Mapping the History of Computing: Software Issues*, ed. Ulf Hashagen, Reinhard Keil-Slawik, and Arthur L. Norberg (Springer, 2002); Ulf Hashagen, "The Computation of Nature, Or: Does the Computer Drive Science and Technology?" in *The Nature of Computation. Logic, Algorithms, Applications*, ed. Paola Bonizzoni, Vasco Brattka, and Benedikt Löwe (Springer, 2013). The philosophical status of early Monte Carlo simulation was recently explored by Isaac Record in a PhD thesis titled Knowing Instruments: Design, Reliability, and Scientific Practice (University of Toronto, 2012).

4. The jump takes place at the bottom of page 130. Pages 130–135 then discuss the application of Monte Carlo methods to the Super, including ENIAC calculations performed in 1950.

5. Fitzpatrick, *Igniting the Light Elements*.

6. Donald MacKenzie, "The Influence of Los Alamos and Livermore National Laboratories on the Development of Supercomputing," *IEEE Annals of the History of Computing* 13, no. 2 (1991): 179–201.

7. Stanislaw M. Ulam, *Adventures of a Mathematician* (Scribner, 1976), 148.

8. Fitzpatrick, *Igniting the Light Elements*, 269.

9. Ulam, *Adventures of a Mathematician*, 196–201. Another firsthand account is given in Nick Metropolis, "The Beginning of the Monte Carlo Method," *Los Alamos Science*, Special Issue 1987. Several secondary treatments are cited in subsequent notes.

10. Aspray, *John von Neumann and the Origins of Modern Computing*, p. 111 and p. 288 (note 50). This public mention of Monte Carlo simulation seems to precede the well-known paper published as Stanislaw M. Ulam and John von Neumann, "On Combination of Stochastic and Deterministic Processes: Preliminary Report," *Bulletin of the American Mathematical Society* 53, no. 11 (1947): 1120.

11. Cuthbert C. Hurd, "A Note on Early Monte Carlo Computations and Scientific Meetings," *Annals of the History of Computing* 7, no. 2 (1985): 141–155. The report reproduced in that article is the source for much subsequent discussion of the computing plan, including Galison, "Computer Simulation and the Trading Zone," 129–130 and Record, "Knowing Instruments," 137–141.

12. Richtmyer's reply (also reprinted by Hurd in his 1995 article) points out that the "slower-down material" could be omitted for "systems of interest to us [at Los Alamos]"—that is, bombs. This suggestion was followed in the first version of the program, though the layer was eventually re-introduced to allow simulation of bombs with uranium hydride cores.

13. Von Neumann also proposed recoding the current zone number, to save having to derive this from the neutron's position.

14. R. D. Richtmyer, "Monte Carlo Methods: Talk given at the American Mathematical Society, April 24, 1959," SMU-APS, series 15 (Richtmyer, R.D. "Monte Carlo Methods"), 3.

15. Hurd, "A Note on Early Monte Carlo," 152 and 149.

16. Ibid., 152.

17. Dyson, *Turing's Cathedral*, 210.

18. J. von Neumann to Ulam, March 27, 1947, SMU-APS, Series 1, John von Neumann Folder 2.

19. "I am hoping to hear very soon from the 'Princeton Annex' some word of the first Monte Carlo." Mark to von Neumann, March 7, 1948, JvN-LOC, box 5, folder 13.

20. Dyson, *Turing's Cathedral*, 175–189 focuses on Klara von Neumann, as does Marina von Neumann Whitman, *The Martian's Daughter: A Memoir* (University of Michigan Press, 2012), 22–23, 38–39, 48–54.

21. A letter from Armand W. Kelley to Richtmyer dated August 28, 1947 confirms that the "necessary approvals have been obtained" for her employment by Los Alamos. JvN-LOC, box 19, folder 7. However, her informal involvement seems to have preceded this letter.

22. Klara von Neumann, "A Grasshopper in Very Tall Grass" (undated memoir), KvN-MvNW. Transcription by Marina von Neumann Whitman.

23. Ibid.

24. William Aspray and Arthur Burks, "Computer Programming and Flow Diagrams: Introduction," in *Papers of John von Neumann on Computing and Computer Theory*, ed. Aspray and Burks (MIT Press, 1987), 148.

25. The best-developed flow diagram produced for the first run measured approximately 24 inches by 18 inches in size, and is neatly written in the hand of Adele Goldstine with the heading "MONTE CARLO Flow Diagram 12/9/47," JvN-LOC, box 11, folder 7. We have made an electronic reproduction available from www.EniacInAction.com. A copy with two later handwritten annotations is in HHG-HC.

26. Ten manuscript pages numbered I, II.a—II.g, III. and IV, JvN-LOC, box 11, folder 8. An undated manuscript page on squared paper in JvN-LOC, box 11, folder 8, contains a plan of ENIAC's three function tables, labeled "FT I," "FT II," and "FT III." Common practice, followed in the Monte Carlo programs, was to use two tables to store the program code and the third "numeric function table" to hold data describing a particular physical situation.

27. Undated manuscript page headed "Refresh Random No." JvN-LOC, box 11, folder 8. John von Neumann was working personally on the methods for the generation of random numbers, so this might well have been written before or separately from the rest of the program.

28. Seven undated manuscript pages numbered 0 to 6 and a single page headed "Shifts," JvN-LOC, box 11, folder 8. The structure of the overview flow diagram on page 0 is reproduced in the shaded area of our figure 8.5. Additional diagrams on pages 1–3 represented the operation boxes and the connections between them in each of the twelve regions. Pages 4–6 contained detailed timing estimates for each box and region.

29. Two storage tables can be seen in our figure 8.1, one attached by a dashed line to the line between boxes 1* and 1.2* and one to the right of box 7*.

30. Von Neumann talks about the "square and take the middle digits" approach to generating pseudo-random numbers, and about testing the resulting distribution, in letters to A. S. Householder (February 3, 1948) and C. C. Hurd (December 3, 1948). See *John von Neumann: Selected Letters*, ed. Miklós Rédei (American Mathematical Society, 2005), 141–145.

31. This was another minor optimization—two of the four points at which new numbers had been generated were, by late 1947, modified to make use instead of particular digits within the number already generated.

32. The idea of a subroutine was familiar within the ENIAC team as early as 1945: "It is possible to have the main routine divided into sub-routines, in which case one stepper is used to feed another stepper, thus allowing the proper sub-routine to be chosen in the course of a regular routine." Eckert et al., *Description of the ENIAC (AMP Report)*, 3–7. This predates the earliest occurrence of the term recorded in the *Oxford English Dictionary*, a 1946 use by John von Neumann.

33. Martin Campbell-Kelly, "Programming the EDSAC: Early Programming Activity at the University of Cambridge," *Annals of the History of Computing* 2, no. 1 (1980): 7–36, at 17. Campbell-Kelly attributes the terminology used for the two types of subroutines to Douglas Hartree.

34. To be fair to Wheeler, who has been credited as the inventor of the closed subroutine, we should note that the Monte Carlo programs used a simple method to process the return address and relied on global variables as parameters and arguments. Campbell-Kelly shows that EDSAC practice soon moved beyond these particular mechanisms. Also, ENIAC's use of function-table memory eliminated the possibility of automatically relocating subroutines from a library, which was a major focus of early work on subroutines both by Goldstine and von Neumann (in the final installment of the "Planning and Coding … " reports cited earlier) and by the EDSAC team. The loss of this particular "first" takes little away from the substance of Wheeler's innovations.

35. The original simple sequence of operation box numbers was confused by alterations to the original diagram. Small insertions were placed in new boxes with decimal numbers, such as 20.1*. More radical changes led to new numbering sequences distinguished by overlining, or the use of the symbol °. For the second run, the boxes were renumbered sequentially, each functional region being allocated a block of ten numbers. As before, though, modifications soon led to the introduction of a variety of ad hoc symbols.

36. Hurd, "A Note on Early Monte Carlo," 155.

37. K. von Neumann, "Actual Running of the Monte Carlo Problems on the ENIAC," JvN-LOC, box 12, folder 6. An electronic reproduction of this document has been made available by the authors from www.EniacInAction.com.

38. For a comparison of alternative techniques of census taking, see E. Fermi with R. D. Richtmyer, "Note on Census-taking in Monte-Carlo Calculations" (LAMS-805, Series A), Los Alamos, July 11, 1948.

39. "Now the speed of a 1 MEV neutron is about 1.4×10^{-9} cm/sec and the mean free path between fissions is about 13 cm so the mean time between fissions is about 10^{-8} sec." Robert Serber, *The Los Alamos Primer (LA-1)* (Los Alamos National Laboratory Research Library, 1943), 2.

Chapter 9

1. For example, he wrote "Klari survived the Aberdeen expedition this time better than the last one" (letter to Ulam, November 18, 1948, JvN-LOC, box 7, folder 7). The word seems to

have been in common use in the von Neumanns' circle. Carson Mark also referred to a series of "rather major calculation expeditions" from Los Alamos to ENIAC in his testimony during the 1971 ENIAC patent trial ("Testimony: September 8, 1971," in volume 48 of *Honeywell vs. Sperry Rand*, 7504, ETR-UP). A meteorologist who worked with John von Neumann also wrote later of "ENIAC expeditions," the first of which was a "remarkable exploit" that "continued 24 hours a day for 33 days and nights." George W. Platzman, "The ENIAC Computations of 1950—Gateway to Numerical Weather Prediction," *Bulletin of the American Meteorological Society* 60, no. 4 (1979): 302–312, quotations from pp. 303 and 307.

2. Fitzpatrick, *Igniting the Light Elements*, 268.

3. Ibid.

4. Von Neumann to Bradbury, February 6, 1948, HHG-APS, series 1, box 3.

5. Von Neumann to Simon, February 5, 1948, HHG-APS, series 1, box 3; Simon to von Neumann, February 9, 1948, JvN-LOC, box 12, folder 3.

6. Von Neumann to Mark, March 13, 1948, JvN-LOC, box 5, folder 13.

7. "Operations Log."

8. The use of certain accumulators for the temporary storage of variables, the usage of the various digits of the random number ξ, the layout of the numeric function table and the constant transmitter registers, and a few numeric constants are listed on four undated manuscript pages on squared notepaper in JvN-LOC box 11, folder 8. The punched-card layout is described in the December 1947 flow diagram.

9. Richtmyer, 1959, "Monte Carlo Methods," p. 4.

10. "Receipt of Classified Materials," January 16, 1948, in JvN-LOC, box 19, folder 7.

11. "Operations Log," entries for April 1 and 2, 1948.

12. J. von Neumann to Ulam, May 11, 1948, SMU-APS, series 1 (John von Neumann Folder 2).

13. J. von Neumann to Ulam, May 14, 1948, SMU-APS, series 1 (John von Neumann Folder 2).

14. J. von Neumann to Ulam, May 11, 1948, SMU-APS, series 1 (John von Neumann Folder 2).

15. K. von Neumann to Ulam, June 12, 1948, ETE-UP.

16. JvN-LOC, box 12, folder 6, contains a seventeen-page manuscript titled "Actual Technique" and a typewritten transcription of the manuscript with insertions and corrections by John von Neumann numbered from x1 to x83 noted in the right margin. Eight larger passages of handwritten text on separate sheets are marked for insertion at various points. This document evolved into "Actual Running of the Monte Carlo Problems on the ENIAC," which will be discussed below.

17. Fitzpatrick, *Igniting the Light Elements*, 269.

18. J. von Neumann to Ulam, November 4, 1948, SMU-APS, series 1, box 29.

19. Three drafts of this report are held in JvN-LOC, box 12, folder 6. One of these is a manuscript in the hand of Klara von Neumann; the other two are typed versions of the same text. One typescript has been annotated and corrected all the way through, primarily by Klara von Neumann. Those corrections are incorporated into the version at

www.EniacInAction.com. Metropolis later wrote to Klara: "Here is your manuscript together with a rough typewritten copy … . The flow diagrams will definitely be finished on Monday and will be sent to you on that day." Metropolis to K. von Neumann, September 23, 1949, JvN-LOC, box 19, folder 7.

20. K. von Neumann, "Actual Running … " (typescript version), JvN-LOC, 5–6.

21. When a neutron reached a census time, ENIAC still interrupted the calculation of its course, resuming only when the card it had just punched was read back in. It appears it would have been possible simply to output a census card for analytical purposes, and then to proceed immediately to determine the fate of the neutron during the next census period. We conjecture that this was not done because it would have eliminated the possibility of doubling the neutron's "weight" between census periods, described below.

22. The team assumed that running a simulation through 13 census cycles would be enough for the second run problems. K. von Neumann, "Actual Running … " (typescript version), JvN-LOC, 13. This set a bound on the exponential growth in card numbers implicit in the doubling technique. Even so, 15,000–20,000 cards would be needed for each simulation.

23. J. von Neumann to Ulam, November 18, 1948, JvN-LOC, series 1 (John von Neumann Folder 1).

24. These documents are all found in JvN-LOC, box 11, folders 7 and 8. The program code has a title page reading "Card Diagram//FLOW DIAGRAM//Coding/Function Table III Values//Monte Carlo//Second Run." Of these, only the Coding section remains. A note added by John von Neumann reads "Will be needed in LA in early January, but should then come to Princeton for reporting, etc. JvN." An annotated version of this program code is included in Mark Priestley and Thomas Haigh, "Monte Carlo Second Run Code: Reconstruction and Analysis," available from www.EniacInAction.com. The earlier draft flow diagram is a little messy, and can be distinguished from others in that folder by its lack of numbering. The later version is a mirror image negative that has corrupted somewhat over the years and is hard to read without image processing.

25. "Modular" in the sense that it appears to have been quite easy to restructure the program between the two runs by splitting one region into two, and reordering several of the regions, for example.

26. Some instructions included addresses or data as well as a two-digit operation code, but most did not. The program for the second run used approximately 2.5 digits per instruction.

27. Teller's campaign for hydride weapons is discussed in Gregg Herken, *Brotherhood of the Bomb: The Tangled Lives and Loyalties of Robert Oppenheimer, Ernest Lawrence, and Edward Teller* (Holt, 2003).

28. J. von Neumann to K. von Neumann, December 7, 1948, KvN-MvNW.

29. J. von Neumann to K. von Neumann, December 13, 1948, KvN-MvNW.

30. Ulam to J. von Neumann, February 7, 1949, JvN-LOC, box 7, folder 7.

31. LAMS-868, "Progress Report T Division: 20 January 1949–20 February 1949," March 16, 1949, quoted in Fitzpatrick, *Igniting the Light Elements*, 269. The original report remains classified.

32. Maria Mayer, "Report on a Monte Carlo Calculation Performed with the ENIAC," in *Monte Carlo Method*, ed. Alston S. Householder (National Bureau of Standards, 1951).

33. J. von Neumann to K. von Neumann, December 7 and December 13, 1948, both in KvN-MvNW. The word "pedaling" appears several times in the ENIAC Operations Log as work is starting in a particular calculation. We believe that it meant stepping through a program slowly for diagnostic purposes.

34. J. von Neumann to K. von Neumann, March 27, 1949, KvN-MvNW.

35. Ulam to J. von Neumann, May 16, 1949, JvN-LOC, box 7, folder 7.

36. K. von Neumann to Mayer, April 8, 1949, KvN-MvNW.

37. J. von Neumann to K. von Neumann, March 27, 1949, KvN-MvNW.

38. K. von Neumann to Dederick, May 16, 1949, JvN-LOC, box 19, folder 7.

39. We have located in JvN-LOC what appears to be a flow diagram for this run, which followed John von Neumann's advice in sticking with the established time-based census method. The diagram is undated and untitled but is neatly stenciled, has nodes numbered 1 to 98, and includes a penciled note reading "The revised diagram will follow when completed in all its beauty. J." As well as a number of general refinements it includes a representation of the code for scattering in "light materials" missing from the flow diagrams for the second run but present as an optional code block within the corresponding program. This fits with the established need to repeat the hydride calculations performed during the second run, and an observation by Fitzpatrick that the 1949 calculations concerned, at least in part, a bomb design code-named Elmer with a hydride core. Fitzpatrick, *Igniting the Light Elements*, 269.

40. "Operations Log."

41. Letter of June 28, quoted in Dyson, *Turing's Cathedral*, 198.

42. J. von Neumann to Ulam, November 4, 1948, SMU-APS, series 1 (John von Neumann Folder 2).

43. Fitzpatrick, *Igniting the Light Elements*, 143.

44. J. von Neumann to Ulam, May 23, 1949, SMU-APS, series 1 (John von Neumann Folder 3).

45. Fitzpatrick, *Igniting the Light Elements*, 143–149, quotation from p. 149.

46. J. von Neumann to Teller, April 1, 1950, JvN-LOC, box 7, folder 4.

47. J. von Neumann to Mark, April 19, 1950, JvN-LOC, box 5, folder 13.

48. Evans to K. von Neumann, February 8, 1952, JvN-LOC, box 19, folder 7.

49. As reconstructed for the fiftieth-anniversary celebration, the Baby's first program consisted of 19 instruction lines, read no input (understandable as switches were the only input device), and ran for 52 minutes with the intention of giving the hardware (particularly the novel memory unit) a thorough workout. (See http://www.computer50.org/mark1/firstprog.html.) The programs run at the EDSAC's inaugural demonstration on June 22, 1949, which printed tables of squares and prime numbers, were longer, consisting of 92 and 76 instructions respectively, much of which was code to print the results in an attractive format. W. Renwick, "The E.D.S.A.C. Demonstration," in *The Early British Computer Conferences*, ed. M. R. Williams and M. Campbell-Kelly (MIT Press, 1989), 21–26.

50. One exception is Crispin Rope, "ENIAC as a Stored-Program Computer: A New Look at the Old Records," *IEEE Annals of the History of Computing* 29, no. 4 (2007): 82–87.

51. Galison, "Computer Simulation and the Trading Zone," 120.

52. The von Neumanns and the Goldstines were married before engaging with ENIAC. Others found love within the ENIAC teams at the Moore School and at the Ballistic Research Lab. Within a few years, the Holbertons, the Spences, the Reitwiesners, and the Mauchlys (John Mauchly having remarried after the sudden death of his first wife) were all brought together by their shared connection to the machine. Light ("When Computers Were Women," note 37) discusses this and also mentions other examples of scientific couples during the era.

Chapter 10

1. "Operations Log," May 17 and 18, 1948.

2. "Description of Orders for Coding ENIAC Problems," July 6, 1948, HHG-HC, box 1.

3. "Operations Log," July 12–14, 1948.

4. Ibid., July 22 and August 5, 1948. Results from Clippinger's calculations were published in Richard Clippinger and N. Gerber, *BRL Report No. 719: Supersonic Flow Over Bodies of Revolution (With Special Reference to High Speed Computing)* (Ballistic Research Laboratory, 1950).

5. "ENIAC Details of CODE In effect on 16 September, 1948." The new instruction set allowed some use of the master programmer to control fixed loops, and contained alternate delay and halt instructions.

6. "Operations Log," October 9, 1948.

7. Bergin, ed., *50 Years of Army Computing*, 35.

8. Melvin Wrublewski, "ENIAC Operating Experience," *Ordnance Computer Newsletter* 1, no. 2 (1954): 9–11 (in HHG-APS, series 4, box 1).

9. Clippinger, *A Logical Coding System*.

10. The Operations Log for April 20, 1948 records "Talked with Clippinger and Dimsdale about new developments in the new code designed for use with the register." The planned instruction set was described in B. Dimsdale and R. F. Clippinger, "The Register Code for the ENIAC," in *BRL Technical Note 30: Report on the Third Annual Meeting of the Association for Computing Machinery* (Ballistic Research Laboratory, 1949): 4–7, 11–14. The ACM did not yet produce conference proceedings, so this was a summary prepared by members of the BRL staff in attendance.

11. EDVAC had acquired short tanks by September of 1945, perhaps in response to von Neumann's experiments in coding Eckert and Mauchly, Automatic High-Speed Computing. Turing employed the same strategy in his ACE report, written toward the end of the year.

12. Nancy Stern, "The BINAC: A Case Study in the History of Technology," *Annals of the History of Computing* 1, no. 1 (1979): 9–20.

13. "Operations Log," January 10 and January 20, 1949.

14. Ibid., June 29, 1949.

15. G. W. Reitwiesner, "Stand-by Plan for Operation of the ENIAC," April 1, 1949, ENIAC-NARA, box 2, folder 3. This proposed new designs to provide storage more efficiently than the existing accumulators.

16. Homer W. Spence, "Operating Time and Factors Affecting It, of the ENIAC, EDVAC, and ORDVAC During 1952," ENIAC-NARA, box 2, folder 10.

17. A total of 87 problems are known to have run on ENIAC. We believe that it tackled about a dozen of them in its original mode. Thus, it appears that 75 problems were tackled in the first four years after conversion to the modern code paradigm.

18. Kempf, *Electronic Computers Within the Ordnance Corps*, 34.

19. Akera, *Calculating a Natural World*, 100–102.

20. Representatives of MIT's Whirlwind project paid great attention to the manufacturing standards used on the 7AK7 to verify its suitability for their new computer as a long life tube. Brown et al. to Forrester, "Investigation of 7AK7 Processing, Emporia, PA," March 16, 1948, in Project Whirlwind Reports, MIT Libraries. Online at http://dome.mit.edu/handle/1721.3/38986.

21. Richard F. Clippinger, ENIAC Trial Testimony, September 22, 1971, ETR-UP, p. 8888.

22. "Aberdeen Proving Ground Computers: The ENIAC," *Digital Computer Newsletter* 3, no. 1 (1951): 2.

23. "Aberdeen Proving Ground Computers," *Digital Computer Newsletter* 3, no. 3 (1951): 2.

24. "Operations Log," December 13, 1948.

25. Bergin, *50 Years of Army Computing*, 154–155.

26. Ibid., 45.

27. Ibid., 153.

28. "Operations Log," July 28, 1949.

29. Bergin, ed., *50 Years of Army Computing*, 54.

30. During the Cold War the National Center for Atmospheric Research never received funding on the scale of Los Alamos, but it was a lead customer for Cray supercomputers and the only site ever to receive a Cray-3 supercomputer (in 1993).

31. Aspray, *John von Neumann and the Origins of Modern Computing*, 137.

32. Ibid., 121.

33. Sayler to Richelderfer, September 29, 1949, JGC-MIT, box 9, folder 299.

34. Jule G. Charney, Ragnar Fjørtoft, and John von Neumann, "Numerical Integration of the Barotropic Vorticity Equation," *Tellus* 2, no. 4 (1950): 237–254, quotation from p. 254.

35. Harper, *Weather by the Numbers*, 141.

36. Clippinger to Charney, December 12, 1949, JGC-MIT, box 9, folder 299.

37. Holberton to Charney, February 7, 1950, JGC-MIT, box 9, folder 299.

38. Ibid.

39. Platzman, "The ENIAC Computations of 1950—Gateway to Numerical Weather Prediction," quotation from p. 307.

40. Charney to von Neumann, July 15, 1949, JvN-LOC, box 15, folder 2.

41. "Skeet" (Hauff) to Charney, April 26, 1950, JGC-MIT, box 9, folder 302. Charney wrote back with fond memories of their "shenanigans together" and inquiries as to Hauff's wife

and her baby, suggesting a fairly warm relationship between the visiting scientist and the computer operator.

42. Platzman, "The ENIAC Computations of 1950—Gateway to Numerical Weather Prediction."

43. Charney to von Neumann, July 15, 1949, JvN-LOC, box 15, folder 2.

44. Aspray, *John von Neumann and the Origins of Modern Computing*, 143. Platzman, "The ENIAC Computations of 1950—Gateway to Numerical Weather Prediction" mentions the difficulties caused by scaling on p. 311, and this is confirmed by the log-book entries.

45. Charney to Hauff, September 6, 1950, JGC-MIT, box 9, folder 302.

46. "Operations Log," March 9, JGC-MIT, box 9, folder 301.

47. Ibid., March 13.

48. "The time interval used was at first one hour but was increased to two and then three hours when it was found that the larger intervals gave practically identical forecasts and did not lead to computational instability." Charney, Fjørtoft, and von Neumann, "Numerical Integration of the Barotropic Vorticity Equation."

49. Platzman, "The ENIAC Computations of 1950—Gateway to Numerical Weather Prediction," quotation from p. 310.

50. Ibid. The log book records several instances of procedures being repeated because steps had been missed in preparing the input deck.

51. Charney, Fjørtoft, and von Neumann, "Numerical Integration of the Barotropic Vorticity Equation."

52. Platzman, "The ENIAC Computations of 1950—Gateway to Numerical Weather Prediction," 310.

53. Joseph Smagorinsky, quoted in Aspray, *John von Neumann and the Origins of Modern Computing*, 143.

54. Aspray, *John von Neumann and the Origins of Modern Computing*, 146–147.

55. Ibid., 146. According to Charney, Fjørtoft, and von Neumann ("Numerical Integration of the Barotropic Vorticity Equation"), an ENIAC forecast took a little over 24 hours, but it was estimated that "with a thorough routinization of operations" the time taken using ENIAC could be halved.

56. The Institute for Advanced Studies' computer had 1,024 words of delay-line storage and 2,048 words of drum storage, with 40 bits per word (ibid., 87). ENIAC took about 20 add times, or 4,000 microseconds, to multiply at the time that the forecasts were run. Fritz, *Description of the ENIAC Converter Code*, 24. The IAS computer is reported to have taken 713 microseconds.

57. Relative timings of ENIAC versus the IAS machine are from ibid., 145.

58. Brainerd to Goldstine, May 6, 1944, MSOD-UP, box 48 (PX-2 General Jan-Jun 1944).

59. Goldstine, *A Report on the ENIAC*, VII-13.

60. J. von Neumann to K. von Neumann, December 7, 1948, KvN-MvNW.

61. Fritz, *Description of the ENIAC Converter Code*, 7.

62. ENIAC followed something akin to the later technique of "prefetching" instructions from memory, in that execution of one instruction overlapped with fetching of the next. The durations quoted assume sequential execution. Thus, the times given for the simplest operations such as addition (six add times after the initial conversion) were fixed by the time taken to fetch the next instruction. For more complex operations such as multiplication (twenty add times after the initial conversion), ENIAC triggered its "basic sequence" (analogous to later fetch and decode cycles) part way through so that the next instruction would arrive just when it was needed. Executing a branch would mean that the next instruction to be executed had not already been fetched, causing it to take longer than usual. "Detailed Programming of Orders, ENIAC Converter Code," ENIAC-NARA (ENIAC Converter Code Book Used Before Installation of Shifter and Magnetic Core Memory).

63. "Aberdeen Proving Ground Computers: The ENIAC." An early design for the high-speed table is given in an untitled document in ENIAC-NARA, box 4, folder 14. This notes that it would take one add time to transmit the desired address to the high-speed function table and half an add time to receive its contents, though it also noted further modifications that could reduce the total to one add time. Instruction durations late in the machine's career are given in "Listing of Add Times of ENIAC Converter Code," June 1, 1954, ENIAC-NARA, box 4, folder 1.

64. J. Cherney, "Computer Research Branch Note No. 40: High Speed Shifter," ENIAC-NARA, box 4, folder 1.

65. "Changes to BRLM 582 'ENIAC CONVERTER CODE'," circa June 1954, ENIAC-NARA, box 4, folder 1.

66. Wrublewski, "ENIAC Operating Experience." We are not sure what might have been eliminated.

67. "Sidelights on the Financial and Business Developments of the Day: Military Memory," *New York Times*, December 20, 1952.

68. "Revised Specifications for Static Magnetic Memory System for ENIAC," October 9, 1951, ENIAC-NARA, box 4, folder 1.

69. The new instructions defined two versions of store and two of extract. One variant of each used indirect addressing and the other acted on a fixed address specified as an argument stored immediately after the instruction. These took between five and seven add times to execute, even though the memory itself could retrieve a number in only one add time. That made the core memory about twice as slow as accumulator memory. "Changes to BRLM 582 'ENIAC CONVERTER CODE'," circa June 1954, ENIAC-NARA, box 4, folder 1.

70. Wrublewski, "ENIAC Operating Experience." Specific reliability issues with the core memory were discussed further in Melvin Wrublewski, "An Engineering Report on the ENIAC Magnetic Memory," *Ordnance Computer Newsletter* 2, no. 2 (1955): 11–13 (in HHG-APS series 4, box 1).

71. Fritz, *Description of the ENIAC Converter Code*.

72. Michael R. Williams, "The Origins, Uses, and Fate of the EDVAC," *IEEE Annals of the History of Computing* 15, no. 1 (1993): 22–38.

73. Kempf, *Electronic Computers Within the Ordnance Corps*, 54.

74. Williams, "The Origins, Uses, and Fate of the EDVAC," quotation from p. 37.

75. Kempf, *Electronic Computers Within the Ordnance Corps*.

76. Williams, "The Origins, Uses, and Fate of the EDVAC."

77. Spence ("Operating Time and Factors Affecting It … ") gives a figure of 3,063 tubes in ORDVAC as of early 1953. The number would vary over time as new capabilities were added to the machines.

78. "Aberdeen Proving Ground Computers," *Digital Computer Newsletter* 5, no. 2 (1953): 7–8.

79. Ibid.

80. When the BRL tallied the results for that year, ENIAC continued to spend less time on problem set-up and code checking than either of the new machines. In an average week it spent 79.4 hours running production jobs, versus 30.4 for EDVAC and 53.7 for ORDVAC. "Aberdeen Proving Ground Computers," *Digital Computer Newsletter* 6, no. 1 (1951): 2.

81. Williams, "The Origins, Uses, and Fate of the EDVAC."

82. Kempf, *Electronic Computers Within the Ordnance Corps*.

83. J. F. Cherney, "Branch Report No. 48: Modifications of the ENIAC's IBM Input-Output Sign Sensing System," November 9, 1953, NARA-ENIAC, box 2, folder 10.

84. "Aberdeen Proving Ground Computers," *Digital Computer Newsletter* 6, no. 4 (1954): 2. EDVAC's speed seems to have overwhelmed the supply of coded problems, as it spent 60 hours a week idle to ENIAC's two

85. Wrublewski, "ENIAC Operating Experience."

86. "Aberdeen Proving Ground Computers," *Digital Computer Newsletter* 7, no. 3 (1954): 1.

87. Computer History Museum, "ENIAC (in online Revolution exhibit)," n.d., accessed January 23, 2015 (http://www.computerhistory.org/revolution/birth-of-the-computer/4/78). The same claim is made in Williams, "The Origins, Uses, and Fate of the EDVAC."

Chapter 11

1. Doron Swade, "Inventing the User: EDSAC in Context," *Computer Journal* 54, no. 1 (2011): 143–147, quotation from p. 145.

2. Eckert, "The ENIAC." Eckert also noted that von Neumann was "particularly interested" in the "three-address instruction code" they had already formulated for EDVAC in which "we were going to tell the computer the location of two operands and the location for storing the result." However, as Burks later noted, von Neumann is explicitly credited with the substitution order, the basis for address modification, in Eckert and Mauchly, Automatic High Speed Computing. That is a crucial feature, without which the radical simplicity of the modern code paradigm would not be possible.

3. Mauchly, "Amending the ENIAC Story."

4. Notes of meeting with Dr. Von Neumann, March 14, 1945, AWB-IUPUI.

5. This is easiest to find as a reprint at the end of Eckert, "The ENIAC." However, a draft copy, with certain corrections marked up, can be found as "Disclosure of Magnetic Calculating Machine", January 29, 1944, UV-HML, box 7 (ENIAC Moore School of Electrical Engineering Disclosure of Magnetic Calculating Machine).

6. Stern, *From ENIAC to Univac*, 75.

7. McCartney, *ENIAC*, 124.

8. Burks and Burks, *The First Electronic Computer*, 150 shows Mauchly making this point during his testimony in the patent trial.

9. Burks and Burks, *The First Electronic Computer*, 265-267.

10. For example, "the instructions given to a single program control are referred to as a *program*," Goldstine, *A Report on the ENIAC*, I-21; "accumulator 3 is programmed to transmit," "ENIAC Progress Report 31 December 1944," IV-21.

11. "ENIAC Progress Report 31 December 1943," III-3. Note the distinction made here between the "programs" (individual operations) and "interconnections" (to make a set-up for a problem).

12. "ENIAC Progress Report 30 June 1944," IV-10.

13. Eckert, "Disclosure of Magnetic Calculating Machine."

14. "The Function Generator," PX Report, November 2, 1943, MSOD-UP, box 3 (Reports on Project PX). By the end of the year, this had been superseded by a more passive "function table" which did not provide built-in interpolation facilities. "ENIAC Progress Report 31 December 1943," chapter XI.

15. Staff of the Harvard Computation Laboratory, *A Manual of Operation for the Automatic Sequence Controlled Calculator* (Harvard University Press, 1946), 28, 50.

16. Quoted in Burks and Burks, *The First Electronic Computer*, 101.

17. In January of 1944 the ENIAC team was in close contact with the team at Bell Labs working on calculators controlled by paper tape (Herman H. Goldstine, "Report of a conference on computing devices at the Ballistic Research Laboratory on 26 January 1944," February 1, 1944, ETE-UP). Although the text provides no specific evidence it is certainly plausible to suppose that Eckert imagined that a calculator equipped with paper tapes might read instructions from them as well as numbers.

18. The text of the disclosure provides only one reason to believe that he imagined using its disks or drums to store what we would think of as programs. Although Eckert focused on permanently etched disks for "automatic programming" he mentioned as an aside that record-able magnetic disks could also be used. Erasable disks hold an obvious appeal for the storage of what we think of as programs, but it is also quite possible that he imagined updating the control codes to develop new mathematical functions for the calculator or to modifying existing ones. The benefits of this approach were well established in later generations of technology, for example the IBM 370 mainframes of the 1970s read their microcode from floppy disks and modern computers and smartphones can flash upgrades to firmware.

19. An initial list of patentable ideas from ENIAC and early work on what became EDVAC was prepared by Eckert and Mauchly as "Main Outline of Material for Patent Applications." This was presented "roughly in the order in which they should be considered" and bore a note that it was typed later from an original dated February 5, 1945. The ideas included delay-line registers, delay-line computing circuits, ideas on the use of tubes for computing, electronic ring counters, various features of the designs for ENIAC's accumulators, function tables, multiplier, cycling unit, "programming system, divider, and master programmer" (such as "digit control of steppers") and a long list of "input and output devices" such as "super-sonic card readers." The final item was a list of "design considerations." In other words the list included a lot of speculative new ideas on components connected with EDVAC but the only control innovations mentioned were from ENIAC. A later and better-developed list was headed "Supplemental Outline—Devices for Computing" and included dozens of ideas over

eight pages such as schemes for detecting errors in pulse trains and devices for printing from magnetic tape at high speed. Again, no discussion of new control systems or architecture was included. We located copies of both documents in AWB-IUPUI with stamps showing that they had been reproduced from UV-HML but are unsure of the box number within the original collection.

20. Von Neumann, "First Draft of a Report on the EDVAC," section 1.2.

21. Campbell-Kelly and Williams, eds., *The Moore School Lectures*.

22. Michael R. Williams and Martin Campbell-Kelly, eds., *The Early British Computer Conferences* (MIT Press, 1985); Hartree, *Calculating Machine*; Hartree, *Calculating Instruments and Machines*; Engineering Research Associates, *High-Speed Computing Devices*.

23. Engineering Research Associates, *High-Speed Computing Devices*, chapter 10, pp. 182–222.

24. W. H. McWilliams, "Keynote Address," *Review of Electronic Digital Computers: Joint AIEE-IRE Computer Conference (Dec. 10–12, 1951)* (American Institute of Electrical Engineers, 1952): 5–6.

25. Nathaniel Rochester, "A Calculator Using Electrostatic Storage and a Stored Program," May 17, 1949, From the IBM Corporate Archives, Somers, New York. Its system of two-digit instruction codes and three-digit addresses for the stored program was very similar to the format adopted for the converted ENIAC.

26. This was in an end-of-year summary of developments in "Electronic Computers" for an engineering audience. "Radio Progress During 1950," *Proceedings of the IRE* 39, no. 4 (1951): 359–396, quotation from p. 375.

27. C. E. Frizzell, "Engineering Description of the IBM 701 Calculator," *Transactions of the IRE* 41, no. 10 (1953): 1275–1287, quotation from p. 1275.

28. J. W. Sheldon and Liston Tatum, "IBM Card-Programmed Calculator," in *Papers and Discussions Presented at the Dec. 10–12, 1951, Joint AIEE-IRE Computer Conference* (Association for Computing Machinery, 1951): 30–36, quotation from p. 35.

29. Walker H. Thomas, "Fundamentals of Digital Computer Programming," *Proceedings of the IRE* 41, no. 10 (1953), quotations from pp. 1245 and 1249.

30. Willis H. Ware, *The History and Development of the Electronic Computer Project at the Institute for Advanced Study* (RAND Corporation, 1953), p. 5.

31. International Business Machines Corporation, "Magnetic Drum Data Processing Machine Announcement," IBM Archives, 1953, accessed November 11, 2014 (https://www-03.ibm.com/ibm/history/exhibits/650/650_pr1.html). This is an interesting place in which to discover the term as the 650 combined computer and punched-card technologies, storing a program internally on a drum while relying on external plugboards to configure its input and output formats. This dual system echoed the two kinds of program control on the test assembly that had originally motivated the new coinage. The release observed that the 650 "combines one of the advanced memory devices and the stored program concept of IBM's big '701' … with new high speed reading capacity in the conventional punched card equipment."

32. Goldstine, *The Computer*.

33. Burks and Burks, "The ENIAC," p. 385.

34. Comment by B. Randell, *Annals of the History of Computing* 3, no. 4 (1981) 396–397.

35. Brainerd, "Project PX—The ENIAC."

36. Campbell-Kelly, "Programming the EDSAC."

37. Campbell-Kelly and Aspray, *Computer*, 104.

38. Allan G. Bromley, Stored Program Concept: The Origin of the Stored Program Concept, Technical Report 274, Brasser Department of Computer Science, University of Sydney, modified November 1985 (http://sydney.edu.au/engineering/it/research/tr/tr274.pdf).

39. B. Jack Copeland, *Turing: Pioneer of the Information Age* (Oxford University Press, 2013).

40. Campbell-Kelly and Aspray, *Computer*.

41. Mark Priestley argues in *A Science of Operations: Machines, Logic, and the Invention of Programming* (Springer, 2011) that the general connection between Turing's computational model and actual stored-program computers was only widely recognized after 1950.

42. For example, in Raúl Rojas, "How to Make Zuse's Z3 a Universal Computer," *IEEE Annals of the History of Computing* 20, no. 3 (1998): 51–54.

43. Wikipedia, "Stored-Program Computer," accessed October 17, 2012.

44. Paul Ceruzzi, *Computing: A Concise History* (MIT Press, 2012), 29.

45. Swade, "Inventing the User," quotation from p. 146.

46. That claim is discussed further in Thomas Haigh, "Actually, Turing Did Not Invent the Computer," *Communications of the ACM* 57, no. 1 (2014): 36–41.

47. Bartik, *Pioneer Programmer*, xx.

48. Clippinger, Oral History Interview with Richard R. Mertz, 11–12.

49. Goldstine, *The Computer*, p. 233. Goldstine's personal papers, HHG-APS and HHG-HC, include several documents that confirm the earlier operation of ENIAC with the new control method. The date he gave in the book appears to be based on the title of a BRL document in HHG-APS titled "ENIAC: Details of CODE In effect on 16 September, 1948." That, of course, provides no more than a later bound for its first operation after conversion to the modern code paradigm.

50. Neukom, "The Second Life of ENIAC."

51. Metropolis and Worlton, "A Trilogy on Errors in the History of Computing," quotations from pp. 53–54. This was originally presented at a conference in 1972. At that point Metropolis may not have been aware of the Manchester Baby.

52. Goldstine, *The Computer*, 233.

53. Aspray, *John von Neumann and the Origins of Modern Computing*, 238–239.

54. Burks, unfinished book manuscript, appendix B.

55. Burks, "Review of William Aspray Ms. 'The Stored Program Concept,' for Spectrum," July 11, 1990, AWB-IUPUI.

56. The influence of the Williams Tube on the work of von Neumann's group at the Institute for Advanced Studies is related in Dyson, *Turing's Cathedral*, 142–148.

57. The Baby's parts were soon used to build a complete and useful computer, now known as the Manchester Mark I, which was fully operational by late 1949. However, we focus here on the Baby, as it is generally accepted as the first "stored program" computer to operate, or

in some formulations the first machine to run a stored program, and hence it provides a natural comparison point.

58. Allan Olley, "Existence Precedes Essence—Meaning of the Stored-Program Concept," in *History of Computing: Learning from the Past*, ed. A. Tatnall (Springer, 2010).

59. For a nuanced account of the SSEC's use of relay memory for instructions, see Charles J. Bashe, Lyle R. Johnson, John H. Palmer, and Emerson W. Pugh, *IBM's Early Computers* (MIT Press, 1986), 586–587. This account describes a procedure by which a five-instruction subroutine could be executed from relay memory, but admits that "it is more likely, in fact, that all but the final line [an instruction in which the source of the next instruction was modified to terminate the loop] would be stored in a pair of subsequence tapes."

60. Comprehensive technical details on the SSEC, even on basic elements such as its instruction set, have not been published. The most detailed surviving descriptions we were able to locate are in an incomplete, unpublished, undated manuscript by A. Wayne Brooke, "SSEC. The First Selectronic Computer (with markup from C. J. Bashe)," in AWB-NCSU, box 1, folder 14.

61. Descriptions respectively from Paul E. Ceruzzi, *Computing: A Concise History* (MIT Press, 2012), 50, Campbell-Kelly and Aspray, *Computer*, 104, and Campbell-Kelly and Aspray, *Computer*, photo inset.

62. David Hartley, "EDVAC 1 and After—A Compilation of Personal Reminiscences," University of Cambridge Computer Laboratory, last modified July 21, 1999, accessed January 23, 2015 (http://www.cl.cam.ac.uk/events/EDSAC99/reminiscences/).

63. Campbell-Kelly, "Programming the EDSAC."

64. For example, once a virtual computer built within Conway's Game of Life was shown to be computationally equivalent to a Universal Turing Machine, that single fact told us that with sufficient time and a large enough cellular matrix that computer could execute the same algorithms as any machine built from conventional components.

65. Michael S. Mahoney with Thomas Haigh, ed., *Histories of Computing* (Harvard University Press, 2011).

66. Ibid., 91.

67. Rojas, "How to Make Zuse's Z3 a Universal Computer."

68. Zuse claimed to have devised the "stored program concept" in 1937 but decided that "in 1938, given the state of the technology, it would not have been wise to use the von Neumann architecture." Konrad Zuse, *The Computer—My Life* (Springer, 1993), 44 and 50.

69. For example, the entry on ENIAC in Wikipedia (accessed January 23, 2015) asserts that "it was Turing-complete, digital, and capable of being reprogrammed." A Web search locates hundreds of instances of the same claim.

70. Calvin C. Elgot and Abraham Robinson, "Random-Access Stored-Program Machines, an Approach to Programming Languages," *Journal of the ACM* 11, no. 4 (1964): 365–399.

71. Raúl Rojas, "Who Invented the Computer? The Debate from the Viewpoint of Computer Architecture," *Proceedings of Symposia in Applied Mathematics* 48 (1994): 361–365.

72. By contrast, the read-only memory in the function tables was fully addressable, and "modern" search algorithms, for example, could be (and in the Monte Carlo programs, were) written in the converter code.

73. "Changes to BRLM 582 'ENIAC Converter Code'," circa June 1954, ENIAC-NARA, box 4, folder 1.

74. What if one plays the theorists' traditional game of exploring what a machine could do if granted vast amounts of time and storage but left otherwise unchanged? To make the accumulators addressable, one could simply write a pair of subroutines: one to store and one to load. Each would take as a parameter an accumulator number, which would be used to calculate a jump to the function-table address at which the appropriate "listen" or "talk" instruction has been placed. That would tie up two rows of a function table for each accumulator rendered addressable, but unlimited storage would already have been assumed. See our online appendix "How to Make ENIAC's Accumulators Addressable Using a Subroutine," available at www.EniacInAction.com.

75. For a rather aggressive critique of the impressionistic use made of the ideas of the universal computer and Turing machine by some prominent historians, see Edgar G. Daylight, "Difficulties of Writing About Turing's Legacy," Dijkstra's Rallying Cry for Generalization, last modified September 3, 2013 (http://www.compscihistory.com/DifficultTuringLegacy).

Chapter 12

1. D. R. Hartree, "The ENIAC: An Electronic Calculating Machine," *Nature*, 157 no. 3990 (1946): 527; "The ENIAC: An Electronic Calculating Machine," *Nature*, 158 no. 4015 (1946): 500–506; *Calculating Machines; Calculating Instruments and Machines*.

2. Berkeley, *Giant Brains or Machines That Think*, p. 113.

3. David H. Ahl, ed., *The Colossal Computer Cartoon Book* (Creative Computing Press, 1977).

4. Internet users have formalized this joke as an apocryphal war of press releases between Microsoft and General Motors. See, e.g., http://www.snopes.com/humor/jokes/autos.asp.

5. Lynn Grant, "Conserving ENIAC (aka Project CLEANIAC)," http://www.penn.museum/blog/museum/conserving-eniac-aka-project-cleaniac/, accessed June 30, 2014.

6. Geise to Burks, April 8, 1960, AWB-IUPUI.

7. Burks to Giese, February 18, 1985, AWB-IUPUI.

8. An online version of the museum's display can be found at http://www.nwmissouri.edu/archives/computing/index.htm.

9. Brendan I. Koerner, "How the World's First Computer Was Rescued from the Scrap Heap," *Wired*, November 25, 2014 (http://www.wired.com/2014/11/eniac-unearthed/).

10. Mitch Meador, "ENIAC: First Generation of Computation Should Be a Big Attraction at Sill," *Lawton Constitution* (swoknews.com), October 29, 2014.

11. Burks, *Who Invented the Computer?*

12. Larson, *Findings of Fact*, section 11.13.

13. Most recently, though without apparent conviction, in Smiley, *The Man Who Invented the Computer*.

14. McCartney, *ENIAC*.

15. Burks, *Who Invented the Computer?*

16. "Preliminary Announcement: International Research Conference on the History of Computing," in AWB-IUPUI.

17. The three credentialed historians were I. Bernard Cohen, Henry S. Tropp, and Kenneth O. May.

18. In collection of material from the Los Alamos conference in AWB-IUPUI.

19. Goldstine to Smith, May 14, 1959, HHG-APS, series 6, box 1.

20. Randell, "The Colossus."

21. Burks and Burks, "The ENIAC," 311. "General purpose" is defined on page 385.

22. Paul E. Ceruzzi, *Reckoners: The Prehistory of the Digital Computer, from Relays to the Stored Program Concept, 1935–1945* (Greenwood, 1983).

23. Paul Ceruzzi, then entering the field as a doctoral student, recalls a direct influence from the 1970s discussion of whether programmable calculators were computers (private discussion with authors, November 4, 2011). This is reflected in a contemporary discussion by the computer pioneer Fred Gruenberger, who argued that stored-program capability was the true dividing line between computers and calculators. See Gruenberger, "What's in a Name?" *Datamation* 25, no. 5 (1979): 230.

24. The influence of electronic calculators on the historical debate was mentioned to us by Paul Ceruzzi. Misguided pedants continue to try to impose it—for example, the Wikipedia page for ENIAC has repeatedly been changed to suggest that the C in ENIAC stood for "calculator." The incorrect version is found in many online sources, and even some books present the question as unsettled. "There is some confusion regarding precisely what 'ENIAC' stood for," according to Mike Hally, *Electronic Brains: Stories from the Dawn of the Computer Age* (Granta Books, 2006), 12.

25. Al Gore, "The Technology Challenge How Can America Spark Private Innovation?," *University of Pennsylvania Almanac,* February 20, 1995.

26. Bergin, ed., *50 Years of Army Computing,* vi.

27. The quotations are from Jan Van Der Spiegel, "ENIAC-on-a-Chip," *PennPrintout* 12, no. 4 (1996). The project is described in more detail in Jan Van der Spiegel et al., "The ENIAC—History, Operation and Reconstruction in VLSI," in *The First Computers: History and Architectures,* ed. Raúl Rojas and Ulf Hashagen (MIT Press, 2000).

28. Til Zoppke and Raúl Rojas, "The Virtual Life of the ENIAC: Simulating the Operation of the First Electronic Computer," *IEEE Annals of the History of Computing* 28, no. 2 (2006): 18–25.

29. Jon Agar, Sarah Green, and Penny Harvey, "Cotton to Computers: From Industrial to Information Revolutions," in *Virtual Society? Technology, Cyberbole, Reality,* ed. Steve Woolgar (Oxford University Press, 2004).

30. Huskey is, as of this writing, 98 years old. His name doesn't appear in the Moore School lectures volume either as an instructor or as a student, but he did lead a computer project that began in the 1940s: the Standards West Electronic Computer (SWAC). He may be the last survivor of any computer project of that decade.

31. Burks, *Who Invented the Computer?,* 17.

32. Smiley, *The Man Who Invented the Computer.*

33. A number of Amazon.com reviews by experts on digital computing identify specific errors; see http://www.amazon.com/The-Man-Who-Invented-Computer/product-reviews/ 0385527136. Some non-specialists were also unimpressed. Example: "The narrative shuffles painstakingly along; reading it is like watching a very old man pack for vacation. The characters feel morally and intellectually uninhabited, lighted from without rather than within. The scientific developments at the heart of modern life are never satisfactorily explained (except in the wonderfully lucid appendices)." Kathryn Schulz, "Binary Breakthrough," *New York Times,* November 26, 2010.

34. Fritz, "ENIAC—A Problem Solver" and "The Women of ENIAC."

35. Thomas Petzinger, "The Front Lines: History of Software Begins with the Work of Some Brainy Women," *Wall Street Journal,* November 15, 1996.

36. Light, "When Computers Were Women," 469.

37. *Technology and Culture* is the most respected journal for history of technology. At the time of writing, Web of Knowledge lists Light's as the second most widely cited paper published in that journal and records more citations for it than for any paper ever published in *IEEE Annals of the History of Computing.*

38. Ada Lovelace is described as "computer pioneer" on an English Heritage "blue plaque" attached to her former home in London's St. James' Square.

39. Bartik, "Hendrie Oral History, 2008," 30 and 34.

40. Ibid., 58.

41. Ibid.

42. For a salient discussion, see Judith A. McGaw, "No Passive Victims, No Separate Spheres: A Feminist Perspective on Technology's History," in *In Context: History and the History of Technology*, ed. Stephen Cutcliffe and Robert Post (Lehigh University Press, 1989).

43. Walter Isaacson, *The Innovators: How a Group of Hackers, Geniuses, and Geeks Created the Digital Revolution* (Simon and Schuster, 2014), 107.

Conclusion

1. For example, Abbate (*Recoding Gender: Women's Changing Participation in Computing*, 26) uses a quotation from Mauchly to support the judgment that "programming was an afterthought." According to Nathan Ensmenger (*The Computer Boys Take Over: Computers, Programmers, and the Politics of Technical Expertise*, MIT Press, 2010, 15), the discovery that setting up ENIAC to execute a computing plan would "turn out to be difficult and require radically innovative thinking" was "completely unanticipated."

2. Michael S. Mahoney, "The Histories of Computing(s)," *Interdisciplinary Science Review* 30, no. 2 (2005): 119–135, quotation from p. 121.

3. I. Bernard Cohen, *Howard Aiken: Portrait of a Computer Pioneer* (MIT Press, 1999).

4. Ensmenger, *The Computer Boys Take Over*, 32.

5. "ENIAC Progress Report 31 December 1943," chapter XIV.

6. Stephen R. Barley, "Technicians in the Workplace: Ethnographic Evidence for Bringing Work into Organizational Studies," *Administrative Science Quarterly* 41, no. 3 (1996): 404–441.

7. The incident was described in several oral-history interviews and most recently in Bartik, *Pioneer Programmer*. On page 80, Bartik states that "Kay's exclamation was a breakthrough!"

8. Goldstine, *A Report on the ENIAC*, quotations from pp. I-10, I-20, II-15, and IV-9.

9. Ensmenger, *The Computer Boys Take Over*, 14–15, 36–39. Goldstine and von Neumann ("Planning and Coding Problems for an Electronic Computing Instrument. Part II, Volume 1," 99–104) outline a methodology for planning and coding problems, but do not to appear to propose a firm division of labor or to define coding as a clerical task. They suggest that "every mathematician, or every moderately mathematically trained person, should be able to do [the coding] in a routine manner."

10. See, for example, Abbate, *Recoding Gender* and Beyer, *Grace Hopper*.

11. Light, "When Computers Were Women," 470.

12. Ensmenger, *The Computer Boys Take Over*, 32.

13. Ensmenger, *The Computer Boys Take Over*, 35–39. Ensmenger writes on page 37 that the ability of the operators to recognize a failed vacuum tube suggests that they "were able to interact much more with the computer engineers and technicians than was probably originally intended."

14. Abbate, *Recoding Gender: Women's Changing Participation in Computing*, p. 26 and note 43 on p. 185. In fact the idea of "coding" does not appear to have been applied to the work of producing ENIAC set-ups in project progress reports or in Goldstine's *Report on the ENIAC*. It may have gained currency after the propagation of the modern code paradigm in the First Draft. This makes sense in view of the familiarity of things like Morse Code. EDVAC programs were to be represented as a series of numerical codes, like those of the Harvard Mark I (where the term found an early foothold), whereas ENIAC set-ups were recorded graphically.

15. Beyer, *Grace Hopper*, 52–58. Of course, the task of the Mark I's operators was simpler than that of ENIAC's operators.

16. The argument is made at greater length in Thomas Haigh, "Masculinity and the Machine Man," in *Gender Codes: Why Women are Leaving Computing*, ed. Thomas J. Misa (IEEE Computer Society Press, 2010).

17. Galison and Hevly, *Big Science: The Growth of Large-Scale Research*.

18. Latour, *Science in Action: How to Follow Scientists and Engineers through Society*.

19. Akera, *Calculating a Natural World*; Akera, "Constructing a Representation for an Ecology of Knowledge: Methodological Advances in the Integration of Knowledge and its Various Contexts," *Social Studies of Science* 37, no. 3 (2007): 413–441.

20. Andrew Pickering, "The Mangle of Practice: Agency and Emergence in the Sociology of Science," *American Journal of Sociology* 99, no. 3 (1993): 559–589.

21. Michael S. Mahoney, "The Beginnings of Algebraic Thought in the Seventeenth Century," in *Descartes: Philosophy, Mathematics and Physics*, ed. S. Gaukroger (Harvester, 1980).

22. Michael S. Mahoney, "Calculation—Thinking—Computational Thinking: Seventeenth-Century Perspectives on Computational Science," in *Form, Zahl, Ordnung. Studien zur Wissenschafts- und Technikgeschichte. Ivo Schneider zum 65. Geburtstag*, ed. Menso Folkerts and Rudolf Seising (Frank Steiner Verlag, 2004).

Index